Technology and Diversity in Higher Education:

New Challenges

Yukiko Inoue
University of Guam, USA

 Information Science Publishing

Hershey • London • Melbourne • Singapore

Acquisition Editor:	Kristin Klinger
Senior Managing Editor:	Jennifer Neidig
Managing Editor:	Sara Reed
Assistant Managing Editor:	Sharon Berger
Development Editor:	Kristin Roth
Copy Editor:	Julie LeBlanc
Typesetter:	Marko Primorac
Cover Design:	Lisa Tosheff
Printed at:	Yurchak Printing Inc.

Published in the United States of America by
> Information Science Publishing (an imprint of Idea Group Inc.)
> 701 E. Chocolate Avenue
> Hershey PA 17033
> Tel: 717-533-8845
> Fax: 717-533-8661
> E-mail: cust@idea-group.com
> Web site: http://www.idea-group.com

and in the United Kingdom by
> Information Science Publishing (an imprint of Idea Group Inc.)
> 3 Henrietta Street
> Covent Garden
> London WC2E 8LU
> Tel: 44 20 7240 0856
> Fax: 44 20 7379 3313
> Web site: http://www.eurospan.co.uk

Library of Congress Cataloging-in-Publication Data

Technology and diversity in higher education : new challenges / Yukiko Inoue, editor.
    p. cm.
  Summary: "This book examines current and effective educational practices as well as new challenges involving emerging technologies in increasingly diverse learning environments in higher educationand the impact of the explosion of technology. These challenges are well documented in this collection of essays, case studies, and research reports"--Provided by publisher.
  Includes bibliographical references and index.
  ISBN 1-59904-316-5 -- ISBN 1-59904-317-3 (softcover) -- ISBN 1-59904-318-1 (ebook)
  1. Education, Higher--Computer-assisted instruction. 2. Educational technology. I. Inoue, Yukiko.
  LB2395.7.T423 2007
  378.1'734--dc22
2006027709

British Cataloguing in Publication Data
A Cataloguing in Publication record for this book is available from the British Library.

Dedication

To old friends, good friends and the best friends

Technology and Diversity in Higher Education:
New Challenges

Table of Contents

Foreword

Education in general and, more specifically, higher education, faces new challenges and is at a critical juncture in its evolution. Today we are experiencing what Ervin Laszlo (1989) called a "convergence" in his book, *The Inner Limits of Mankind*. We are at a time when a number of parallel forces are coming together and intensifying the chaos occurring in higher education. Several primary elements of this convergence are the rapid advancement of technology; the collapsing of barriers, both natural and man made, that has kept humanity separated; and the educational opportunities that are now available to anyone-anywhere-anytime.

With the advancement of technology, instructional delivery to a diverse student population is currently a reality. Consequently, it is often difficult for students enrolled in online classes to visualize or relate to fellow classmates representing cultural differences and/or alternate geographical locations. Is this a new challenge? I think it is. Some might say that the very structure and function of higher education are being threatened. I would prefer to think that we are experiencing the collapse of one approach to instruction and learning to adapt to an emerging one. This book is a collection of essays, case studies and research that reports on many elements of this evolution involving higher education in an increasingly diverse learning environment.

Technology, economic needs and ease of travel have made our world, for all intended purposes, one country. The major issues that prevent this changing world from embracing a new identity are humanity's inability to communicate and socialize on an acceptable or genuine level. These issues have prompted the increase in the use of educational technologies, intensifying the cultural encounters that universities experience in a variety of applications. This has had the advantage of imposing on higher education the need and ethical responsibility to confront limitations in programmatic offerings both curricular and extracurricular, particularly as they impact issues of diversity. Recently, accrediting agencies have recognized this challenge and required all institutions of higher learning to include dispositions in their conceptual framework that support goals involving diversity. Higher-education communities are concerned less with a person's attitude than the behaviors that issue or evolve from that attitude.

As a consequence of today's technology, universities have entered markets that would never have been considered a decade ago, often driven by an economic force that universities face today. I teach at a small university in western Kansas, with a dwindling population. Due to economic circumstances, this institution was forced to examine and potentially attract other markets and populations as candidates for offered academic programs. This examination mandated major commitment from the faculty and the institution to adjust in significant ways. As a result, we found ourselves playing an increasing role in regional economic development, in the delivery of life-long learning and in the development of "connectivity" to rural communities, while addressing issues of concern. In a manner of speaking, we have become more relevant to our regional needs while at the same time reaching out to international markets for economic enhancement. It is interesting to note, in fact, that the international connectivity has brought many fringe benefits to the regional community. The products of our institution are now more marketable, while simultaneously providing economic "connectivity" and resources to the small rural communities of western Kansas.

A decade ago, the president of our university set out a vision of "High Tech—High Touch" as a goal to drive future development. Technology has, in fact, facilitated interpersonal and inter-social exchanges and provided general access to information, which has the effect of blurring the distinction of nation, race or culture. Universities of the future will be required to develop many more and different kinds of links with surrounding society. Their success will be determined increasingly by their ability to deliver distant learning opportunities and their relevance to the local and regional communities in which they reside. And here lies a threat to the conventional way of doing things. Soon, my university, Fort Hays State University, will have more students enrolled in our courses from China (6,000) than from Kansas (5,000). This was driven, in the beginning, out of economic necessity, but has greatly changed the way we do business regionally and dramatically affected our existing programs, curriculum and faculty. Our universities today extend far beyond our regional and state markets, and offer courses and degree programs nationally and internationally; and, many on-campus courses have added a "virtual" element to their current course structures in addition to face-to-face environments.

My contact with students has changed dramatically with the use of e-mail and computer-based communication, such as computer conferencing programs. Technology has provided mechanisms for distance delivery of education that has improved the frequency and quality of communication with students and colleagues within my department and internationally.

Other challenges reported in this book are what we have learned about learning and its application to the explosion of technology. Globally, these *new challenges* we face should be viewed as an opportunity and not one that has threatened our very survival. The insights emerging from this experience are well documented in this collection of essays, case studies and research reports. Several chapters explore the issues around these challenges, and between these pages you will encounter several very able endeavors to offer solutions and suggestions to improve our understanding and effectiveness in delivery of post-secondary instruction to diverse populations. As a result, people of every background have been exposed to the cultures and norms of others, which may be the most valuable element of the learning experience.

So, are these new challenges in higher education or are they perhaps an opportunity given the tools of technology available to us today?

Ray Johnson
Educational Administration
Fort Hays State University

Reference

Laszlo, E. (1989) *The inner limits of mankind: Heretical reflections on today's values, culture and politics*. Oxford: Oneworld Publications.

Preface

Although cooperate America has witnessed increased productivity and effectiveness from investments in information technology, higher education is still trying to cope with applying it to its core processes: teaching and learning. ... There is little doubt that technology has the potential to enhance teaching and learning, but there is a lack of agreement on how it should be used for improving academic productivity and enhancing higher learning. (Ma & Runyon, 2004)

Diverse Learners

The United States (U.S.) is a veritable "salad bowl" of humanity and, in fact, diversity is an established characteristic of American higher education. The diversity currently found on college and university campuses takes into account not just differences in race or ethnicity; it also includes the greater representation of women than in generations past as well as increased educational access to nontraditional students and those with handicapping conditions.

In the early 1960s, most college students were men; but the late 1960s and 1970s witnessed the entrance of women into American higher education in unprecedented numbers. In the present day, the majority of U.S. college and university students are female (Durrence, 2005). Open recruitment of older students in the late 1970s and 1980s swelled the ranks of college attendees by including more nontraditional students, returning students and those wishing to pursue a second degree, thus shifting the demographics of the typical university student. A concerted effort to entice ethnic minorities in the 1980s and 1990s further broadened the diversity and enriched the population of university campuses across the land (Musil, 1996).

Today's schools, colleges and universities are called on to serve a more ethnically, linguistically and culturally diverse student population than ever before. Racial diversity in American higher education has the powerful consequence of breaking down patterns of racial separation in neighborhoods, employment settings and within social groups of graduates from racially diverse colleges and universities. For many students, the college and graduate school years represent the first extended period of time spent in an environment other than their home communities (U-M Marketing Communications, 2005). A survey released by the Business Higher Education Forum shows that a majority of Americans think that *diversity*—and many methods taken by institutions to ensure it—is important in business and higher education (Yates, 2000). It should be further noted that the technology age of today is making *new* demands on the higher education system in a diverse environment, requiring radical changes in *what* is taught and *how* people learn.

Shift in Faculty Roles

The faculty makes up a dynamic system within higher education, and each faculty member has to continuously strive to enhance teaching, research, scholarship and service by engaging in the activities of professional development, instructional development, personal development and curriculum development. It needs to be recognized that one of the most critical elements of education in teaching is self-development of the teacher; and, the ultimate goal of education is to enhance the students' development and learning. By sharing their technological integration and experience, individual faculty members can become resources for each other.

In the book *Promotion, Tenure, and Faculty Review Committees,* an essential resource rich in valuable suggestions, Diamond (2002) emphasizes that for improving students' learning experiences and enhancing faculty teaching effectiveness, "changes" have important implications for faculty roles in the information age. Diamond summarizes the current trend well:

Dramatic increases in enrollment, increasing diversity of student bodies, more competition among institutions and, from the private sector, growing demands for institutional accountability, diminishing government support, and increasing availability of technology and associated options for the design and delivery of instruction will all affect institutional priorities and faculty roles. (p. ix)

Faculty and administrators are paying greater attention to evaluating interdisciplinary work and technology-based teaching and research as well as the changing roles of faculty (Diamond, 2002). Computer-based environments provide a variety of ways to reach learners with different backgrounds, ages, learning needs, external demands from family and employers, linguistic capabilities and personal expectations. As technology continues to enhance the teaching-learning process, "there is an expanding recognition of its potential value in establishing and supporting a student-centered environment" (Spodark, 2001, p. 46).

Table 1. Fundamental shifts in the role of the professor

Traditional (20th-century learning)	Resource based (21st-century learning)
Teacher as expert model	Teacher as facilitator or guide
Textbook as primary source	Varity of sources or media
Facts as primary	Questions as primary
Information is packaged	Information is discovered
Emphasis on product	Emphasis on process
Assessment is quantitative	Assessment is qualitative/quantitative

With the advent of the Internet, the effective integration of the ever-changing world of information technology (IT) into higher education has become an increasingly challenging—but increasingly necessary and rewarding—task. Ma and Runyon (2004) suggest the establishment of a *new* instructional paradigm—a paradigm that transforms higher-learning institutions from schools that rely on the traditional, individual-oriented teaching model to institutions that use a synergistically discipline-oriented teaching mode.

In this kind of teaching mode, providing computers, software and networked classrooms is certainly necessary, but simply providing hardware, software and a high-speed Internet connection does not bring about the desired integration of technology into higher education. Three elements are essential to provide effective teaching and learning: (1) all faculty members must be able to use the same Internet teaching resource site; (2) collaboration among faculty members should be encouraged and supported, even to the extent of class coverage if necessary, thus, program coordination becomes much easier; and (3) the combined resources of all the technologies available should benefit all faculty members' teaching and enrich all students' experience, creating unprecedented synergetic value (Ma & Runyon, 2004).

The fundamental shifts in the role of the professor (from expert dispensing knowledge to a resource or a guide) are illustrated by Janicki, Schell, and Weinroth (2002) in Table 1.

Technology-Based Teaching

In the educational environment of today, particularly in higher education, technology is still underutilized as a pedagogical tool and, in many cases, remains for the most part untapped (McVay, Snyder, & Graetz, 2005). Many faculty members use IT only for sending and receiving e-mail, browsing a World Wide Web site, providing basic course information and processing text with software like Microsoft Word; beyond those, however, the steep learning curve is a strong deterrent for faculty members to adopt instructional technology (Strauss, 2005). Why have more faculty members, who clearly have the ability to master IT, not taken more advantage of it? Strauss identifies five answers to this intriguing question:

- Faculty do not know what is possible (do not have a clear vision of what IT can do).

- Faculty cannot always tell what is easy to do with IT and what is hard.

- Faculty believe that technology will hurt them.

- Faculty are not interested in IT that is not relevant to their short-term needs (e-mail, Web browsers and the basic of course-management systems are commonly used).

- IT changes too rapidly, and change is disruptive (and faculty may be willing to learn how to use some new software).

Furthermore, maintaining that basic computing support is a utility like water and electricity, Strauss (2005) states that a reasonable goal for an IT staff is to help move faculty members in the right direction with small, even tiny, steps and to provide them with training and software that they can readily use. The ultimate goal is greater instructional quality and capability on the part of the teachers and greater opportunities for learning and achieving on the part of the student.

With greater attention given to the near overwhelming number of technologies available, it still remains of utmost importance for higher education to focus on meeting the academic needs of teacher and student: effective *and* advanced teaching. McVey et al. (2005) suggest five practices that may enhance instruction and have a positive impact on student outcomes:

- Encourage student-faculty contact.

- Encourage cooperation among students.

- Encourage active learning and give prompt feedback.

- Emphasize time on task while communicating high expectations.

- Respect diverse talents and ways of learning.

Advances in IT have presented universities with *new* opportunities and challenges, and *new* vehicles to increase academic productivity and enhance teaching effectiveness in higher learning. Demographic trends in colleges and universities indicate that the student population is becoming more ethnically, culturally and racially diverse. Curriculum designers and instructors are extremely challenged to provide meaningful, relevant and motivating educational opportunities to *all* learners. The integration of technology into teaching is forcing faculty members to make changes as it increases the *quality, diversity* and *availability* of information; at the same time, an increasing dependence on technology can change the teacher-student relationship in student-centered learning environments (Moore, 1999).

To sum up, it is the faculty member's responsibility to create the conditions in which real and meaningful learning is possible; and, the student's responsibility to take advantage of that (Laurillard, 1998). Certainly, it is a useful notion.

Purpose of the Book

No matter how it is presented, designed and implemented, technology does play an ever-increasing and necessary role in higher education. Nevertheless, every university teacher faces at least four common areas of academic concern: preparing and organizing courses; teaching and providing assignments; assessing student learning; and evaluating the effectiveness of teaching (Ramsden, 1999). In the present day, in all areas of the curriculum, "teachers must teach an information-based inquiry process to meet the demands of the technology age. Meeting this challenge will be impossible unless educators are willing to join the revolution and embrace the new technology tools available" (Bill Gates, cited in Shelly, Cashman, Gunter, & Gunter, 2004, p. 6.10). Higher education in general and faculty members in particular must be the leaders in the integration of technology in diverse learning environments.

Keeping the above-mentioned four areas of concern facing faculty members in mind, this publication, *Technology and Diversity in Higher Education: New Challenges,* focuses on educational research and teaching practices of the digital age with the following objectives:

- Discuss theoretical and practical complicity of technology integration for diverse learners in higher education.

- Disseminate current research and analysis in technology and diversity in higher education.

- Examine a technology-mediated teaching in increasingly diverse learning environments.

- Present case studies of online and technology-based education for diverse students.

- Provide future trends and new challenges in implementation of technology and diversity in higher education.

Organization of the Book

Educators have increasingly recognized the importance of accommodating learning diversity in technology-enhanced learning environments. Each chapter of this book touches on an important theme—effective and advanced practices in the information age—through teaching, research, application and integration. This book, consisting of 13 chapters, is divided into six sections: (1) literary reading and technology; (2) case studies in technology and diversity; (3) evaluating the role and impact of technology in medical education; (4) questionnaire research in technology and diversity; (5) development and implementation of technology and diversity in learning; and (6) opportunities and new challenges in technology and diversity.

Chapter I inquires as to whether the cognitive and cultural changes incurred by reading fewer books are significant relative to the overall gains yielded by technological change in the classroom learning environment. The author presents evidence that suggests the indispensability of literary reading experience alongside technologically enabled or enhanced modes of learning. While heralding the positive learning outcomes of computer-aided instruction, the author emphasizes that rigorous assessment must also monitor the changes in literacy that accompany it and which qualify the benefits of technical content delivery.

Chapter II documents the successful formation of an intergenerational computer-tutoring project between college preservice teachers and senior adults living in a retirement community. Service-learning methodology used as a framework is described and the results of the first year of implementation are documented. The authors explain the knowledge, skills and dispositions gained by the college students in the process of tutoring and the project benefits enjoyed by the senior adults. The authors also hope that this can be a model for other universities interested in community-based learning projects.

Chapter III details the project and experience of developing post-secondary distance education in a diverse setting where the author has been involved in the design and implementation of the technology-based education. The author demonstrates how challenges for generating engagement with Web-based online courses can be met and overcome, describing the analysis of the developers' and students' experiences. The factors to strengthen and reinforce learning are judged in contributing to student achievement in meeting learning objectives.

Chapter IV describes the challenges and successes involved in crossing the digital divide from traditional to Web-based portfolios in a diverse student environment. The authors emphasizes that traditional portfolios, typically in the form of three-ring binders, are now being replaced with electronic versions on CD-ROM, DVD and the Internet. Two directions for electronic portfolios are those created with software tools found on computers or Web-based storage systems generally accompanied by data management systems that allow assessment of portfolio data. The use of electronic portfolios offers great promise but also poses significant challenges.

Chapter V provides a case study of the design and delivery of a course called "Learning with Information and Communication Technologies" (ICTs) guided by a mediated learner approach using new approaches to using ICTs and assessment *for* learning as key course design drivers. The course aims to prepare future teachers who demonstrate strong theoretical and practical understanding of designing and creating effective ICT teaching and learning experiences. The authors also provide an analysis of the implementation of that course through the presentation of the learning stories and reflections of students.

Chapter VI begins with the statement that medicine is one of the most demanding fields a person can enter. How physicians are trained has been heavily influenced by the advent of the technology era. Technology has progressed faster than society has been able to integrate it. The same is true within schools of medicine and residency training programs. The author emphasizes that many technological advances are available to medical educators and the goal of the chapter is to make educators aware of possible educational tools in the medical program.

Chapter VII examines students' perceptions of technology experiences based on three important inquires: Are today's students well prepared for the challenges of the information age? Do students possess the skills and motivation required for self-directed, life-long learning? How can educators help students to better prepare and improve information literacy skills? Data are analyzed based on four variables—gender, ethnicity, academic status and age. Qualitative data (student essays on technology use) are also analyzed to support quantitative student data from a survey questionnaire. Implications for practices are discussed, and future trends are identified.

Chapter VIII presents an analysis of Internet overuse on college campuses in general based on a survey of university students regarding their Internet use. The author emphasizes that one side effect of the technological revolution with the potential to cause harm is an inclination by some people, most notably students in higher education, for excessive and compulsive Internet use. Often called Internet addiction, this disorder is particularly prevalent on the campuses of colleges and universities and, for some students, it has the potential to be as destructive as excessive use of alcohol, tobacco or drugs.

Chapter IX evaluates the state of readiness towards adopting online distance courses between business students and faculty based on the following questions: At what stage of the undergraduate program do students recognize the importance of using the Internet for online education use? What factors explain the rate of adoption towards Internet use by students and faculty? Are there significant differences between undergraduate business students and faculty in the readiness of adoption of online education? The study is timely, given the infancy planning stage of online education delivery at the University of Guam.

Chapter X presents the case of virtual learning environments, which provide electronic access to some or all aspects of campus life. The San Diego State University Interwork Institute is partnering with community colleges in the western Pacific to offer degrees using a unique educational model. Through partnership and technology, this model blends virtual technologies with site-based facilitators and services, enabling Pacific islanders to access advanced degrees without having to travel abroad. It also allows regional 2- and 3-year colleges to build capacity to meet critical local educational challenges.

Chapter XI highlights the technological methods used to collect data from staff members who provided on-site professional development to improve teachers' knowledge and instructional practices in early reading. Data are collected via video cameras that offered immediate feedback to teachers regarding strategies acquired during professional development activities. Also described are the rewards and potential pitfalls of utilizing technology for both formative and summative uses within diverse contexts, with a focus on the incorporation of cultural, language, political, social and environmental realities of the Pacific.

Chapter XII discusses the different uses of video technology for instruction and assessment. The uses of video provide ways for students with different backgrounds and experiences as well as language differences to effectively engage with their performance and develop their skills, knowledge and dispositions. Through engagement in performance recorded via video technology, students become more motivated to prepare effectively. Their skill level rises both from the motivated preparation and through interaction with the product. The author emphasizes that each of the uses for video technology utilizes different strategies and techniques.

Chapter XIII documents the complexity of concepts of diversity and technology within the context of higher education in the Pacific. The authors identify the challenges and opportunities that a Pacific island university faces as it attempts to address the unique multicultural landscape of the region and its technological realities. The authors further explore the possibilities inherent in directly addressing issues of diversity and technology while at the same time accomplishing the courses' prescribed academic goals. The authors also provide 10 important lessons learned from the capstone course experience from which others can benefit.

It should be noted that many authors of this publication are from the University of Guam. Although it was not the editor's intention, it is understandable because faculty members at the University are in a diverse student environment and the issues of technology and diversity are part of their daily teaching. The university is fertile ground for diverse experiences, practices, discoveries and challenges for teaching and learning. The faculty is eager to discuss the issues and concerns and to make a positive impact on teaching, learning and teacher education.

Advances in technology will constantly bring new challenges to higher education, simply because teaching with technology is inevitably a dynamic, ever-changing process. It is sincerely hoped, in today's digital age, that each author's experiences and observations will stimulate the readers to rethink the way it thinks about technology and diversity in higher education.

Yukiko Inoue
Mangilao, Guam

References

Diamond, R.M. (2002). *Promotion, tenure, and faculty review committees.* Boston: Anker.

Durrence, L. (2005). Colleges show way up for women. *The Ledger Online.* Retrieved June 5, 2005, from www.theledger.com

Janicki, T.N., Schell, G.P., & Weinroth, J. (2002). Developing of a model for computer supported learning systems. *International Journal of Educational Technology, 3*(1). Retrieved June 18, 2005, from www.outreach.uiuc.edu/ijet/v3n1/janicki/index.html

Laurillard, D. (1998). *Rethinking university teaching: A framework for the effective use of educational technology.* New York: Routledge.

Ma, Y. & Runyon, L.R. (2004, July/August). Academic synergy in the age of technology: A new instructional paradigm. *Journal of Education for Business,* 367-371.

McVay, G.J., Snyder, K.D., & Graetz, K.A. (2005). Evolution of a laptop university: A case study. *British Journal of Educational Technology, 36*(3), 513-524.

Moore, D. (1999). School + technology = changes. *School Planning & Management, 38*(3), 11.

Musil, C. M. (1996). The maturing of diversity initiatives on American campuses. *American Behavioral Scientist, 40*(2), 222-232.

Ramsden, P. (1999). *Learning to teach in higher education.* New York: Routledge.

Shelly, G. B., Cashman, T. J., Gunter, R., & Gunter, G. A. (2004). *Integrating technology in the classroom.* Boston: Thomson Learning.

Spodark, E. (2001). The changing role of the teacher. *Foreign Language Annals, 34*(1), 46-51.

Strauss, H. (2005, June 24). Why many faculty members aren't excited about technology. *The Chronicle of Higher Education, 51*(42), B30-B32.

U-M Marketing Communications. (2005). *The compelling need for diversity in higher education.* Retrieved June 18, 2005, from www.umich.edu/~urel/admissions/legal/expert/intro.html

Yates, E. L. (2000). Survey shows support for diversity in colleges, business. *Black Issues in Higher Education, 17*(2), 17.

Acknowledgments

The production of a book is exciting, but complex. The editor would like to thank all the staff at Idea Group Inc., especially Mehdi Khosrow-Pour, Jan Travers, Amanda Kirlin, Andrew Bundy, Jennifer Neidig, and, particularly our development editor, Kristin Roth (who worked with me from beginning to end), for their constant assistance and expertise throughout the production process, from developing a book prospectus to completing the book editing procedure. I have thoroughly enjoyed working with such a reliable and high-energy publishing team.

The production of a book involves many individuals. Special thanks go to all involved the collation and review process of the book, without whose critical and valuable comments and suggestions book production could not have been satisfactorily completed. Special thanks also go to Ray Johnson at Fort Hays State University for his foreword to the book. Johnson has extensive experiences in diversity and technology in higher learning. He also provides workshops nationally on issues of diversity and development of strategic plans for educators, charitable organizations and business groups. I certainly value his voice when speaking of visions and challenges involving technology integration for diverse learners.

I would like to particularly express my appreciation to all of the chapter authors who wrote, revised, clarified and responded to my many inquiries during the editing process. Many contributors were also chapter reviewers. This publication and its value are truly built around such excellent contributors. Most contributors would not identify themselves as technologists; rather, they use technology to deliver or reinforce the content in which they are experts, focusing on learning engagement in diversity. Each author has shared practices, applications, discoveries and challenges encountered in improving the post-secondary teaching and learning process while making a positive difference through higher education.

In closing, I would like to thank my colleagues in the College of Professional Studies at the University of Guam, and Mary Spencer, dean of the College of Liberal Arts and Social Sciences), for their support and encouragement during the development of this manuscript. I would also like to express my thanks to all of the staff of the interlibrary loans department at the University of Guam for their constant assistance for getting references and materials. Finally, my special thanks go to Kazuko Onodera, my academic and lifelong mentor, who never lost faith in my scholarly endeavors and personal actualizations.

Section I

Literary Reading
and Technology

Chapter I

Scanners and Readers:
Digital Literacy and the
Experience of Reading

Christopher S. Schreiner, University of Guam, USA

Abstract

While heralding the positive learning outcomes of computer-aided instruction, rigorous assessment must also monitor the changes in literacy that accompany it and qualify the benefits of technical content delivery. A decline in literary reading, recently documented by a National Endowment for the Arts study, is a case in point. This chapter inquires as to whether the cognitive and cultural changes incurred by reading fewer books are significant relative to the overall gains yielded by technological change in the classroom learning environment. It argues that the impressive focus on multimodal literacy in classrooms from elementary levels through college, which seems to favor diversity of content, is prone to exclude the analytic challenges that literary reading and the growth of historical consciousness demand. This chapter presents evidence that suggests the indispensability of literary reading experience alongside technologically enabled or enhanced modes of learning.

Introduction

It is increasingly the case that to speak of "technological education" is to commit a tautology, like saying "green grass" or "the salty ocean." A recent headline says it all: "Arizona School Trades Textbooks for Laptops." This is not to say that all classrooms, especially those in less-privileged school settings, have reached the cutting edge. Even for fairly advanced or tech-savvy instructors in well-funded programs, their practical relationship to innovational methods and machines is asymptotic, always out of reach just as they purchase the most recent version of software. Nevertheless, it can be argued that the technological transfiguration of education as such is the rule, not the exception, and with it the rise of digital literacy, and that the only variable to be noted in this evolution is the specific timing of its institutionalization, with some schools or sectors lagging others due to geographic and socio-economic factors.

Regardless of whether some schools have fully computerized learning environments, most administrators, teachers and students desire to have computers and Internet capability. Try to imagine a situation in which new computer equipment is offered by the administration to faculty to upgrade their classroom, and a teacher replies, "I would prefer not to. Just give us more books." Such a preference seems almost unimaginable. In this regard, it is not an aberration but a general trend signified in the title of the following article: *Packing Up the Books: University of Texas Becomes the Latest Institution to Clear Out a Main Library to Make Room for Computers* (Mangan, 2005). This trend, which we will have occasion to call, tongue-in-cheek, stealth *Fahrenheit 451*, evinces the usurpation of literary space by digital media and, as such, poses a challenge to educational diversity insofar as infrastructure becomes pervasively technical and students themselves become "scanners" and "Web hounds" as opposed to "readers." These are no longer labels, but identities, with specific cognitive styles and moral dispositions. No in-depth study has yet been written that describes and evaluates the differences between these forms of subjectivity. This chapter will highlight problems and raise questions in preparation for such a study. It will also argue for the value of literary reading as a necessary counterbalance to technical content delivery.

Other than Information

That there are positive educational aspects of technical instruction and media is not in question here. To be sure, a book such as Steven Johnson's *Everything Bad is Good for You* goes too far in heralding the cognitive advantages associated with using new digital media such as video games, downplaying the fact that the cultural content of video games is still largely based on male combat or arcade scenarios narrow in moral and intellectual scope compared to the rich diversity of world literature. It has been argued that playing intricate computer games mimics the experience of reading great literature. But anyone who has seen an avid gamer hurry to "beat" a new game and then trade it in for another knows that such games cannot be compared to unbeatable novels like *Moby-Dick* or *Middlemarch*, which invite repeated and remarkably different readings over the course of a lifetime from the same reader.

No one will deny that there are specific problem-solving skills amounting to a type of "literacy" learned in computer labs and video games and invaluable for the workplace. But in the enthusiasm to usher in educational change, it is necessary to be vigilant that a lowering of expectations or degradation of book-based literacy (including literary-critical consciousness) does not occur under the guise of technical progress or conceptual re-description under rubrics such as "multimodal literacy." Even when an author like Steven Johnson (2005) touts the benefits of reading, as when he remarks, "I believe the printed word remains the most valuable vehicle for conveying complicated information—though the electronic word is starting to give printed books a run for their money" (p. 23), his exclusive focus on "information" reveals a blindness to the different role of print literature in education and personal development. His reductive thinking, which places all media in a frenzied competition of conveying messages between sender and receiver, overlooks the fact that literary works convey something *other* than information, called *meaning*, conveyed *indirectly* in ways that challenge and diversify human cognition. Different media have different educational uses, and it nullifies the distinctiveness of literature to place it in a race with informatics. It is worthwhile to provisionally describe this distinctiveness to begin to assess the qualitative changes in the educational experience of students for whom reading books is no longer the primary modality of learning.

The Challenge to Cognitive Diversity

The problem of the hegemony of technical content delivery has been convincingly argued in Heidegger's writings on technology; for example, *The Question Concerning Technology*. For Heidegger, technology always has "planetary dominion" (Lingis, 1968, p. 132) whether or not certain classrooms have computers. The encompassing nature of technology is so inexorable and ubiquitous that it is largely deceptive to suppose we have an option to be technical or not, since our thinking and discourse are themselves technical. What Heidegger and his commentators mean by this is that human cognition and understanding have, over the course of centuries, become determined by the lure of technique, mistaking method for truth. Objectification, calculation, numerical and statistical assessment, demographic analysis, information retrieval and surveys are the primary methods of determining meaning. It is no wonder that when students are asked to explicate a story, they submit papers replete with information about the author and topics derived from the Web, but devoid of critical insight into the meaning of the work. Information gives them a sense of control, but they have no personal stake in the material, which has not required exegetical struggle but only information retrieval. Their sense of control or mastery in the assignment, then, is partly a delusion, for much in the story escapes them, and even what they capture is not "theirs" (intellectually or emotionally) but only material they have scanned and printed. This is to say that their technique of Web mastery (information retrieval) is nothing human, according to Heidegger, although it appears to be so; the human subject is itself an agency of the *Ge-Stell* or Enframing (Heidegger, 1977): "In this way the impression comes to prevail that everything man encounters exists only insofar as it is his construct" (p. 27). This illusion gives rise in turn to one final delusion: It seems as though man everywhere and always encounters only himself. Such a development leads Heidegger to ask: "What shall we do? *How must we think*?" (Heidegger, 1977, p. 40).

To use a contemporary expression, Heidegger seeks to discover how we can think "outside the box" such that thinking is not merely a process of objectification. He has written controversial essays that argue for the necessity of a poetic way of thinking and writing, even as we stand with one leg within the Set-Up (variant translation of *Ge-Stell*). It should be evident that the mandate for instructional and cultural diversity so often heard in educational contexts is rendered problematical by the notion of technical enframing. According to Heidegger (1977), technology holds sway to such an extent that thought and, therefore, the humans that think, whatever their ethnic origin, become uniform or standardized: "This uniformity becomes the surest instrument of total, that is, technological, rule over the earth. The modern freedom of subjectivity vanishes totally in the objectivity commensurate with it" (p. 152).

It follows from this philosophic analysis that the question of an alternative to technically facilitated education, of the relative merits of technical vs. some other mode of education, is, when it arises, largely delusory. To be sure, technical diversity within a technological environment is not hard to achieve. There can be different technical methods and machines deployed. But can there be different cognitive styles in a technical environment that are not technical, except in a fugitive or marginalized mode? The existence of that which is ostensibly unrelated to or different than everything technical becomes questionable or irrelevant, banished to the realm of myth and poetry. This is indeed close to the truth of the matter, as we learn from a recent National Endowment for the Arts (NEA) survey (to be discussed later) that shows the declining *literary* reading of young people.

The Challenge to Educational Diversity

Heidegger's analysis of the inexorable influence of technology in modern life makes Todd Oppenheimer's essay, *The Computer Delusion*, all the more provocative, for he argues that we have a choice in the use of technology, and that contemporary educators have become delusional about the benefits of computers in education. As we will see in a moment, this idea of choice is guardedly echoed by Heidegger, who speaks of the freedom of thought to deem appropriate uses for technology. But this freedom is not easily gained or exercised because of its increasing marginalization.

First published in the *Atlantic Monthly* magazine, Oppenheimer's essay has since become a cornerstone in the Internet site *Arts and Letters Daily*, posted as a link in the left-hand column under the sub-heading, "Classics." Oppenheimer (1998) makes claims such as the following:

There is no good evidence that most uses of computers significantly improve teaching and learning, yet school districts are cutting programs—music, art, physical education—that enrich children's lives to make room for this dubious nostrum, and the Clinton Administration has embraced the goal of 'computers in every classroom' with credulous and costly enthusiasm. (p. 45)

What most concerns Oppenheimer is the gradual decline in the diversity of educational resources as computers and technical programs replace books and traditionally humanistic courses of study. In *a poll taken early last year,* Oppenheimer (1998) writes:

U.S. teachers ranked computer skills and media technology as more 'essential' than the study of European history, biology, chemistry and physics; than dealing with social problems such as drugs and family breakdown; than learning practical job skills; and than reading modern American writers such as Steinbeck and Hemingway or classic ones such as Plato and Shakespeare. (p. 46)

This is a serious matter that he raises, one with which this chapter is likewise concerned. Yet, as we will see, it is literary reading—however endangered—that offers the greatest opportunity for diversity. Whatever the pessimistic excesses of Oppenheimer's essay, it reminds us to be critically aware. The integration of education and Internet technology in classroom instruction remains uncritical without objective long-term studies of the learning outcomes of the proliferation of Internet access on campuses, computer-facilitated instruction and the technological classroom. The studies that Oppenheimer criticizes are largely inconclusive, some being seriously biased by corporate funding, such as Apple Computer's famous "Classrooms of Tomorrow." It is Oppenheimer's finding that after enormous expenditures for computer apparatus, there is scant evidence of greater student achievement. The most common outcome that he finds reported in the literature is the entertainment value of the computers and related equipment. Hence, he quotes Clifford Stoll's anecdote (Oppenheimer, 1997): "We loved [computers] because we didn't have to think for an hour, teachers loved them because they didn't have to teach, and parents loved them because it showed their schools were high-tech. But no learning happened" (p. 49).

Literary Experience Diversifies Thought

Although Heidegger's (1966) analysis of the sovereignty of technique is fatalistic, he does leave open the possibility that thinking can strive to operate *otherwise*, differently, even as it remains under the influence of technology:

Still, we can act otherwise. We can use technical devices, and yet with proper use also keep ourselves free of them, that we may let go of them at any time. We can use technical devices as they ought to be used, and also let them alone as something which does not affect our inner and real core. (p. 54)

By "inner core," Heidegger means the freedom of thought open to the unexpected, which he calls the "mystery." This is a difficult freedom, to be sure. Thinking is capable of a difficult process of release, discovery and invention that both produces and uncovers meaning in poetry and literature, but that also enables technical innovation. Thought cannot be trapped by, yet depends on, what it already knows if it wishes to progress. It must be self-critical and flexible, aware of how its habitual methods and assumptions determine the objective truth of its investigations. Genuine literature demands more than habitual response and slogans. The singularly demanding linguistic experience that has come to be associated with the reading of classic literature and poetry compelled Heidegger to search history for a time when thought was not yet determined by Enframing.

To fathom the diversifying power of literary experience, Heidegger (1977) goes far back to the historical origins of thought in *poiesis*, the bringing forth of meaning. Originally, in pre-Socratic times, poetry and scientific invention arise from the same freedom of thought, but gradually across the centuries they are separated into *poiesis* and *techne* (poetry and technology), after which *techne* (technique or method) comes to dominate. Their original reciprocity or codependence is forgotten. But *poiesis*, the freedom of primal questioning, has not become extinct so much as hidden from mankind. The mystery is preserved even today by literary experience in which thinking (*Denken*) and poetizing (*Dichten*) are joined (Birault, 1972). Reading genuine literature—symbolically and semantically difficult material that requires interpretation—awakens the process of thought stimulated by mystery, the unexpected and unknown.

Literary experience is a source of diversity. It diversifies cognition via rhetoric and allusion. The diversifying power of literature of which we speak, that Heidegger calls *poiesis*, is also called "literariness." The literariness of literature, which Paul de Man (1982) defines as "the use of language that foregrounds the rhetorical over the grammatical and logical function" (p. 283), challenges thought, whose calculations and conventions meet resistance in a great novel or poem. Thought encounters something "other" in literature, something deep, unfathomably ambiguous. Although Herman Melville's story "Bartleby the Scrivener" strikes a student as devoid of meaning when initially encountered ("At first I didn't know what to say about this story …"), she comes to see that this apparent *lack* of meaning is only cognitive resistance to unfamiliar material which, when overcome with patient analysis and discussion, experiences a *surplus* of meaning ("I had no idea there is so much to say about this story!").

Different kinds of literary-critical approaches are useful to ascertain the meaning of literary episodes and the obscure motivations of their characters, but the first criterion is *active reading* that sincerely engages with the matters at stake in a given text. We will have occasion to define this concept more specifically later. For now, it is sufficient to point out, with the aid of research in phenomenology, the focus of such a concept is on the "role of the reader" (Iser, 1978, p. 11), and not on the traditional (passive) notion of reading that uncovers a hidden meaning. This is the idea behind my own prefatory advice to students in literature classes that they will get out of a text what they bring to it. This "bringing" refers to an attitude and stock of historical knowledge. One brings not only enthusiasm but an intellectual openness and repertoire of previous learning. Also required is a kind of hospitality that respects whatever the literary work offers in its historical and linguistic specificity. The surplus of meaning associated with a text gives it a creative potential that represents a sort of collaborative possibility for a reader. This, of course, makes reading always also a kind of writing, by which the reader inscribes his or her thoughts and impressions in the future of the book being read. To be sure, informed literary reading requires advanced diction, psychological acuity and historical understanding. Often, cognitive resistance to a literary work is secretly a call-up of these powers of analysis ("look up that strange word"; "check your history book") declined by a passive reader. These powers are, as it were, "called out" of the active reader, in their nascence, and exercised in the process of assiduous reading.

If such powers are largely unavailable, as with young readers, the imperative to do additional research (part of this call-up of powers necessary for active reading) needs to be encouraged or enforced by their instructor until an active "habit" develops. Such an active reading habit will not only make a reader conscious of his or her own ignorance and prejudices, but will bring the reader's historically aware consciousness into a refreshing encounter with the alien but stimulating past embodied in a literary work. In this regard, the hermeneutic concept of a "fusion of horizons" (Gadamer, 1985, p. 272) has not yet been discredited and remains a valuable pedagogical approach in the advancement of literacy, for it promotes diversity of content in learning.

It can be suggested from what has been said here that practice in reading novels by the likes of Melville, Austen and Tolstoy makes us philosophers and psychologists while providing us with a detailed sense of robust language and the historical period in which the novels take place. Such reading does not in any case follow a prearranged format or sequence of programmatic deductions and conclusions, however much it is influenced by our cultural pre-conceptions and, for example, the guidance of an instructor.

It follows from the preliminary observations made above that it is not only English students who can benefit from reading literature. Scientists too, exercise their imagination when reading complex and suggestive literature, as if briefly reviving the atmosphere from which early science and mathematics arose. It is all the more ironic, then, that it is technical science which, having become eminently successful in shaping the world we live in, excludes literary experience as something fanciful and fictive. The success of technology has brought about an "ideological victory and the domination of a single cultural type" (Serres, 1989, p. 19). In other words, its influence is hegemonic, while poetry and literature are minor, largely obscure powers in the world.

It is for this reason that Michel Serres worries that technology, as the single way of living, speaking and learning in the world today, excludes all other ways of thinking and learning. We saw this was a concern of Todd Oppenheimer. But like Heidegger, whose philosophy is echoed in his writing, Serres values literary experience as something absolutely rare and precious, indispensable to the freedom of human thought. While he acknowledges that literature is endangered, he is less critically naïve than Oppenheimer, who vehemently criticizes the spread of technology. Serres (1989) knows that we cannot exclude technology. He says that science is right—it deserves its victory because it works so effectively in the world. But Serres also argues that "literature is a resource for science" (p. 7). Anyone who carefully reads the writings of Heidegger and Serres knows that these thinkers are not opposing technology. They are, however, arguing for the preservation of literary experience to achieve a balance in cultural life and education. If this balance is not achieved, literacy as traditionally understood will change so drastically that literary experience will itself become extinct.

Fundamental Changes in Literacy

What are the changes in literacy that accompany technological integration on campus? It is now almost a banality to observe that today's college students represent a generation whose primary knowledge base and discourse community is not book learning, but telematic and digital databases and media sources, including televisual and Web-based sources. The ability to manipulate these sources is called digital literacy. This impressive paradigm shift is problematical to book-oriented scholars. Anthony Grafton, a professor of history at Princeton University, has said, "My students come to college less and less able to negotiate a book landscape and more and more adept at negotiating the Web" (Carlson, 2005, p. 2). This means that students are ever more proficient at managing information and responding to the rapid, multifarious cues of an electronic environment of graphic images and hypertexts. It also means that students read fewer books, as a recent study funded by the NEA reveals (Bradshaw, 2004). Dana Gioia (2005), chairman of the NEA, says: "The concerned citizen in search of good news about American literary culture will study the pages of this report in vain" (p. 2). The study *Reading at Risk: A Survey of Literary Reading in America* shows that among respondents who responded to a survey of their reading habits, 54% had read some type of literary work in 1992, whereas in 2002 this number had declined to 46.7%. Another author (McLemee, 2004) says, "If present trends continue, American aliteracy will only deepen over the next generation: The steepest decline in reading has occurred among young adults, ages 18 to 24" (p. 1).

Based on my observations as a college English professor for more than a decade, students are prone not only to read fewer books, but shorter ones. There is increasing resistance to longer works of literary or philosophical content. This resistance was a problem I observed in the mid-1980s before the popularization of the Internet, which means that other pervasive cultural and socio-economic factors were attenuating college student literacy, such as television viewing, the popularity of home video systems and obligations to part-time jobs. In the mid-1990s, I received a letter from a former professor of mine that a novel I had read with pleasure in her seminar in 1978, Malcolm Lowry's *Under the Volcano*, was no longer teachable—students cannot get past the first chapter. Nevertheless, later in this chapter an optimistic account of literary reading by students in a recent class of mine will be described, in which textual difficulty is a source of stimulation and discovery.

The particular decline in book literacy remarked by Grafton is worrisome if book learning is something *more* or *other than* information management, if the experience of reading books such as novels, essays, and historical and philosophical works contributes something additional to human life than information. If so, the question must be asked: What is lost, if anything, in the transition from book-based to digital literacy? Is the loss compensated by the gain in digital literacy? Furthermore, when Grafton says digitally literate students are less able to "negotiate a book landscape," he does not just mean that students are no longer inclined to read books, but that they are less inclined to visit the library except to use the Internet, less able to use book-based library facilities, less skillful with book-based bibliographic and archival source retrieval (Carlson, 2005). This tendency is correlative with the actual removal of books from libraries to make room for computers and an "information commons," reported by Katherine Mangan (2005). She quotes Fred Health, vice provost for libraries at the University of Texas at Austin: "All of us are dealing with a creative tension between our commitment to this great print collection and the digital tsunami that's bearing down on us" (p. 1).

The Decline of Historical Consciousness

It is noteworthy that Thomas Bisson, a professor of medieval history at Harvard University, recently observed the avoidance of pre-modern history by students at Harvard. He speaks of the insidious crush of the present in the lives of the students. He says we have become "careless of those distant pasts, humanly imagined and imaginatively reconstructed, that alone can place our fragile present in perspective" (Bisson, 2005, p. 17). Another history professor writes:

Anyone who has taught history to college students for more than 40 years, as I have, has watched a steady decline in the background they bring to the subject. Increasingly, their studies have been geared to contemporary issues like global interactions rather than a sustained immersion in the rich variety of the past. (Rabb, 2004, p. 7)

It follows that the problem is not only a question of books not being read and libraries being underutilized. It is also the case that effective historical consciousness is diminishing. Even if one equates scanning with reading (and we will explain why this should not be done), the material read on screen is by and large not historical. It is contemporary, associated with current events and popular culture, except when an assignment specifically calls for historical research.

Multimodal Literacy and Literary Reading

A second case in point that exemplifies a change in literacy is the development of the concept of multimodal literacy. This concept does not signify progress in literacy so much as a euphemistic description of the state of affairs by which book literacy has beaten a gradual retreat from the classroom due to competing modalities (mostly electronic) that command and distract student attention. The merits of this new pedagogy, which are especially salient in small projects done by students at school and home, have already been concretely demonstrated, as the volume *Multimodal Literacy* attests (Jewett & Kress, 2003). The most heuristically valuable message of this study in multimodal literacy is that it is helpful when learning Shakespeare for students to become involved in the performance of the text. This technique of enactment has been a standard and highly successful practice of Shakespearean pedagogy. While by no means innovative, it is an unquestionably effective method to get students involved in the text by performing it.

Yet when it comes to the replacement of focused literary study with a multimodal activity, as occurs in a reported case of Shakespeare pedagogy, it appears that a new technique is actually a concession to a decline in literacy. In one study, a teacher acknowledges that the students suffer from a handicap when reading Shakespeare:

The text presents students with archaic forms of language and historically remote cultural conventions, and so it is difficult stuff to 'penetrate' ... Teachers often want to mobilize their students' experience and knowledge of the world, of home and school, of other texts—books, film and television—and bring them to bear on their reading of the printed page. Sometimes, teachers decide that students will better understand the meaning of the text if they move beyond sedentary readings toward acting out some part of Shakespeare. Through the processes of dramatization, the bodily enactment of the text in voice, action and interaction, value might be added to the reading of Shakespeare. (Franks, 2004, p. 155)

This seems like a fairly harmless passage conveying the difficulty of teaching Shakespeare and the strategies for ameliorating the situation. The fact that it is written by a British teacher in the homeland of Shakespeare makes us wonder how much more difficult it is for an American teacher to teach Shakespeare. It is crucial to observe several simultaneous messages being conveyed here, the sum total representing a sort of stealth *Fahrenheit 451* by which the challenging prolixity of book reading is withdrawn from the landscape of learning, diminishing linguistic and historical consciousness.

There is, first of all, the observation that Shakespeare confronts students with "difficult stuff to penetrate." This difficult stuff is "archaic forms of language" and "historically remote cultural conventions." Difficulty is a well-known characteristic of reading Shakespeare. What, therefore, is the intention of such an otherwise banal observation? It is unfortunately the case that these observations are made to gather textual obstacles to learning to justify a change in educational materials that would no longer be historical, or be originally penned by Shakespeare. Some contemporary version might be suitable, a film or CD-ROM. The observations are defensive; students are to be protected from difficult learning experiences. Archaic language and remote cultures are not seen here as forces of positive anachrony, by which a student experiences a break with his or her own historical horizon, its cultural practices and world view, a break that would refresh his or her own views and invigorate their perception and linguistic ability. Rather, the context of the passage makes it all too evident that "archaic forms of language" and "historically remote cultural conventions" are seen as troublesome idiosyncrasies whose specific challenges need to be filtered, softened or transfigured into a preferably electronic format and modality.

Later in this chapter, we will see student testimonies from one of my literature classes, which appreciate the anachrony of literary language. Nevertheless, since some students are more comfortable with the technological amenities that engage them at home and in school than with reading historical, densely composed verbal artifacts, their teachers want to bring the study of Shakespeare to this comfort level, this zone of stimulating gadgetry and televisual imagery. The effort is to bring Shakespeare to the level of the students, rather than the students to the level of Shakespeare. Such is the pedagogical concession, the capitulation, as it were, that operates under the rubric of multimodal literacy. The fact of the matter is that literary experience is not convenient. The focus of attention demanded by genuine literature, whatever its potential benefits for a generation of distracted students, is being forfeited for the sake of convenience.

Insofar as multimodal literacy seeks to secure a new comfort level for students, it represents a potentially catastrophic acquiescence in the face of widespread, generational problems, such as attention deficit disorder and hyperactivity. It has been suggested that in some cases these problems do not originate in inborn psychophysical conditions but in cultural problems, such as dysfunctional family life, informational overload, nutritional imbalance and multimedia-induced cognitive distraction. In other words, multimodal literacy might well be exacerbating the mental and behavioral conditions it struggles to ameliorate.

The key adjective applied to the reading of Shakespeare that raises our suspicion is "sedentary." The term is used negatively in the context of highly restless students, for whom sitting still and pensively reflecting is a challenge. All serious reading is experienced by such a group as a "sedentary" activity—as indeed it should. But the term should not have a negative connotation, which remains blind to the truth value of Pascal's (1966) remark that, "The sole cause of man's unhappiness is that he doesn't know how to stay quietly in his room" (p. 67). Sedentary refers to the mood and bodily disposition of meditative, philosophical lucubration. Is this mood and all such sedentary "states of the soul" to be avoided by young students? What are the consequences of demoting sedentary activity, the pace and mood of all serious indoor study? Again, we see here an acceptance of hyperactivity rather than an effort to temper it with literary experience and other cognitively demanding analytic endeavors that focus attention.

As said above, the gradual exclusion of book-based learning by multimodal literacy strikes as a sort of Stealth *Fahrenheit 451*. Readers will recognize this reference to the title of Ray Bradbury's famous novel (1953) about the suppression of book culture caused by a political ideology that seeks a mollified, shallow, acquiescent and uncritical populace—in short, a culture of illiteracy. Bradbury's grim futuristic scenario remains too extreme to serve as an allegory for the effect of technology on education and the concomitant decline of book literacy and a culture of reading in schools. In any case, the long-term results are not known. But the bookless landscape Bradbury melodramatically evokes comes all too easily to mind when we read in the *Chronicle of Higher Education* articles entitled, *College Libraries Set Aside Books in a Digital Age* (Blumenthal, 2005).

Scannable Discourse
(Maximizing the Efficiency of Digital Literacy)

Observations about the decline of historical literacy remind us that certain technologies seem to enrich and diversify learning (for example, different search engines) yet arguably reduce its scope insofar as both imagination and effective historical consciousness are attenuated. In this case the appearance, of diversity would mask a horizon limited to what is contemporary.

No doubt the purchase and installation of technologies that replace traditional library content is motivated by noble intentions, and the almost infinite material that can be discovered by careful searching is of great depth and diversity. But the actual habits, tastes and priorities of contemporary users prevail to delimit the depth potential of what is installed. Furthermore, design features are being implemented on the Web that encourage what can only be called a simplification of content and the thought it is meant to arouse. Web design, knowingly or not, is in complicity with the "dumbing down" of cultural life.

To show this complicity, we have to inquire as to the phenomenal format of digital literacy —how it shows itself, or appears to the reader and the user. The problem that arises here is the stylistic homogeneity of what appears and appeals to students during Web-based browsing, surfing and searching. This is not to say that there is not diverse material on the Web, but that the specific structures and formats of the hegemonic search engines (*Yahoo* and *Google*) constrain heterogeneity and reinforce the standardization of the learning experience, especially with regard to the material acquired by scanning. It seems obvious to point out that search engines are configured to command the search strategy of searchers and not be commanded by the searchers, although the illusion persists of a clever searcher searching. To be sure, there can be clever searchers for information, and these types will outperform on the new SAT being prepared by the Educational Testing Service to test digital literacy. But without long-term assessment of outcomes, this cleverness cannot be assumed to be a replacement for analytic thought, much less for what Heidegger calls *der Dichtungschar-ackter des Denkens* (Birault, 1972), the poetic character of thought.

What characterizes the process of reading (browsing, surfing and searching) on the Web? The research brief of Morkes and Nielsen (1997b), titled, *How Users Read on the Web*, explains their title with the following reply: "They don't." Users don't read when they use the Web. According to Morkes and Nielsen (1997a), people rarely read Web pages word by word; instead, *they scan the page*, picking out individual words and sentences. The research, which found that 79% of the Web users tested "always scanned any new page they came across" and only 16% of tested users "read word by word," is guided by the following purpose: to maximize the efficiency of Web usage using a highly scannable text. Morkes and Nielsen argue that because "really good writing" rarely appears on the Web, it is best to streamline Web text so readers can find useful information as soon as possible.

The primary role of the Web is assumed to be the delivery of information, for which streamlining serves an indispensable role. But with the increasing use of the Web by billions of users, the market sets its own demands, with accessibility (clarity and concision) and performativity (usefulness) becoming the criteria of choice for publishing and education.

In keeping with their discovery of the habits of Web users, Morkes and Nielsen prescribe a scannable format and style incorporating the following features:

Scannable Format

1.   Highlighted key words (hypertext links serve as one form of highlighting; different typefaces and colors are others)

2.   Meaningful subheadings (not "clever" ones)

3.   Bulleted lists

4.   *One idea* per paragraph (users will skip over additional ideas if they are not caught by the first few words in the paragraph)

5.   The inverted pyramid style, *starting with the conclusion*

6.   Half the word count (or less) of conventional writing

(Morkes & Nielson, 1997a)

In light of such prescriptive stylistics, it needs to be asked if scanning, which used to be a specialized technique for "speed reading," is becoming a normative practice in digital literacy in reading and writing. For the sake of argument, it can be suggested here that the technical format recommended above concretely embodies Heidegger's abstract notion of "Enframing" (*Ge-stell*). In other words, although Heidegger saw all thought and perception as filtered and framed by technical objectification, he did not foresee and describe a literal *style* for such framing. Morkes and Nielson go further than Heidegger dared by prescribing a literal format and style for the Information Age. This format, we have seen, simplifies our cognition (access and processing) of what is available on the Web: highlighted text; one idea per paragraph; half the word count of conventional text; and conclusions presented first.

What are the implications of maximizing the cognitive efficiency by which Internet content is assimilated? The most general consequence of making everything scannable is that all Web content is treated as information, converted into information that is simple and easily summarized. Conclusions, offered in advance, foreclose critical analysis of a given state of affairs. As a rhetorical option, the "scannable" style of display represents the choice of a "synthetic arrangement" (Knoblauch & Brannon, 1984, p. 39) of material over an "analytic presentation." The synthetic arrangement depends on the recognition that a reader who is either ignorant of a subject matter or impatient to learn the writer's most important information will find it more satisfying to see generalities first. An analytic textual presentation, on the other hand, requires more work from readers and is considered a more sophisticated style of presentation; its strength lies in engaging readers' interest by giving them some responsibility for anticipating where the writer is headed. It is for this reason that Oppenheimer (1997) cites Larry Cuban of Stanford University: "Schooling is not about information. It's getting kids to think about information. It's about understanding and knowledge and wisdom" (p. 60). Also cited is Yale's David Gelernter, who complains about the time wasted by students surfing the Internet. "We need less surfing," Gelernter is quoted as saying.

The danger of scanning uniformly formatted material is that diverse information is reduced to more or less the same value and significance. In this regard, Morris Berman (2000) observes: "Most of Generation X lacks all sense of history or cultural continuity. Increasingly, we live in a 'weightless order,' in which all information is equally significant" (p. 49). Berman is rightly worried about an erosion of critical and historical consciousness. We find this erosion epitomized today in the booming market for the *Dummies Guide* series. Examples of these texts include *The Complete Idiot's Guide to American Literature*; *World History for Dummies*; *Mythology for Dummies*; *The Complete Idiot's Guide to Philosophy*; and *Philosophy for Dummies*. These simplified works, written in a "boiled down" style, reflect the technical format recommended by Nielson for the Web, and represent an ominous convergence of Internet content and book publishing. When Heidegger (1968) speaks of poetry, thought and science "assimilated to one another" through literature, he is referring to precisely this convergence of genres and formats engineered by publishing corporations, which even he could not have imagined would have become, as they are today, media conglomerates such as Time Warner. Literature loses its literariness and becomes technical writing and cinematic versions of literary masterpieces. It has been noted by more than one author that the potential for a film contract is the primary criterion for publishing contracts. Such observations suggest that the film industry will determine the future of literary experience for coming generations.

Morris Berman (2000) takes such developments as grave indicators of the decline of American culture, with individuals experiencing the loss or denigration of their powers of judgment, imagination and historical awareness:

If my colleague at a Midwest university now has a student who never read a novel, how long before he has a student who asks him, "What's a novel?" (In fact, millions of Americans don't know the difference between fiction and nonfiction.) If the students don't recognize Browning now, how long before they have never heard of Shakespeare? ... In his introduction to the book Dumbing Down: Essays on the Strip-Mining of American Culture, *John Simon notes that a world of learning is disappearing before our eyes, in merely one generation. We cannot expect, he says, to make a mythological allusion any more, or use a foreign phrase, or refer to a famous historical event or literary character, and still be understood by more than a tiny handful of people.* (p. 41)

Although teachers are becoming aware of the developments noted by Berman, the empirical and phenomenological differences between literary reading and digital literacy are not self-evident to today's college students, whose growing competence in multimodal digital "literacy" masks, with its progressive rhetoric, the decline of literary consciousness. Peter is robbed to pay Paul. There is a lack of self-awareness on the part of the student body regarding what their developing technical literacy excludes—an experience of the depth dimension of literary discourse. The *Dummies Guides* are taken for granted as legitimate means of primary access to classic works in history, literature and philosophy. Students need to be aware of these changes in literacy and the growing corporate complicity between scannable Web-based content and print culture. Only seen in this context of competing value claims will the simplifying and de-historicizing effects of today's specific practice of digital literacy not be taken as normative for future learning.

The Reading Experiences of Scholars (The Growth of Literary Consciousness)

To explain the meaning of reading as an act and process, to fully grasp what kind of experience is endangered with extinction when we speak, for example, of the "decline of reading" as does the NEA report, we need to go directly to readers' narratives, biographical testimony. Our first example is the reading experience of Janna Levin (2004), professor of physics at Columbia University. Her personal narrative discloses the world or culture of reading manifested in family life, as it were as a *form of family life.* Her father had "enormous medical reference books" that she perused after he went to work. She found them intimidating and attractive.

Inside were hieroglyphs. I tried to read the entries—Pancreatic Adenocarcinoma, Cerebellar Vermis Hypoplasia, Myeloid Myelodysplatsic Syndromes—but never could understand a significant word. I was jealous that someone else could access the ideas and knowledge trapped in the Latin inscriptions. ... I knew that those drab, heavy books were somehow connected to a real place—a hospital. ... In the evenings, my mother would read books, so many books. She'd settle on the couch and stretch her toes away from the back of the novel. If she finished a book, she managed to find a place for it on already full bookshelves. One day, nosing around, I saw that they were stacked three or four deep on the shelves: Toni Morrison, Philip Roth, Joyce Carol Oates. It would be many years before I would succumb to such capacious reading—an avarice on the verge of addiction, including compulsive spending in bookshops and hoarding of books to ensure that the supply never diminished. Books in drawers, under the bed, in boxes under the stairs. Books high and low for sheer pleasure. Lust almost. Many, many years later, I would write a book. The intimacy of those books would migrate from memory to influence to experience, until they were digested and stored in my fibers, an integrated part of who I am. (pp. 171-172)

The reading experience described by Levin consists of an emotional and intellectual transition from incomprehension ("never understand a significant word ...") to intimacy. There is an inner relation between these feelings. Difficulty, in the process of being overcome, intensifies the engagement with the material, not only through a feeling of mastery, of achievement, but a sort of bonding, as if an intimacy is developed along the way as the adversary becomes a dear friend. It is striking to note that household space in the Levin home, with shelves full of books, conforms to the desires of readers in a family.

A similarly positive encounter with difficulty occurs in the reading experience of the young R. G. Collingwood (1939)—later a world-famous historian—who was home-schooled until the age of thirteen:

My father had plenty of books, and allowed me to read them as I pleased ... One day when I was eight years old, curiosity moved me to take down a little black book lettered on its spine Kant's Theory of Ethics. *It was Abbott's translation of the* Grundlegung zur Metaphysik der Sitten*; and as I began reading it, my small form wedged between the bookcase and the table, I was attacked by a strange succession of emotions. First came an intense excitement. I felt that things of the highest importance were being said about matters of the utmost urgency: things which at all costs I must understand. Then, with a wave of indignation, came the discovery that I could not understand them. Disgraceful to confess, here was a book whose words were English and whose sentences were grammatical, but whose meaning baffled me. Then, third and last, came the strangest emotion of all. I felt that the contents of this book, although I could not understand it, were somehow my business: a matter personal to myself, or rather to some future self of my own. It was not like the common boyish intention 'to be an engine-driver when I grow up,' for there was no desire in it; I did not, in any natural sense of the word, want to master the Kantian ethics when I should be old enough; but I felt as if a veil had been lifted and my destiny revealed. There came upon me by degrees, after this, a sense of being burdened with a task whose nature I could not define except by saying, 'I must think.'* (pp. 3-4)

It was Collingwood's experience to become compelled, not disgusted or bored, by the formidable abstraction and difficulty of the philosophical classics in his father's library. His struggle to read philosophy, which initiated the growth of his literary consciousness and his destiny, was an emotional, intensely complex encounter with something incomprehensible that spoke to his innermost self, albeit obscurely. Kant's writings were not, like a video game today, solved and discarded by Collingwood. Rather, his engagement with them led to a life-long intellectual attachment. It is also noteworthy that as in Levin's experience, the young Collingwood's literary development was encouraged and influenced by the mere presence of many books in his home.

For our third example of literary consciousness, it is worthwhile to cite Freud's appreciation of the fiction writer, who:

can keep us in the dark for a long time about the precise nature of the presuppositions on which the world he writes about is based, or he can cunningly and ingeniously avoid any definite information on the point up to the last. ... The storyteller has a peculiarly directive power over us; by means of the moods he can put us into, he is able to guide the current of our emotions, to dam it up in one direction and make it flow in another. (Mahoney, 1987, p. 177)

One of the features of fictional narrative that appeals to Freud is the *uncertainty of sense-making* in the narrative, in the way a world takes form, due to the nuanced temporality of the narrative flow and the craft of the author. This keeps the reader off balance, or guessing. Freud savors the unpredictability of fictional prose, one of the intrinsic qualities of its literariness. The narration of details concerning character behavior, event, setting do not have a predictable tempo. Furthermore, Freud speaks of a "directive power" associated with *emotionally engaging* material. He recognizes the power of reading to shape his thought and motivate his own writing. Overall, what strikes about Freud's reading is that it is not a quest for certainty, but a participation in speculative thought. His own prose in such famous works as *Beyond the Pleasure Principle* reflected this speculative propensity.

Freud was also particularly enthralled with the literary criticism of Stefan Zweig. Take note of what impressed Freud in Zweig's critical prose:

I have read it with exceptional pleasure, otherwise there would hardly be any point in writing to you about it. The perfection of empathy combined with the mastery of linguistic expression left me with a feeling of rare satisfaction. What interests me especially are the accumulations and increasing intensity with which your language keeps groping closer to the most intimate nature of the subject. (Mahoney, 1987, p. 178)

It is the intensity of empathetic linguistic description that captivates Freud as he reads Zweig's literary criticism. The descriptive prose of Zweig is empathetic, yet accurate, true to its subject. In short, Freud thinks it an admirable thing for a writer to be fully spellbound by a work of literature and yet write convincingly about it, such that another reader would also be inspired to read that literary masterpiece. Notice the word "groping" that Freud uses to characterize Zweig's critical approach. The struggle with hermeneutic difficulty—what does a text mean?—is appreciated as a professional and artistic necessity.

We learn from readers like Freud that one does not shirk difficulty because it is inconvenient; rather, one struggles to understand what is being said on the page in a process called "active reading" (Ingarden, 1973, p. 38), thereby sharpening one's mental powers in the cognition of the literary work. Active reading is an encounter with semantic difficulty that is much different than in "passive" reading, which is a purely receptive process, like scanning. The reading of a literary work of art, Ingarden says:

can thus be accomplished 'actively' in the sense that we think with a peculiar originality and activity the meaning of the sentences we have read; we project ourselves in a co-creative attitude into the realm of the objects determined by the sentence meanings. (p. 40)

The youthful reading experiences of scholars can be summarized as follows:

Reading Experience of Scholars

1. Movement from humble incomprehension to intellectual mastery
2. Difficult text does not alienate so much as attract and stimulate
3. Emotional/intellectual relation to books resulting in intimacy and life-long attachment
4. Reading as a cultural practice, family activity and source of community
5. Analytic exercise in search of a mystery that beckons active reading
6. Pleasure in semantic analysis, textual interpretation and the life of language

The literary experience of scholars documented in personal narratives offers a lesson to the teacher of literature who is intimidated by changes in the literacy habits of her students, for whom "short and simple" texts are preferable. The lesson is, *do not compromise. Teach the difficult texts whose rhetorical material poses an analytic challenge.* Do whatever it takes, such as reading the text aloud in its entirety, with discussions clarifying words and context, as the class I describe below does when reading Herman Melville. But remember: Reading is less a quest for certainty than intellectual challenge and emotional satisfaction.

Reading Melville: Encounters with Anachrony and Rhetorical Intricacy

It was the purpose of the above section to foreground the educational importance of difficult literary experiences for eminent scholars and professionals. The kind of reading material that stymied and then engaged them was patently analytic in its discourse, not synthetic, in the terms we cited above from Knoblauch and Brannon (1984). Recall that analytic material requires intellectual engagement, whereas synthetic material is already processed as it were (like fast food for the mind). These scholars and thinkers did not grow their intellects by passively reading summaries or bulleted lists, but by actively reading prodigiously challenging texts. We see in their experiences that there is a "residue of indetermination" associated with literariness (de Man, 1982). Literature, whether fictional, philosophical or historical, is not, according to Paul de Man, a "transparent message in which it can be taken for granted that the distinction between the message and the means of communication is clearly established" (p. 285). How something is said is integral to its semantic comprehension. This compounding of sound and sense is part of the original literary experience that students need to encounter to fully develop their cognitive and linguistic powers (which are hardly distinguishable in any case). Its importance for cognition is such that to convert it to a simple language or scannable format is to reduce its power to sharpen our powers of analysis.

In my *Introduction to Literature* (EN 210) class at the University of Guam, consisting mostly of first- and second-year General Education students, Melville's story *Bartleby the Scrivener*, published in 1853, has proven to be both a tremendous hurdle and rewarding experience for students. It is the obstacle overcome, they say, that makes the reward more rewarding. The primary obstacle is the noncontemporaneity of Melville's prose, the persistent anachrony of its legalistic style and diction, which veers into parody. We read the entire story aloud, and students often stumble over the sentences and their recondite sounds. I ask them to look up all the words they don't know, and some students find more than 130 words. We define words in context and often uncover the roots of most of the words in class discussion, some of which appear on a quiz. From the obscurity of literary language emerges a certain charm of description, "whiskered, sallow and, upon the whole, piratical-looking," "unwarrantable usurpation," "unnecessary maledictions," all associated with a clerical character named Nippers, whose colleagues (fellow scriveners) are Turkey and Ginger Nut. A student *in Introduction to Literature* offers the following observation about Melville's language.

I have to admit that I was taken aback by the language in Bartleby *at first. But after the first couple of lines, the story grew on me, and I fell into the rhythm of it. I love the way the lines feel, the way all the words and voices blend together in a harmony that isn't heard anymore. Overall, I enjoyed* Bartleby—*it was a refreshing break from contemporary literature. As students, our job is to learn. While new and contemporary and clear are all very good, we must consider the quality of thought we are promoting if we simply stick with whatever we already know and understand.* (EN 210 student, University of Guam, 2005)

The "rhythm" and "harmony that isn't heard anymore" are integral to the flow of the narrative. Narrativity—the process and effects of narration—not only involves the reader in the unfolding of events and meaning from beginning to end; it also creates, in this story by Melville, a tightly woven world within a world, a small office space in the heart of Wall Street. It was Melville's art to convey the antic, vapid atmosphere of clerical life on Wall Street in the nineteenth century as something cozy. In the boredom of the workplace without windows, the traits and speech habits of characters become exaggeratedly significant to each other, as a sort of dynamism of the trivial, and these traits and habits comprise a community.

Herman Melville has an ear for the idiosyncratic ruminations of a boss with a conscience, who waxes philosophical over a new employee named Bartleby. The latter, a "scrivener" or copyist, eventually refuses to perform his duties at work, but does so politely in a stance of non-violent resistance. His behavior is perplexing to all of his co-workers, but especially to his boss. I quote a passage as follows:

Nothing so aggravates an earnest person as a passive resistance. If the individual so resisted be of a not inhumane temper, and the resisting one perfectly harmless in his passivity, then, in the better moods of the former, he will endeavor charitably to construe to his imagination what proves impossible to be solved by his judgment. Even so, for the most part, I regarded Bartleby and his ways. Poor fellow! Thought I, he means no mischief; it is plain he means no insolence; his aspect sufficiently evinces that his eccentricities are involuntary. He is useful to me. I can get along with him. If I turn him away, the chances are he will fall in with some less indulgent employer, and then he will be rudely treated, and perhaps driven forth miserably to starve. (Melville, 1969, p. 50)

In this passage the rhetorical intricacies of self-persuasion, which arise from the sympathetic understanding and charitable impulses of the firm manager, are expressed in a prose whose archaism is in the very length and syntax of its sentences. Students don't write sentences like that. And they are not accustomed to reading such sentences. The incomprehensible obduracy of Bartleby is interpreted as harmless passive resistance. There is a leap from rational judgment into hospitality in such an interpretation. Bartleby's motivation never becomes completely clear, but the narrator's encounter with otherness evokes hospitality. It is his first response. What strikes students is the generosity of this response, which, embedded in anachronistic language, teaches them about a moral sensibility that existed in an age before theirs. To read old-fashioned sentences with patience, to pronounce and define obsolete or underused words, rewards the reader with insights into a moral world no longer here, yet accessible in books. The most common response to this passage is, "The boss would quickly fire Bartleby today," and "No boss would contemplate his employee's disobedience with such thoughtful patience. The bosses must have been more caring in Melville's time." It deepens the learning experience of students when they learn, on the contrary, that tolerance was not normative for Melville's time, but atypical, and that the behaviors narrated by Melville run counter not only to his time but our own time. As Wolfgang Iser (1978) says of the eighteenth-century novel *Tom Jones*, "it does not refer directly to one dominant thought system" but is concerned with "the deficiencies produced by a number of systems. It shows the gulf between the rigid confines of principles and the endless fluidity of human experience" (p. 77). In other words, a story like *Bartleby the Scrivener* does not only reflect the social norms of its time, but also the particular philosophical ideas and opinions of its author, Melville, which create interpretive opportunities for understanding human behavior in a horizon of historical perspective. "The concept of the horizon," says Gadamer (1985), "suggests itself because it expresses the wide, superior vision that the person who is seeking to understand must have. To acquire a horizon means that one learns to look beyond what is close at hand—not in order to look away from it, but to see it better within a larger whole and in truer proportion" (p. 271).

How did students respond to the question, "Describe your experience reading *Bartleby the Scrivener*"?

When reading Bartleby the Scrivener *I found a lot of old text that I wasn't familiar with and had to look up. Although this is true, the context of the story was laid out in class in a manner that was understandable. From the beginning,* Bartleby *was an interesting story. It made you wonder why Bartleby did what he did. When I finished the story, I was disheartened by the situation but I was also moved by his motives, which were never clearly stated.* (EN 210 student, 2005)

The old-fashioned sound of Melville's prose involved this reader in an experience of defamiliarization. She gradually finds her bearings with the help of class discussion and a dictionary. Bartleby's repeated phrase, "I would prefer not to," is compared in class to today's slogan, "Whatever." The students ascertain that Bartleby's phrase is polite refusal, whereas "whatever" expresses a lack of respect. The linguistic comparison generated intense classroom discussion. But it wasn't only the anachronistic diction of Melville's story that seemed unfamiliar to this student. Bartleby's inscrutable behavior, which compels him to withdraw from the world, and then to starve to death curled up in a prison yard, is oddly moving, not in spite of but *because of* the obscurity of his motives and feelings.

A common experience for students in the Introduction to Literature class was incomprehension when confronted with unfamiliar "literary" words. But for most, this was not a learning situation of which they disapproved. The demand to look up obscure words was met with hesitant vigor, and then increasing satisfaction as the course progressed. This aspect of literary reading is perhaps the most noteworthy element in the student responses to reading Melville's story:

My first impression of Bartleby the Scrivener *was "Oh no! I don't understand anything!" It made me question my knowledge of words; "Have I learned enough?" It was difficult to read the story by myself; it needed time and word-for-word understanding, but I figured this (Melville) is what literature is all about. Nobody takes time to read Melville anymore. ... It is really worthwhile to educate students on words they don't learn in high school. Schools should require us to read more books by famous authors like Melville.* (EN 210 student, 2005)

Another student appreciates the fact that reading Melville's language broadens her historical understanding and knowledge of the evolution of culture.

Bartleby the Scrivener *was a difficult text because of the language used, but I found the story to be very interesting. The language really shows the culture at the time and is actually a sort of history lesson. In all of my English classes I haven't read a story like this one. The language sets a tone for the story ... I think these are very important texts to read because that is what we have evolved from. We have to know our history, where our thinking comes from.* (EN 210 student, 2005)

The following features epitomize literary experience in the classroom and challenge students in ways they are unaccustomed:

Student Literary Reading Experience

1. Difficult, sometimes anachronistic diction and style of literary prose

2. Ambiguity, allusion and indirect language; obscurity of human motives

3. Rhetorical effects and tropes, including irony, parody, metaphor, sarcasm

4. Emotionally engaging material of a turbulent, tragic or comical nature

5. The exercise of analytic and philosophical reflection in the discovery of meaning

6. A sense of total involvement for the reader in the flow of narrative

It is noteworthy that although the scholars we cited read somewhat different, more essayistic literature than the students, who read literary fiction, both groups share an appreciation for the active, participatory nature of the reading process, and for the intrinsic value of overcoming semantic and analytic challenges. Furthermore, for both groups an emotional attachment was associated with the most satisfactory reading experiences.

Conclusion

A major conference about the role of technology in academia has a keynote panel devoted to the following question: What is the role of the humanities in an era dominated by technology? The present essay has proposed a basic answer: Educators need to insist on literary reading as a necessary analytic exercise, and for the development of moral and historical awareness. Within a balanced or "multimodal" curriculum, there should be time for scanning *and* reading. This balance recognizes and respects the difference between information management and the interpretation of literary material, different but indispensable cognitive experiences for a quality education. The present study has sought to explain that the powerful effects of "literariness" are not limited to fictional novels and other genres associated with English class, but to analytic material found in history, science and philosophy books as well, the kind read (as we saw) by scholars and thinkers in their youth. Such literary discourse, which is often allusive, indirect and prolix, cannot be easily scanned as can many other textual forms on the Web. But its difficulty involves the reader in a meaning-making process that forces personal involvement, something sorely lacking from information retrieval. This personal involvement, we saw in young readers, has lasting consequences that shape a destiny.

The technical conversion of material associated with the scannable format movement, and Web-based initiatives to provide summaries of classic literature instead of the entire works, press our reading experiences ever closer to conforming to the criterion of performativity that J. F. Lyotard (1992) says defines postmodern knowledge, which is forced to fit a pragmatic function. It must be amenable to coding and scanning, or be excluded. This is a later stage of the Enframing that Heidegger foresaw in the rise of technological culture: Literary forms are rendered irrelevant. It means that a story like *Bartleby the Scrivener* will not fit the curriculum due to its semantic and psychological obscurity. Its meanings and Bartleby's motives are too allusive and incalculable. To be coded or not to be coded (machine code), to be bulleted or not, to end up with nothing but *Dummies Guides* or not: That is the question for literature and the people who read it. Bartleby would say: "I would prefer not to."

It is noteworthy that the defining crisis of Melville's career was when he was confronted with the decision as a writer to write popular novels that conformed to current tastes or philosophical, densely symbolic works of literature. His early career in the 1840s had been blessed with the popular success of novels based on his youthful voyages in the South Seas. These were largely replete with local color, adventures of runaways experiencing tribal customs and the passions of exotic life in the islands before returning to ship. Melville's decision is now literary history: *Moby Dick,* which appeared in 1851, was a publishing failure due to its robust literariness, selling a few hundred copies. His later novels fared more or less the same dire reception due to their difficulty. Thus, Bartleby's "I prefer not to" on Wall Street was also Melville's position as a writer. He preferred not to accommodate his novel writing to the popular demands of the marketplace. He wanted readers (or "thought-divers," as he called them), not scanners. "Any fish can swim near the surface, but it takes a great whale to go down stairs five miles or more" (Sealts, 1982, p. 261).

References

Berman, M. (2000). *The twilight of American culture.* New York: Norton Books.

Birault, H. (1972). Thinking and poetizing in Heidegger. In J. Kockelmans (Ed. and Trans.), *On Heidegger and Language.* Evanston: Northwestern University Press.

Blumenthal, R. (2005). *College libraries set aside books in a digital age.* Retrieved May 14, 2005, from www.nytimes.com

Bradbury, R. (1953). *Fahrenheit 451.* New York: Ballantine Books.

Bradshaw, T. (2004). *Reading at risk: A survey of literary reading in America.* Washington, DC: National Endowment for the Arts.

Carlson, S. (2005, March 14). *Scholars note decay of citations to online references.* Chronicle of Higher Education (p. 2). Retrieved March 18, 2005, from http://chronicle.com/daily2005/03

Collingwood, R.G. (1939). *An autobiography.* Oxford: Oxford University Press.

De Man, P. (1982). The resistance to theory. In P. Rice & P. Waugh (Eds.), *Modern literary theory* (pp. 272-289). London and New York: Oxford University Press.

Gadamer, H.G. (1985). The principle of effective history. In K. Mueller-Vollmer (Ed.), *The hermeneutics reader* (pp. 267-273). New York: Continuum Publishers.

Gioia, D. (2005). *Why literature matters. Boston Globe.* Retrieved April 10, 2005, from www.boston.com/news/globe/editorial_opinion/oped/articles/2005/04/10why

Heidegger, M. (1966). *Discourse on thinking* (J. Anderson and H. Freund, Trans.). New York: Harper & Row.

Heidegger, M. (1968). *What is called thinking?* (J. G. Gray, Trans.). New York: Harper & Row.

Heidegger, M. (1977). *The question concerning technology and other essays* (W. Lovitt, Trans.). New York: Harper & Row.

Ingarden, R. (1973). *The cognition of the literary work of art* (R. A. Crowley and K. R. Olson, Trans.). Evanston: Northwestern University Press.

Iser, W. (1978). *The act of reading: A theory of aesthetic response.* Baltimore: Johns Hopkins University Press.

Jewett, C., & Kress, G. (2003). *Multimodal literacy.* New York: Peter Lang.

Johnson, S. (2005). *Everything bad is good for you: How today's popular culture is making you smarter.* New York: Riverhead Books.

Knoblauch, C. H., & Brannon, L. (1984). *Rhetorical traditions and the teaching of writing.* Upper Montclair: Boynton Cook.

Levin, J. (2004). A day in the life of a child. In J. Brockman (Ed.), *Curious minds: How a child becomes a scientist* (pp. 171-176). New York: Pantheon Books.

Lingis, A. (1968). On the essence of technique. In M. Frings (Ed.), *Heidegger and the quest for truth* (pp. 126-138). Chicago: Quadrangle Books.

Lyotard, J-F. (1992). *The postmodern explained* (J. Pefanis, Trans). Minneapolis: Minnesota University Press.

Mahoney, P. (1987). *Freud as a writer.* New Haven: Yale University Press.

Mangan, K. (2005). Packing up the books … . *Chronicle of Higher Education, 51*(45). Retrieved June 30, 2005, from *http:/chronicle.com/weekly/v51/i43/43a02701*

McLemee, S. (2004). *Americans found to read less literature than ever.* Retrieved July 16, 2004, from http://chronicle.com/weekly/v50/i45/45a00101.htm

Melville, H. (Ed.). (1969). *Great short works of Herman Melville.* Warner Berthoff. New York: Harper & Row.

Morkes, J., & Nielsen, J. (1997a). *How users read on the Web: Reading on the Web alert box.* Retrieved June 16, 2005, from http://useit.com/alertbox/9710a.html

Morkes, J., & Nielsen, J. (1997b). *Concise, scannable, and objective: How to write for the Web.* Retrieved June 16, 2005, from http://useit.com

Oppenheimer, T. (1997). The computer delusion. *The Atlantic Monthly, 280*(1), 45-62.

Pascal, B. (1966). *Pensées* (A. J. Krailsheimer, Trans.). New York: Penguin.

Rabb, T. K. (2004). What has happened to historical literacy? *Chronicle of Higher Education.* Retrieved March 14, 2005, from *http://chronicle.com/weekly/v50/i39/39b02401.htm*

Sealts, M. M. (1982). *Pursuing Melville.* Madison: University of Wisconsin Press.

Serres, M. (1989). Literature and the exact sciences (R. Lapidus, Trans). *Substance, 18*(2), 3-34.

Section II

Case Studies in Technology and Diversity

Chapter II

Intergenerational Learning:
College Students and Older Adults

Joyce McCauley, Sam Houston State University, USA

Marilyn Rice, Sam Houston State University, USA

Abstract

This chapter describes the successful formation of an intergenerational computer-tutoring project between college pre-service teachers and senior adults living in a retirement community. Service-learning methodology used as a framework is described and the results of the first year of implementation is documented. The authors hope that this can be a model for other universities interested in community-based learning projects. First, the authors give the need for computer training for senior adults. They describe the process of matching college students enrolled in technology courses with residents of a local retirement home. They explain the knowledge, skills, and dispositions gained by the college students in the process of tutoring and the project benefits enjoyed by the senior adults. Popular Internet sites for the elderly user are listed and improvements for future implementation are noted.

Introduction

I saw her sitting there. Mary Rose. Age 91. Her eyes were on the computer screen in front of her. She shook her head, looked down at the keyboard and back up to the screen. Her hands were folded in her lap. I leaned in the door. "Hey, Mary Rose. What are you working on so diligently?"

Oh, I can't remember what my son told me about this contraption. I know I'm supposed to press something so I can answer my e-mail from my granddaughter, but I can't remember. I just can't remember.

I sat with her for a while in the activities room of the retirement home, showing her an operation that is quite a part of my life: "HIT REPLY." Seems easy enough. But, perhaps, when I'm 91, I might forget too. Although I gave Mary Rose a short lesson in replying to her e-mails, she started me on an adventure that day—a journey teaching computer technology through service learning. This chapter shares that journey.

Background

There are many more Mary Roses today than before. Advances in medicine and healthier life styles have made living longer possible. "The likelihood that an American who reaches the age of 65 will survive to the age of 90 has nearly doubled over the past 40 years—from just 14% of 65-year-olds in 1960 to 25% at present" (Adler, 2002). In the 1990s, there were about 5 million Americans older than age 85, and by the year 2040, this number will increase to 24 million (Schneider, 1991). By 2020, there will be 53 million Americans older than 65, and that number will rise to 77 million by 2040, more than double the number today (Adler, 2002). The vast majority of these senior adults want to be active participants in life; they want to continue learning. The American Association of Retired People reports that more than 90% of adults older than age 50 want to continue to learn to keep pace with the world (AARP, 2000). Knowledge of computers can help older adults be full participants in this Age of Information (Timmermann, 1998) and might well be the reason that this age group is the fastest growing segment of computer users (Mayhorn, Stronge, McLaughlin, & Rogers, 2004). In addition, computer activities provide mental, creative and psychomotor challenges that help to enrich the brain's abilities (Adler, 2002; Jenevein, 1993). Even something as simple as playing computer games entertains and encourages seniors to practice spelling, memory and concentration skills as well as improves feelings of self-worth (Lawhon, Ennis, & Lawhon, 1996; Peniston, 1990). Learning new things slows specific aspects of aging (Schneider, 2003), and learning to surf the Internet can result in more positive attitudes toward aging (Cody, Dunn, & Hoppin, 1999).

But learning how to operate "this contraption" (as Mary Rose said) and learning the new vocabulary associated with cyberspace can be a daunting task. What was the best method for senior adults to learn how to use and understand computer technology?

Finding a Solution: Service-Learning

As I sat talking with Mary Rose that day, an idea came to me. "Mary Rose, how would you like a tutor? We have university students who want to become teachers. I bet one of them would be glad to practice their teaching skills on you." She was thrilled at the prospect. First of all, she would be getting personal attention to learn computer technology, and second of all, she would be getting it free! My journey had begun. My next stop was to my colleague's office at the university.

The College Connection

Marilyn Rice teaches the technology courses that our college students must take to graduate with a teaching degree. I took a few moments to explain the dilemma that Mary Rose was having, and asked her if some of her students might be willing to help her. Luckily, Rice had just added another requirement to her course she called the "Technology Assistant Assignment," in which each student was required to help someone with his or her computer/technology skills. She had anticipated that this 10-hour requirement would be carried out by working in the public schools, but she could see that encouraging some students to work with a senior adult would also fulfill her course requirements.

As Rice and I talked, we realized this project could be more than just a class assignment. If carefully planned and implemented, it could be a service-learning experience for those students in her technology classes. Service-learning is a teaching method that connects the academic requirements/objectives of a course with a community need. Students apply what they have learned to a real situation and then reflect on the experience (Seifer, Hermanns, & Lewis, 2000). In our case, the college students would apply their skills and knowledge learned in the technology class to helping senior adults understand how to use the computer and utilize the Internet. With the added power of writing a reflective piece, students would increase their understanding of teaching and enhance their sense of civic responsibility (Karp, Pedras, Heide, & Flottermesch, 2001). One of the purposes for higher education is, indeed, to help college students see themselves as more than just a teacher, nurse, businessman, lawyer, computer analyst; but rather, see themselves as a connected, important and positive force in the world—citizens who contribute, who help solve community problems. Service-learning projects help this connection to happen. By working with the elderly, our students will begin to understand issues of aging on a deeper level and will realize that by applying their knowledge, skills and dispositions, they can make a difference.

There are other desirable outcomes from the application of a service-learning teaching model. Service-learning helps college students improve academic performance and learn critical thinking, time management, decision-making, problem solving, self-confidence and communication skills (Aspras, 1997; Colby, Ehrlich, Beaumont, & Stephens, 2003; Covan, 2001; Lewis, 2002). The efficacy of service-learning is reflected in the increase in the number of colleges promoting these programs (Enos, 2003).

Rice and I also realized that this tutoring project was an opportunity to bring young college students and older adults together. Very rarely do college students get a chance to experience being a part of an extended family; they live apart from their families and lose the natural intergenerational composition. This is the norm for the American society today. "Practically non-existent are the networks of economic, educational and cultural interdependence previously established by households composed of grandparents, parents and children" (Strom Thurmond Institute, n.d.). This age segregation provides few opportunities for intergenerational interaction (Generations United, n.d.) and may be a cause for the growing bias against the elderly. "Instead of regarding seniors as wise and acknowledging their experience, they are often thought of as senile" (Levine, 2004, p. 9). Cross-age learning experiences, such as our project, have shown to improve the students' sense of responsibility toward others (Aspras, 1997). In addition, a commonly cited benefit of service learning has been reducing barriers between those serving and those being served (Lewis, 2002). Perhaps, by creating this tutoring opportunity for the two generations to interact in a positive learning environment, attitudes toward the elderly may improve.

The senior adults participating in our project would benefit in several ways. The first, of course, would be by receiving computer tutoring—10 hours of free private lessons per college student. Second, to continue to remain healthy in advanced years, seniors are encouraged to remain active and engaged. By working with young college students, older adults would be participating in an ongoing meaningful activity. This can decrease loneliness, boredom and depression while increasing self-esteem (Generations United, n.d.). Finally, our senior adults would benefit by experiencing a service-learning project as well. Unlike "most service learning programs that involve older adults as only recipients of a service" (Lewis, 2002, p. 658), we wanted our seniors to have a stake in the project—to be active participants. In addition to learning computer technology, the seniors would be serving our students by allowing them to practice their course content and by helping to evaluate these college students' teaching skills. We would ask the senior adults to reflect on their experiences with our college students and on their own learning. The Computer Tutors Project, as we would name it later, appeared to be a win/win situation, in which all participants would give and all participants would receive.

Yes, it seemed that this project could help more than one Mary Rose; it had the potential of impacting many—other senior adults, our students and our community. Our Computer Tutors Project could serve as a model for our university colleagues, helping them see the power of matching course standards with community needs. We decided to take the challenge and move forward. In doing so, however, we had to answer a few more questions: Was there a need for this tutoring project? How many Mary Roses were there?

Matching the Players

My next stop was back at the retirement home. I met with the activities director and explained the Computer Tutors Project. She thought it would be an excellent collaborative and scheduled me to talk to the residents at their meeting the following month.

As I planned for this first meeting, I had to make certain that I would say the right thing, that I would explain the project in such a way that the senior adults would believe it was worth their time and effort. Seniors rarely rush in to be the first to try out new gadgets, so my initial approach would have to be well designed. I would need to hit some key factors—that computers are affordable, easy to use and capable of delivering significant benefits (Adler, 2002). Additionally, I wanted to make sure the senior adults believed that they had a stake in the success of this project too, that they understood we needed them to help us evaluate these future teachers. My introduction to the project at the meeting was the following:

Hello everyone. I'm Joyce McCauley and I teach college students how to become teachers at Sam Houston State University (SHSU). I've come to your meeting today because I need your help. One of the courses we teach at the university is computer technology. The students are learning how to teach someone how to use the computer and all the new vocabulary that's part of this new technology. We are looking for people that would volunteer to work with our students, allowing them to practice the teaching skills they're learning in class. I thought, since you have computers in the activities room, some of you might like to learn how to use them by having a university tutor. The computers are free, the Internet access is free, and you'll have your own private tutor! I bet some of you would love to learn how to send e-mails to your grandchildren. But, more importantly, if you volunteer for this project, you'll help us. At the end of November, you'll be asked to evaluate these future teachers by filling out an evaluation on their teaching skills. They get a grade on how well they explain things to you, how clear they are, and how patient they are. If you're interested in helping on this project, please come to the first meeting next week. I need you!

Several residents stopped to talk with me after the meeting. They seemed eager to join the group and give computer literacy a try. This enthusiasm was in line with the research: "Nearly two in three 50- to 75-year-olds view 'retirement' as a time to begin a new chapter, start new activities and set new goals" (Novelli, 2001, p. 33). I was hoping our project would be a *new chapter* for those that had never used a computer.

The following week, there were 24 senior adult volunteers on the sign-in sheet. All were at different levels of computer literacy—from knowing nothing about computers to wanting help on spreadsheets. All were different ages—from 63 to 96. Mary Rose was among them. We were thrilled. The need was there.

The final puzzle piece was to talk to the college students in Rice's classes. The second week of classes, I went to each of the three technology classes and explained the project. The majority of the students who were interested were also very reluctant. Since they had seldom been around older people, the students were hesitant about what to expect and had many concerns such as: How will these old people act? Will they be nice or contrary? Will they physically be able to do this? Are they bed-ridden? Are they all in wheelchairs or on walkers? What kind of environment will I be working in?

Rice and I spent some time talking with the college students about the facility, its organization and the residents. We talked about a few issues of aging and how many older adults experience loneliness, loss of purposefulness and reduced self-esteem. We made it a point to emphasize that this special project was an opportunity to give something back to the community. Soon, many of them began to understand a little more about what to expect, decided they were willing to pilot this project, and were asking when they could start. We had 26 volunteers. All the pieces were falling into place. We were ready to begin.

First Meeting at the Retirement Home

They all arrived at 7 p.m. to meet each other—the senior residents of the retirement home and the university students. Walkers and wheelchairs interspersed with laptops and backpacks, each eyeing the other, wondering how they were going to get paired. Small bits of conversations could be heard:

"So what do you study now-a-days at the university?"

"If I wore those high heels, honey, I'd be flat on my back before I'd walk a block."

"Why do you have two holes for earrings?"

The frankness of the seniors surprised some of our young college students. Soon there was a nice hum of chatting and chuckling between the two groups. After a quick welcome, I began:

"OK, everyone. Here's the way we're going to find the computer tutors that best fit your needs. I'll ask each senior adult to stand up and tell what you'd like to learn. College students will listen and if you think you can teach the skill, raise your hand and we'll get you together. We'll start with you, Mr. Davis."

One by one, the senior adults stood. There were many and varied requests for help, such as the following:

"I could use a little help on saving my files. Sometimes I'm not sure where the heck these things go."

"I want to learn how to play games. My son says it's fun."

"I just want to be able to send an e-mail to my granddaughter."

"Can someone help me find things about Medicare and medicine?"

"I don't know a darn thing. You don't have to be very smart to help me."

Each of the 24 senior adults talked a bit about what they wanted to learn, and gradually each was paired with a college student. Soon the room was buzzing with conversation and plans for the next meeting. The students set their tutoring schedule with their senior adults. Some decided on 1-hour blocks of time; some wanted 2-hour blocks. We had a few extra students who posted their hours in the activities room so anyone could come for help.

The tutoring continued over the next two weeks of the semester. The college students realized that their teaching methods and techniques needed to be adapted to the learning

Figure 1. Intergenerational learning: College student and older adult

styles and needs of the senior adults. Several suggestions for teaching older adult learners, proposed by the Texas Department of Aging (2002), proved to be helpful to our students. These included:

- Allowing more time for learning
- Helping learners organize the material
- Permitting and promoting self-pacing
- Using concrete examples and basing them on past experiences of the learner
- Using various cueing devices (e.g., encouraging the learner to use visual images, rhymes, acronyms and other self-designed coding schemes)
- Making appropriate environmental adjustments (e.g., extra voice and media amplification, high contrast on visual materials, present using both audio and visual techniques, minimize distractions, provide appropriate lighting and incorporate breaks)

Results of the Tutoring:
The Senior Adult Perspective

The results of our tutoring sessions were more successful than we anticipated. According to our pre- and post-computer literacy surveys, the senior adults who knew nothing about computer use when the project began reported that they had learned how to use e-mail. Communicating with relatives through e-mail seemed to be one of the most compelling reasons that motivated them to take the tutoring sessions.

The second most-popular activity for new users was understanding and using the Internet. There were a variety of sites of interest and the college students placed icons on desktops or bookmarked many, including:

- **AARP:** www.aarp.org/—An informative Web site by the AARP that includes articles and links, games, technology lessons, health information and travel opportunities.

- **Elderhostel:** www.elderhostel.org/welcome.asp/—Focuses on travel opportunities accompanied by instructors who offer lectures, courses and workshops.

- **Genealogy:** www.geneaology.com/index_n.html/—A free and fee-based site that helps start family trees, locate information and build Web sites.

- **Seniors-site:** http://seniors-site.com—Informative Web site that includes poetry, jokes and an extensive message board with subcategories (medical insurance, drugs, veterans)

- **Medline Plus:** http://medlineplus.gov/—Includes more than 4,000 illustrated articles about diseases, tests, symptoms and surgeries.

- **Medicare:** www.medicare.gov/—Answers frequently asked questions about billing, Medicare appeals and enrollment options

- **SeniorCom:** www.xplore.com/xplore500/reviews/01.24.1998.html/—A search engine for "people who weren't born yesterday."

- **SeniorLaw:** www.seniorlaw.com/—Web site for answers to legal questions.

Part of the fun of surfing the Internet was locating and playing games. No longer would senior adults need to feel isolated, since many sites offered multiplayer games in which you could be playing with family members who lived across town or opponents on the other side of the world. Some sites offered free playing, while others had nominal fees. Popular sites were:

- **ACBL - Play Online:** www.acbl.org/play/playOnline.html/

- **Addicting Games:** www.moneygaming.com/

- **Coffee Break Arcade:** www.coffeebreakarcade.com/

- **GamesDex:** www.gamesdex.com/

- **Ok Bridge:** www.okbridge.com/

- **Play Free Games:** http://lovefreegames.aavalue.com/processflow.cfm/
- **Play Free Games Online:** www.MrSuperGames-Jump.com/
- **Yahoo Games:** http://games.yahoo.com/

In addition to the e-mail and Internet lessons, the college students also helped seniors learn word processing, managing folders, scanning, copying information to a disk, and creating tables and spreadsheets. One of the most celebrated lessons, perhaps, was creating desktop screen savers from family photos.

At the conclusion of the tutoring sessions, we interviewed the senior adults to record their overall opinion of the Computer Tutors Project. Their responses were encouraging:

- "Wish more of us would do this ... because ... you know— 'Use it or lose it.'"
- "I didn't learn to use the computer when I was young. Just now and I'm in my 80s. I have to live long enough to learn all that stuff on the computer. There's so much to learn."
- "My girls [tutors] were absolutely wonderful. If they didn't know the answer to something, they'd just go up to the university and find out. The next day they'd be back with the answer and show us how."
- "I never heard of e-mail. Then Manny [tutor] came and we kept a notebook. (I had to write it down 'cause I could get lost real quick, you know.) She taught me loads of things. We had so much fun together. Now here I can pop a button and answer people all over the world. It really goes there. I know everything about e-mail now."
- "I was able to pull up a girl's finishing school I went to and look at all the pictures they have on the Web site. It was fun."
- "It breaks my heart to watch my friends playing solitaire hour after hour when they could learn the computer and go all over the world."
- "I firmly believe this program will be a boon to the senior community. And now, I can help my group join the world of the future right now. I know we have just touched the surface of electronics as we know it today, and I feel any help we can be to my population will give us a hand up to the present, and make us feel 'with it.'"
- "What you have brought to us here is the opportunity to learn a skill that is invaluable. May this be the beginning of a new adventure."

Results of the Tutoring:
Evaluation of the College Students as Tutors

The senior adults knew from the beginning of the project that they would be asked at the end of the tutoring sessions to evaluate our college students. We asked the following questions:

1. Would you sign up again for tutoring from another SHSU student?
2. Was the SHSU student genuinely interested in teaching you?

3.   Was the SHSU student patient in teaching you?

4.   Was the SHSU student able to break down the steps needed to teach you what you wanted to learn? In other words, was the instruction clear and easy to understand?

5.   Would you recommend this SHSU student for the teaching field?

In 100% of the written surveys and oral interviews, the senior adults answered YES to all survey questions. Many participants added additional comments to the survey questions that were equally positive and described the students using adjectives such as helpful, courteous, patient, punctual, lovely, kind, cooperative, delightful, eager, capable, sincere and pleasant. These characteristics are certainly dispositions reflected in good teachers.

Results of the Tutoring: The College Student Perspective

Also at the end of the semester, we asked our college students to reflect on the experience. In reading their response papers, we found the college students learned quite a bit about teaching others. They learned patience, flexibility, the power of motivation, the importance of building self-esteem and the challenge of meeting the needs of a variety of learners.

•   "What I really learned from this experience was the power of background knowledge. I take for granted that I grew up while computers were coming about and don't realize just how complicated they are. Because [senior adults] didn't have the same background as I have, I could not say things like 'click and drag' and expect them to know what I was talking about. In my classroom, I will remember this experience when working with my students."

•   "The experience as a whole was a positive one, though at first I didn't quite see it that way. It was hard to make the connection between teaching the elderly and teaching children. However, I learned you have to know the person and how that person learns—the same will work for your students. Every student is different and they don't all learn in the same ways at the same pace. Different people have different learning styles."

•   "I learned just because I might think something is easy—it's not easy for others. I now have learned how to teach a program slowly and in depth to a person/child that does not know how to use it."

•   "I discovered what I do and do not know about the computer. After trying to answer other people's questions, I determined what I do know how to do on the computer and what I need to learn. I should brush up on my computer literacy skills before entering the class-room."

Our college students also learned other things through this service-learning experience—things about themselves, about the elderly and about life. They learned about empathy, understanding and the gratification received knowing they contributed to helping someone learn. Perhaps this, really, is the heart of teaching. Perhaps these lessons are the ones that shape their civic and moral values and have a long-lasting impact on their sense of who they are and what they want to be.

- "One thing I liked about this assignment was working with the elderly. They are so sweet and I just felt so appreciated. I really felt like I was doing more than teaching them about computers. I was giving them some much-needed company."

- "The second lady I worked with stayed with me the rest of the time. Every time I signed up, she made sure she put her name down with mine. What an ego boost that was for me."

- "I had such a great time during the technology assistant part of this class. I had planned on getting a mentor teacher [in a public school], but I signed up for the retirement home instead. To my surprise, I had a wonderful time. I was thinking stereotypical when I signed up for it. I thought it was going to be so boring—you know— old people. I was completely wrong. Those men and women are so wise. They even taught me!"

- "I enjoyed every minute of working at the retirement home. Just seeing their faces light up when they saw me and how excited they were when I taught them something they could share with others. That's the best."

- "I cannot tell you how much I enjoyed working with Mrs. Lowrey. She was very enthusiastic about learning the computer, and she caught on pretty quick. The time flew by for the two of us. Not only was it nice for the residents to say, 'Oh, thank you for coming into our lives' —but I feel the same way about her. I now have a new friend. It was such a rewarding feeling for me knowing I was helping another human being. That is why I choose teaching as my profession."

- "It has been such a blessing to me to become a part of these women's lives. Believe it or not, I always leave there feeling refreshed. If I have had a tough day, these women just give me a boost of energy! (Sounds crazy, I know.) I have even told them that after my duties are complete for this class I am still going to tutor them (not as often but when I have some spare time). I even have a friend of mine from church who wants to start going with me."

- "I feel that even if you are not teaching someone computer skills, you are still touching their lives because just smiling, telling them hi or waving at them makes them happy."

One surprise that we had was the interest taken in our Computer Tutors Project by the children of the senior adults. Several times, these "children" would stop by during the lessons and encourage and compliment the college students. As new residents would move into the retirement home, the "children" would be eager for their parents to sign up for tutoring lessons. One note was received that said, "Please establish a user ID and password for my father and insist that he start using e-mail so that he can correspond with his three sons and daughter." Here again is the need to stay connected and to be a part of this fast-paced Age of Information.

Computer Tutors Project: Changes

Each semester, Rice and I have tried to improve on the Computer Tutors Project. Many suggestions came from the senior adults and the students in their final reflection on the experience. Below are the ideas that we have already implemented or are planning on implementing in the semesters to come:

1. **Brochure:** Produce a brochure explaining the project to distribute to visitors to the retirement home. Have photos of the residents, comments and lesson topics.

2. **Posted times:** Post the times of lessons on specific topics such as cut and paste, saving a file, surfing the Web.

3. **Best times:** Survey residents for best times for lessons. Avoid busy evenings, special events or times during meal hours.

4. **Location:** Use only the computers in the activities room. Avoid going to individual apartments (liability issues).

5. **How-to posters:** Create big posters to display on the "how-to" of various software applications like Word and Excel.

6. **Note-taking:** Encourage the residents to write their own notes while being tutored. Helps with retention of material.

7. **Strategies:** Create a list of learning strategies from education courses that could be applied in the tutoring sessions. Post these by the computers as a reminder to the college students to use them in teaching.

8. **Popular sites poster:** Display a poster listing the most popular URLs, such as AARP or Bridge Online.

9. **Bulletin board:** Hang a small bulletin board for the residents and college students to post notes to each other about Web sites that are particularly interesting or easy to use.

10. **Suggestion box:** Place a suggestion box in the activities room for residents to give ideas for future lessons.

11. **Web site:** Create a resident home Web site that can be managed by the residents themselves. They will decide the design and content.

12. **Newsletter:** Collaborate on the production of a resident home newsletter. Tutoring sessions can be aligned with this activity.

13. **Monthly documentary:** Assign a few students to help residents produce a documentary of the resident home activities. Take digital photos of these monthly activities (plays, concerts, art activities, for example) and help create a photo show or digital scrapbook that can be played at the information desk.

Future Trends

The age of information, sustained and accelerated by computers and the Internet, changed our lives in the 20th century and will have an even greater impact in the 21st century. As a larger portion of our population lives longer, "the notion that 'retirement' at age 60 or 65 generally marks the end of an individual's productive life is rapidly becoming obsolete" (Adler, 2002, p. 6). Senior adults are still a very important and active part of community life. However, as of 2003, only 22% of senior adults age 65 and older are online (Madden et al., 2003). This is not a surprising statistic when you take into consideration older adults have not grown up with these technologies. Their college years and working careers are completed and they now live in environments where computers are less available. Unfortunately, this lack of Internet savvy results in a large percentage of our population at a distinct disadvantage in terms of acquiring knowledge, communicating, shopping, banking and investing.

Learning to use technology is certainly a challenge for the older generation. A recent survey of computer usage indicated that senior adults believed that one difficulty they had was the lack of support, both during learning and on-going use (Goodman, Syme, & Elsma, 2003). The complexity of these technologies and the time and effort required to learn to use them remain huge barriers (Adler, 2002).

Organizations concerned with aging are finding ways to encourage seniors to become computer literate by offering online lessons and courses. The AARP, because of the growing interest in online learning, has added free lessons to its Web site that include how to access e-mail, restore deleted files, navigate Web pages, capture information and customize your computer. According to AARP, senior adults are "not technology-averse consumers" and are ready for more now that they really understand the empowering value of these technologies (Rossman, 2004).

Generations on Line, a national non-profit organization, has created specially programmed software for senior centers, retirement homes, libraries or other institutions in which senior adults cannot afford or choose not to enroll in computer training courses. Using familiar images and large type instructions, the program guides elders who have no computer experience through four basic Internet functions: simplified e-mail (easy registration, no attachments, which can pose problems for facilities); Memories: Generation to Generation (posted questions and answers in which supervised fourth-grade children ask seniors about their memories of the past in four categories); a multi-lingual search in 36 languages (through a partnership with Yahoo!); and links to sites of interest to seniors (including social security and Medicare, veterans affairs, newspapers around the world and health portals) (Generations on Line, n.d., p. 5).

Many high-tech companies are increasing their efforts to tap into the expanding senior market, packaging software, training and peripherals designed specifically for the older adult. One common complaint from older users is the complexity and technical jargon related to computer use (Goodman et al., 2003). To that end, some companies offer free clinics to demystify the use of technology through mobile clinics, in-store advice sessions and other community outreach activities (Gateway, n.d.).

Internet marketers, too, are targeting the senior population. According to the United States (U.S.) Census data, even though a small percentage of seniors use the Internet, 80% of those are in the top 30% income bracket. As one marketing company stated, "They have the money. They are retired. They have time to be online" (Marketing VOX, 2003, p. 3).

A further support for the elderly is an increase in grant opportunities at high schools, colleges and universities. Computers Made Easy (For Senior Citizens) is one such project that developed from a college foundation grant. This has become a non-profit organization (www.csuchico.edu/~csu/seniors/computing2.html) designed to help senior adults learn computer technology and locate resources. Another non-profit organization that began from a grant is Senior-Net (www.seniornet.org/php/default.php). Its mission is to provide older adults education for and access to computer technologies to enhance their lives and enable them to share their knowledge and wisdom (Senior-Net, n.d.). Not only is the Web site a source of technology information, but the organization also supports learning centers throughout the U.S. and other countries. Senior-Net also publishes a newsletter and sponsors conferences for ages 50 and older participants.

Finally, community service-learning is increasingly becoming a part of required coursework on college campuses (O'Grady, 2000). There is an expanding body of quantitative and qualitative research that shows service-learning as effective in motivating students in their coursework and strengthening the relationships between colleges and the communities they serve. Campus Compact, a national coalition of more than 950 college and university presidents, has taken the lead in this research and in challenging higher-education institutions to make service-learning a part of college life. Membership in the organization provides campuses with resources, model programs, funding, workshops, recognitions, professional development and technical support (Campus Compact, n.d.). Three examples of Campus Compact members engaged in promoting civic engagement are Temple University, Earlham College and Mount Union College. Project SHINE at Temple University in Philadelphia has developed a program linking its college students with elderly immigrants who hope to pass the citizenship exam. Both Earlham College in Richmond, Indiana, and Mount Union College in Alliance, Ohio, encourage their students to engage in service-learning projects and suggest community organizations that assist the elderly. The Office of Service-Learning and Community Service at Mount Union College also assists faculty in developing service-learning connections to course content, posting model syllabi and suggesting a variety of student reflection ideas including journaling, class presentations, art, drama and storytelling (Mount Union College, n.d.).

The Computer Tutors Project at SHSU will continue in the semesters to come. It has become a model service-learning experience for our college students and an excellent learning opportunity for senior adults. In the words of Marion Lowrey, of one of our participants, "Many of us have watched this incredible means of rapid communication emerge since leaving our working days. Surely your students can scarcely imagine the life we knew without it—so it is wonderful to have help bridging a really big gap." Our hope is to keep adding these bridges by expanding the Computer Tutors Project to other retirement centers and senior centers in the surrounding communities.

Conclusion

The Computer Tutors Project has been wonderfully successful. It is in its fourth year now and has tutored more than 100 residents. The continued presence of our college students has given these senior adults the courage and support they need to continue to understand, in the words of Mary Rose, "this contraption." More importantly, perhaps, we found this intergenerational service-learning project has helped dispel inaccurate stereotypes that the college students had toward senior adults, and vice versa. Working together and sharing stories and laughter encouraged tolerance and helped create a bond between the two generations. Many of the college students still keep in touch with their senior adults, even though the requirements of the course are finished. We also found connecting academic requirements to real-life experiences helped our students gain a deeper understanding of the knowledge, skills and dispositions of the course.

Mary Rose did not know it, but she taught me something that day. I learned that there are incredible resources out there among senior adults just waiting to be tapped. I learned that a good thing for university professors is to find ways to utilize our expertise to meet community needs. And finally, I learned that our college students and I appreciate an opportunity to give back to the people who helped build this country and gave us the freedom we enjoy. It was a good thing I stopped in to see Mary Rose that day. It was a good thing I hit REPLY.

Author Note

The Computer Tutors Project is a part of the Full Circle Literacy Program, initially funded by a grant from SHSU. For the past 3 years, The Forum at the Woodlands, a senior retirement community located in The Woodlands, Texas, has supported the Project. Correspondence concerning this chapter should be addressed to Joyce Mc-Cauley, Department of Language, Literacy and Special Populations, Sam Houston State University, Box 2119, Huntsville, TX 77341. E-mail: mccauley@shsu.edu

References

Adler, R. (2002). *The age wave meets the technology wave: Broadband and older Americans*. Retrieved August 10, 2005, from www.seniornet.org/php/default.php?PageID=6694

American Association of Retired Persons (AARP). (2000). *Survey on lifelong learning*. Retrieved August 10, 2004, from http://research.aarp.org/general/lifelong_1.htm

Aspras, M. (1997). Cross-age teaching + community service = enhanced self-esteem. *Journal of Family and Consumer Sciences, 89*, 28-31.

Campus Compact. (n.d.). *About us*. Retrieved August 8, 2005, from www.compact.org

Cody, M., Dunn, D. & Hoppin, S. (1999). Silver surfers: Training and evaluating Internet use among older adult learners. *Communication Education, 48*(4), 269-286.

Colby, A., Ehrlich, T., Beaumont, E., & Stephens, J. (2003). *Educating citizens: Preparing America's undergraduates for lives of moral and civic responsibility.* San Francisco: The Carnegie Foundation.

Covan, E. K. (2001). Employing service-learning to teach research methods to gerontology students. *Educational Gerontology, 27*, 623-627.

Enos, S. (2003). *Service-learning on American campuses: Challenges for pedagogy and practice.* Retrieved August 25, 2004, from www.ric.edu/itl/issue02/authors.html

Gateway. (n.d.). *Gateway launches technology training initiative for AARP members: Gateway and AARP aim to make technology more accessible and less complicated.* Retrieved June 25, 2005, from www.prnewswire.com/cgi-bin/stories.pl?ACCT=104&STORY=/www/story/10-022000/0001327835&EDATE=

Generations on Line. (n.d). *About us.* Retrieved August 1, 2005, from www.generationson-line.com/aboutus.html

Generations United. (n.d.). *Fact sheet: The benefits of intergenerational programs.* Retrieved September 1, 2003, from www.gu.org/projg&ofaqs.asp

Goodman, J., Syme, A., & Elsma, R. (2003). *Older adults' use of computers: A survey.* Retrieved May 30, 2005, from www.dcs.gla.ac.uk/~joy/research/2003_bcs_hci

Karp, G., Pedras, M., Heide, T., & Flottermesch, K. (2001). *Meeting NCATE standards through service-learning: Dispositions.* Retrieved August 17, 2005, from www.clemson.edu/ICSLTE/ resources/docs/sldispositions.pdf

Lawhon, T., Ennis, D., & Lawhon, D. (1996). Senior adults and computers in the 1990s. *Educational Gerontology, 22*, 193-201.

Levine, R. (2004). *Aging with attitude.* Westport: Praeger.

Lewis, M. (2002). Service learning and older adults. *Educational Gerontology, 28*, 655-667.

Madden, M. (2003). *American's online pursuits: The changing picture of who's online and what they do.* Retrieved June 20, 2005, from www.pewinternet.org/report_display.asp?r=106

Marketing VOX. (2003). *Don't forget senior citizens when planning online.* Retrieved July 12, 2005, from www.marketingvox.com/archives/2003/01/13

Mayhorn, C., Stronge, A., McLaughlin, A., & Rogers, W. (2004). Older adults, computer training, and the systems approach: A formula for success. *Educational Gerontology, 30*(3), 237-254.

Mount Union College. (n.d). *Service-learning: Reflection ideas.* Retrieved August 21, 2005, from www.muc.edu/academics/service_learning/service_learning_at_mount_union_college/information_for_faculty_and_staff/resources_for_faculty_and_staff/reflection_ideas

Novelli, W. D. (2001). *Beyond fifty: American's future.* Retrieved May 2, 2004, from www. aarp.org/Articles/a2003-01-03-beyondfifty.html

Peniston, L. C. (1990). The mental, social and emotional benefits of computers in a recreational program for senior citizens. In G.K. Palmer (Ed.), *Proceedings from the Intermountain Leisure Symposium* (pp. 122-139). Provo: Brigham Young University.

Rossman, L. (2002, April). *What's next?* Presentation at the American on Aging and National Coalition on Aging, San Francisco.

Schneider, E. L. (1991). Cutting the costs of aging. *Issues in Science and Technology, 7*(4), 47-49.

Schneider, K. (2003). The significance of learning for aging. *Educational Gerontology, 29*(10), 809-824.

Seifer, S., Hermanns, K., & Lewis, J. (Eds.). (2000). *Creating community-responsive physicians: Concepts and models for service-learning in medical education.* Washington, DC: American Association of Higher Education.

Senior-Net. (n.d.). *About senior net.* Retrieved August 17, 2005, from www.seniornet. org/php/default.php?PageID=5005

Strom Thurmond Institute. (n.d.). *The intergenerational movement.* Retrieved August 13, 2005, from www.strom.clemson.edu/teams/risl/intmove.html

Texas Department of Aging. (2002). *Workforce and older Texans.* Retrieved March 3, 2005, from www.dads.state.tx.us/services/agingtexaswell/publications.html#best

Timmermann, S. (1998). The role of information technology in older adult learning. *New Directions for Adult and Continuing Education, 77,* 61-71.

Chapter III

Developing Technology-Based Education for Adult Learners in Micronesia:

A Case Study for Learning Engagement in Diversity

Lucyann Kerry, University of Guam, USA

Abstract

The purpose of this chapter is to present the project work and experience of developing post-secondary distance education in a challenging and diverse setting where the author has been involved in the design and implementation of the technology-based education. The experience of the project demonstrates how challenges for generating engagement with Web-based online courses can be met and overcome. Online learning activities were analyzed in light of student feedback. This feedback, collected over the length of the project, indicated the positive and negative factors for the design, execution and revision of the online learning environment. These factors, to strengthen and reinforce learning, were judged successful in contributing to student achievement in meeting course and program learning objectives. The chapter concludes with a more general discussion of relevant development issues. This work is supported by a review of relevant literature.

Introduction

As distance education in the form of technology-based higher education expands globally, it offers new learning opportunities to under-served, more diverse populations of students. With trans-border, international choices in education growing through greater transmission capacities and educational entrepreneurship, new alliances and relationships are taking place between traditional educational institutions and the developing world (Potashnik & Capper, 1998). The western Pacific, also known as Micronesia, is one such region. It is being confronted with new possibilities for higher education while at the same time having limited resources. Spanning 3,000 miles of Pacific Ocean with scattered islands and a dispersed population of 300,000, its major urban center is the island of Guam, a United States (U.S.) territory. Learning engagement is considered an initial stage to actual learning, the internal process, evidenced by learning performance outcomes. This need is driven by the North American model of education and its educational trends, which the region uses as its basis for educational standards. However, because of ongoing questions and issues regarding the nature of the educational market demand, cost effectiveness, the prioritization of limited resources and how best to address pressing societal needs, the allocation of resources and efforts for developing and offering technology-based education should have clear justification as meeting the region's educational goals.

This chapter proposes a preliminary strategic approach to address the above challenges as a starting point for further work. This strategy is the result of the research and experience generated by a 3-year project based at the University of Guam (UOG) developing online courses for students in Micronesia. The courses were developed and offered by UOG with its regional partners, Palau Community College (PCC) and the College of Micronesia – Federated States of Micronesia (COM-FSM). The initial target population of regional students was agriculture teachers needing a degree qualification. The university developed online courses in the agriculture sciences that were part of its bachelor's degree program in secondary education emphasizing agriculture. The courses developed by PCC were for general education requirements in math, English and science that articulated or transferred between the institutions as prerequisites for UOG's degree program. The initial pilot course that served as the development model for the other courses was UOG's Introduction to Agriculture, AG101.

Research data was generated from the participants through observation, course performance assessment, surveys and interviews. The long-term societal goal of the project was to promote increased food production for the region. This was to be attained through an increased agriculture knowledge base for students of the region's tertiary and secondary educational systems. Thus, the U.S. Department of Agriculture (USDA) funded the project through its Higher Education Challenge Grant Program. Course development was subsidized by government and was not funded as an investment in educational products for an entrepreneurial global market. This is an important distinction to be made, since there are misconceptions and myths about the profitability, revenue stream or cost-savings value for investing in distance education and technology-based education (Bates, 1997).

Background

Micronesian adult students took part in this USDA higher-education project, *Promoting Agriculture Education in the Western Pacific,* # 2001-38411-10714,[1] which initiated the first online courses within the region. There was both diversity among the students and diversity between students and the educator-developers. The latter were predominantly American and European faculty, although there were some Filipino and Chamorro, the island ethnicity of Guam. These differences included culture, language, gender, age, economic level, technology experience and educational frames of reference. Nevertheless, how significant were these differences for constructing an effective instructional process?

The Digital Divide

These differences reflect an inherent disparity in the *global schoolhouse* of the *haves* and *have-nots,* represented by the term *digital divide.* This divide exists with technology infrastructure and access for the haves on one side and lack of access on the other side for the have-nots. Identified as an issue by Roblyer, Dozier-Henry and Burnette (cited in Marshall, 2001), technology has evolved historically as tools of a white male elite, generating problems of access and equity—access and equity being jointly held values to actuate in the democratic model of society. This dichotomy is seen in the challenge of integrating technology-based education with the emerging practice of multi-cultural education in the U.S., where a gap exists between the access and use of technology with the teaching of diverse students (Brown, 2002). Although the term *digital divide* has been used to refer to the technology-access inequity that exists in the world, it has been reframed to refer to greater educational and societal inequities of those most disenfranchised groups, whether internal or external to the U.S. or other developed nations (Gorski, 2001). Micronesia is a representative group, being one of the most isolated and under-developed areas of the world; it is the last area to become self-governing, only establishing democratic representative governments in the 1990s. For these disenfranchised populations, access to technology is not only from lack of physical access but is also based on a context of lack of support and value for their technology access (Facey, 2001; Gorski, 2001). The concern is that technology is carving a deeper divide along lines of historical disenfranchisement, including race, ethnicity, age and generational shifts, language, gender, the physically challenged and economic class (Brown, 2002).

Challenges

There are parallels between indigenous populations, such as the First Nations of Canada, Micronesians and South Pacific Islanders, as they face the dilemma of slipping further behind in attributes denoted as Western quality-of-life standards, being limited in responding to rapid changes of social, economic and environmental conditions or in the continuation in loss of traditional ways of life. This loss is impacted through the influence of the euro-centric imbalance of educational content and the lack of access to technology. For many diverse populations globally, higher education is not a part of the cultural process from within the society but is imposed from the outside, with alien conventions, operating principles and traditions of the world of strangers and outsiders. This was the case for the Micronesians. A key question in this dilemma of indigenous peoples is how do they maintain their distinctive aspects of culture yet absorb useful outside information (Banks, 2003)? However, it is not so easy to generate or integrate content and knowledge construction that shifts from the prevalent and established world-view model to a more compatible model that acknowledges the world of different peoples. The prevalent model reflects major global power structures. Higher education as an extension of this dominant model or what is referred to as *imperial culture* may inherently reinforce rather than reform or adapt the status-quo model to the realities of diverse populations. How technology can be used to address this issue has yet to be determined (Marshall, 2001).

In the global environment, educators are now confronted with the emerging challenges of how to overcome the digital divide and how best to design, develop and implement technology-based education for diverse populations in the world. When this project for Micronesia began, its educational partners, the designer-developers, faculty, coordinators and participating students had to take on these unstated, but real, challenges. The project could be described as being *on the digital divide*, the island of Guam being on one side with developers and faculty, and the other side being the islands states of Palau, Chuuk, Yap, Pohnpei, and Kosrae with students and local coordinators. The project management and instructional development resources at the UOG were clearly on the developed side of the digital divide, the U.S. territory of Guam having an infrastructure and developed economy intrinsic with that of the U.S.

The Project

The project consisted of 3 years of work to initiate, design, develop and implement the distance education. Distance education had been generated at UOG at specific times during the previous 20 years, with a variety of delivery methods in different curricular areas. These attempts had occurred only sporadically on a non-sustained basis, never becoming an integral part of the institutions' academic programs and administrative processes. As the project began, there was only a limited technology and organizational infrastructure to support its work. The first year was a planning year, initiating the regional coordination framework and organizational elements. It was also the year that the technology model was created with a locally designed delivery platform called Pacific Regional Outreach Architecture (PROA). Site visits were made by the project's design team to assess the resources of science labs, agriculture research stations and central technology infrastructures. The assessment of student learning need would come later. The second year was a development year for the specific instructional design of the courses, refining the technology delivery design, and establishing a project home page and Web address. This provided for student access to the PROA courseware, which would frame the individual courses.

The Design Problem

By the beginning of the second year, faculty at the community-college level with experience in classroom teaching of large populations of Micronesian students provided feedback for the course design. The challenge was to determine what would be an appropriate design for a Micronesian distance learner. The preliminary course design was based on clarity of English language in text content, an easy-to-read screen layout and icons, and a clear pattern of progressive tasks for the performance of each individual lesson of the course. It should be noted that in the initial design stages, the developers had great difficulty separating in their minds delivery design from instructional design; these designs being integrated in the technology examples reviewed by the developers. Because the costs of commercial courseware, such as Blackboard or WebCT, had been prohibitive, a local vendor was contracted to develop the PROA customized software design. Internal interactivity in the software proved too complicated initially, and the courseware became a static Web page holding course content. Limited regional bandwidth proved an added barrier for Internet communication with large files. The static Web page and its text files did not need as much transmission capacity as the more commercial educational software platforms. This gave it a transmission advantage against delays. Eventually, the delivery design consisted of the PROA courseware being accessed through an open Web page URL address. This pragmatically meant that passwords and user identifications were not necessary for student access and use. Nor was there a need for software management by the institution, as it had a limited capacity to perform this management. The local IT contractor managed the Web page site whose HyperText Markup Language (HTML) files sat on a server located in California. When super typhoons battered the region, the server was not affected and the online courses were still running. If electricity, phone and satellite transmissions were stable locally, students could continue to access the courses.

The Issue of Learning Engagement as a Fundamental Design Concept

As Ingram (in press) explains, "*Engagement* is thought to be a key variable for enabling and encouraging learners to interact with the material, with the instructor and with one another, as well as for learning generally" (p. 2). But what does this variable mean for instructional design in the cross-cultural learning context with diverse students such as Micronesians? Students cannot learn if they are not engaged in an instructional program; they cannot learn if they are not engaged with the tertiary institution. Retention and sustaining enrollment for degree completion are related issues to the issue of generating learning engagement. In total, engagement can be considered a complex, integrative process between the student and higher education. One prevalent use of the term is that the students are paying attention to their instructional tasks; that is, they are *engaged*. In the traditional classroom, the instructor may identify the engagement variable when the students appear interested, listening with concentration and asking questions in response to the events of instruction. This understanding was used for direct observations of the Micronesian students for the evaluative process of this project. With the separation of instructor and students by distance, this scenario does not take place. How, then, does the instructor know the students are interested, paying attention and, thus, being *engaged*? Another understanding of the term *engagement,* found in the literature of technology-based education, is that of a *meaningful dialog* between student and instructor or between student and student. The presence of *interactivity* is one possibility that may produce this dialog and reflect the face-to-face classroom. Establishing and maintaining interactivity has been one course attribute identified as the means to learning engagement in online courses. In this scenario, the responsibility for learning shifts from instructor to student. It becomes *learner-centered.*

The key questions related to the term *learning engagement* are, ultimately: Is learning taking place? and What is the quality of this learning? Although the precise answers to these questions may continue to defy educators, groups of educators within the field are trying to answer these questions around certain theoretically based practice models (Wilson & Cole, 1996). A range of models and theories of learning are threaded around the two major concepts of *behaviorism* and *constructivism*. These terms represent two parallel teaching methodologies in tertiary education. Grouping related theories with common attributes result in two categories: (1) *transmissive, objectivist, behaviorist;* and (2) *collaborative, constructivist.* Both threads may be found in the design, development and practice of distance education and technology-based education. Design is not standardized. Because of the emerging dichotomy between the established practices of pedagogical tradition and innovative methodology, the design and development of distance and technology-based education may become a challenge in selecting and using a consistent methodology. Faculty, who have been teaching for many years in one style, may be reluctant or inflexible to make a major change to the other; even if there is the expectation that students are flexible to shift from one approach to the other.

Pedagogical Models of Practice

Can this ongoing dialog hold keys for useful development of technology-based education for diverse populations? It may be helpful to identify the pedagogical models that have emerged from the theoretical threads and drive the design process (Wilson & Cole, 1991). Practice methods rather than theory pragmatically form the basis for institutional expansion of their technology-based curriculum. In the research work of this project, there were indications that instructional elements based on constructivist learning theory would support learning and that the learner population could possibly adapt to a mix of elements in a pedagogical design based on both theories rather than only one or the other. Pedagogical models used in a design may be assumed intuitively from the prevalent teaching practice at a given institution or with a group of faculty in a given discipline. Teacher-centered considers the instructional process to be one of transmission of information that the passive student absorbs or accumulates, then replicates.

Another group of educators considers engagement to primarily take place in a social context with group learning. Referred to as *social constructivism*, there is an emphasis on cooperative, collaborative learning and learning communities. The last characteristic would include the interactivity of people. The term *learning communities* is problematic, as it is not a standardized term or concept. Yet, this does not describe all learning situations in which learning engagement is expected as part of the instructional process. Although there is the need to restructure the teaching environment for technological change (Bates, 1997), one solution to all learning scenarios is not only limited but may ultimately be counterproductive, leading to student disengagement out of frustration in the learning experience. With the challenges of the digital divide, the separation of distance, different understandings of appropriate behavior cross-culturally and limited resources, this constructivist model and its theoretical base may be an unrealistic pedagogical model to assume for any given context. Claims are made of the primacy value of collaborative, cooperative learning and peer interaction (Ewing, Douling, & Coutts, 1999), but solid research evidence has yet to be generated (Stacey, 1999).

For this project, the overall design goal was to establish distance education with Web-based courses. At the time, the design group was not consciously identifying learning engagement as a goal, but rather assuming it on an intuitive level. We wanted to make the course usable and accessible for the student; emphasis was on individual interactivity with the online instructional material and the instructor. The design constructed and communicated the expectation for performance outcomes; for example, compare and contrast animal cells and plant cells.

The Pilot Course Design

The Introduction to Agriculture online course emulated, in its online design, the model of a traditional lecture course, structured with weekly class lessons and assignments. Instructors' lectures were replaced with online text lecture content; content summaries were used for reinforcement and clarity; there were self-testing quizzes for feedback and reinforcement of the English and scientific vocabulary; there were assigned readings and homework from the course textbook. This design was instructionally accessible across the digital divide. It worked. The lab component, however, was conducted during the on-site programs. This design from the traditional pedagogical model was most familiar to faculty and students in the region; it supported the behavior pattern for learning instilled from use in a face-to-face setting. This transmissive model of pedagogy has been in dominancy as the characteristic model for teaching online courses throughout the 1990s in higher education (Green, 1999). In the debates over learning engagement, this model, typical of higher education, would be criticized for producing only superficial learning, simply because knowledge or information is presented as static, unrelated to context and unquestionable as facts to be memorized and restated rather than applied or transformed. However, within the context of Micronesia, it functioned successfully according to the standards used in higher education. The student learning assessment was based on homework completion and exam performance, acceptable evidence of learning for the existing standards of higher education in North America. For the project, an ongoing design issue was the online discussion forum. It never functioned as planned for use as group interactivity.

Establishing the Relationship with Student Users

During the second year of the project, student involvement began. It included an identification and recruitment process that resulted in the formation of the pilot group of students.

College entrance testing results for potential students produced low scores in math and English. This represented inadequate preparation for learning achievement in higher education, and indicated the overall inequity of education for the region. The design response was to include vocabulary building and textual content reinforcement into the first online course. The research work of Lankbeck and Mugler (2000) with students in the South Pacific suggests that deep understanding of course material cannot occur without ease of readability. This may be an ongoing issue in attempting to meet the learning needs of diverse populations that are emerging as *English-as-a-second-language* students. English is the predominant language in distance education either as course content or in the use of technology and software. To engage and perform the learning outcomes for the online course work, Micronesian students have to face a multi-fold learning curve. They need to learn how to be a distance education student; how to use the computer technology for the online instruction; and, they would need to learn more specialized areas of language. The language challenges consisted of learning specialized English for the use of the computer, specialized English as scientific vocabulary in course content, and the use of the new language of Latin as a scientific communication.

Not all potential students teaching in the island schools had even attended college. A high school diploma was the only teaching qualification required on one island. Thus, there was a range of experience in being a college student. Lack of experience in the conventions of higher education was a possible student characteristic as well as the problematic situation of a student having completed far more than enough college credits numerically for graduation without obtaining the required courses. This last example was not atypical in a region where many teachers had been working on a bachelor degree through on-site professional development, sometimes taking courses over 20 years without achieving degree completion. As degree requirements changed over 20 years, they had to continually play catch-up in achieving changing prerequisites. This had become an issue that inflexible administrative processes had failed to address. Coordination resources and student support services for the project were developed further in the second year. However, from the beginning of the project, these areas did not get the attention or resources that the technology and the instructional design received. Although this is often the case in developing distance education, logistical support and coordination communication would prove to be critical for continued student engagement.

Textbooks and course materials were extremely weighted to the industrial agriculture production model of North America. The practice of this agriculture was a strong contrast to the village-based sustainable, subsistence agriculture practiced on Pacific atolls. Island farming consisted of gardens with crops of taro, cassava and sweet potato rather than thousands of acres of wheat or corn. Citrus, banana and coconut trees were productive and widespread. Island households have small numbers of pigs and chickens. But, horses, steers and dairy cattle were non-existent. Fishing was a major food production activity, but formal aquaculture operations were few. The course designer-developers were aware of these discrepancies and did include some text content and relevant regional agriculture examples when it could be integrated with established field knowledge. This was difficult, however, because (1) the primary development team members generating the online course were not indigenous to the region, and (2) the project planners had not allocated time and financial resources for this type of work.

At the beginning of the third year, a pilot group of 13 students was formed, primarily comprised of teachers and island educators. They were flown to the UOG for a face-to-face orientation. The pilot group consisted of 12 men and one woman, representing the islands of Palau, Yap, Chuuk, Pohnpei, and Kosrae. The common language base was English and there was some multi-lingualism among the students in different Micronesian languages. It was during the orientation process that the project developers began a critical relationship with the learner, a relationship that had not existed in the first year and was slowly evolving in the second year. The course design and development had been a parallel process with student selection, but the face-to-face orientation allowed the digital divide to be crossed so that developers and faculty of the project could have direct interaction with pilot students for the first time. From data collected in exit interviews with students who completed the first online course, the orientation event was critical for their successful learning engagement and eventual course completion. It provided computer training in the use of the online course and gave the students a head start with coursework. For the developers, the orientation served as a trial run for the initial design of the online course. As students first saw and then immediately used the design, it served as a validation of its effectiveness. Although revision work for the course design had been planned to take place after the introduction of the design to the students, this revision was not needed. This first use of the design was observed as successful, because the students remained attentive to the screen, they performed the coursework of the first lesson; they did not turn to other activities or distractions. Once they had accessed the Web pages, they moved easily around the platform design. They could follow the instructions and tasks of the course and the individual lessons.

Until the orientation, no one, including many of the institutional administrators and faculty, had experienced this type of education. Until they saw it and used it, they simply did not know what it was and how it operated. Since technology-based education is not for technology's sake, but a human experience, the orientation served to provide both new exposure to technology and generate relationship building across the digital divide. These new and ongoing relationships were based in trust among the project participants. This trust is considered crucial for substantive engagement of participants in an educational dialog (Barab, Hay, & Duffy, 1998). What was problematic was that one-quarter of the students, the older ones in their 40s and 50s, had never touched a computer prior to orientation. It was also discovered that most of the students did not have personal e-mail accounts, nor did they use e-mail on a regular basis for communication. Accounts were set up for them at this time. Being physically removed from their island and placed in an intensive learning environment may have accounted for their rapid use of the new online learning environment. Although computer literacy had been expected of students as a selection criterion, this did not prove to be the case. The initial lack of proficiency in using computers and e-mail eventually was an indicator for future success in completing the first online course.

The third year saw implementation of the pilot online course and the general education courses with formal enrollment. The performance and experience of the pilot students was monitored and evaluated during this third year from orientation until the following summer when the students had completed the course and took part in a second face-to-face summer program.

Of the original 13 pilot students, six immediately dropped out after the end of the orientation when they returned to their islands. In practical terms, this amounted to no further direct e-mail communication or response to project communication. There was an assortment of reasons for this. In the case of participants from one island nation, Chuuk, their participation ended when their island's electronic transmission and communication infrastructure collapsed. Telephone, electricity and satellite communication were not functioning. Out of the remaining seven in the pilot group, five went on to successfully complete the first online course. The other two had taken the course previously and did not need it for their degree programs.

Learning on the Other Side of the Digital Divide: The Issues of Student Disengagement

The Story of Joseph of Malek

This is a composite account representative of the experience of several pilot students. As project director, the researcher made a site visit to Island 5 (Note: to hide the identity of the subjects, the location is not specifically defined). This was the home island for Joseph. He lived in the village of Malek and taught at the local school. We were concerned he was disengaging but we did not know why. All his past academic records showed that he was successful doing college coursework. During the orientation he had been admitted to UOG and was enrolled in AG101; he had received training in the distance instruction and had successfully started the coursework while at the orientation. Then he left Guam and nothing came back from across the distance that separated his island from Guam. I had checked with the course instructor at UOG and there had been no communication from him regarding the coursework. No homework was sent back, no response to e-mails. It was as if he had dropped out of sight in the deep blue western Pacific Ocean. There was no response from the local coordinator, either.

Why wasn't he doing the coursework? Were the conditions on the island preventing his participation in the coursework? He was an adult student considered most likely to succeed. Seeking answers to these questions, I traveled by air 1,500 miles to an island located at the farthest corner of the region. I received a warm welcome from the local coordinator, but he did not have any definite answers. From our discussion, it was clear that time and distance were relative, there was a contrast in expectations and cultural orientations. The coordinator explained that he did not read his e-mail. He had limited access to the local campus computers. He did not feel under any pressure to check very often. Perhaps the phrase "out of sight, out of mind" describes the coordination scenario. Because this was to be a cost-effective project, coordination had been one more responsibility added to his schedule without any further remuneration. Joseph's village was so far away, at the end of the island's only paved road. He had not been communicating with Joseph on a regular basis. This distance was about 10 miles, but the psychological and contextual distance could be described as very far locally. It was the most distant municipality from any of the island services and infrastructure. It could be described as one of the most remote, inhabited corners of one of the most remote global regions. Because I was on the island, the coordinator called ahead to the village school to see if Joseph was there. Driving a rental car on the only paved road on the island, I passed thick jungle on slopes of volcanic mountains to the right, ocean waves splashed over the reef to my left, the road continued through the mostly thick jungle or swampy taro patches.

I was greeted in Malek by students singing a cappella as they marched out of the gated compound of school buildings sitting between the only road and the sea. Joseph was waiting; he was surprised that I had traveled to see him. I told him I had to know; why was he not doing his online course, especially after we had flown him to Guam, given him training and readmitted him to the university to do coursework for his college degree and his teaching qualification?

He looked guilty, he was sorry. We went to his classroom to talk. The classroom was dark, there was no air conditioning and it was warm. A ceiling fan was turned on for my comfort. Joseph was proud of the table in the corner. It held his classes' textbooks and curriculum materials, used books donated from schools in Hawaii. The only other things in the room were desks, chairs and a blackboard. I asked him if he had seen my e-mail. No, he did not use e-mail or check it on any sort of regular basis. It just was not part of the lifestyle. Not even after the orientation to its use. And, what about his access to a networked computer? This was understood as necessary from the orientation and each student was interviewed about their access situation. Yes, but he had not been able to travel to the local campus. Transportation was always a problem. No, computers were not at their homes, no one owned their own computer. There were no monthly Internet accounts with the island service provider. It was a non-competitive government telecommunications monopoly that kept rates high. With wages of $200 a month and yearly household incomes of $2,000 to $5,000 for those who were lucky to be on the government payroll, such as teachers, these items were still too expensive to afford.

But, yes, there was a computer lab for the school. Could he show it to me? And, why did he not use it for his online course? There was an access problem; it was about security. At the end of the day, the keys to the doors went with one villager who was responsible for all the school security. Therefore, it became a problem for Joseph to be at the school after work hours when he had the time to do the coursework. Even if he had access, he had no time to do the online course, because his employer required him to take another professional development course. Two courses had been too much to do on top of his other responsibilities of job, church, community and family. There were too many competing factors for his time. He pulled out a correspondence course and proudly showed me the correspondence course workbook with all his written performance work for an education course. The security person was still on the school grounds, so I asked to see the school computer lab. Experienced faculty in the region had assured me that schools had IT resources. I tried to access the online course but the speed of the computer and the bandwidth were so slow; after almost 10 minutes of sitting in the dark, warm room waiting for course pages, I gave up. Joseph promised that he would try to do the online course the next semester. He would have more time then. Before I left, he gave me a tour of his school garden. He used it to teach agriculture with his students; the garden was abundant with peppers, eggplant and cucumbers, their vines tied to neatly arranged trellises made from bamboo. His students marketed the produce, making extra money for their school activities. It was a successful learning environment. Later, during the visit to this island, I tried to send e-mail to the project office. Nothing was available at the hotel. The local campus was locked up; the staff had left. It was the weekend. Computer access might be available at the island's central telecommunications office,

I was told. When I arrived, I found the equipment broken. The parts had been ordered but they had not arrived. Yes, the island had Internet. It had computers. But their use was still problematic for basic communication, not only for an online course.

By the end of the project 1 year later, Joseph had still not done any of the online coursework. He had disengaged. For this region, a frail thread exists for a baseline type of learning engagement. It can be traced. If the student could access the course, then the course functioned as a learning vehicle. If the student could not access the course, there was no engagement. These multiple contextual barriers on any island worked against the teaching and learning process. The contextual factors of the digital divide were not only from under-developed technology but logistical factors that varied from island to island. Some students disengaged but others did not; those who remained engaged completed the pilot course.

The Student Experience of Engagement: Who is the Engaged Micronesian Student?

Technology-based instructional design does not function in a vacuum but in an external learning environment. For these Micronesian students, the learning environment was challenging beyond what is representative of a technologically developed society. Only with high motivation, dedication and maturity were students able to overcome many of the elements that were creating barriers to their learning experience. The external learning environment and the internal learning process need to be in harmony and integrate to achieve learning for a given student. After working directly or at a distance with the pilot students for a year, the project had gained a deeper understanding of the students and the Micronesian people.

Who was the engaged student in Micronesia? Using the pilot group as representative, he was about 25 to 35 in age with several years of community college, a family man and a teacher. He had a wife who might be a working professional; he had at least two or more children. He had many responsibilities. He understood the sea, fishing to feed the family. He understood the land, raising taro and pigs. Sunday meant going to church, it could be protestant or Catholic. He did not eat river fish. This was a traditional taboo. He had to answer to a village chief in a command- and authority-based society; his status and relationship to others was established at birth or via marriage. He existed in a framework of obligations, in a social fabric where, in his traditional group, family was identity and support. Family needs and obligations overrode the responsibilities of work and school. In this diverse society, the Internet, video games, television, reading books and newspapers do not compete for an individual's attention, but social interaction and responsibility does.

The Micronesian student liked to read quietly; the reading process appeared to be the strongest English language proficiency skill area. He was reflective and could be described as internalized rather than verbally articulate. He expressed himself in dance. It was also important to the student to have a good pair of sunglasses, athletic shoes and the right baseball cap. He was fatalistic, accepting the inevitable, walking away from problems rather than being confrontational. Student names were not consistently used in records and transcripts. A father's family name might be used or the mother's family name could be used. This posed problems for institutional processes of registration and advisement. There is almost no research in the area of Micronesian adult learners (Sukrad, Timarong, & Temaungil, 2002). What can be identified is that the Micronesian student shared many of the same traits that adult students in developed countries have: for example, openness for new ideas and experiences, looking for ways to improve life and livelihood, balancing many competing responsibilities and having limited time to do all that was necessary. Students thought professionally about their own educational experience in the project. As recounted in their responses to exit interviews, their teaching experience made them sensitive to pedagogical issues and made them better students in recognizing the commitment and motivation necessary to succeed at learning. Being teachers gave them an ability to articulate their frustrations as well as their positive achievements in learning with the online course. Yet, there were differences for the Micronesian adult students compared to adult students in developed countries. These can be identified as contextual differences. They did not have the same background of experiences and a comparable foundation in knowledge or its use. This was vividly revealed when I stood on a California beach during a study tour to the U.S. with the pilot students during the second summer program. We were on the edge of the continent. A student who was one of the most successful adult learners in the project asked me: "Where is the other side of the island?" For someone who had never traveled off of an island, the concept of a continent was not part of his frame of reference. Information acquisition is referenced to other information. The other side of the island was 2,000 miles east. There were differences related to the lack of a material culture. Their goods were limited to what is grown, produced locally or brought in as imports in shipping containers. These imported goods are not cheap. The islands lack dollar stores that can provide them with low-priced items, items that could be used as basic instructional materials. Thermometers, paper goods, measuring sticks, scales, even access to a microscope posed problems for these students. What is abundant in developed nations is hard to get in under-developed nations. Assumptions of what was affordable and available locally for students to individually purchase proved to be unrealistic.

Collective action took the place of individual initiative. I saw students collectively pool all their money to purchase meat for a barbecue during orientation. I saw collective action as they quickly and easily formed teams for a course lab project, growing sprouts from a $1 bag of mung beans. They would not have been available on their local island. I saw them start to think about ways to intervene with the parents of their students; they hoped to change attitudes about environmental use that was affecting public health, such as the placement of piggeries next to rivers. But they thought carefully about ramifications and how this could be perceived. Islands are small places and you do not disturb the existing balance without considering possible problems that might be generated. The overall instructional goal for the development and design of this technology-based education was to engage the student in a teaching and learning process that would result in relevant and useful learning. This seemingly simple goal may be elusive to achieve for many different reasons, including those related to the issues of the digital divide and multicultural education. Identified by Lankbeck and Mugler (2000), distance-learning conditions were difficult for South Pacific island students because of a lack of technology infrastructure, student isolation, and a lack of guidance and feedback for performance.

These learning issues were compounded by the use of course design formulated by designers who were not islanders. The designers simply did not understand these conditions when structuring expected performances into the courses. This paralleled the experience of the Micronesia project. Since very little information was at first available regarding the students who would be taking these courses, design decisions were based primarily on a North American model of Web-based online course design and the body of research for learning engagement from the North American student experience. The design emphasized individual coursework and interactivity between the student and instructor. Local campuses and personnel were part of a coordination framework but were not originally planned as significant instructional support; rather, as logistical or administrative support. Although what is called equity pedagogy has identified the advantage of using technology to address the needs of different learning styles and intelligence skills (Ukpokodu, 1996), there is the issue of whether technology can adequately address this equity need in environments of pervasive limited resources. This issue was raised by Marshall (2001). The Micronesian regional environment proved too difficult to attempt a design for the online course environment using more individualization. Increasing choices of designed components would have been unmanageable. For the online course to be transmitted and the coursework to be returned, it used a clear progression of constants and tasks for instructional performance. It was limited in the variables that it could offer in a merger of instruction and technology. A more customized multicultural educational experience using technology-based education poses challenges for the future.

The Gender Issue:
A Choice between Democratic Equity for Women
or a Traditional Culture of Male Hierarchy Rewards

The initial group of pilot students were identified and selected by local officials. It produced 12 male students and one female student. When the local community college and university offered the online courses to the general student populations, it produced a population predominately of women. The percentages shifted dramatically both for the Introduction to Agriculture Course offered to students on Guam and to the online courses offered by PCC. Why did this occur? What produced such a big gender shift in enrollment? Was it status placement in the cultural hierarchy or the result of traditional roles of men and women in the culture? Although gender was not a direct research area of the project, it is an aspect of diversity. Agriculture was the women's traditional occupation; fishing was done by men. However, all the teachers in agriculture were men. And, the opportunity to raise qualifications and advance through new educational opportunities was happening for men. To be a pilot student in this instance may have been perceived as a privileged opportunity. It provided new studies opportunities as well as the resources to travel off island for the beginning and ending summer programs.

The perks and advantages may have been going to the men based on cultural status, and women were disproportionately excluded. Equity access was not part of their traditional relationship to the power structures and this contrast in participation may represent the conflict of tradition with the democratic equity model. The common experience in the region was that men selected men. Opportunities had been made available to men. Of note is that the United Nations has identified these island republics in the top 10 for the disadvantage of women. In could then be pointed out that the primary disenfranchised population of Micronesians is also perceived to generate internally disenfranchisement of another population, women. As caste systems exist in these cultures, there may be other disenfranchisement occuring that outsiders would find hard to identify. Nor in this context of traditional values would this be perceived internally by the members of the society as disenfranchisement and inequity. At least, not by those who benefit.

Factors Supporting Engagement

The project research has been used to identify the factors and contextual elements that supported engagement. In contrast to Joseph of Malek with his struggle to engage in the coursework, there was the experience of the student who succeeded in completing the course. It was not an easy accomplishment. There were accounts of heroic measures to get the education and to ensure their successful completion of one course. What made the difference for success with engagement for these Micronesian students? Design and course development efforts focused primarily on course content and delivery technology. This may be typical for a technology-based course. If the larger frameworks of support that include communication and technology infrastructure are too fragile in the learning environment, problematic elements in the teaching and learning dynamic may be generated. This is an ongoing challenge to develop for regions with limited communication, economic and energy resources. It was factors related to these frameworks and occurring at critical points in the course experience that became most evident for promoting engagement or disengagement. By the end of the third year, engaged pilot students able to complete the first online course cited what factors kept them engaged doing their coursework and the points at which they would have left the project. Based on student feedback, the critical factors for engaging the students can be summarized as follows:

- **Personalization of the educational process:** The human factor and socialization played a deciding role in engagement. Relationships other than the central relationship of instructor to student were significant. Although the students were not interacting online, they developed a friendship with the other distance students in the project. It allowed them to get to know Micronesians from different regional cultures, but it also allowed them to share their similar experiences as islanders. There was interrelatedness in diversity.

- **A sense of comfort with reading materials and the flexibility of print or book materials:** Book use was cited as a necessary factor. Albeit books are a technology that is 2,000 years old, their significance to a technology-based course should not be discounted. They had easy portability, their access was available whenever student time permitted in contrast to an online edition, English could be reviewed again and again for translation needs; the text served as an inner-voice type of interactivity. The course textbooks overcame a sense of isolation. Books and bookstores are not as readily available in this regional setting compared to the developed world. Books are easily damaged or destroyed by typhoons and the daily climate; paper molds. Large personal libraries or accumulations of books in households are atypical.

- **A sense of security or validity generated by a physical place, such as a local center at a campus or a community computer center:** This focus or connection to a physical place strengthened student resolve to continue with the coursework, overcoming the insecurity generated by isolation; these locations offered a setting for instructional guidance, mentoring and peer interaction to support their individual instructional needs.

- **The positive experience of the initial resident orientation:** The intensive preparation resulting from the residential orientation, a 2-week program at UOG, was repeatedly cited by students as a highly valued support feature of the project. According to those who finished the course, it gave them the necessary course guidance, coordination orientation, confidence and contextual understanding of the new technology-based learning environment to continue successfully with the distance process.

- **More individual control of learning, with time flexibility:** This positive aspect of the technology-based learning that allowed student access outside of a formal meeting time should be paired with their wish for an increased ability to work at home. The computer technology was only accessible at the local community college or community computer center. Computers and home networking was almost non-existent in the region. It was pointed out by students that their various schedules of professional development were not coordinated; there had been no realistic planning for their multiple enrollments in other courses locally or for the more hectic times in their school work schedules. They did not know what they could do to resolve issues that arose only at specific times or during a limited period.

- **User-friendly courseware:** All students cited the courseware design as accessible and easy to use; they understood what was expected for course performance in terms of homework completion and exam assessment. The emulation in the course design of a known traditional education model that existed in their frames of reference was deemed successful. What proved more difficult for students were issues of access to the technology and the inter-related course coordination and course communication. The communication issues revolved around student work and the online course, and the relationship of the student to the educational institution. The technology was cited as a learning engagement problem. It posed a barrier; access to it was a frustration point. It brought the instruction, but at times, it also prevented or interrupted the instructional process. With the ongoing social context and the experience gained in technology use by the students, communication did evolve and improve over time. But, online interactivity was minimal during the duration of the piloting course. Attaching the homework to e-mail was a serious learning curve initially for some of the students, and they did not communicate the problem. The roles and responsibilities over the administrative relationship were not always clear, nor had they not been established for at-a-distance operations. Students did not know how to communicate about their issues and the developers had not realized that these issues existed. They arose during the implementation stage.

Planning, design and development can have the following issue areas: logistical support, student support, faculty support, evaluation and laboratory experiences. Across the digital divide, these issue areas are compounded by unexpected local conditions. For instructional design to be effective or optimal in its ultimate use, it must develop and integrate a supportive framework appropriate to the student's environment. The societal differences need to be planned; on the next level of design are individual differences or preferences. Although there was the hope that the project would become a self-sustaining program beyond the end of the project, it had been funded for only 3 years. This lack of stability and the inability to plan on a long-term basis among institutions has become a weakness that creates a potential for student disengagement. Because this project began to address these challenges for the region of Micronesia, further work is needed. The response to these challenges is hampered because of a lack of qualitative research on the effectiveness of online instruction for substantive learning, and the lack of clarity in the education profession for the concepts, terminology and practice of learning engagement (Ingram, in press). Only by going through the process could one actually obtain the needed information that would have been useful at the very beginning. This is a problematic aspect with any type of start-up operation; longevity provides an experiential base. Even with the above limited results, one can attempt to formulate a future strategy for the use of technology-based education with Micronesians and possibly with other diverse populations.

Implications for a Learning Strategy: Deep vs. Superficial Learning

In the context of the challenges of limited resources, a weak infrastructure, a lack of a strong coordination framework and limited organizational experience, the project's achievement of instructional objectives can become a useful experiential base for future planning. Best practices in the US as related to assessment and accountability appear to be influenced by the position that constructivism is a more effective theoretical base. Its application may generate stronger engagement, deeper learning and relevant student performance. In terms of a global classroom, its effectiveness may depend on the development level of critical thinking and the context of the learning environment. For this project's online courses, the instructional process functioned for knowledge transmission; there had been the possibility that the courses would not function at all and the students would disengage. This did not happen. The transmissive model was the model the instructors and designers understood and were most comfortable using. The students intuitively understood how to be students. There are lingering questions about developing online courses in this region that would support more complex courses with a different type of critical thinking and deeper learning. The experience of this factual overview course (AG101) and its emphasis in sending information content to students may not reflect the challenges represented by advanced coursework. The lab component of the first agriculture course proved so challenging its student performance was accomplished in the summer programs when the students were flown in to university facilities, a costly activity that was done on a one-time basis.

Lankbeck and Mugler (2000) identified and examined the University of the South Pacific student conceptions of their own learning and understanding as it occurred under the learning conditions of the islands. For this identification, the above authors used the six conceptions of learning: (1) increasing one's knowledge; (2) memorizing and reproducing; (3) applying; (4) understanding; (5) seeing something in a different way; and (6) changing as a person. They categorized these conceptions into the two contrasting groups that they identified as reproductive learning (transmissive, behaviorist) and transformative learning (constructivist). Although this objectivist or behaviorist model is criticized as needing to be reformed in higher education, it is clearly a functional model in these conditions. Micronesian pilot students paralleled the South Pacific islander responses in describing their learning experience by indicating the first four responses, especially increasing one's knowledge and understanding. Seeing something in a different way or changing as a person was considered deeper learning experiences in this scale, and were not representative of Micronesian student responses.

Do the challenges, then, limit the ability to use technology-based education to produce deep learning? Or, is there a way to address this instructional need given the inherent challenges of the digital divide? The question lingers of how to design for deep learning given the problematic conditions reflected by this experience. With the research of the Micronesian as an adult learner being almost nonexistent, this project does expand a qualitative knowledge base. Although according to Zemke and Zemke (1984), a characteristic of instructional design best suited for the adult learner is one of self-directed and self-designed learning projects, the Micronesians showed a strong preference for group work and the group social relationship; they were more reluctant to self-direct. However, this indicates a possible affinity for a constructivist approach. This was evident with the hands-on practical work, peer help with English and sharing information about course logistics. The group experience anchored them with confidence and a perception that they were doing the work appropriately; this provided an avenue that broke away from the problems of isolation and the lack of tutor or instructor feedback as observed by Lankbeck and Mugler (2000) in the South Pacific. Another curriculum preference of North American adult learners, according to Zemke and Zemke (1984), is the single concept or theory course rather than survey courses; coursework would focus heavily on concepts relevant to problems. This North American assessment indicates that a constructivist design approach might be more appropriate with its emphasis on applications of knowledge and learner-centered education. Knowledge construction rather than reproduction is emphasized for deep learning.

Cognitive teaching models that represent the constructivist design for teaching and learning identified by Wilson and Cole (1991) have concepts that include embedded learning in an authentic problem-solving environment that is learner relevant for the complexities of the real world, some type of learner control and use of errors as a mechanism to provide feedback on learners' understanding but do not disrupt the reflective process. Since relevancy was a major challenge for adapting course content for Micronesia, the constructivist design provides a mechanism for relevancy. Because the project research results indicate that there are affinities with characteristics found in both approaches, this poses a strategic consideration for re-designing and re-developing an appropriate learning experience more appropriate for this distinctive Micronesian population using the expanding knowledge base about how these learners learn. The survey course's transmissive design was not as problematic for content development and presentation compared to the possible demands and needs using a constructivist approach. At least initially, the alternative constructivist approach may be too complex to coordinate; it may be overly challenging to generate learning engagement for students unfamiliar with the practice of this pedagogical model. However, a strategy is suggested, emerging from the student learning response. Because the student responses indicate an affinity for some of these constructivist design elements, these elements may be more applicable and appropriate if integrated progressively into an evolving learning experience, thus making the design of the instructional framework better adapted for a diverse population across the digital divide; a diverse population with different frames of reference and contextual differences.

Solutions and Recommendations

A Progressive, Integrative Three-Stage Strategy

From an analysis of the project results, the use of a hybrid strategy is proposed. Until more research can be done, this is a proposed strategy to address the dilemma of how to develop more effective design of technology-based education across the digital divide. This preliminary strategy can combine elements of both pedagogies, using learning evidence for effectiveness in challenging learning conditions. This is not a design as replacement for transmissive pedagogy, but rather, a design as a hybrid model that integrates constructivist elements that would be manageable and intuitively favorable for the diverse populations' *learning characteristics*. This strategy would use a multi-stage integrative progression of design steps for the hybrid model. This model is made up of factors in a matrix of constants and variables identified as favorable based on the start-up experience. The proposed strategy consists of three stages for evolving levels of engagement. Course design and development would evolve as the program is generated.

Stage one: Start up and learning foundation development. This stage would establish the initial learning engagement. It would have a strong orientation component and student needs assessment. Its critical objective is to get to know the student and establish a relationship with the student, even at a distance. Personalization, faculty guidance and the communications infrastructure would be emphasized. Flexible time management elements would be constructed as part of the logistical framework. Factors of the materials' culture and the economics of the setting would be identified for impact on the learning experience. Fundamental transmissive pedagogy is established.

Stage two: Intermediate development for course revision and additional courses—patterning learning engagement. This stage emphasizes a planning focus on establishing detailed interactivity with course content, the social elements and greater course logistical communication. Course content, projects and logistical support involve more group activity; this can be group support external to the course or internally designed; mentors are identified and established in the design as student advocates. Center support may be identified or expanded for added activities. Constructivist elements are introduced, such as a team-based exercise. More focus and details of the institutional student services and administrative processes are designed to support learning achievement.

Stage three: Advanced design and development with critical thinking level. Engagement development is expanded for more constructivist factors of authentication, problem solving and relevant knowledge areas in group projects or team exercises. This would emphasize generating knowledge rather than absorbing it. Emphasis in course design and development for this stage includes a more intensive support component for expanded individual advisement.

In determining a strategic choice, different but possibly more effective forms of education and technology-based education should not be dismissed as unfashionable or old fashioned. Other delivery models of technology-based education should be assessed and determined for suitability to meet the local need. It must be asked if the goal is to provide effective education or impose technology use, which could be more problematic than productive.

Future Trends

As reflected in the experience of Micronesia, the globalization of distance education and technology-based education is an expanding, ongoing trend. It will continue to generate cross-cultural communication and integrative work processes for diverse staff, faculty and students. Even as new alliances are being formed for the enhancement of the human resource and employers demand better qualification and certification for the global workforce, the lack of funding and limited resources will continue to impact these trends. Thus, societies will be faced with band-aid solutions to problems that will not go away unless structural reform and overhaul with massive reallocation of resources takes place. There are no precedents. The financial model for this kind of educational overhaul does not exist, and these learning contexts may continue to lag behind in appropriate development for bridging the digital divide.

The requirement of return on investment for Web-based courses will limit their development unless governments and aid organizations are prepared for the allocation of funds and subsidies. It does not readily appear that this will be the case. Consumer marketing of technology to emerging and niche markets may guide the development as corporations make investments for a profitable return when market research indicates this potential. With pressures of limited resources, these highly turbulent learning environments will not be supportive of complicated design elements in the long run. To make instructional design and development functional, it may need to be structured in a lean and trim manner. Patterning, replication, repetition and organizational stability in support of sustainability are key factors that, in the long run, may ensure successful trans-border learning. The North American model and its traditional disciplines are being presented to a wider and more diverse global population as strategic alliances and power structures evolve to include different regions and populations. But the merging of teaching and multicultural education in a shifting, at times confrontational, global framework may well stay problematic. The use of education for propagandistic purposes may transcend a humanist democratic tradition in the conflicts over divergent ideologies.

Key issue areas revolving around content, delivery and infrastructure will inhibit accessibility. Needed research for determining strategy and design may remain neglected. Significant questions remain about the reliability and effectiveness of technology-based education to meet expectations. Competition and fragmentation are conditions of the global distance-education landscape that may continue on a chaotic and disorganized course unless major leadership and guidance emerges. An expanding population may present societies and developers with unattainable educational goals. Concerns of corruption, the management of resources, a lack of effective planning and coordination are framed in the problematic conditions of a troubled world, confronted by eroding civil society. Although there is the possibility of the expansion and deepening of the digital divide into a two-class structured globe, there are, nevertheless, voices in institutions of higher education and the educational profession expressing the need for productive action and the re-allocation of resources to address the inequity.

New Challenges and Learning Engagement

A new challenge now becomes one of how to evolve the education design structure and development process to incorporate an expanding matrix. In this matrix, there are more variables, but the matrix is more compatible with the needs of local conditions and multiple groups of diverse learners. Meeting this challenge should not underestimate the barriers presented by manners, customs, language, gender and other differences. It should not be left to chance or to assumption. Albeit challenging, compatibility of design elements can be attained in terms of the specific learner population or its specific mix of diverse learners.

Initial identification of local, relevant content could be crucial for instructional effectiveness, but it means stepping over the divide by the developers and designers to become better informed to a given society's economic, cultural and political contexts. Learning is a two-way street. It may be challenging to identify and design for the learning characteristics of diverse student populations; it may be challenging assessing local resources. However, for more effective results, these challenges may need to be taken on and met to ensure engagement.

These new challenges raise the questions of how customized and how great a range of design variation will work for larger, more diverse and dispersed populations with any specific course or program structure. The industrial model of open learning, replicated at the University of the South Pacific, consisting of print correspondence materials with tutored, center support, has made substantial progress in expanding access to higher education in Southeast Asia. In looking at these alternative models, there remain questions in assessing their effectiveness for learner engagement and the levels attained in the quality of learning. A standardized model may be more efficient for the developers, but may not match the student need nor ensure engagement and learning success. The challenge is to apply the wisdom of experience and knowledge as a bridge in determining which model to follow, and under what conditions for the given situation. An overemphasis of technology as an end in itself may result in the cost of the learner's engagement.

Not only will the question continue of how best to use limited resources, but there will be long-range-planning questions; resources cannot only increase, but they can become slimmer; they may shift dramatically and unexpectedly both in the short-term and long-term plans. In other words, there may be unpredictable challenges that planning does not presently consider. Political upheaval and natural disasters can unexpectedly affect the shape of the educational climate. Student diversity may present advantages rather than disadvantages. It opens up new knowledge bases and greater realities of experience to share through the instructional experience. However, it should not occur at a loss, but for enhancement.

Conclusion

With the establishment of the Northwest Territories in the U.S. after the American Revolution, the guarantee of free access to education and literacy became the right of the citizen rather than exclusive to a priest or elite ruling class. This principle extends to the use of technology, shaping expectations in global higher education as it reaches new and diverse populations.

This expectation of access was realized, albeit in a small way, for the agriculture teachers of Micronesia, with the new resource of online education. The limited research and proposed strategy presented in this chapter may indicate new ways to develop technology-based education and shift a pedagogical model to a more instructionally productive experience for a diverse population. The need is for more definitive research. Fashion should not dictate when pragmatism may be needed. Clearly, it takes careful thought and planning rather than quick, short-term solutions for substantial progress in making contributions to societies that technology-based education claims to help. Trust and relationship building, continuity and stability should be major concerns. The goals and purpose of education should fit the realities of the learning context. Unless major changes occur in the global landscape, serious questions will continue to exist about the use of this ideological model and its access to technology; historical inequities may continue to limit the realization of progress and societal rewards with the use of technology-based education. Disenfranchisement rather than empowerment is not an absolute status quo; possibility offers hope. A continuing examination, dialog and transformation of education are required to bridge the gap of ideal and reality. Ultimately, the future challenge is to provide educational opportunities that balance diversity with cultural, political and economic rights.

References

Banks, J. A. (2003). Educating global citizens in a diverse world. *New Horizons for Learning Online Journal, 9*(2). Retrieved April 25, 2005, from http://home.blarg.net/~building/strategies/multicultural/banks2.htm

Barab, S. A., Hay, K. E., & Duffy, T. M. (1998). Grounded constructions and how technology can help. *Tec Trends* (Technical Report # 12-00). Retrieved April 25, 2005, from http://cee.indiana.edu/publications/tr_12_00.pdf

Bates, A. (1997). *What kind of university?* Retrieved May 2, 2005, from http://bates.cstudies.ubc.ca/carnegie/carnegie.html

Brown, M. (2002). Multicultural education and technology: Perspectives to consider. *Journal of Special Education EJournal, 17*, Article 3. Retrieved April 25, 2005, from http://jset.unlv.edu/17.3/asseds/smith.html

Ewing J. M., Dowling J. D., & Coutts, N. (1999). Learning using the World Wide Web: A collaborative learning event. *Journal of Educational Multimedia and Hypermedia, 8*. Retrieved May 5, 2005, from www.dundee.ac.uk/education/jewing

Facey, E. (2001). First nations and education by Internet: The path forward, or back? *Journal of Distance Education/Revue de l'enseignement a distance*. Retrieved May 5, 2005, from http://cade.athabascau.ca/vol16.1/facey.html

Gorski, P. C. (2001). Understanding the digital divide from a multicultural education framework. *Digital Divide and EdTech*. Retrieved May 2, 2005 from www.edchange.org/multicultural/net/digdiv.html

Green, K. C. (1999). High tech vs. high touch: The potential promise and probable limits of technology-based education and training on campuses. *U.S. DOE EdPubs Online Ar-*

chives. Retrieved July 12, 2005, from www.ed.gov/pubs/Competence/section4.html

Ingram, A. L. (in press). Engagement in online learning communities. *Elements of Quality Online Education: Engaging Communities, 6*. Retrieved May 5, 2005, from www.albertingham.com/Engagement%20in%20Online%20Learning%Communities%20PaperFinal.doc

Lankbeck, R., & Mugler, F. (2000). Distance learners of the South Pacific: Study strategies, learning conditions and consequences for course design. *Journal of Distance Education/Revue de l'enseignement a distance*. Retrieved May 5, 2005 from http://cade.athabascau.ca/vol15.1/landbeck.html

Marshall, P. L. (2001). *Multicultural education and technology: Perfect pair or odd couple?* Retrieved May 5, 2005, from www.ericdigests.org/2002-3/odd.htm

Potashnik, M., & Capper, J. (1998, March). Distance education: Growth and diversity [Electronic version]. *Finance and Development*. Retrieved May 2, 2005, from www.worldbank.org/fandd/english/0398/articles/0110398.htm

Stacey, E. (1999). Collaborative learning in an online environment. *Journal of Distance Education/Revue de l'enseignement a distance*. Retrieved May 2, 2005, from http://cade:athbascau.ca/vol14.2/Stacey.html

Sukrad, W., Timarong, A., & Temaungil, M. (2002). *Adult learning and learners*. Honolulu: Pacific Resources for Education and Learning.

Ukpokodu, N. (1996). Equity pedagogy: Successfully educating America's diverse students. *The Professional Educator, 18*(2). Retrieved July 14, 2005, from http://edstar.ncrel.org/mn/ViewEssay.asp?IssueID=43&EssayID=250

Wilson, B. G., & Cole, P. (1991). A review of cognitive teaching models. *Educational Technology, Research and Development 39*(4), 47-64. Retrieved July 14, 2005, from http://carbon.cudenver.edu/!bwilson/cogapp.html

Wilson, B. G., & Cole, P. (1996). Cognitive teaching models. *Handbook of Research in Instructional Technology*. Retrieved July 14, 2005, from http://carbon.cudenver.edu/~bwilson/hndbkch.html

Zemke, R., & Zemke, S. (1984). Things we know for sure about adult learning. *Innovation Abstracts, 6*(8). Retrieved May 5, 2005 from http://nonolulu.hawaii.edu/intranet/committees/FacDevCom/guidebk/teachtip/adults-3.htm

Endnote

[1]   This material is based on work supported by the Cooperative Research, education and Extension Service, USDA, under Agreement No. # 2001-38411-10714. Any opinions, findings, conclusions or recommendations expressed in this publication are those of the author and do not necessarily reflect the view of the USDA.

Chapter IV

Crossing the Digital Divide:
Online Portfolios in a Diverse Student Environment

Catherine E. Stoicovy, University of Guam, USA

John Sanchez, University of Guam, USA

Abstract

Traditional portfolios, typically in the form of three-ring binders, are now being replaced with electronic versions on CD-ROM, DVD and the Internet. Two directions for electronic portfolios are those created with software tools found on computers, or Web-based storage systems generally accompanied by data management systems that allow assessment of portfolio data. The use of electronic portfolios, either Web-based or software generated, offers great promise but also poses significant challenges. This chapter describes the challenges and successes involved in crossing the digital divide from traditional to Web-based portfolios in a diverse student environment in higher education.

Introduction

Over the past two decades, American education has seen tremendous demographic changes that have created a student population more racially, ethnically and culturally diverse than ever before. According to the National Center for Education Statistics (NCES, 2005), 42% of public school students were considered to be part of a racial or ethnic minority group in 2003, an increase from 22% in 1972. In comparison, the percentage of public school students who were White decreased from 78% to 58%. At the college level, student diversity is also on the increase. According to the American Council on Education's (ACE) *Minorities in Higher Education Twenty-First Annual Status Report* (ACE, 2005), college enrollment of minorities rose by nearly 1.5 million students (52%) to more than 4.3 million from 1991 to 2001.

Working with a diverse student population presents unique challenges in that students differ in terms of educational experiences, levels of income, home language, culture and ways of learning. Given the growing diversity in campuses across the nation, educators are beginning to legitimize multiple paths to learning and the notion of multiple literacies. With the grow-ing acceptance by educators of the theory of multiple intelligences as developed by Howard Gardner (1983, 1999), the tide is rising in favor of capturing the wisdom of our students in multiple ways (Roach, 2001). The challenge for educators is how to capture the varied backgrounds and strengths inherent in a diverse student population. Traditional measures of assessment (i.e., paper-and-pencil tests) do not enable students to use and demonstrate a broad range of abilities. In today's digital world, however, educators are discovering that technology offers great promise for diverse student populations. "Today's technologies are capable of giving full recognition of student achievements that can capture a 'snapshot' of the multiple literacies of our students that have been neglected or limited by the traditional measures used to demonstrate or measure performance" (Roach, 2001, p. 2).

Electronic portfolios are an increasingly popular way of using technology to display and assess students' abilities, particularly in teacher education programs (Barrett, 2005). Portfolios are purposeful collections of student work that demonstrate effort, progress and/or achievement (Barrett, 1999; Russell & Butcher, 1999). Two directions for electronic teaching portfolios are those created with software tools found on computers or Web-based storage systems generally accompanied by data management systems that allow assessment of portfolio data (Gibson & Barrett, 2003). Web-based assessment systems support consistent, secure storage and ag-gregate reporting of assessment information and are likely to be increasing in significance due to the requirements of accrediting agencies for institutions of higher education and the advantages of Web-based portfolios over more traditional modes of assessment.

The purpose of this chapter is to describe the challenges and successes involved in cross-ing the digital divide to Web-based portfolios in a diverse student environment in higher education. We will begin with a review of the benefits of technology and a discussion of electronic portfolios as an emerging educational tool for teacher education. We will then provide an account of one school of education's journey from traditional portfolios, typically in the form of three-ring binders, to Web-based portfolios with a student body primarily comprised of Asian-Pacific Islanders.

Technology and Multiple Paths to Learning

In today's digital age, technology has contributed to the notion of multiple paths to learning and an expanded definition of literacy. Technology and the Internet are transforming the way students organize and seek knowledge (International Society for Technology in Education, 1999). "Adolescents today navigate through multiple formats of literacy—films, Web sites, television, CD-ROMs, books, magazines, music, videos and newspapers" (Taylor, 2005, p. 1). Taylor describes these tools as artifacts of our changing literacy. Students with laptops, MP3 players, cell phones, flash drives, handheld organizers and calculators are the norm. Both in and out of the classroom, students are using technology for communicating, investigating, accessing and using information. An added bonus is that technology can be successfully used regardless of whether the classroom setting is mainly bilingual or contains an English as a second language (ESL) component (Svedkauskaite & Reza-Hernandez, 2003). Through technology, limited English-proficient (LEP) students can learn in a rich linguistic environment and find opportunities to interact with the multicultural world and extend their language skills (Padrón & Waxman, 1996).

Electronic Portfolios for Teacher Education

The use of portfolios to document teaching development and expertise has surged in recent years (Barrett, 2005; Roach, 2001). Portfolios are now used for many purposes, including admission into teacher education programs, documenting student teaching, showing in-service development, interviewing, accreditation and certification by the National Board for Professional Teaching Standards (McLaughlin & Vogt, 1996). Traditional portfolios, typically in the form of three-ring binders, are now being replaced with electronic versions to provide evidence of a student teacher's development as a professional. Like their paper predecessors, electronic portfolios are collections of work used to showcase students' performance and demonstrate progress toward meeting degree requirements. Barrett (2005) defines an electronic portfolio as follows:

An electronic portfolio uses electronic technologies as the container, allowing students/ teachers to collect and organize portfolio artifacts in many media types (audio, video, graphics, text); and using hypertext links to organize the material, connecting evidence to appropriate outcomes, goals or standards. (p. 5)

The contents of electronic portfolios can now include video, digital audio, multimedia presentations and hyperlinks to word documents and the World Wide Web, enabling students to learn and be assessed in multiple ways.

Literature Review on Electronic Portfolios

Much of the growing body of literature readily found on electronic portfolios is geared with the student teacher in mind (Barrett, 1999, 2005). The national movement toward performance-based standards has prompted interest in the use of electronic portfolios by pre-service teachers to document their knowledge and teaching performance. Another reason for this growth in popularity is the broader, more contextualized view of teaching that portfolios provide as compared to traditional assessments, such as standardized tests (Shulman, 1998). While the current literature on electronic portfolios in teacher education is limited, it does support the many advantages offered by technology. Creation of electronic portfolios has been found to be "positive and useful" (McKinney, 1998, p. 85) and "constructivist, demanding and multifaceted" (Milman, 1999, p. 1). Portfolio-based assessment is beneficial pedagogically because the format can encompass evidence from a wide variety of sources, provides a richer picture of the student and actively involves students in the learning process (Barrett, 1999, 2005). Electronic portfolios teach valuable technology skills; allow electronic storage; provide potential employers with examples of applicants' knowledge, skills and dispositions; and document that students have achieved designated assessment standards. As teachers, they will be better prepared to meet the National Educational Technology Standards (NETS) for Teachers and to help their students meet the NETS for Students. Warner and Maureen (1999) suggest that by developing an electronic portfolio, teacher candidates will learn important computing skills and knowledge that can directly impact integration into their own classrooms. They believe candidates will be motivated to implement electronic portfolios for assessing their own students.

Crossing the Digital Divide: One School of Education's Journey

Despite the increasing use of electronic portfolios in teacher education programs, implementation can be challenging. The following account describes one school of education's challenges and successes in implementing a Web-based portfolio system with a diverse student body. In a university student population of about 3,000, 85% are of Asian-Pacific Islander ethnicity from Guam and the Northern Mariana Islands, the Philippines and the Micronesian islands of Chuuk, Palau, Pohnpei, Kosrae, Yap and the Marshalls. Moreover, a significant segment of the population can be referred to as generation 1.5 students, because they share characteristics of both first- and second-generation immigrants (Rumbaut & Ima, 1988). Equipped with social skills in English, generation 1.5 students often appear in conversation to be native English speakers. However, they are usually less skilled in the academic language associated with school achievement, especially in the area of writing (Harklau, 2003). Harklau further describes the diversity among generation 1.5 students in terms of their educational experience, native and English language proficiency and academic literacy:

There is great diversity among them in terms of their prior educational experience, native and English language proficiency, language dominance and academic literacy. Some of these students immigrated to the United States while they were in elementary school; others arrived during high school. Still others were born in this country but grew up speaking a language other than English at home. They may see themselves as bilingual, but English may be the only language in which they have academic preparation or in which they can read and write. One of the most common traits among generation 1.5 students is limited or no literacy in the first language. (p. 1)

The limitations in writing skills pose challenges for educators. Generation 1.5 students do not fit the typical profile of ESL students, and so are not usually placed in ESL courses, yet they are often unprepared for writing at the level demanded in college (Harklau, 2003; Valdés, 1992). With regard to Pacific islanders, many of whom may be grounded primarily in oral traditions, students may not see any well-defined purpose for writing. Despite limitations with written language, however, these culturally diverse learners come to college with a wealth of prior knowledge, experiences and modes of learning. For example, like their mainland counterparts, students in our teacher education program are quite capable of navigating through multiple formats of literacy with the latest tech gadgets on the market.

Our hunch (Wolcott, 1991) was to build on students' technological skills as a way to tap diverse ways of learning and knowing. Web-based portfolios would allow students to demonstrate what they know in multiple ways via audio, video, graphics and text. Moreover, the use of Web-based portfolios would help the school of education meet the National Council for Accreditation of Teacher Education's (NCATE) accreditation requirements. Teacher education programs seeking NCATE accreditation must establish an electronic assessment system that collects and analyzes data on applicant qualifications, candidate and graduate performance, and unit operations to evaluate and improve the unit and its programs (NCATE, 2005).

We were excited, but where to start? While several faculty members had dabbled with electronic portfolios on CD-ROM, requiring them in one or two courses, most had been using the traditional three-ring binder portfolio as a course requirement. A small cohort of interested faculty, pioneers as we like to call ourselves, initiated the process. The first step was to introduce the idea of Web-based portfolios to faculty members during faculty meetings and retreats. Short multimedia presentations and discussions served to inform faculty about the merits of using Web-based portfolios to develop, manage and assess the school's program and student achievements, especially with regard to NCATE accreditation. The next step was to find a reputable commercial Web-based portfolio system tailored to the particular needs and challenges of the education profession, and backed by a company willing to do business with an institution thousands of miles across the Pacific Ocean. After numerous e-mail messages and long-distance phone calls, we found a system that met our needs. However, that was just the beginning of a long process. What we thought would be an easy road turned out to be longer and bumpier than we had expected. But like true pioneers, our small cohort forged ahead.

Despite a general recognition of the usefulness of Web-based portfolios, the key to success is how well the faculty and students are prepared for using this new learning and assessment tool. Even if faculty are enthusiastic about implementing the system, they need to be prepared for the significant amount of time, effort and communication needed to make it happen. A lot of work had to be done that first year to set a framework that would support the growth of the project over the next couple of years. At the onset, we managed to schedule several teleconference-training sessions for faculty, but the training was ill attended and insufficient. We needed face-to-face on-site training. So began the next step in the journey. Due to the university's location, it is expensive to provide on-site training. With a tight budget, where would we find the funds for such an expensive endeavor? With much persistence, we finally obtained the funding from administration and other sources, and in spring 2005, the off-island trainer arrived. Faculty who were interested in piloting the Web-based portfolios in their courses attended the sessions with their students. While the trainer was excellent and faculty and students learned the basic skills for navigating the Web-based tools, it became evident that more training was needed. Once again, the funding issue emerged, so we came up with the idea to use several members who had become adept at using the system to provide faculty training. Two faculty, one full-time and one part-time, took on the responsibility of teaching the others to navigate and implement Web-based portfolios in their courses. Before we could begin the training, however, we encountered another obstacle. The operating system in faculty computers and those in the computer lab could not support the Web-based portfolios. Fortunately, a new computer lab with state-of-the-art equipment was nearing completion and administration found funds to purchase new laptops for faculty. The trainers were now well on the way to faculty and student development.

Faculty Development

The training of faculty has its own issues. Adults, usually entrenched in their own style, are reluctant to change. So, instead of trying to implement systemic change all at once, the task was handled individually. The training began on a one-to-one basis with the initial cohort group. The key was to create a situation in which faculty requested the training rather than viewing it as a top-down mandate for already overburdened professors. The trainers were given release time to schedule training sessions at times convenient for faculty. In addition, the trainers simplified the training by creating portfolio templates for faculty and assuring them that they did not have to be experts in technology to get started. The trainers then gave one-on-one assistance for using the suite of tools embedded in the Web-based assessment system. To get all faculty on board, the trainers conducted multiple workshops, demonstrations, announcements and discussions.

It was essential to make the training as easy as possible for faculty. Most faculty were not so much interested in the development of Web-based portfolios as they were in how this new technology could be used to streamline their work. Once they recognized the advantages of using a Web-based assessment system for reviewing and assessing students' performance in meeting the course standards, faculty became more motivated to use it.

Student Development

The training of students was a much easier task. When students enroll in school, there is an expectation that they will be learning new things. The students were eager to be on the cutting edge with the newest technologies. Already familiar with the latest tech gadgets, they embraced the training sessions as a way to become even more tech savvy. The trainers scheduled 1-hour sessions in the computer lab, where students learned how to navigate the suite of Web-based tools to create a customized portfolio aligned with national standards. The implementation of portfolios was first introduced in an entry-level foundations class to establish the expectation that candidates will maintain a Web-based portfolio throughout their professional preparation program. Gradually, faculty required students to maintain portfolios in other courses. The goal is to have all students maintain a Web-based portfolio for the duration of their program of study. In addition, students will have access to their portfolios for a full year after graduation, which will allow them to showcase their work to prospective employers.

Portfolio Content

The faculty built program curricula around the Specialized Professional Association's NCATE approved standards and developed course assignments that allowed students to showcase the full range of their abilities, aligned with the standards. With the help of the faculty trainers, portfolio templates were developed for both graduate and undergraduate courses. Portfolio templates and guidelines for artifact selection and evaluation, what and how to choose, and how evidence connects to outcomes were provided. These were specific enough to give needed support and general enough to invite student creativity and ownership.

Faculty Development for Portfolio Content

During one-on-one training sessions, faculty identified one key artifact, for each course they taught and the grading criteria for the artifact. The trainer created a template to allow for the submission of the assignment from the students. While the template provides a framework for submission of artifacts, the software is flexible enough to allow students to post the artifacts, too. When data is analyzed after 1 year, the faculty and programs will revisit the content of each course and make informed decisions about modifying the content for each course portfolio. The use of technology to create a portfolio does not take the place of the intent of the portfolio. The faculty decides on the type of portfolio the students will maintain. This can run the gamut, from a showcase portfolio where only "best work" is kept to a developmental portfolio in which students submit first, second and third drafts of projects with the portfolios highlighting the development that occurred over the semester. Again, the key to successful implementation of any change is that that users find the change useful. Faculty assumes the responsibility of helping students develop their portfolio. Once faculty loses control of this aspect, they no longer have a sense of ownership and will quickly lose interest in the process.

Student Development for Portfolio Content

After identifying key artifacts to be included in the portfolio, faculty instructed students to include exemplary work in their portfolios that demonstrates their competency in meeting the standards. Since a key part of portfolio assessment is developing tasks that will enable students to use and demonstrate a broad range of abilities, students may use video, digital audio, multimedia presentations and hyperlinks to word documents and the Web to show evidence of their performance. The Web-based portfolios allow students to move or copy artifacts from a portfolio developed in one class and combine it with artifacts from other classes to develop a new portfolio. Course requirements for the pilot courses required students to create a table of their field experience hours and a two-page reflection of their experiences, submitted electronically. The table will continue to grow each semester, culminating in one document summarizing a student's four years of field experiences. The reflections allow the faculty advisor to review students' writing and help them develop the skills of a reflective practitioner. A review of the first set of portfolios submitted during the pilot year revealed students were utilizing technology in creative ways. While most portfolios were standardized in their presentation, as they were using set templates, some took it a step further. As a number of students already owned digital cameras or cell phones/camera combo units, most loaded photos of their experiences. With scanners available in the computer lab, students scanned their original field notes and loaded those for additional documentation. As a course requirement, students produced a multimedia presentation of their experiences. A graduate course designed for technology integration encouraged students to develop lesson plans utilizing the tools in the Web-based assessment system. They were able to include video streaming into their plans. A format for Web quests and Web pages was also available, and students utilized these as well.

Assessment

The Web-based assessment system will improve the school's ability to create and manage an assessment system that is valid, fair and consistent. The students' work (artifacts) must be evaluated using well-developed rubrics with identifiable and specific criteria. Faculty evaluate the artifacts and portfolios by means of electronic rubrics, cross-referenced with student demographic information that enable collection and analysis of large amounts of data on students, programs and the institution. The artifacts and assessments in each individual course provide the groundwork for the data to be used at the program and unit (or School) level.

The school's assessment system is designed to monitor students' developmental performance at appropriate benchmarks over the length of their program. Using multiple assessments with multiple indicators allows the school to collect both qualitative and quantitative data as a student progresses through the program. A standard syllabus is used for all sections of each course, including content and assessments aligned with the standards of the Specialized Professional Association, performance measures and common rubrics. Individual professors customize the teaching methods, strategies, resources and tools to support student learning and performance.

In the school of education, there are three major assessment points for students. The first is upon completion of four required "education" courses. A committee of faculty members evaluates the new portfolio created by the student. To make an informed decision on whether or not the student should proceed through the program, the committee need only request a report of how the student performed on each assignment submitted to their electronic portfolio. This type of assessment occurs again before the student is allowed to student teach (mid-point) and, finally, upon graduation (exit). The Web-based system allows for the aggregation and disaggregation of data for decision-making purposes.

Student Perspectives

The buy-in from students is essential to the successful implementation of Web-based portfolios. To obtain student feedback, we distributed questionnaires in several undergraduate classes that had piloted the portfolios in key courses. The students' responses were analyzed for emerging patterns. The next section illuminates the following emergent themes: (1) reproduction, (2) organization, (3) access, (4) navigation, (5) creativity and (6) challenges.

Reproduction

A recurring theme was the notion of reproduction. The fact that students no longer had to print out copies of their portfolio contents was seen as a big advantage for using Web-based portfolios. Comments include the following:

- "Basically, you do not have to make copies to pass it on."
- "I wouldn't have to go through the hassle of printing everything out."
- "Don't have to spend for ink or paper or binders."
- "Instead of printing all my documents, I can just enter it into the portfolio online."
- "I won't have to make photocopies if I want other people to read it."
- "Not having to purchase a binder and paper, assignments are turned in neatly and typed out."
- "I would prefer an online portfolio and getting updated with the use of technology nowadays. I think it's convenient as far as saving paper and time when having to type out some things for the traditional three-ring binder."
- "The advantage for the online portfolio is that you do not have to carry a big binder around, and how convenient it is to just type everything in and put them in as attachments."

Organization

Students consistently commented on the usefulness of Web-based portfolios to organize their work in a systematic manner:

- "I kept all my work neat and organized."
- "A majority of college students are busy people, and organizing an online portfolio takes less time than a traditional one. When done typing a document, one can just connect to the Internet, log into the portfolio account and submit it instead of printing it, punching holes and then inserting it into a binder."
- "I would prefer to create an online portfolio, since it takes less time to organize and I won't have to worry about it getting lost or damaged. Plus, with the Internet being the way it is, I know everything I left in the portfolio will still be there for many years if the company in charge of the account doesn't shut down."
- "I was already stressing out about completing all the work from all my other classes. But anyway, after a while though, I realized how beneficial an electronic portfolio really is. The time put into creating it was well worth it. I kept all my work neat and organized. Plus, I was able to make it look great on PowerPoint!"
- "It saves space and could be easily organized in a systematic manner."
- "The e-portfolio can hold a large amount of artifacts and if the person creating the portfolio did it correctly, it is very organized."

- "Everything is better organized and you can add so many neat graphics."
- "I would definitely prefer to create an electronic portfolio over the traditional three-ring binder simply because it's neater, more organized."
- "Once you have all your documents saved and ready to go, all you have to work on is organizing the material and hyper-linking them together. No more sheet protectors and 5-inch three-ring binders."

Access

Students indicated that Web-based portfolios are easily accessible. They enjoy the convenience of online accessibility for a variety of reasons:

- "I won't have to make photocopies if I want other people to read it; I can just give people a code to access the online portfolio."
- "Many people can view it at once; there is no mess involved when fixing it up for future references."
- "Turning in assignments just at your very home."
- "It takes up less space and is, of course, compact."
- "I like the access you can give people and people you can block from sharing your portfolios with."
- "Having several links included, such as access to other people's creations online."
- "With an electronic portfolio, it has easy portability. It does not take up as much space as a three-ring binder. It is neater, easily accessible for professors to look at … Three-ring binders take up too much space and are sometimes too heavy."
- "The main advantage is that the computer is so compact and easy to carry around."
- "You can access it online with corrections made by your teacher."
- "Does not take up too much space, lightweight, and is easily accessible for anyone to view."

Navigation

Ease of navigation was another theme. Students' comments revealed that learning how to use the tools for Web-based portfolios was quite easy and that being computer literate helped them with the process. Several noted their surprise at how easy it was to learn the steps.

- "It's like writing e-mail—easy."
- "I would have to say that the biggest surprise for me had to be how easy it was to hyperlink all the documents together."
- "My biggest surprise is how simple and convenient it is."

- "The steps are easy to follow and you can always refer back to the CD-ROM for instructions in case you forget."
- "At first, it was a bit confusing. But when I got the hang of it, it was pretty simple."
- "I felt a little frustrated at first when creating my online portfolio, but as soon as I got the hang of it, it became easy and more fun to compile information."
- "Fellow students helped me to understand [e-portfolios] better."
- "I would say I had the skills to develop my online portfolio; taking a computer class and being literate in computers helped me to do just this."
- "I had taken programming classes prior than this course, which helped me to even create our own group Web site at Geocities."
- "I knew how to get around a computer. After a few trials, I was able to understand how to go about the program. So, in a sense, I did have the skills to develop such a portfolio."

Creativity

Creativity was a major theme that emerged from the data. Students provided numerous comments about the potential for creativity with Web-based portfolios and the excitement about customizing their portfolios for greater diversity:

- "I felt excited creating my portfolio online because it was a total different thing for me. It's actually fun because you can do all sorts of things on it."
- "I would say it does not matter whatever background you come from; as long as you know how to use a computer would be pretty much useful. I think the online portfolio would be beneficial with students from diverse backgrounds."
- "I would probably say that I was impressed with the way [the e-portfolio] turned out, especially when I presented it. With my ideas and creativity, it was personalized and I was able to animate it as well."
- "It would give students more of an opportunity to be creative and search for ideas they never thought they could put together. It becomes very personalized, and with students from diverse backgrounds, I'm sure if they learn the skills to put one together, they would definitely enjoy using the computer."
- "I would say I especially liked the features of adding video clips and incorporating other things from the online references."
- "E-portfolios allow for a greater diversity of expression."
- "E-portfolios are easy to create once you know the basic steps. After that, you can become as creative as you want to make your portfolio one of a kind."
- "My biggest surprise when creating my electronic portfolio was how good our end product looked and the creativity of everyone involved."
- "Electronic any day. You are allowed more creativity and autonomy in expressing what you have learned."

- "I enjoyed it quite a bit. I felt it allowed us to utilize all the skills we had learned in one project."

- "I would say I especially liked the features of adding video clips and incorporating other things from the online references."

- "Having several links included, such as access to other people's creations online."

- "I think it can work with students from diverse backgrounds if they all spend a couple minutes a week playing around with the portfolio."

- "We may learn something from students with diverse backgrounds."

- "Creating an online portfolio was very inviting for me. In a sense, it made technology a reality to applying for a teaching career."

- "I knew the very basics. The more we went over how to create one by looking at electronic portfolios created in the past, the more excited I got to make mine spectacular."

Challenges

While acknowledging the advantages of Web-based portfolios, several students noted challenges associated with its use:

- "In time, the online portfolio will work for all backgrounds of students. The only way I don't see it working in an array of backgrounds is if a certain culture has not been exposed to much technology, so going about and taking remedial courses for the technology will be a hindrance; also, if the site is not catered to their language. (It would be great if the site was able to translate languages!)"

- "The only problem I can think of would be the cost and having access to a computer, but other than that, it can work if students just put some time to adjust to it. I think it will work. Technology is now all over the world; people will prefer to use it for its convenience."

Analysis

A review of the literature addressing pre-service teachers' responses to electronic portfolios is scant, yet positive. McKinney's (1998) analysis of pre-service teachers' electronic portfolios, interviews and surveys led her to conclude that creating electronic portfolios is positive and useful. Electronic portfolios have a positive impact on preservice teachers' self concepts (Ryan, Cole, & Mathies, 1997). Preservice teachers who create electronic portfolios learn an alternative way to think about and display their accomplishments (Richards, 1998; Wright, Stallworth, & Ray, 2002). Teacher education students who experience technology become more comfortable with it and are more likely to use technology in their teaching (Goldsby & Fazal, 2000; McKinney, 1998). An analysis of the students' responses is consistent with past research in that they are enthusiastic about the use and advantages of Web-based portfolios. Students were particularly impressed with the opportunity to demonstrate their skills creatively in a variety of formats and they expressed pride in their finished products. They were surprised at how easy it was to navigate and use the portfolios. Any frustrations associated with learning how to use Web-based portfolios dissipated with use. Once they "got the hang of it," students found the portfolios quite easy to use, especially since they were already familiar with computers and other technology tools. Of particular interest were the positive remarks with regard to the use of Web-based portfolios for a diverse student body. Students' responses supported our hunch (Wolcott, 1991) that Web-based portfolios would enable a diverse student body to use and demonstrate a broad range of abilities. For example:

- "I think it can work with students from diverse backgrounds. We may learn something from students with diverse backgrounds."

- "E-portfolios allow for a greater diversity of expression. I would say it does not matter whatever background you come from, as long as you know how to use a computer, [it] would be pretty much useful. I think the online portfolio would be beneficial with students from diverse backgrounds."

- "With my ideas and creativity, it was personalized and I was able to animate it as well."

- "It would give students more of an opportunity to be creative and search for ideas they never thought they could put together. It becomes very personalized, and with students from diverse backgrounds, I'm sure if they learn the skills to put one together, they would definitely enjoy using the computer."

- "Electronic any day. You are allowed more creativity and autonomy in expressing what you have learned."

Critical Issues

Several issues and concerns regarding Web-based portfolios emerged during the school's transition from traditional to Web-based portfolios. Training was an issue for both faculty and students with regard to financial and geographical factors. With much persistence and perseverance, however, the school obtained the financial support necessary for the initial training. To augment the training, two faculty members took on the responsibility of providing additional training to faculty and students. Another issue was that using an online database aligned with standards might be too structured, leaving the learner with limited flexibility and creativity. On the contrary, students' responses revealed that standards provide an ideal structure for electronic teaching portfolios while allowing a great deal of flexibility. Students consistently commented on the creative opportunities that Web-based portfolios provide. The student registration fee for Web-based portfolios was an initial concern; however, a number of students qualify for financial assistance from teacher preparation scholarships that fund the portfolio fees. For those students who do not qualify for scholarships, the one-time portfolio registration fee is much less expensive than maintaining traditional, three-ring binder portfolios. An issue that has come up in past discussions with students and faculty is whether students can continue developing the portfolio once they are out of the educational system. The system the school adopted allows student access to the portfolio for 1 year beyond graduation, with the option to extend registration indefinitely. Based on both the findings and the limitations of the pilot study, several directions for future research seem appropriate. Additional surveys on students' perceptions about the use of Web-based portfolios are recommended. Additionally, studies to explore faculty perceptions would provide valuable insights as the school continues its journey.

Future Trends

Despite predictions that electronic portfolios were just another trend in the search to enrich the assessment of student achievement, they continue to offer powerful possibilities for improving teaching and learning (Michelle, 2000). According to Michelle (2000), electronic portfolios will continue to survive for several substantial reasons: First, advances in Internet-based technology—and the evolution of the Web as a commercial venue in particular—have irreversibly affected the way our society communicates and shares information. Improvements in the tools used to create multimedia and Web site documents have opened new authoring possibilities to non-expert users of technology. Second, the ongoing concern over standards and student achievement in a global economy has provided a steady motivation for educators to explore alternative modes of assessment. With the adoption of performance-based accreditation systems, teacher education programs face the challenge of authentically assessing the knowledge, skills and dispositions of teacher candidates. The NCATE, the National Board for Professional Teaching Standards and State Professional Standards Boards have adopted performance assessment strategies requiring teacher candidates to demonstrate their knowledge, skills and dispositions and the impact of teacher education candidates on K-12 student achievement. Electronic portfolios show promise, today and for the future, as a way to meaningfully compile, document and analyze teacher candidate performance for a diverse student population.

Conclusion

Although the school faced challenges in crossing the digital divide, the benefits students reported led the researchers to conclude that the implementation of a Web-based assessment system is well worthwhile. That the students embraced the Web-based portfolios as a significant improvement from traditional portfolios was essential to its implementation. As one student remarked, "Online portfolios have all the advantages and efficiency of electronic media over paper, pencil and binders." Prior to the implementation of Web-based portfolios, each semester found students laden with heavy binders packed with artifacts, rushing off to portfolio conferences to meet with professors. That image will soon be a memory with the school-wide adoption of the Web-based assessment system. No longer will students have to wait in line to showcase armloads of portfolios to their professors. From the convenience of their home or any other location, and with one click of a mouse, students will be able to send their portfolios to faculty and prospective employers. Though the school had to overcome initial stumbling blocks, faculty and students managed to find their way across the divide. We survived the pilot year and faculty has made the paradigm shift necessary to move with our students into the 21st century.

References

American Council on Education (ACE). (2005). *Minorities in higher education twenty-first annual status report (2003-2004)*. Retrieved April 25, 2005, from www.acenet.edu/AM/Template.cfm? Section=Home&TEMPLATE=/ CM ContentDisplay.cfm&CONTENTID=3701

Barrett, H. (1999). *Electronic teaching portfolios*. Retrieved September 20, 2005, from http://electronicportfolios.org/portfolios/site99.html

Barrett, H. C. (2005). *Researching electronic portfolios and learner engagement* (white paper). Retrieved June 18, 2005, from www.taskstream.com/reflect/whitepaper.pdf

Gardner, H. (1983). *Frames of mind. The theory of multiple intelligences*. New York: Basic Books.

Gardner, H. (1999*). Intelligence reframed. Multiple intelligences for the 21st century*. New York: Basic Books.

Gibson, D., & Barrett, H. (2003). Directions in electronic portfolio development. *Contemporary Issues in Technology and Teacher Education*. Retrieved March 20, 2005, from www.citejournal.org/vol2/iss4/general/article3.cf

Goldsby, D. S., & Fazal, M. B. (2000). Technology's answer to portfolios for teachers. *Kappa Delta Pi Record, 36*(3), 121-123.

Harklau, L. (2003). *Generation 1.5 students and college writing*. Retrieved January 2, 2004, from www.cal.org/resources/digest/0305harklau.html

International Society for Technology in Education. (1999). National educational technology standards for students: Connecting curriculum and technology. Eugene: International Society for Technology in Education.

McKinney, M. (1998). Preservice teachers' electronic portfolios: Integrating technology, self-assessment, and reflection. *Teacher Education Quarterly, 25*, 85-103.

McLaughlin, M., & Vogt, M. E. (1996). *Portfolios in teacher education*. Newark: International Reading Association.

Michelle, R. (2000). *Digital portfolios: An enduring promise for enhancing assessment*. Retrieved September 12, 2005, from www2.edc.org/CCT/publications_feature_summary.asp?numPubId=30

Milman, N. B. (1999). *Web-based electronic teaching portfolios for preservice teachers. Proceedings of the Society for Information Technology and Teacher Education 10th Annual International Conference* (ERIC Database # ED432273).

National Center for Education Statistics (NCES). (2005). *Participation in education.* Retrieved July 31, 2005, from http://nces.ed.gov/programs/coe/2005/section1/indicator04.asp

National Council for Accreditation of Teacher Education (NCATE). (2005). *About NCATE.* Retrieved March 15, 2005, from www.ncate.org

Padrón, Y. N., & Waxman, H. C. (1996). Improving the teaching and learning of English language learners through instructional technology. *International Journal of Instructional Media, 23*(4), 341-354.

Richards, R. T. (1998). Infusing technology and literacy into the undergraduate teacher education curriculum through the use of electronic portfolios. *T.H.E. Journal, 25*(9), 46-50.

Roach, V. E. (2001). *Literature review on portfolios. Literature, theory, applications and such.* Retrieved June 23, 2005, from http://webfolios.home.netcom.com/Literature_Review/Literature_Review.html

Rumbaut, R. G., & Ima, K. (1988). *The adaptation of Southeast Asian refugee youth. A comparative study. Final report to the Office of Resettlement.* San Diego: San Diego State University. (ERIC Database # ED 299 372).

Russell, J. D., & Butcher, C. (1999). Using portfolios in educational technology courses. *Journal of Technology and Teacher Education, 7*(4), 279-289.

Ryan, C. W., Cole. D. J., & Mathies, B. K. (1997, February). *Teacher education field experiences: Impact on self-esteem of professional year program interns via electronic portfolios.* Paper presented at the annual meeting of the Eastern Educational Research Association, Hilton Head, SC (ERIC Database # ED405329).

Shulman, L. (1998). Teacher portfolios: A theoretical activity. In N. Lyons (Ed.), *With portfolio in hand: Validating the new teacher professionalism* (pp. 23-38). New York: Teachers College.

Svedkauskaite, A., & Reza-Hernandez, L. (2003). *Critical issue: Using technology to support limited-English-proficient (LEP) students' learning.* Retrieved April 20, 2004, from www.ncrel.org/sdrs/areas/issues/methods/technlgy/te900.htm

Taylor, N. (2005). *Addressing multiple literacies with technology.* Retrieved July 25, 2005, from www.scholastic.com/administrator/success/multipleliteracies.htm

Valdés, G. (1992). Bilingual minorities and language issues in writing. *Written Communication, 9,* 85-136.

Warner, M., & Maureen, A. (1999). Educational progressions: Electronic portfolios in a virtual classroom. *Technological Horizons in Education Journal, 27*(3), 86-89.

Wolcott, H. F. (1991). Posturing in qualitative research. In M. D. LeCompte, W. L. Millroy, & J. Preissle (Eds.), *The handbook of qualitative research on education* (pp. 3-52). San Diego: Academic.

Wright, V. H., Stallworth, B. J., & Ray, B. (2002). Challenges of electronic portfolios: Student perceptions and experiences. *Journal of Technology and Teacher Education, 10,* 49-62.

Chapter V

Information and Communication Technologies:
Towards a Mediated Learning Context

Glenn Finger, Griffith University, Australia

Maret McGlasson, Griffith University, Australia

Paul Finger, Griffith University, Australia

Abstract

Teaching and learning in the 21st century should be markedly different from earlier times through the design of new teaching and learning environments. Through the presentation of three models of technology-rich learning environments (teacher-directed, learner-centered and mediated), this chapter provides a case study of the design and delivery of a course called Learning with Information and Communication Technologies (ICTs) guided by a mediated learner approach, using new approaches to using ICTs and assessment for learning as key course design drivers. That course aims to prepare future teachers who demonstrate strong theoretical and practical understanding of designing and creating effective ICT teaching and learning experiences, and are confident and proficient users of ICTs. We provide an analysis of the implementation of that course through the presentation of the learning stories and reflections of students. Specific discussion is provided about the conceptualization and implementation of an e-portfolio approach to promote deep learning.

Introduction

Through the presentation of three models of technology-rich learning environments, namely, teacher-directed, learner-centered and mediated (see Trinidad, 2004), this chapter provides a case study of the design and delivery of a course called *Learning with ICTs* guided by a mediated learner approach using new approaches to using ICTs and assessment *for* learning as key course design drivers. *Learning with ICTs* aims to prepare future teachers who demonstrate strong theoretical and practical understanding of designing and creating effective ICT teaching and learning experiences, and who are confident and proficient users of ICTs. In terms of diversity, the students who undertake this course enter the university with a very diverse range of ICT knowledge, skills and attitudes. This diversity is discussed together with the conceptualization and implementation of an e-portfolio approach to promote deep learning. Therefore, there is a dual challenge here—first, to use ICTs in the design and delivery of a university teacher education course that caters to a diverse range of student needs and strengths, and second, for that course to promote the development of ICT skills and knowledge for those students as future teachers to be able to design and deliver effective teaching and learning using ICTs with their students.

Teaching and learning in the 21st century should be markedly different from earlier times, as Russell and Finger (2005) have argued that teaching and learning is now occurring in an increasingly online world. Since the penetration of computers in educational institutions, in particular during the last two decades, there has been a dynamic increase in access by teachers and students to ICTs through the purchase of hardware and software, ongoing renewal and upgrading of hardware and software, and large ongoing investments in infrastructure that has dramatically improved connectivity. Traditionally, learning environments were restricted to face-to-face delivery or where distance education was undertaken, delivery was largely characterized by the posting of printed resources, and communication was often slow and cumbersome. However, the move to adopt new and emerging technologies to transform the ways we teach and learn requires improved understanding of how we can best use those new and emerging technologies. For example, Fraser (2003) suggests that, while students spend approximately 20,000 hours in classrooms by the time of their graduation from a university, "educators often rely exclusively on assessing achievement and pay scant attention to the quality of the learning environment" (Fraser, 2003, p. vii). He argues that there is considerable optimism internationally that the integration of ICTs will enable the creation of learning environments, but warns that this optimism needs to be "accompanied by systematic research and evaluation" (Fraser, 2003, p. vii). This caution is echoed in *The Becta Review 2005 Evidence on the Progress of ICT in Education*:

A key challenge for institutions is to develop effective and innovative ways of using ICT to extend learning beyond the boundaries of their organization, and in doing so support practitioners in delivering more learner-focused educational experiences. (p. 5)

Background

The use of new and emerging technologies, referred to throughout this chapter as ICTs, has gained many proponents in higher education as a means for opening possibilities for improved delivery of programs with benefits for educators and students. Chambers, for example, identified education as "the next killer application for the Internet" (Chambers, 2001). There is now a plethora of terms, such as Web-supported, Web-enhanced and Web-based modes of delivery, e-learning and flexible learning, to reflect higher education strategies that utilize ICTs, with many universities developing e-strategies.

According to Bigum and Rowan (2004), the enthusiasm of vice chancellors in universities reflects two drivers: "... a perception that flexible delivery is more effective and efficient in terms of getting teaching resources to students, and secondly, that one form of flexible delivery, online teaching, offers possibilities for generating revenue from overseas fee-paying students" (p. 213).

Bigum and Rowan also cautiously note that the status of the term *flexible learning* is reflected in sayings in some Australian universities as being "inversely proportional to the distance you are from the vice chancellor!" (Holzl, 1999, p. 1). There is an inherent danger that teaching and learning is viewed narrowly as a consumer package to be marketed and delivered to students who become seen as customers rather than learners. Bigum and Rowan (2004) caution that "how we frame this work matters" (p. 223), as we need to be aware in our quest for improved teaching and learning using ICTs that particular performances of flexibility "close down what is possible, rather than, as the rhetoric suggests, open up performances of teacher education" (p. 223).

Similarly, Roffe (2004) adds substantially to the conception of e-learning, as he argues that the "e" term should not be seen exclusively as equating to electronic learning, but rather needs to be understood in terms of the human purpose of learning. Roffe proposes that e-learning should be concerned with more human "e"s—engagement of the learner, enhancement of learning, ease of use, empowerment of the learner to control the learning schedule and execution of the learning program (Roffe, 2002). Then we argue that in designing courses for students in higher education programs, which capitalize on the use of ICTs, a design process needs to be driven by the conceptualisation of a model of an ICT-rich learning environment.

Defining Deep Learning

Throughout this chapter, we will refer to the term deep learning in ways consistent with the definition provided by Education Queensland's *Productive Pedagogies* (Education Queensland, 2002a, 2002b). Deep learning is conceptualized as relating to deep understanding and deep knowledge. For example, students develop deep understanding when they grasp the relatively complex relationships between the central concepts of a topic. Instead of being able to recite only fragmented pieces of information, they understand the topic in a relatively systematic, integrated or holistic way. As a result of their deep understanding, they can produce new knowledge by discovering relationships, solving problems, constructing explanations and drawing conclusions. On the other hand, students have only shallow understanding when they do not or cannot use knowledge to make clear distinctions, present arguments, solve problems or develop more complex understanding of other related phenomena (Education Queensland, 2002a).

Knowledge is *deep* when it concerns the central ideas of a topic or discipline judged to be crucial to it. Deep knowledge involves establishing relatively complex connections to those central concepts. Knowledge is *shallow, thin or superficial* when it is not connected with significant concepts or central ideas of a topic or discipline, and is dealt with only in an algorithmic or procedural fashion. Knowledge is also shallow when important, central ideas have been trivialized by the teacher or students, or when it is presented as non-problematic. This superficiality can be due, in part, to instructional strategies; for example, when a teacher covers large numbers of fragmented ideas and bits of information unconnected to other knowledge (Education Queensland, 2002b). When both deep knowledge and deep understanding are combined, deep learning takes place.

Models of ICT-Rich Learning Environments

Trinidad (2003) notes that in Hong Kong, as with many countries, many leaders and policy makers "correlate the use of technology with pedagogical changes" (p. 101). However, in many Hong Kong classrooms, even with the introduction of new technologies, "… teachers remain teaching in a transmissive, exam-driven culture (teaching for the test) and the technology is used for lower-level activities, such as teachers presenting lectures via PowerPoint and students' word processing assignments and searching the Internet" (Trinidad, 2003, p. 101).

Thus, there is the potential for educators to use ICTs to continue to teach with a subject-centered approach using traditional pedagogies. Trinidad theorizes three conceptions of technology-rich learning environments: (1) teacher-directed, (2) learner-centered, and (3) mediated. The following summaries of these models are drawn from Trinidad's theorizing.

The Teacher-Directed Learning Environment:
ICTs Integrated into Existing Approaches

In this model, teaching, learning and assessment reflect a transmissive approach whereby the educator is expert with a specific knowledge base and the student is seen as a passive receptor of the knowledge to be taught, acquired and assessed. The implication of the use of ICTs in this model is to support a teacher-directed approach. Elsewhere, Roblyer (2004) refers to this as a directed or objectivist approach that views knowledge as having a separate, real existence outside the human mind and learning happens when this knowledge is transmitted to people and they store it in their minds. Drill and practice software, and low-level use of the Internet as a means to obtain information, reflects this approach. Figure 1 provides a visual representation of this model, with the positioning of ICTs as an adjunct

Figure 1. ICTs and the teacher-directed learning environment (Adapted from Albon & Trinidad, 2001)

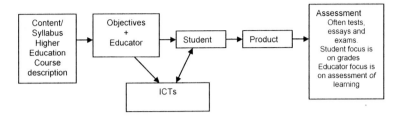

resource for educators and students.

The Learner-Centered Teaching Environment: *ICTs Transform Pedagogy, Curriculum and Assessment*

The learner-centered teaching environment reflects a more constructivist approach, as described by Roblyer (2004), whereby humans construct knowledge by participating in certain experiences that foster creativity, self-analysis and metacognition, and promote problem solving and group collaboration. In this model, according to Trinidad (2004), the educator can be involved in restructuring the learning activities and the curriculum to transform curriculum, pedagogy and assessment. As displayed in Figure 2, adapted from the work of Newhouse, Trinidad and Clarkson (cited in Trinidad, 2003), this learning environment highlights the central importance of a learner-directed approach, and the role of ICTs enables transformation.

The Mediated Learning Environment

Albon and Trinidad (2001) theorize the Mediated Learning Approach (MLA), which "revolves around the learner and the technology, which *drives* the model" (p. 106). Here we

Figure 2. ICTs and the learner-centered learning environment (Adapted from Newhouse, Trinidad & Clarkson, cited in Trinidad, 2003, p. 22)

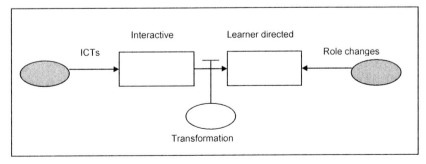

see the "e" word's more sophisticated definition: "There becomes a sense of empowerment and engagement for the learner … where they are no longer dependent on the specific and often limited knowledge of their educator, but work within the community of learners mediated by the educator" (Trinidad, 2004, p. 105). In this model, ICTs become the vehicle for communication, collaboration and the framework for mediated learning, which provides for interactions to assist the development of new and self-sustaining communities of learners to exist alongside established, traditional approaches. Subsequently, not only ICTs are utilized, but multiple information sources are used, ranging from traditional text materials in the form of books to the online resources of the Internet. In this model, ICTs are used as interactive technologies that enable learning communities "that transcends the four walls of classrooms but are not restricted by traditional class timeframes" (Trinidad, 2004, p. 106). It becomes essential, then, that educators design courses that provide learning experiences using forms of communication and facilities to access information at a time and place of the learner's choosing, beyond and in addition to the traditional timetabled face-to-face lectures and tutorials.

In MLAs, the ICTs that drive the design of learning are complemented in the design approach by the assessment *for* learning, rather than assessment *of* learning. Assessment *for* learning, discussed in detail later in this chapter, also drives MLAs. Assessment is seen as more than knowing the content, but becomes integrally interwoven into stories of learning whereby students collect and select authentic and diverse evidence, drawn from a larger archive representing what a person or organization has learned over time and on which the learner has reflected. Figure 3 builds substantially upon the model developed by Trinidad to theorize the importance of assessment *for* learning. The model overcomes the limitation of the earlier Trinidad model, which presented a self-contained model, whereas the model built in Figure 3 highlights the transformations occurring throughout the learning journeys of students within a course, and also articulates the connections between other formal and informal learning, as well as future learning. Too often, we see courses developed as stand-alone courses within higher education programs. Rather, we need to see ICTs and assessment *for* learning drive course design to assist students to synthesize learning among the courses they are studying within a specified study duration (e.g., within a semester) as well as throughout longer learning journeys (e.g., from learning over 3-4 years of a formal university program to life-long learning).

In addition, the model attempts to acknowledge the learning experiences students bring with them to the specified course. That is, students who enter the university program bring a diverse range of ICT knowledge, skills and attitudes. As displayed in Figure 3, this diversity was captured through the use of the *ICT Continua* (Education Queensland, 2003), which commences with a *Minimum* phase, proceeds to a *Developmental* phase, and is ongoing through the *Innovator* and *Leader* phases. Most students entering the program were identified as being at a *Minimum* level of ICT knowledge and skills. Some students were best described as being terrified of using computers, while some had advanced ICT skills and knowledge. Consistent with the conceptualization shown in Figure 3, all students were encouraged to adopt the *Learning Journey* metaphor accompanied by an expectation that there would be transformational learning. Assistance and support was provided through peers, online sources and collaborating organizations.

In this chapter, this model is critically important for analyzing the case study presented,

Figure 3. The MLA

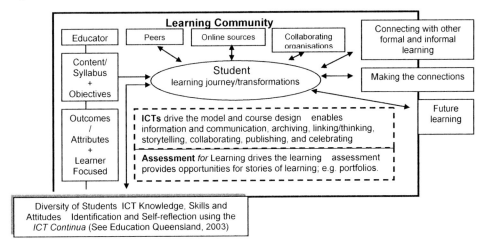

Note: This model builds substantially on the model provided by Trinidad, 2004

as both the ICTs and assessment *for* learning are key drivers in designing the MLA. In the following section, we discuss the use of ICTs and the assessment *for* learning approaches with specific reference to the portfolio process and the development of a learning community through discussion forums.

Case Study:
Designing the Course *Learning with ICTs* – Towards a Mediated Learning Environment

This case study focuses on the design and delivery of the course *Learning with ICTs*. This course is a first-semester, first-year course situated within an eight-semester, 4-year teacher education preservice program at the Gold Coast campus of Griffith University in Queensland, Australia. This course is also delivered from two other Griffith University campuses (Mount Gravatt and Logan), and university policy requires cross-campus consistency in the formulation of the course outline. Semester 1, 2005, was the first time this new course was delivered, due to it being a course within a new bachelor of education (primary) program that commenced in 2005.

The Architecture: Course Design

The course conceptualization was guided by the need for the entire suite of four first-semester courses to have an integrated assessment item so students could make connections between the four courses rather than the courses being delivered as four discrete courses. Also guiding the conceptualization of all four courses was a central question: Who are we as learners? Subsequently, the expectation was that students entering their first semester of the teacher education program would undertake personal and group investigations around that central question through the theoretical perspectives, learning experiences, content and assessment of each course, as well as through making the connections among those courses.

The Assessment

For *Learning with ICTs*, three assessable tasks were required: problem set, Web site development and portfolio. Additional activities students were required to do included attending lectures and workshops. The course was Web enhanced through the provision of the Blackboard platform adopted by Griffith University. Students were provided with additional online learning resources in the form of summaries of lectures, Web links to useful Web sites, and a range of tools, such as the discussion forum. The discussion forums were established by the lecturer around key topics related to the central concepts of the course, and students were expected to engage in these regularly. These were intended to provide students with opportunities to formulate and share ideas with other students in a non-threatening environment and scaffold students into developing more articulate analyses and linkages with theoretical perspectives as they progressed through the course. These enabled informed discussion about the topics posted, contribution of original ideas supported by reference to relevant literature and thoughtful responses to other people's contributions.

The Problem Set

The problem set was undertaken by students using ICTs to formulate their answers to a range of problematic scenarios. An example of a problematic scenario was:

Your school has been expending substantial funds from the school budget to acquire ICTs for some years. However, there are concerns that these ICTs are not being used effectively in classrooms. As an enthusiastic and informed user of ICTs, especially through your deep understandings of learning with ICTs developed throughout your preservice teacher education program, you have been asked to outline a rationale to inform the improved use of ICTs in your school to the school's ICT committee. Your rationale for ICT use needs to be supported by reference to learning theories and theorists, especially those associated with directed instruction and constructivism.

Students were scaffolded into the problem sets through their engagement with the textbook, lectures and discussions in workshops, and through the establishment of online discussion forums. The discussion forums were designed using the Blackboard platform, and students were allowed to make new threads and respond to other students' ideas.

The Web Site: Who are we as Learners?

The assessment task directly linked with the other courses and required students, working in pairs, to design a Web site using Macromedia Dreamweaver. Students were provided with the following design challenge:

As a teacher, you will be required to utilize a variety of tools to promote effective communication. This task exploits some of the communication capabilities of the World Wide Web. In the courses Introduction to Education, Studies in Sociocultural Understandings and Communicative Performance, you have been investigating the question "Who are we as learners?" by investigating your experiences as a learner and your reasons for selecting teaching as a career. You should also have come to realize the diversity that exists between yourselves and your potential students. Your task now is to assemble the discoveries you have made into a series of Web pages. The aim of this task is to use these pages to illustrate the aforementioned diversities and your understanding of your journey, as a learner, to date. Your Web site should also reflect some of the implications of this new knowledge for your professional life as a teacher.

Students created their Web sites around a suggested structure, which included the homepage titled *Who are we as Learners?*, and pages called *Personal Learning Journeys*, *Why Teach?*, *What makes a Good Teacher?* and *Our Professional Futures*. Artefacts in the form of assignments from the other courses, as well as additional information using a variety of media, were collected by students as "assets." The variety of media enabled students to develop interactive multimedia and digital video stories of learning. Students then selected and organized those assets for inclusion in the Web sites. As well as using *Macromedia Dreamweaver*, students used Macromedia Fireworks, Macromedia Flash, Windows Moviemaker, Microsoft PowerPoint, Adobe Photoshop, Adobe Acrobat and Microsoft Photo Editor to create their artefacts. The design of this assessment enabled the Web site to be a central vehicle for the development of students' personal stories of learning with the portfolio described in the following discussion.

The Portfolio

The Portfolio was conceived initially as a showcase piece to demonstrate basic and advanced ICTs skills through developing samples using a variety of software. However, guided by our move to conceptualize the course guided by MLA, students were encouraged to develop the portfolio more as a personal story of learning through the notion of an ICTs journey consistent with the *ICT Continua* (Education Queensland, 2003) used as a self-reflection tool, whereby teachers—in this case, future teachers—can move through *Minimum*, *Developmental*, *Innovator* and *Leader* phases. The ICTs Journey metaphor aligns with the MLA model (see Figure 3).

The portfolio task was established as a foundation for a portfolio students will continue to

Figure 4. Traditional portfolio process: Emphasis is on collection of evidence (Adapted from Barrett, 2005b)

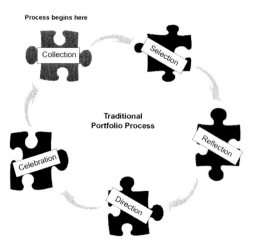

contribute to throughout the 4 years of their program. Therefore, the self-reflection links with prior ICT skills and knowledge and provides the platform for ongoing ICTs learning by linking with future learning. Students were required to demonstrate an extensive range of ICT skills and knowledge, including word processing, desktop publishing, presentation software, multimedia design, spreadsheets, databases, educational software, Internet use and Web site development. The ICT skills needed to be complemented by descriptions of how each ICT application could be used creatively in teaching and learning environments. The Web site development described earlier was integrated into the portfolio, and discussion forum contributions were also required to be included. We continue to investigate how the portfolio enhances students' personal learning journeys and how the format supports this process. The following provides insights into the design of the portfolio in terms of moving towards e-portfolios within the context of assisting the development of an MLA using ICTs.

Defining E-Portfolios

There are many definitions for portfolios within education. The literature ranges from traditional portfolios showcasing assessment through to reflective digital portfolios or e-portfolios that support deep learning. Four major types of portfolios can be identified in the literature.

Traditional Portfolios

In 1991, Valencia (cited in Chatel, 2003) stated that a portfolio is a collection of student work that provides the means for "collecting evaluative information formatively as well as summatively" (p. 33), giving it the unique characteristic of always being a work in progress. It is a collection of physical artefacts that reflect a student's development and progress. Figure

Figure 5. Reflective portfolio process: Emphasis is on reflection (Source: Adapted from Barrett, 2005)

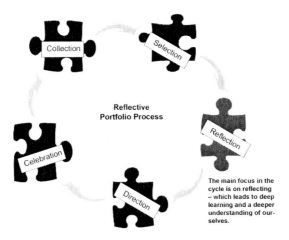

4 demonstrates the traditional approach to developing a portfolio as presented by Barrett (2004a, 2004b, 2005), which commences with collection, selection, reflection, direction and celebration. In the traditional portfolio, emphasis is on the collection of artefacts, with the final product usually presented as a paper copy for assessment.

Reflective Portfolios

Barrett (2005b) advocates that a portfolio should be more than just a collection of data and recommends that the role of reflection in the portfolio is important for promoting deep learning. Barrett states:

... an educational portfolio contains work that a learner has collected, reflected, selected and presented to show growth and change over time, representing an individual or organization's human capital. A critical component of an educational portfolio is the learner's reflection on the individual pieces of work (often called "artefacts") as well as an overall reflection on the story that the portfolio tells. (p. 2)

Figure 5 shows that the emphasis is within the reflection phase of the process.

E-Portfolios

Barrett (2005a) notes that e-portfolios, also known as digital portfolios or electronic portfolios, are defined by the National Learning Infrastructure Initiative (NLII, 2003) as:

Figure 6. E-portfolio process: Enhancing the process through ICTs

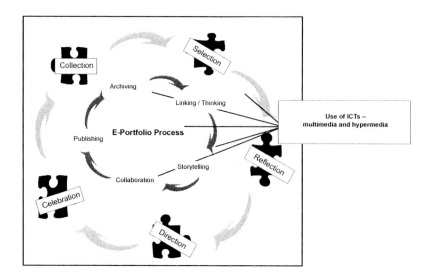

- A collection of authentic and diverse evidence
- Drawn from a larger archive representing what a person or organization has learned over time
- On which the person or organization has reflected
- Designed for presentation to one or more audiences for a particular rhetorical purpose

The traditional process, which involved collecting, selecting, reflecting, direction and celebration, is enhanced through the use of ICTs, according to Barrett (2004a) through the use of multimedia and hypermedia to enable archiving, linking and thinking, storytelling, collaborating and publishing. Figure 6 diagrammatically portrays the enhanced process of creating a portfolio with the added ICT enhancements. This extends the ability to communicate the stories of learning from the restrictions of a predominantly paper or print publication to multimedia, digital stories using video, audio, graphics and text in a Web-based portfolio. The use of hyperlinks through hypermedia can be a powerful means to demonstrate connections and links, rather than being limited to the restrictions of a linear story of learning similar to the teacher-directed learning environment model shown in Figure 1.

Higher Education Portfolios

In the context of higher education, the term portfolio denotes collections of evidence assembled by students, faculty members or entire institutions to enhance the effectiveness of teaching and learning, assess learning effectiveness and demonstrate competence to external stakeholders (DiBiase, 2002). Several types of academic portfolios have received attention in the literature; however, three have become prominent, according to Ketcheson (2001):

- ***Student learning portfolios:*** *Purposeful collections of examples of student work annotated (ideally) with students' reflective commentary. Examples may be drawn from assignments associated with a single course, or from curricular and co-curricular activities spanning a student's entire academic career.*

- ***Teaching portfolios:*** *Consist of course syllabi, assignments, student work and other artefacts, collected by practicing or aspiring teachers with the intent of fostering self reflection and peer review of teaching.*

- ***Institutional portfolios:*** *Contain examples of [an] institution's activities, programs, and initiatives, each expressing an element of reflection and self-assessment. Through its portfolio, an institution documents how it is achieving its stated mission by examples that speak to the interests of various audiences.* (p. 84)

For this case study, these contexts of designing the assessment *for* learning, defining e-portfolios as a process that is learner focused and using ICTs to enable the use of multimedia and hypermedia for students to collect, select, reflect, direct, publish and celebrate their stories of learning merge to inform the design of the course *Learning with ICTs* to create a mediated learning environment driven by the use of ICTs and assessment *for* learning. The key emphasis in the following analysis is to relate stories of personal learning in that course. This is consistent with Barrett's theorizing that any portfolio should be a story of learning that promotes deep learning. Her thoughts are that the portfolio needs to incorporate a section within the reflection phase that focuses on storytelling. Moreover, Barrett refers to the work of Paulson and Paulson (1994), who outline the differences between the positivist and constructivist paradigms of portfolios:

- ***Positivist portfolios:*** *The purpose of the portfolio is to assess learning outcomes, and those outcomes are, generally, defined externally. Positivism assumes that meaning is constant across users, contexts and purposes ... The portfolio is a receptacle for examples of student work used to infer what and how much learning has occurred.*

- ***Constructivist portfolios:*** *The portfolio is a learning environment in which the learner constructs meaning. It assumes that meaning varies across individuals, over time and with purpose. The portfolio presents process, a record of the processes associated with learning itself; a summation of individual portfolios would be too complex for normative description.* (p. 36)

As the course design and delivery takes place within a university higher education context, there is a need to acknowledge both a positivist and constructivist approach. As an institution, we need to meet both certifications as well as promote personal growth and development of students. Therefore, when developing a portfolio, a hierarchical approach could be used. According to Barrett and Wilkerson (2004), the positivist approach is "the floor below which they cannot fall." The constructivist approach is where we hope our teacher candidates will go above the floor, showcasing the many ways that they are going beyond minimum requirements.

Reflections and Narratives: Personal Stories of Learning

As suggested by Holloway and Wheeler (1996), "Narratives and life histories are stories which individuals tell about their condition, work or life" (p. 59). While these are not new forms of data collection, as there is evidence of the use of these, for example, in the form of autobiographies and diaries, Holloway and Wheeler suggest that previously, "narratives were not analyzed systematically; but more recently, they have found a place in naturalistic enquiry for studying "the phenomena of development and transition in people's lives" (Josselson & Lieblich, 1993, p. ix). This approach is adopted here to gain access "to the world of participants and share their experiences" (Holloway & Wheeler, 1996, p. 60). This aligns with the *Productive Pedagogies* (Education Queensland, 2002c) reference to the use of narrative in lessons encouraging the use of personal stories, biographies, historical accounts, and literary and cultural texts. In contrast, an expository teaching style places more emphasis on written, non-fiction prose, and scientific and expository expression by both teacher and students. It involves descriptions, reports, explanations, demonstrations and the use of documentaries (Education Queensland, 2002c).

Students' personal stories of learning were gained from the artefacts collected and selected by them for inclusion in their Websites developed around the focus question *Who are we as learners?*, as well as for their portfolios. A student example of a Web site is provided to illustrate one student's personal story of learning, and examples are drawn from that student's e-portfolio to demonstrate the course in action. Students were also required to engage in online discussion forum topics posted regularly throughout the course. This chapter draws upon their responses in the final forum for the course and presents a synthesis of those responses to portray students talking about their learning.

Web Site: Who are we as Learners?

Generally, students were challenged early in the course with the task of having to design and present a Web site. However, after some scaffolding into the construction process, the Web sites were designed and constructed to provide a means for the collection, selection and presentation of student artefacts related to the focus question and the required questions framed for each of the Web pages. Students used a variety of media and created "assets" and "images" folders for archiving their artefacts. A course, *Sociocultural Understandings*, being undertaken simultaneously by students, required them to provide an autobiographical account of an experience in their lives and analyze this through a sociocultural lens. Students included this in their Web sites as a link from their *Personal Learning Journey* Web page. The following is an excerpt from a student example:

Throughout the development of oneself, each individual person is exposed to an individual set of incidents and circumstances, which occur in social institutions that impacts and defines that person's beliefs and values in a process known as socialization (Holmes, Hughes, & Julian, 2003). A key moment in the development of my beliefs occurred in the event outlined

Figure 7. E-portfolio homepage (Acknowledgment: This Web page was constructed by a co-author of this chapter)

in this account. This very event defined my belief of who I am as a learner. I discovered on reflection of this particular event that society suggests that there are those exposed to advantage in life and those exposed to disadvantage, but our social foundation suggests that the disadvantaged should be supported by the advantaged. (Student sample in Web site)

That Web site included a rich suite of images of the student throughout various stages of learning and growth, together with reflections of his personal learning journeys, key events in his life, including the highs and the lows, the struggles and the achievements, his reasons for wanting to become a teacher, his thoughts on what makes a great teacher and his vision for his professional future.

E-Portfolio: A Student Sample

The portfolio process as described earlier in this chapter required students to portray their personal stories of learning in terms of ICT skills and knowledge through the creation of ICT samples to demonstrate basic and advanced skills and knowledge using a wide range of software. Figure 7 portrays the homepage of a student with navigation to the samples and stories of learning in his e-portfolio. This e-portfolio presented not only a means for the archiving, linking and publishing of evidence of learning unable to be demonstrated through a single essay or end-of-semester exam, but it provided the means for linking with other assessments undertaken in this course, such as the discussion forum contributions and Web site development, and enabled links with other assessments in other courses being undertaken by the student. As indicated earlier in relation to the Web site, the e-portfolio also enables a powerful means for using it as a platform for linking with future learning. Additional pages can be added, additional artefacts can be archived and linked, and the currently stored evidence of learning will provide a rich resource for reflection as the student's learning journey continues.

Students Talking about their Learning

Throughout the course, students participated in an online forum discussion that had to be included in their portfolios. Consistent with the MLA model (see Figure 3), and after the course delivery, the assessment *for* learning experiences provided by the problem sets, the Web site—*Who are we as Learners?*—and the portfolio process, the culminating forum was framed by the course convenor as:

This is the final forum for this course. I am confident that students are making the connections required this semester and can make sense of the ways in which this course has been designed, and the ways in which the four semester-1 courses are attempting to make connections. ... I'd like to think that through your activities, you've made several other important connections—connected with the Teaching Team (lecturers and tutors), and connected with other students ... these connections are critical to assist your sense of belonging and sense of learning community. Finally, the Web site—Who are we as learners?—encourages you to make links (should I say 'hyperlinks'?) with the other courses you are undertaking. So ... the final forum for this course asks you to reflect upon your learning journey this semester in terms of the deep understanding and deep learning (the really important personal and professional growth experienced). You are invited to share some of your reflections about that deep learning. Comment, for example, on the challenges, the highlights and the connections. (Finger, 2005)

The following reflections have been synthesized from the student responses provided to that forum topic.

Discussion Forums: Effective for Communicating Ideas

The online facility provided by the discussion forums was perceived as being extremely effective by students. These perceptions tended to be supported by expressions by students that the forums provided a facility for assisting students to gain confidence in articulating ideas required by the problem set assessment task.

*   "The discussion forums were a super idea to help with the problem set questions. I enjoyed reading other people's input, and it also helped me think about other students' different viewpoints."

*   "These discussion forums are great! There are a number of reasons why I feel this. The first is that it is a non-threatening environment where you can express your ideas . ... The second is that it also allows you to examine other people's ideas at the same time, ideas that you may not have thought of or that could have been presented in the lectures or tutorials. There have been weeks when you come into the forums late and see the quality stuff that others have already written and all you can do is just say 'That's right.' It did also open up our thought patterns in preparation for the problem

set, again giving us greater understanding and deeper thought before confronting the scenarios in the problem set."

- "The discussion forums have provided me with opportunities to write, read and think about my own learning journeys. … I also found that the forum topics complemented the text and lectures very well."

- "I think that the forums gave us all an opportunity to express our opinions and they really helped me to interact with my peers."

- "In addition, I liked the forums because they helped me to get my mind around the concepts I had read or learnt in the lectures. They also meant that I had time to respond to the questions asked in the forums and wasn't put on the spot … they were a non-threatening way to communicate ideas."

Reflections: Who am I as a Learner?

Students reflected that the focus question—*Who are we as learners?*—was effective in linking their learning in this course with the other three courses they undertook during the semester.

- "What a journey. I feel that this course has been very reflective and allowed me to explore who I am as a learner with the help of the other three courses."

- "The overall theme of who are we as learners really makes you think about why we are here, why we made that choice to be part of the education field, and I'm grateful for having the chance to reflect upon it."

Making the Connections

Students generally reported that the focus question—*Who are we as learners?*—facilitated the connections between the courses, and some students indicated that the Web site enabled the connections to be made.

- "To me, this course helped me link all the other courses I am doing because of the Web site having grouped all my ideas of who we are as learners."

- "By looking at the connections between and within each course, I now see that all the courses—despite the different topic areas—are designed to make each of us look at who we are. This course has intrinsically given us a powerful medium for learning."

- Students also mentioned the connections made between assessment items within the course *Learning with ICTs*, connections with the teaching team and connections with other students.

- "The forum topics, lectures and assessment items have all been directly linked."

- "The 'hyperlinks' between the Web site and our other courses are starting to appear at long last. All of our subjects encouraged us to learn about our attitudes, beliefs and values and then challenge them in a new way. It has been an amazing journey, and I am proud of how much I have learnt."

The Challenge of Designing a Web Site

Students enrolled in this course came with a wide range of ICT skills and knowledge. Very few had designed and constructed Web sites. The course required students to create a Web site as described earlier in this chapter using Macromedia Dreamweaver to enable the development of a Web-based means for collecting, selecting, reflecting and publishing artefacts related to the central question of *Who are we as learners?* Many responses from students highlighted the challenge this created, which they overcame, and felt great personal satisfaction with their learning.

- "Week 1 … What do you mean I'll be designing a Web page? Are you out of your mind? Only ICT geniuses can do that stuff … but here I am at the end, having accomplished something I never thought I could, would or should, and I'm really proud of my input and the final result."
- "For me, this course has been an absolute treasure; I started off thinking, they are kidding right—design a Web site! After cursing and grumbling, we started; we made mistakes; we grumbled some more; we continued; we made more mistakes … the final design is ready now. But you know, the road I have traveled to get to where I am with my Web design has been the most stimulating, educational experience I have had since starting my degree … thanks for the challenge and the learning experience; this is precisely why I want to teach, to offer challenge, stimulation and excitement—which you clearly set out and attained with this student."

Stories of Inspiration to Teach

Powerful stories were presented by many students related to becoming inspired to teach from the learning experiences provided in this course. Underlying these reflections were often messages of the importance of the human dimension in teaching the course and the relationships between the lecturer, tutors and the students.

- "I have learnt that anyone can dictate information to students and say 'learn this,' but good teachers inspire deeper learning. They encourage students to explore what they know, explore the unknown and explore what their peers know."
- "Glenn [lecturer] and my tutor should be commended for their fabulous work and their inspiring stories … I don't know what everyone else thinks … BUT I AM INSPIRED."
- "What has been the deep learning for me this semester? It has been making the connections with the various course contents, with the tutors and lecturers, the students,

and how I can use these experiences in my future role as a primary school teacher. But above all, it has been about connecting with me and the deep personal reasons for wanting to enter the profession."

- "Glenn, you have been so approachable and friendly, and many of us have spoken of what a great example of what teachers should be you are; you are interested in more than the surface, thank you!"

- "I would like to thank Glenn and Maret [tutor] for their fantastic teaching efforts this semester; your passion for teaching reminds us all of why we chose to study this course and head in the direction we are going, thank you."

Some students suggested that the success was related to the narratives and sometimes the associated humor provided by the lecturer to illustrate theoretical perspectives. The following reflections are indicative that there is a powerful human dimension required to inspire students. The use of ICTs can assist in achieving this, but are insufficient by themselves to ensure success. Passion, enthusiasm, modeling commitment and the building of authentic relationships with students were seen by students as contributing to their commitment to teach.

- "My tutor, Carmel, should be commended on her kind approach to teaching. ... I feel inspired by her and Glenn ... here's a pat on the back. Your stories have also inspired me ..."

- "Glenn, you mentioned how impressed you were with the tutorial attendance; I think you can take credit for that—your passion and enthusiasm overflowed the lecture theatre and infected all of us."

- "I could not see how anyone, no matter how gifted, would be able to make computers and keyboards and hard drives exciting. But! All credit to Glenn, he pulled it off marvellously! Not only did he make these mundane electrical pieces seem interesting, but explained in his always polite humor how technology has, is and will affect us. One thing that I constantly noticed throughout the semester was Glenn's passion for his course. This came through not only in his lectures, but even when greeting me in the hallway. It was great to meet someone who so obviously enjoyed and loved his career with children, and has made me much more aware of my desire to enter this profession, too. So thank you, Glenn."

Future Trends and Solutions: The Journey Continues ...

Based upon the students' stories, the e-portfolios provide the platform for the personal stories of learning to continue. The continuing collecting, selecting, reflecting, directing and publishing will continue as students proceed through their higher education program on their journeys as future teachers. The *ICT Continua* (Education Queensland, 2003) will continue to provide the self-reflective device for documenting and guiding that journey.

Continuing research and investigation is needed to theorize e-portfolios to promote deep learning by students in higher education. The case study provided here has provided a sense of a road map that has gone some distance along this journey. However, considerable development is required to further explore the ways in which students can collect, select, reflect, direct, publish and celebrate their learning. For example, why might students see some attempts at e-portfolio as simply another requirement or assessment *of* learning.

Similarly, the promotion in this chapter of MLAs requires more theoretical models built to guide and be guided by course design and delivery. There seems to have been some critically important intangibles, almost impossible-to-measure qualities emanating throughout the story provided in this chapter—stories of higher education, humans, humor and stories of passion, challenge, commitment and inspiration. A key challenge is our need to develop improved understandings of the interface between teaching, learning and ICTs. How can ICTs assist in transforming learning in higher education, as Roffe (2002) puts it, so that it engages learners, enhances learning, provides ease of use, empowers the learner to control the learning schedule and assists in the execution of the learning program?

Conclusion

This chapter has outlined a case study of the design and delivery of a course for future teachers undertaking a higher education course. The design of that course—*Learning with ICTs*—was guided by a mediated learning approach in which the design was driven by ICTs and by assessment *for* learning. Through describing the assessment undertaken, complemented by samples, and a synthesis of reflections by students, the chapter has provided some guidance for understanding the importance of the human dimension of technology in higher education. The chapter provided some insights into the potential for the role of e-portfolios theorized as enabling personal stories of learning using multimedia and hypermedia.

References

Albon, R., & Trinidad, S. (2001). Tapping out new rhythms in the journey of learning. In A. Herrmann & M.M. Kulski (Eds.), *Proceedings of the 10th Annual Teaching Learning Forum*. Perth, Australia: Curtin University of Technology. Retrieved November 16, 2005, from http://lsn.curtin.edu.au/tlf/tlf2001/trinidad.html

Barrett, H. (2004a). *Electronic portfolios as digital stories of deep learning*. Retrieved May 3, 2005, from http://electronicportfolios.org/digistory/epstory.html

Barrett, H. (2004b). *Electronic portfolio as digital story of learning: Digital storytelling as reflective portfolio*. Retrieved May 3, 2005, from http://electronicportfolios.org/digistory/eportfoliostory.htm/

Barrett, H. (2005a). *What is an e-portfolio?* Retrieved May 10, 2005, from http://electronicportfolios.org/digistory/epstory.html

Barrett, H. (2005b). *Researching electronic portfolios and learner engagement* (white paper). Retrieved September 13, 2005, from www.electronicportfolios.org/reflect/whitepaper.pdf

Barrett, H., & Wilkerson, J. (2004). *Conflicting paradigms in electronic portfolio approaches.* Retrieved May 3, 2005, from http://electronicportfolios.org/systems/paradigms.html

Becta Review. (2005). *The Becta review 2005 evidence on the progress of ICT in education.* Retrieved June 6, 2005, from www.becta.org.uk/page_documents/researchbecta_review_feb05.pdf

Bigum, C., & Rowan, L. (2004). Flexible learning in teacher education: Myths, muddles and models. *Asia-Pacific Journal of Teacher Education, 32*(3), 213-226.

Chambers, J. (2001). *E-learning takes stage as next killer APP.* Retrieved June 16, 2005, from www.infoworld.com/articles

Chatel, R. (2003). The power and potential of electronic literacy assessment: Eportfolios and more. *New England Reading Association Journal, 39*(1), 51-57.

DiBiase, D. (2002). *Using e-portfolios at Penn State to enhance student learning.* Retrieved May 3, 2005, from www.e-education.psu.edu/portfolios/e-port_report.html

Education Queensland. (2002a). *Productive pedagogies classroom reflection manual: Deep understanding.* Retrieved July 31, 2005, from http://education.qld.gov.au/public_media/reports/cirriculum-framework/productive-pedagogies/html/int-03.html

Education Queensland. (2002b). *Productive pedagogies classroom reflection manual: Deep knowledge.* Retrieved July 31, 2005, from http://education.qld.gov.au/publicmedia/reports/cirriculum-framework/productive-pedagogies/html/int-02.html

Education Queensland. (2002c). *Productive pedagogies classroom reflection manual: Narrative.* Retrieved July 31, 2005, from http://education.qld.gov.au/public_media/reports/cirriculumframework/productive-pedagogies/html/rec-03.html

Education Queensland. (2003). *Information and communications technology continua.* Retrieved June 15, 2003, from http://education.qld.gov.au/cirriculum/learning/technology/cont.html

Finger, G. (2005). *The final forum — learning with ICTs.* Retrieved June 3, 2005, from Learning with ICTs Web site in Learning@Griffith, Griffith University, Gold Coast campus.

Finger, G., & Russell, G. (2005, July). *ICT's and teacher education: Digital portfolios — Digital storytelling, reflection and deep learning.* Paper presented at the Australian Teacher Education Association Conference at Surfers Paradise, Queensland.

Fraser, B. J. (2003). Preface. In M.S. Khine & D. Fisher (Eds.), *Technology-rich learning environments: A future perspective.* NJ: World Scientific.

Holloway, I., & Wheeler, S. (1996). *Qualitative research for nurses.* London: Blackwell Science.

Holmes, D., Hughes, K., & Julian, R. (2003). *Australian sociology: A changing society.* Frenchs Forest: Pearson Education.

Holzl, A. (1999). Flexible learning: Can we really please everyone? *Educational Technology and Society, 2*(4). Retrieved May 30, 2005, from http://ifets.ieee.org/periodical/vol_4_99/formal-discussion_1099.html

Josselson, R., & Liebich, A. (1993). *The narrative study of lives.* Newbury Park: Sage.

Ketcheson, K. A. (2001). Public accountability and reporting: What should be the public part of accreditation? In J.L. Ratcliff, E.S. Lubinescu, & M.A. Gaffney (Eds.), *How accreditation influences assessment* (pp. 83-93). San Francisco: Jossey-Bass.

Paulson, F. L., & Paulson, P. (1994). Assessing portfolios using the constructivist paradigm. In R. Fogarty (Ed.), *Student portfolios.* Palatine: IRI Skylight Training & Publishing.

Roblyer, M. (2004). *Integrating educational technology into teaching.* Upper Saddle River: Pearson Education.

Roffe, I. (2002). E-learning: Engagement, enhancement and execution. *Quality Assurance in Education, 10*(1), 40-50.

Roffe, I. (2004). *Innovation and e-learning: E-business for an educational enterprise.* Cambridge: Cambridge Printing.

Russell, G., & Finger, G. (2004, July). Teacher education in an online world: Future directions. *Paper presented at the Australian Council for Computers in Education Conference, Research, Reform, Realise the Potential,* Adelaide.

Trinidad, S. (2003). Working with technology-rich learning environments: Strategies for success. In M. S. Khine & D. Fisher (Eds.), *Technology-rich learning environments: A future perspective* (pp. 97-113). NJ: World Scientific.

Section III

Evaluating the Role and Impact of Technology in Medical Education

Chapter VI

Technology in Physician Education

Michelle LaBrunda, Cabrini Medical Center, USA

Jose A. Cortes, Cabrini Medical Center, USA

Abstract

How physicians are trained has been heavily influenced by the advent of the technology era. Technology has progressed faster than society has been able to integrate it. The same is true within schools of medicine and residency training programs. Many technological advances are available to medical educators, and the goal is to make educators aware of the possible educational tools. Traditionally, medicine has been a learn-by-doing discipline. This is becoming less and less acceptable in modern society, and new training methods are being sought, developed and implemented. Some of the modalities available to medical educators include intranet, hand-helds, virtual reality, computerized charting, computerized access to information and electronic monitoring student education. Technological advances in medical education have their uses, but there are also many drawbacks, including hardware limitations, computer failure, security issues, patient confidentiality issues, property rights, maintenance and poor attitude of those required to implement new learning systems.

Introduction

In the United States (U.S.), more than $810.7 billion per year is spent on medical expenses (Agency for Health Care Research and Quality, 2005). This is about 8% of our entire gross national income. Technological improvements have allowed for significant advances in all aspects of medicine, which aid in saving many lives each year. However, this same technology is associated with the rising costs of medical care. How this $810.7 billion is utilized within the health care system is largely determined by physicians. A physician in training is taught to use a specific, methodical thought process as part of his or her training. First, all possibilities, even the improbable ones, are considered. The most likely causes of a problem are determined and the best diagnostic tests to verify or disprove clinical suspicions are done. Only then is treatment determined and a course of action implemented. The tremendous infusion of technology into the medical field has complicated physician training by making available a plethora of diagnostic and testing options. Medical educators are faced with the challenge of appropriately integrating technological considerations into a fledgling physician's clinical thought process. This challenge is further exacerbated by the need to educate physicians to utilize appropriate technology in training and in practice among patients from a multitude of educational, cultural and linguistic backgrounds. In a nation where hospitals and medical centers must serve the needs of an enormously diverse population, it is important to be aware of the interaction of medical technology and culture.

This chapter describes the structure of medical education and the way technology is being used in the education of physicians. It discusses some advantages and disadvantages of technology in medical education and how these technological advances may impact a culturally diverse population.

Background

It has been difficult for the medical education community to keep pace with the ever more sophisticated technologies developed on a seemingly weekly basis. There are more and more tests that can be ordered, increasingly innovative procedures that can be performed, and the emergence of new treatments that can be offered. Keeping in mind that all medical interventions have side effects, some of which are predictable and others not, where is the line to be drawn between what is medically warranted and what is too invasive, too unlikely or too expensive? As a physician, these issues must constantly be addressed, and often, a concrete demarcation does not exist. Promoting skill in the use of decision-making technology while continuing the intense depth and scope of traditional physician training is a major challenge facing medical educators today. Technology is seen in all facets of medical education, and it affects medical students on at least two levels. First, in the continually evolving world of medicine, students must not only be aware of new advances but must also learn when to apply them. Second, technology may be used to assess the quality of training or to evaluate the learning and performance of a medical student. An intranet, personal digital assistants (PDAs), virtual reality and computerized charting, as well as other available technologies, have the potential to revolutionize not only the way medicine is practiced, but the way it is taught, as well.

Medical technology, however, is not without some controversy. Unfamiliarity of some patients with the imposing appearance of even common technologies does little to promote a healthful and healing experience. While technology is generally touted as a marvelous educational and diagnostic tool, it can also have the effect of interfering with the learning process of a physician in training. Physicians must be able to function effectively while utilizing the latest technological innovations; custom and language cannot be barriers. It is equally important, however, that physicians be able to function effectively without an abundance of technological gadgetry. Verbal communication is still the cornerstone of the patient-physician relationship, and all too frequently, this relationship is sacrificed on the altar of technological advances.

It is important to remember when training physicians that emergency situations often arise at places where the latest technology is not readily available. Although there are many benefits to using technology over more invasive, traditional methods of diagnostic assessment, treatment and diagnosis of patients is trending toward an over-reliance on technology. This over-reliance is being perpetuated in the way medical students are being trained. The medical education community must determine how to most effectively optimize the use of technology without forgetting to look at the face of the patient on the other side of the device; in other words, how to practice the science of medicine without losing the art of medicine. The art of medicine includes empathy, communication skills and bedside manner. This is particularly essential in cases where patients do not have a clear command of English and may not have a full understanding of what is occurring. Technology should assist in the utilization of both clinical acumen (the science) and productive patient-physician relationships (the art), not handicap the problem-solving skills of medical students. With time, a proper balance will be found between the integration of technology and traditional medical skills, but the technological explosion has been so rapid that medical educators have been struggling to keep up.

Structure of Medical Education

Becoming a physician in the U.S. is a lengthy process, requiring years of formal education and practical training. First, the student has to complete at least 3 years of undergraduate work, although most students typically complete a bachelors of science degree in a biological science. Next, a satisfactory score on the arduous Medical College Admission Test (MCAT) exam must be achieved. The MCAT is a 1-day exam consisting of multiple-choice blocks of questions on the physical, biological and chemical sciences as well as an essay writing section that demonstrates proficiency in written communication. Once the required transcripts documenting sufficient grade point average have been compiled with MCAT test scores and letters of recommendation, a student wishing admittance to medical school may then fill out the lengthy application form and, if accepted, enter medical school.

Most medical schools are designed so that the first 2 years consist of the basic sciences and the second 2 years comprise the clinical sciences. The basic sciences are the building blocks of medicine, and include subjects such as biochemistry, histology (the study of tissues), pathology (the study of diseased tissue), physiology (the study of normal functioning) and statistics. The clinical sciences can be considered application of the basic sciences. These courses tend to focus on how to examine a patient, the recognition of disorders and diagnosis of disease. They teach skills that bridge the basic sciences and their application at patient bedsides. Courses in legal medicine and ethics are usually included throughout the curriculum and, increasingly, sensitivity to and awareness of cultural diversity is entering the course of study. After graduation from medical school, the medical doctor (MD) or doctor of osteopathic medicine (DO) is granted and the student is considered a physician, but for many, this may only be the halfway point of their education. Most physicians choose to specialize by entering into a residency program. A residency program consists of physicians with minimal clinical experience practicing medicine in a specific specialty under close supervision of more experienced physicians. Depending on the area of specialization, residency may last anywhere from 3 to 5 years. In addition, after residency many physicians choose to enroll in a fellowship program. A fellowship allows a physician to sub-specialize after residency. It is like residency in that a more experienced physician supervises a less experienced one. A fellowship usually lasts 1 to 3 years, but could be longer, and multiple fellowships may be completed by a diligent physician.

To become a physician in the U.S., mastery of academic medical content as well as effective application of knowledge and skill must be demonstrated by satisfactory scores on a rigorous series of medical examinations. Passing scores on four exams are required to obtain a professional license to practice medicine: the U.S. Medical Licensing Exams (USMLE) Step 1; USMLE Step 2 Clinical Knowledge (CK); USMLE Step 2 Clinical Skills (CS); and USMLE Step 3. Three of the four exams are multiple choice in format and computer based. USMLE Step 2 CS involves actors feigning illnesses and an evaluation of the future physician's ability to interact with a patient, perform an adequate physical exam and determine appropriate diagnostic steps. USMLE Step 3, in addition to the multiple-choice blocks, has a section of interactive case studies that require insightful application of academic knowledge and competent judgment in the assessment of patient treatments. Step 1 evaluates the basic sciences, Step 2 (CK and CS) the clinical knowledge base and skills, and Step 3 the application of the clinical sciences. Additional exams are administered after the completion of residency and fellowship. These additional examinations are not required to practice medicine within the area of specialization, but are required if the physician wishes to be board certified.

The requirements for licensure vary from state to state. All states currently require that the USMLE exams or equivalent be passed. Some require additional years of supervised training, especially if the physician graduated from a foreign medical school.

On July 1, 2003, the Accreditation Council for Graduate Medical Education imposed a new set of guidelines limiting the workweek of physicians in residency to 80 hours. Prior to this date, residents were often required to work many more than 80 hours per week. This exposed them to the largest number of clinical scenarios possible during their years of residency training and maximized the hands-on learning experience. With the new restrictions on resident work hours, new, more efficient methods must be employed to ensure sufficient, practical physician training.

Technology in Medical Education

Traditionally, medicine was a learn-by-doing discipline. This has become less and less acceptable in modern society due to risks associated with inexperience. To cover any possible gaps in the training of resident physicians, new training methods are being sought, developed and implemented. There are a variety of technology modalities through which medical education may be enhanced. PDAs, virtual reality and computerized charting are technologies gaining a strong foothold in the diagnosis of patient ailments, the organization and availability of pertinent patient records and the training of new physicians.

Intranets

Many medical schools and hospitals have installed campus-wide intranet networks. The intranet systems are similar to the Internet except they have more limited access. These local systems provide a structured environment for residents and allow great access to information. This information pertains specifically to issues of importance to medical students. It could be information on schedules, required reading, lecture notes, photographs, or audio and video clips. Since many medical students are off campus for the last year of medical school, these local networks give the possibility of a virtual campus and provide continuity of education (Ward, Gordon, Field, & Lehmann, 2001). Medical tasks now require more processing, communication and transfer of greater amounts of information. Intra-institutional communication systems, such as intranets, are useful in organizing this information. Intranets can allow the most current information on a patient to be immediately available to many people at various sites. This allows laboratory values, radiology results and consultations from specialists to be available to both students and medical workers at the same time. Patient care is increasingly shifting from inpatient to ambulatory care, and training models have not kept up with the change. Hospital settings create a "captive" population from which medical students can learn. As medicine shifts toward a more outpatient-oriented environment, physicians in training have less access to patients undergoing treatment. Intranets make possible a simplified media through which many people may have access to an interesting case while respecting the patient's right to privacy. An intranet has much more utility for medical students than just permitting access to patient information. It can serve as a repository for evaluation forms, instruction, schedules, directory, and as a bulletin board for transmitting important information (Zucker, White, Fabri, & Khonsari, 1998). Intranets increase the accuracy of information, because the data is only entered one time rather than being transferred and transcribed numerous times as seen in traditional paper-based systems.

PDAs

PDAs include the Palm system and Pocket PCs. Both are being used more and more commonly in the field of medicine. PDAs have many utilities in the field of medical education. They allow for quick access to medication information, including drug-drug interactions, diagnostic manuals and medical calculators.

Currently, there are programs integrating physicians' PDAs into the hospital computer system. This permits rapid and accurate access to patient information as well as bedside data entry. Wireless communication is rapidly facilitating communication between health care providers of different departments, even though they are not able to see the patient at the same time. It is common during physician education that a student is only exposed to one aspect of a patient's care. The surgery residents are minimally exposed to a patient's other medical problems, and the medical residents are peripherally aware of the surgical issues. PDA systems allow students and residents to have access to all pertinent information simultaneously. Legibility problems are corrected by the typed format and subsequent errors are minimized. PDAs have other useful purposes in the education of physicians. They can serve as a procedural log. As a log, it has been shown that PDAs have high reliability, dependable data integrity, low data-entry workload and rapid feedback for residents and program directors for residents' procedural experience (Nicolaou & Davis, 2001). They are relatively low in cost, are very easy to use and require minimal or no training. It is clear that soon physicians will use PDAs for prescribing, ordering studies, checking results, capturing charges and dictating notes. Information can be integrated from multiple sites and gives students and residents access to pertinent information, scientific calculators and drug interaction information, and alerts physicians and pharmacists of potential conflicts with medications. Basic clinical guides and medication prescribing information may be stored on PDAs and quickly accessed. This is important, since medical residents are usually responsible for initiating therapy in emergency situations at hospitals with residency programs. PDAs are increasingly being integrated into the hospital environment, and it is important that medical students become confident in employing them as effective tools that provide access to critical information, even when they are not integrated into hospital databases.

Virtual Reality

As technology has progressed, so have the available treatment and diagnostic modalities. The traditional learning-by-doing methodology has become less acceptable as more invasive and delicate procedures are required for optimal patient care. Students are expected to master complex skills with no errors and minimal experience. Medical educators are forced to create options other than practicing on live patients. These alternative options include Web-based education, virtual reality and high-fidelity human patient simulator. An additional benefit of this training is the ability to practice patient comfort in the presence of technological devices. Care for the patient includes more than just the application of modern technologies. A patient's background, experience and command of English can have a significant influence on his sense of well-being during treatment and can affect the success of an important procedure. A trusting patient-physician relationship is especially important when working with patients with different cultural and linguistic backgrounds.

One of the most promising types of virtual reality is called augmented reality. Augmented reality consists of superimposing a virtual world on the real one so both are experienced simultaneously (Vozenilek, Huff, Reznek, & Gordon, 2004). For example, a virtual image of a complicated fracture may be superimposed on a patient's leg, allowing a surgeon to "see" the broken bone before beginning a surgery. Fluoroscopy is an X-ray that may be taken during surgery. It has many applications, most of which are related to placement of external devices into the body. Fluoroscopy allows the position of these devices to be observed and adjusted while a surgical procedure is still in process. The disadvantages include radiation exposure of medical personnel and patients from the fluoroscopy machine and poor quality of fluoroscopic images. Continuing with the broken leg example from above, virtual reality allows a surgeon to take an initial set of fluoroscopic images and load them into a virtual reality program, then observe an image of the broken bone projected by the virtual reality simulator. These virtual images can be used during surgery to obtain proper alignment of the bones while minimizing radiation exposure. These true life images can be recorded and used by medical faculty for educational purposes while avoiding exposure of students and residents to radiation (Gruntzner & Suhm, 2004).

Most virtual reality has been designed with particular surgical specialties in mind, although some are also useful for emergency medicine. Many of these virtual-reality systems have been designed with the goal of producing high-fidelity patient simulators that can give real-istic tactile, auditory and visual stimuli. Full-body simulation allows physicians to practice procedural skills with no patient risk. Immersive simulators are emerging that may also be useful in emergency medicine. They provide a complete computer-generated environment, not just a specific portion of the environment, which allows for organized team simulations (Vozenilek et al., 2004; Medical Readiness Trainer Team, 2000).

Medical schools in the field of psychiatry are also beginning to integrate virtual reality into their programs. One of the treatments for phobias is to gently expose a patient to that which he or she fears. Traditionally, this was done through photographs and visualization tech-niques. Virtual reality is being used by many psychiatrists as part of the treatment regime. Immersing a patient with a phobia into a virtual simulation requires a delicate approach, and medical students clearly must be adequately supervised and trained (Krijin, Emmelkamp, Olafsson, & Biemond, 2004; Klinger et al., 2005). Rehabilitation medicine is also adapting virtual-reality training to assist recuperating patients. Virtual reality enables patients to try motor skills without risk of injury. Although there may have been some initial doubt as to the effectiveness of this treatment, it has been shown that patients can learn motor skills from virtual reality (Holden, 2005). Medical students need to be aware that these types of rehabilitation options exist, and rehabilitation residents should have some exposure to virtual rehabilitation as part of their training.

Simulated patients made out of electrical conductors, computer chips and circuits all wrapped in a thin layer of plastic emulating human skin have been designed for use in training medi-cal personnel in various diagnostic simulations. There are a number of types of these patient simulators and each is designed for educational accommodation in a specific medical area. They may be used to learn how to place IVs, for auscultation of heart sounds and for practic-ing management of a patient whose heart stops, among other uses. Depending on the model, different degrees of reality are mimicked and students can practice procedures related to both common medical situations and emergencies. Interactive patient simulators allow students to learn to anticipate common reactions, avoid common mistakes and become acquainted with high-risk, adrenaline-filled situations in a safe environment.

Integration of simulators into medical programs is becoming more and more common, but is still a slow and expensive process. Currently, robotic surgeries are being done and robotic surgery simulators are being implemented in a number of programs. Both in the simulator and during the real surgery, robotic arms are controlled at a console. The advantage of the simulator in this case is that the simulator can be set on record mode and can give feedback as to whether or not the surgical movements were safe. Also, alternate options and approaches can be explored by the physician. What would have happened if X or Y had been performed are questions that cannot be answered using patients as practice subjects, but simulators can answer these sorts of questions. Currently, each surgical robot costs about $1.2 million (Conn, 2004), but as technology advances the price will drop, making these robots available to more training programs.

Pulmonologists who train on bronchoscopy simulators are just as fast and competent as someone who had done several bronchoscopies on human subjects (Conn, 2004). It can be inferred from the very limited amount of data available that high-quality patient simulators would decrease the number of procedural complications by allowing physicians with less experience to master difficult skills in a non-life-threatening environment. It is possible that as technology progresses, simulator training will become so integrated into the medical system that it will become part of the certification process for medical specialties that require procedural skills. In fact, expertise with video games has been shown to enhance surgeons' skills. Surgeons who spend more time on video games work 27% faster and make 37% fewer mistakes than those who do not (Conn, 2004).

Computerized Charting

Currently, many hospitals are converting from a paper-based charting system to computerized patient tracking. Electronic medical records give medical staff easy access to all patient information at one site. The information can be accessed from computers throughout the hospital or from physicians' PDAs. In hospitals, there is often difficulty assembling all pieces of information relevant to a patient because there are a number of different departments and sources of information involved. Specialists are consulted, radiographs taken and blood work drawn, and decisions are made by a number of different medical services. A large portion of a student physician's time may be spent trying to get all relevant information together in one place at one time for any specific patient. To provide the optimum care, access to information from a patient's previous admissions should be readily available and consulted. Computerized charting gives students and residents access to all relevant patient information, allowing for a more comprehensive understanding of each case. From an economic standpoint, computerized charting saves money. It decreases the rate at which diagnostic tests are inadvertently repeated on the same patient, helps prevent tests from being performed on the wrong patient or at the wrong site, and generally decreases the total length of hospital stay. Medical education must include training for students in how to deal with financial issues within the hospital as well as in the outpatient clinics if the future physician is to achieve economic stability. Part of this training should include how to utilize computerized charting to manage patient care in an expedient, practical and economical form.

Another technological advance is the picture-archiving and communication system. This system allows x-rays and other radiological studies to be viewed on computer rather than via printed films. A picture-archiving communication system makes it easy for students to compare films from various patients with similar diseases or from one patient over a period of time, both of which are important in clinical diagnoses as well as in learning to read radiological studies. This system is slowly being integrated by many institutions and is preferred by physicians over regular films (Nissen, Abdulla, Khandheria, Kienzle, & Zaher, 2004).

Access to Information

The current model in medical education is the mentored student. In this model, the one with least experience is responsible for undertaking all the responsibilities of patient care. When a challenge is met that the student/resident is unsure how to handle, he or she contacts the next higher-up doctor in the chain of command, and so on. On rounds, the physician with the most experience takes time to go over the individual cases and redirect medical care if needed.

This system presents a number of difficulties. Recently, there has been a move towards treating patients in a more outpatient environment. There are fewer hospitalizations, so physicians in training have less access to patients. Conversely, these patients have significantly less opportunity for treatment from a senior or highly experienced physician. The tolerance of mistakes in medicine is zero. In an effort to reduce medical mistakes so the number of errors is as close to zero as possible, physicians with more experience may be reluctant to allow residents to manage their patients. Physicians at various times are expected to care for their patients in the hospital, see patients in their office, supervise residents, perform and publish leading-edge research, and write grant proposals that bring funding to the hospital. Often, one or more of these services is performed with no compensation. The demands on a physician's time are enormous and seem to be increasing all the time. Physicians have less and less time to devote to supervision and teaching. Because of the new direction medicine is taking, all learning opportunities must be fully utilized and new learning opportunities made available. One way to maximize the learning process is through improved access to information. The paperless charting systems, intranet and PDAs already mentioned are examples of improved access to information, but other information modalities are available. For example, sound and video clips may be integrated into presentations. Some computer systems even allow for interactive videos (Nissen et al., 2004). A newer approach to teaching medicine is problem-based learning (Ward et al., 2001). Problem-based learning is different from the traditional approach to medicine in that a specific problem is simultaneously addressed from multiple vantage points. Environmental, behavioral, nutritional, social, economic, cultural and religious factors can be taken into consideration, as well as any obvious medical problems. Technology allows a single problem to be addressed from many perspectives. Chat rooms and video conferences allow experts from various fields in geographically distant locations to interact with each other, provide consultation advice and give feedback to medical students (Whitcomb, 2003).

A shortcoming of many medical education programs is the failure to treat medical students as adults (Barnete, 1995). A student's unavoidable and inevitable lack of experience is sometimes confused for ignorance. Partially because of this attitude, and partially because of the sheer amount of material that must be mastered, students are increasingly finding the lecture-based method of education unsatisfactory. Strømø, Grøttum, and Lycke (2004) showed that the introduction of computer-supported, problem-based learning systems had a positive influence on student learning. The students tended to increase their use of Web-based resources, expand their interaction with experts and lessen the use of textbooks, which are often outdated by the time they are in print (Strømø et al., 2004). Lectures can be informative, but applying skills and knowledge to case studies and interactive simulations can be much more meaningful and effective. Health care professionals must continually learn new skills, procedures and diagnostic techniques. Education never actually ends. Physicians must frequently update their knowledge base and train in new techniques. Modern communication and computerized learning tools help achieve these goals (Zak, 2004). In addition to requiring re-certification exams, many states also require practicing physicians to participate in a program of continuing medical education credits. These credits are becoming increasingly available through Web-based teaching environments. This makes both delivering and receiving the required medical education credits easier and more flexible. These more accessible educational credits may help improve compliance of physicians with the credit requirements. This requirement also offers opportunities for residents and physicians to enhance their knowledge of how cultural and religious traditions among diverse patients can impact medical treatment, and how best to respectfully and appropriately treat an individual rather than a disease or disorder.

Monitoring Student Education

Computer technology can be used to directly monitor students' progress through their academic studies. There are numerous computer applications available, such as access to journal articles and abstracts, downloadable textbooks and drug information databases that can be consulted to improve educational outcomes and enrich the educational experience. Also, problems that result from poor penmanship are avoided. Presently, when one medical shift changes to another, a process called sign-out occurs. During sign-out all relevant patient information and a to-do list is passed from one shift to the next. It is done by medical residents, attending physicians, nursing staff and anyone else responsible for patient care. Medical mistakes may result if important information is not transmitted correctly or is forgotten by either shift. Technology, especially PDAs, allows for electronic sign out. Specific data on each patient may be transferred electronically. A resident, especially during off shifts, may be responsible for the well-being of 50 or more patients, often on different wards. Electronic access to basic patient information, such as a list of medical problems, current medication list and any active issues (such as a blood transfusion, for example) minimizes the risk of medical errors made due to lack of information on a specific case. In addition, electronic sign-out allows alarms to be set, reminding on-call residents of tasks that need to be done or patients that need to be checked.

Databases can be accrued for each student that monitor clinical experience and ensure that students receive comprehensive training. Students can enter patient contacts and residents can log procedures into PDAs for easy evaluation, allowing any omissions in education or experience to be identified (Fischer, Stewart, Mehta, Wax, & Lapinsky, 2003). Additionally, computers and PDAs can be used in data collection for research. Every year, more than 2 million medical journal articles are published (Hancock, 1996). This is in addition to the existing base of medical knowledge. Medical educators are already maximizing the amount of information that a student can learn in the amount of time allotted. It is impractical to extend the length of time of medical training, so methods of being more efficient must be evaluated. Technology plays a primary role in this trend toward greater efficiency.

Disadvantages

People today are living longer lives than ever before, and the productive period of those lives has been greatly extended. Survival rates of the ill or injured are at an all-time high. A major contributor to this happy state of affairs is technology. This includes not only technology for diagnostic and treatment purposes, but also innovations used for development of medications and training of highly capable physicians. Technological advances have led the way to many improvements in modern medicine. However, there are also drawbacks to a dependence upon technology. These include hardware and software limitations, computer failure, security issues, patient confidentiality issues, property rights, maintenance and poor attitude among those required to implement new learning systems (Ward, Gordon, Field, & Lehmann, 2001). Currently, one of the primary problems in medical technology is lack of bandwidth. Adequate bandwidth is required for proper data transfer (Fischer et al., 2003). Also, the resources required to develop a specific technology can be prohibitively expensive (Whitcomb, 2004).

Technology is not without patient risk. Risks and costs are often underemphasized in medicine for financial and social motives (Schroeder, 1981) or because the health care provider underestimates or is unaware of the risks associated with a given technology. For example, a full-body computed tomography (CT) scan has a 0.08% chance of causing cancer (Brenner & Elliston, 2004). Students must be well aware of the potential side effects of all diagnostic procedures and treatments, and must learn to convey this information in an understandable manner to the patient.

As the health care industry evolves, the demands on physicians continue to grow, and time constraints in the physicians' day are surfacing as a common and worsening problem. In order to adapt to new technologies directed at enhancing medical education, instructors must spend additional time learning the technology themselves. Extensive training may be required of physician educators to gain adequate mastery before introducing procedures to students. Many health care professionals simply do not have time to devote to this requirement. Medical education includes extensive role modeling and learning through observation. It is through this role modeling that students learn bedside manner and communication skills with both patients and other physicians (Zucker et al., 1998). The introduction of many of the technologies previously described decreases the amount of role-model learning and peer interaction. Strømø et al. (2004) showed that the introduction of computer-supported, problem-based learning made students' attitudes towards cooperation more negative, making them less likely to work together (Strømø et al., 2004). Technology that decreases role modeling could hinder the acquisition of patient-doctor interaction skills. This may be particularly significant in treating those whose linguistic abilities limit their ease of understanding physicians and procedures in the first place.

The medical field tends to attract science- and technology-directed thinkers, but these individuals may not be the best people for treating a patient in a holistic manner. In medicine, there is a need to treat the whole patient, and treatment often includes behavioral modifications. The vast majority of disease is preventable through proper diet, regular exercise, not smoking, consuming little alcohol and safe sexual practices. It seems most people are not taught good habits as children. Changing behavior to promote healthy lifestyles does prevent disease. Behavior modification requires educating patients so they are convinced they need to change bad habits. As technology becomes more advanced, the tendency is toward a deterioration in close patient-doctor relationships, which can result in lessening ability to persuade patients toward long-lasting behavioral changes. In addition, patient diversity is greater than ever, and medical students might never learn proper communication skills that allow them to influence their patients' choices. Preventive medicine is the discipline where the greatest impact can be made in improving overall health. The science-geared minds frequently attracted to medicine tend to be less interested in preventive care than in the challenges of curing disease (Clawson, 1990). To adequately apply preventive medicine, social, cultural, ethnic and behavioral factors affecting a patient's life must be weighed equally with scientific knowledge, or the desired change in patient attitude or behavior is less likely to occur. That is to say, someone with a solid grounding in patient care and communication skills but possessing minimal clinical knowledge can have a more profound impact on long-term health of a patient than a doctor with outstanding clinical knowledge who lacks interpersonal skills. As technology increasingly enters into the educational process there, is the possibility that health care providers may continue to become more science-centered and less person-centered.

Medicine is taught as both an art and a science. The science in medicine is obvious, but the importance of non-scientific factors within the field of medicine is underestimated by both medical personal and the lay person. Traditionally, doctors accept a sick person as a patient and then try to treat the medical condition. The best doctors also identify risk factors for disease and try to prevent disease. The preventive branch of medicine includes vaccination, smoking cessation programs, diabetes screening and education, weight loss promotion, nutrition counseling, regular Pap smears and exercise consultations. Communication, not technology, is required for disease prevention. Medical technology becomes important primarily when prevention has failed. The art of medicine requires physicians to learn how to conduct an interview with an endless variety of patients in a non-judgmental format. This puts the patient at ease with him or herself and the physician. The interview must follow a well-organized format, so relevant medical information is extracted and a trusting doctor-patient relationship is forged. Technology may misguide inexperienced physicians and medical students into forgetting that it is the subjective symptoms of the patient that first and foremost lead to the correct diagnosis. Only with this basic piece of information clearly in mind is the physical exam and laboratory data of any value. The principle skill used in clinical work is problem solving. Medicine is like detective work. First, information must be obtained from the patient and his or her family. Next, that information, which may or may not be completely accurate, has to be combined with the physical exam, laboratory and radiology studies. A physician must be able to combine all the information, look for the source of the problem and determine possible treatments, then select the one most suitable for the individual patient. Technology is a master at providing useful information, but the physician must solve the problem (Clawson, 1990). With the pervasiveness of advanced technologies, there is a risk of over-reliance on computer-generated information and an under-emphasis on transmission of thinking and problem-solving skills.

An additional problem with technology is equitable application; economically underprivileged patients often have a medical disadvantage. However, there is a tendency when new technology is found to be advantageous to utilize that technology at every promising opportunity. Over time, the expense of the technology is spread out over many patients, and the price gradually decreases, making it available to more people. During the price-dropping interim, the poorer population may have less access to cutting-edge technology. The medical residents and students who train in facilities serving a lower socioeconomic population will also have less opportunity to work with high technology, resulting in a potentially poorer education.

Other problems exist associated with the integration of technology into medical education. One of these is that students are sometimes more experienced with common technologies than their teachers (Salas & Anderson, 1997). Or, sometimes educators lack enthusiasm for new technological concepts and this is inevitably conveyed to the students (Moberg & Whitcomb, 1999). Occasionally, technology projects are promoted by an individual instructor who leaves that teaching position and the technology component falls by the wayside, which indicates a lack of long-term support and organizational interest (Barnete, 1995). In addition, it is very expensive to fund medical education, and most of this expense is shouldered by the student physician. It is a problem if the cost of medical education sees a significant increase due to more technological requirements (Jones & Korn, 1997). Educating future doctors is a difficult task. Technology provides an almost limitless number of directions educator can pursue. The key is to be aware of available options and the advantages and disadvantages of each, and choose the options most likely to provide long-term educational benefit to the educator, future physicians and the great diversity of patients whose lives this physician will impact. It is inevitable that technology will play a vital role in medical education, and educators must be ready for the challenge.

Future Trends

There is much promise on the horizon in medical technology. Technological improvements include better organization of data and improved access to information; collegial exploration of ethical, cultural and social issues; improvements in communication and consultation capabilities; an increase in online educational opportunities; and the evolution of medical technology itself.

One of the major problems in the utilization of technology in physician education is organizing the amount of available information into a usable format. The organizational systems available are lagging behind the technological advances. An expanding number of organizational systems to enhance a physician's ability to effectively utilize technology will be emerging in the near future. One method the medical community has employed to help assimilate and utilize the body of available information is through an approach called evidence-based medicine. Evidence-based medicine is relatively new and operates by collecting all the available research studies on a topic, rating them according to their quality and combining them into one easily accessible location so the work can be summarized and meaningful conclusions can be drawn from the combined findings of all the studies. This is a large change from the mentor-based system, where medical traditions were passed on, often without question, from one generation of physicians to the next. There is considerable enthusiasm for evidence-based medicine. It helps to provide optimum care for patients, and in the future is likely to become even more well known.

Future applications of medical technology contain a number of ethical issues, and the study of ethical implications is already on the rise. Ethics is generally an understudied aspect of technology, because there is little to be gained financially by research sponsors. Ethical issues will play a growing role in medical education as technology and the procedures that technology makes possible continue to evolve. Stem cell research, deoxyribonucleic acid (DNA) testing, preserving the lives of comatose patients indefinitely and replacement organs for treatment of the elderly or infirm are but a few of the issues already at hand, and the list is growing daily.

Newer, faster, smarter, better, smaller, more powerful and so forth are descriptions antici-pated in the future of medical technology. In general, physicians and medical students even in the near future must be prepared to work with computers in ways we can hardly imagine today. The trend is a move toward exclusively electronic data storage and retrieval in all aspects of patient care. Basic keyboarding, once a class only for secretaries, is now one of the most important preparatory classes a student can take. Even now, it is often being taught in elementary school, where traditionally it was a high school course. Innovative technologies emerge more rapidly than an educator can master, so training must focus on basic technological skills with an accent on thinking logically and adapting creatively to new circumstances.

It is becoming apparent that the federal government may have a greater regulatory hand in technology and its application in the future. At a national level, the U.S. government is proposing standards for health information technology (HIT) and backing it up with legisla-tive proposals. The National Health Information Incentive Act of 2005 aims to facilitate the development and adoption of national standards in health technology, provide initial financial support and ongoing reimbursement incentives for physicians in smaller practices to adopt the HIT policies, and support quality improvement activities (ACP Press release Feb 11, 2005). The National Nanotechnology Initiative (NNI) (www.nano.gov) is a federal research and development program established to coordinate the multi-agency efforts in nanoscale science, engineering and technology. The goals of the NNI are to maintain a world-class research and development program intended to realize the full potential of nanotechnology, and to facilitate the transition of new technologies into products for economic growth, jobs and other public benefit. These goals include development of educational resources, train-ing of a skilled workforce, creation of a supporting infrastructure, development of tools to advance nanotechnology and finding ways to support responsible development of nanotech-nology. Awards have been given to medical schools and research institutes to establish new research initiatives focusing on creating advanced nanotechnologies to analyze and detect arterial plaque formation on the molecular level in its early stages. Another group has been awarded grants to detect, monitor, treat and eliminate vulnerable plaques. Nanotechnology clearly has a large role in the future of medicine, and is already used for noninvasive imag-ing and sensing, targeted therapies and drug delivery systems, as well as for treatment of heart, lung, blood and sleep disorders.

At this point, there is limited application for nanotechnology in the training of medical students. The field is in its infancy. It is important though, that students are aware that the technology exists and to understand the tremendous potential it holds in the field of medicine.

Conclusion

Looking back to the earliest days of modern medical science, we can see that the progress of medicine, as it evolved from conjecture and superstition into a science of diagnosis and treatment, has been fueled by daring minds that had the courage to question, challenge, explore, postulate new ideas, try new approaches and prove to others the need for change. We have moved from an informal, poorly structured and chaotic system to one that attempts to tie the clinical practice of medicine to the scientific evidence available. Technology has stoked the current momentum and provided a fertile environment that fosters the exploration of new frontiers in health care. During the renaissance period, we ventured into the "inner sanctum" of the human body to learn its anatomy; we printed materials to distribute to others; we expanded knowledge and communicated theory; all of which obligated us to ask more questions. We have moved at the pace our technology has allowed and grappled with serious ethical dilemmas along the way. As a society, we have had to make room in our ideals to evaluate and assimilate current technologies and develop plans for future advances we can only imagine. Those who work as medical educators and health care professionals are obligated to create an ethical balance and provide safeguards for society while preserving life through available technology.

One can only wonder at the expanse of the unknown and where current technology will take us. Medical students are becoming familiar with a virtual world that makes information available immediately. Medical educators are earnestly responding by integration of evidence-based educational tools into the medical school curriculum and teaching early on the need to discern the true quality of the evidence being presented by a publication. This is a life-long skill needed by every physician. Physicians as a group have embraced the concept and practice of intranet, handheld devices, virtual teaching, microsurgery and technology-dependent modalities. Technology will continue to push the boundaries of diagnosis and treatment of diseases and, in the hands of a caring and skilled physician, can foster the treatment of people as diverse, unique individuals rather than emphasizing treatment of disease.

References

Agency for Health Care Research and Quality. (2005). *Health expenditure statistics*. Retrieved May 26, 2005, from www.meps.ahrq.gov/papers/st61/stat61.pdf

Barnete, G. O. (1995). Information technology and medical education. *Journal of the American Medical Informatics Association, 2*(5), 285-291.

Brenner, D. J., & Elliston, C. D. (2004). Estimated radiation risks potentially associated with full-body CT screening. *Radiology, 232*(3), 735-738.

Clawson, K. (1990). The education of the physician. *Academic Medicine, 65*(2), 84-88.

Conn, J. (2004). The games doctors play. *Modern Healthcare, 34*(30), 32-33.

Fischer, S., Stewart, T. E., Mehta, S., Wax, R., & Lapinsky, S.E. (2003). Handheld computing in medicine. *Journal of the American Medical Informatics Association, 10*(2),
139-149.

Grutzner, P.A., & Suhm, N. (2004). Computer aided long bone fracture treatment. *Injury,
35*(1), S-A57-64.

Hancock, L. (1996). *Physicians' guide to the Internet.* Philadelphia: Lippincott-Raven.

Holden, M. K. (2005). Virtual environments for motor rehabilitation: Review. *Cyberpsy-
chological Behavior, 8*(3), 187-211, 212-219.

Jones, R. F., & Korn, D. (1997). On the cost of educating a medical student. *Academic
Medicine. 72*(3), 200-210.

Klinger, E., Bouchard, S., Legeron, P., Roy, S., Lauer, F., Chemin, I., et al. (2005). Virtual
reality therapy versus cognitive behavior therapy for social phobia. *Cyberpsychologi-
cal Behavior, 8*(1), 76-88.

Krijin, M., Emmelkam, P. M., Olafsson, R. P., & Biemond, R. (2004). Virtual reality exposure
therapy of anxiety disorders. *Clinical Psychology Review, 4*(3), 259-281.

Medical Readiness Trainer Team. (2000). Immersive virtual reality platform for medical
training: A killer-application. *Studies in Health Technology and Informatics, 70*,
207-213.

Moberg, T. F., & Whitcomb, M. E. (1999). Educational technology to facilitate medical
students' learning: Background paper 2 of the medical school objectives project.
Academic Medicine, 74, 1145-1150.

Nicolaou, D. D., & Davis, G. L. (2001). A distributed asynchronous resident procedure log
for hand held devices. *Academic Emergency Medicine, 8*(8), 1200-1203.

Nissen, S., Abdulla, A., Khandheria, A., Kienzle, M., & Zaher, C. (2004). Working group
6: The role of technology to enhance clinical and educational efficiency. *Journal of
the American College of Cardiology, 44*(2), 256-260.

Salas, A. A., & Anderson, M. B. (1997). Introducing information technologies into medical
education: Activities of the AAMC. *Academic Medicine, 72*(3), 191-193.

Schroeder, S. A. (1981). Medical technology and academic medicine: The doctor producers'
dilemma. *Journal of Medical Education, 56*(8), 634-639.

Strømø, H. I., Grøttum, P., & Lycke, K. H. (2004). Changes in student approaches to learning with the introduction of computer supported problem based learning. *Medical
Education, 38*(4), 390-398.

Vozenilek, J., Huff, J. S., Reznek, M., & Gordon, J. A. (2004). See one, do one, teach one:
Advanced technology in medical education. *Academic Emergency Medicine, 11*(11),
1149-1154.

Ward, J. P., Gordon, J., Field, M. J., & Lehmann, H. P. (2001). Communication and information technology in medical education. *Lancet, 357*(9258), 792-796.

Whitcomb, M. (2003). The information technology age is dawning for medical education.
Academic Medicine, 78(3), 247-248.

Whitcomb, M. (2004). More on competency based education. *Academic Medicine, 79*(6), 493-494.

Zak, R. (2004). Continuing medical education. *Healthcare Informatics, 21*(7), 40.

Zucker, S., White, J. A., Fabri, P. J., & Khonsari, L. S. (1998). Instructional intranets in graduate medical education. *Academic Medicine, 73*(10), 1072-1075.

Section IV

Questionnaire Research
in Technology and Diversity

Chapter VII

University Students' Perceptions of Computer Technology Experiences:
Questionnaire Results and Analysis

Yukiko Inoue, University of Guam, USA

Abstract

On the basis of a survey as a research method (from designing surveys to reporting on surveys), the author examined students' perceptions of computers and information technology (IT). In fall 2005, a survey questionnaire was administered to students enrolled in education courses at a university in the western Pacific. Attention was given to four variables—gender, ethnicity, academic status and age. A Likert-scale instrument was designed for data collection. Overall, students of this sample (N = 174) had positive perceptions toward using computer technology. The results of the analysis of variance (ANOVA) analyses indicated, however, that none of the four variables were statistically significant. There were no gender, ethnicity, academic status and age differences in perceptions of technology experiences for this sample. Qualitative data (students' essays on the use of technology) were also analyzed to support quantitative data. Implications for practice were discussed, future trends were identified and recommendations were made for further research.

Introduction

The concept of research in education has changed over the past 100 years but, in essence, educational research is divided into three phases: The first phase focused on psychological studies of training and of fatigue in learning; the use of tests and the reliability of examinations were features of the second phase (research came to be viewed as the work of specialists and experts involving complex statistical procedures); and in the third phase, during the 1950s and 1960s, sociological aspects and different styles of research came to be accepted (Nisbet, 2005). Nisbet further describes the third phase as follows:

This third phase has brought research into closer partnership with policy and practice. ... At the same time, the teacher-researcher movement, which initially aimed to support teachers in carrying out research studies themselves, has developed into something more fundamental: a view of research as a key element in a professional approach ... (p. 42)

There are many ways to obtain data from individuals in educational research. The most common methods are interviews (including focus groups and personal interviews) and surveys of various kinds (including telephone surveys, mail surveys and e-mail surveys). A survey is a "system for collecting information to describe, compare or explain knowledge, attitude and behavior" (Fink, 1995a, p. 1). A survey probably is the single most widely used research method in educational settings; survey questionnaires especially can reach large numbers of people at relatively low cost, can ensure anonymity and can be written for specific research purposes (Wiersma, 2000).

In today's knowledge age, university administrators and educators have been committed to finding ways to make learning more meaningful, more transferable to various situations out of a specific context and more conducive to self-directed, life-long learning (Lim, 2004). There is no question that information and communications technology (ICT)—which is characterized as "service" and "product" specifically designed to organize and speed up the flow of information—is a valuable, useful resource and tool for learning and teaching (Kompf, 2005). The following three intriguing and constructive inquiries posed by Roldan and Wu (2004) are the special interest of the study reported in this chapter:

1.   Are today's college students well prepared for the challenges of the information age?

2.   Do students possess the skills and motivation required for self-directed, life-long learning?

3.   How can educators help students to better prepare and improve information literacy skills?

Guided by these inquiries, and at the same time on the basis of a survey as a research method, the author examined students' perceptions of computer technology experiences. A survey questionnaire was administered to students enrolled in education courses at a comprehensive university in the western Pacific. Attention was given to four variables—gender, ethnicity, academic status and age. A Likert-scale instrument was developed to collect student data that were analyzed using ANOVA. Qualitative data (students' one-page essays on the use of technology and self-directed learning) were also utilized to support quantitative data.

The present study, therefore, is based on the general procedure of questionnaire research, such as the design of questionnaire items, collecting and analyzing the data, and writing reports, in addition to concerning the validity and reliability issues. Implications for educational practice are discussed, future trends are identified, and recommendations are made for further research.

Background

When computers were first used in the classroom, they were used more like "entertainment" centers rather than instructional or educational tools; computers and other sources of technology can now truly enhance instruction (Madsen, 2004). When Madsen was preparing her students for their field trip to a symphony concert, she was able to go "online" and take the students to a site that showed them the diagram of the seating arrangement of the orchestra, the sounds of each instrument that they would be hearing as well as samples of the music. As Madsen's experience indicates precisely, optimal learning may *not* have taken place when only traditional lectures were employed in the classroom. Obviously, students today embrace a more holistic manner of presentation styles by combining text, visual imagery and multimedia text utilizing PowerPoint, VHS/DVD and Internet presentations.

Technology in Higher Education

Technology is intended to serve human purposes, and the burden of technology use is that people must choose carefully *how* to apply it so that they do not sacrifice individuality (Agre, 1999). The integration of technology into education systems is forcing colleges and universities to make dramatic changes, increasing the *quality*, *diversity* and *availability* of information, and altering the teacher-student relationship; technology should be used to leverage the existing knowledge base; to enrich, expand and extend the curriculum from educators' perspective; and to engage interest for investigation and in-depth understanding from students' perspective (Moore, 1999). Technology in education is a necessity for up-to-date learning and teaching, but it is argued that it should be used as part of education, not as a viable substitute (Kompf, 2005).

Delamarter (2005) recognizes four reasons why teachers and professors need to get more involved with technology to:

1.   Meet student expectations
2.   Enrich the classroom experience by engaging the visual learners

3.   Enhance the traditional course through richer pedagogical strategies available with technology

4.   Offer online distance programs

Professors, therefore, need to get themselves trained with IT and into a position to discuss intelligently what sorts of scenarios and policies are the best practice that can be sustained to produce quality teaching and learning (Delamarter, 2005).

Many researchers have made empirical attempts to investigate, explore, expand or evaluate the integration of technology into education and learning. Eynon's (2005) study has found that the most common faculty use of ICT in all subjects is to provide students with access to a range of online resources. It has also showed that faculty motivations for using ICT are to enhance the educational experience for students and to compensate for some of the changes occurring in higher education (such as the rise in student numbers, and demand for flexible learning opportunities). According to Metzger, Flanagin, and Zwarun's (2003) report, college students rely heavily on the Web for both general and academic information, and they expect this usage to increase over time. The report has further stated that college students tend to believe information from the Internet more fully than do people from a more general adult population.

Sheard and Lynch's (2003) study on learner diversity has indicated that different students experience and react to an online environment in different ways, depending on their previous experience, and no one format is going to meet the needs of all students. Therefore, constant challenges for online learning are students' familiarity with the learning environment and their skills and confidence with the Internet and IT. Van Soest, Canon, and Grant (2000) strongly suggest that using a Web forum can encourage dialog among students as well as between students and the professor, and thus can enhance learning within a safe environment.

Designing the technology infrastructure for institutions of higher education is a strategic decision that affects the quality of the educational experience for students and faculty (Demb, Erickson, & Hawkins-Wilding, 2004). In their study on students' reactions to a campus-wide laptop computer initiative, Demb et al. have found that the laptop computer is an "essential" part of college learning for students (i.e., for typing papers, accessing the Internet, searching for research references, making PowerPoint presentations and storing information), making a significant difference in students' study habits as well as their academic and social lives. In other words, the laptop computer extremely helps college students with classroom assignments, e-mail messages and individual research or projects for the course. The above study has also found that student perceptions of the value of the laptop computer to their academic success are tightly correlated with their perceptions of the success of faculty in integrating the laptop computer into classroom activities. However, the strength of student frustration about the cost structure of the laptop usage was one of the most striking findings. In conclusion, Demb et al. have emphasized that gaining sufficient experience with a new computer system to achieve "teaching fluency" requires a substantial investment of time and attention on the part of the instructor.

Stafford's (2005) study found that digital content is highly sought after by students in Internet-supported distance education courses and that distance-education students are motivated to use Internet communication resources to offset the lack of interactions found in the normal classroom. Stafford strongly believes that distance education combines teleconference and Internet-based resources to maximize the combined effect of instructor guidance and Internet-based content delivery. Many studies comparing teaching from a distance with teaching face-to-face indicate the following to be true (Williams, Paprock, & Covington, 1999):

- Quality of learning is as good or better.
- Students are highly motivated (because of appreciation of opportunity or convenience).
- Instructors are better prepared and more well organized.
- Instructional resources are enhanced.
- Collaborative teaching is encouraged.

With online learning, students control when, where and what they learn, as well as how often and how quickly—and this level of control is what creates satisfied students (Peters, n.d.).

Dodds (2003) points out the startling growth of new technologies and the popularity of open- and distance-learning delivery approaches. Online distance learning provides answers to the problems of *availability* (such as accessibility and cost) and the demand for *flexibility* (such as time, place and pace) of higher learning, and technology-mediated learning and online distance education are becoming major vehicles for fulfilling the needs of life-long learning (Beller, 1998).

The term *life-long learning* first appeared in the 1973 United Nations Educational, Scientific and Cultural Organization (UNESCO) report of the international commission on the development of education; life-long learning—a wide variety of types of learning opportunities shaped significantly by learner-directed requirements and contexts—has since played an important role in policy discussions as well as in studies of the sociology and economics of education (Friesen & Anderson, 2004). Highlighting the positive potential of the semantic Web for life-long learning as a future trend, Friesen and Anderson have further described as follows: "The profound flexibility associated with life-long learning (i.e., the need for it to take place *anywhere*, *anytime* and *anyhow*) can be addressed with the help of semantic Web technologies" (p. 684).

Nevertheless, the challenge is more than just to adapt and integrate new technologies into education, but to also find ways in which teaching methods can change fundamentally with the use of technology. In this regard, the connection between inquiry-based learning and electronic learning (e-learning) should be recognized. Inquiry-based learning is a recent manifestation of self-directed, life-long learning, and is characterized as an instructional approach in which inquiry *does* function as a main vehicle for teaching and learning; e-learning has enormous potential to augment inquiry (Lim, 2004). Based on the notion that e-learning can empower students' ownership and self-directed learning by increasing student involvement and responsibility for their own learning, Lim defines the following five stages of the inquiry-based learning process:

1.   Ask (learners articulate their own problems or questions)
2.   Plan (learners design their problem-solving strategies within a certain time frame)
3.   Explore (learners explore resources for solving problems using their background knowledge)
4.   Construct (learners synthesize resources and provide solutions)
5.   Reflect (learners discuss the implications for further refinement)

These stages are useful to understand the concept of a self-defined learning approach. Colleges and universities can help individuals become life-long learners, emphasizing that educational or learning opportunities are available throughout the individuals' lives (Dodds, 2003).

Technology and Diversity in Higher Education

Characteristics of online distance learning related to research studies vary, yet reflect some combination of demographic variables, such as age, gender and ethnic background (Thompson, 1998). According to Thompson, (1) researchers generally agree that distance education students are, on average, older than typical undergraduate students; (2) most studies of distance learners in North American higher education report that more women than men are enrolled in courses delivered at a distance, making generalizations about the relative participation of ethnic minorities in distance education difficult; and (3) distance education is an especially appealing way for students from disadvantaged socio-economic groups to enter higher education. Although comprehensive accurate statistics are not yet available on women learning through distance education, most distance learners are women and distance education continues to offer women opportunities to enrich their lives and to expand their earning power (Burge, 1998). Even though computer technology experiences are as varied as the individuals who use computers, both men and women voice positive attitudes toward online learning—that is, despite many variables, gender does *not* significantly affect student perceptions of distance education (Peters, n.d.).

Advocating that there is no gender difference in the use of e-mail, Gefen and Straub (1997) suggest that gender should be included in IT diffusion models along with other cultural effects, and that the same mode of communication may be perceived differently by the genders. Generally, boys love the computer or the machine for itself and like to spend long hours tinkering and game-playing on computers, whereas girls are far more likely to reject emotional identification with the computer or the machine as a second self and instead think of it in dispassionate and instrumental terms as just a tool (Sofia, 1998): "Gender differences in attitudes toward computers and styles of computer learning could be interpreted differently from a perspective that is critical of *technotopianism* (technological utopianism), alert to *masculinist* bias and more sensitive to the relations between individual and cultural imaginaries" (p. 30).

Koohang's (2004) study focused on students' perceptions toward the use of the digital library in the weekly Web-based distance-learning assignments portion of a hybrid instructional program and found that age is not a significant factor, but gender and prior experience with the Internet are significant factors. In other words, male students have significantly higher positive perceptions toward the use of the digital library, and students who have more prior experience with the Internet have significantly higher positive perceptions toward the use of the digital library.

Inoue's (1999-2000) study searched for an answer to the question of whether or not gender differences would associate with academic status (graduate vs. undergraduate students) on university students' preference for learning by computer-assisted instruction (CAI). The results of ANOVA have found that the main effect of gender is not significant, whereas the main effect of academic status is significant. This means that graduate students do favor CAI more than undergraduate students. The study has further indicated the significant differences between undergraduate females and graduate males, supporting the assumption that computer experiences have a stronger effect gender differences on attitudes toward the use of computers in learning. It may be that graduate students have more computer experiences. Since computer literacy skills increase as time passes, the chance of "give CAI a try" becomes higher. Although Inoue's study does not reveal exactly why graduate students favor CAI more than undergraduate students, such learning experiences as using CAI give maximum opportunities to all students with different backgrounds and academic expectations in the graduate program.

Finally, the importance of recognizing the cultural diversity of students has inspired much recent discussion and research in higher education; racially diverse environments, when properly nurtured, lead to both quantitative and qualitative gains in educational outcomes for all students, including higher retention rates and greater overall satisfaction with college (Ila Parasnis, 2005).

The Survey

Method

Fink (1995b) has identified six requirements for a useful survey: (1) specific, measurable objectives; (2) sound research design; (3) sound choice of population or sample; (4) reliable and valid instruments; (5) appropriate analysis; and (6) accurate reporting of the results. Each of these requirements was considered in relation to the survey questionnaire for this chapter.

The Questionnaire

Specific, measurable objectives. Preparing specific, measurable objectives is the first step in a good survey project. Patten (2001) has made the following pertinent observations in this regard: If the objective is too broad, it is difficult to provide questionnaire items that are effective and relevant; the objectives, as developed, should be reviewed by external experts before proceeding; and the literature relevant to the objective should be thoroughly reviewed. The questionnaire in the present study was designed to answer the following specific questions:

1. Is there a difference in perceptions of computer technology experiences between females and males? (1 = Female; 2 = Male)

2. Is there a difference in perceptions of computer technology experiences among various ethnic groups? (1 = Chamorro; 2 = Asian Filipino; 3 = Other Pacific Islander; 4 = Asian Other; 5 = Caucasian; 6 = Black; 7 = Other)

3. Is there a difference in perceptions of computer technology experiences among various academic status groups? (1 = Freshman; 2 = Sophomore; 3 = Junior; 4 = Senior; 5 = Graduate)

4. Is there a difference in perceptions of computer technology experiences among various age groups? (1 = 20 or younger; 2 = 21-25; 3 = 26-30; 4 = 31-39; 5 = 40-49; 6 = 50 or older)

Sound research design. With respect to this second criterion, Fink (1995b) has observed that a survey design is "a way of arranging the environment in which a survey takes place" (p. 3). In designing a survey questionnaire for the present study, account was taken of the basic question of the feasibility of administering the survey questionnaire to the population of interest, and the questionnaire design was modified appropriately. Although the *five* choices are adequate for most research purposes, Likert-scale items can have up to about *seven* choices without requiring respondents to make falsely fine distinctions: "very strongly agree," "strongly agree," "agree," "neutral," "disagree," "strongly disagree" and "very strongly disagree" (Patten, 2001). In Patten's (2001) words, "Since 1930, other item types have been developed to measure attitudes. Interestingly, however, extensive research indicates that none of them are clearly superior to Likert-scale items, which are easy to write and easy for respondents to understand" (p. 34).

Along with demographic question items (gender, ethnicity, academic status and age), this survey had 62 Likert-scale questions (such as "I am very comfortable using a personal computer"), allowing participants to respond to each question in terms of five degrees of agreement (ranging from 1 = strongly disagree to 5 = strongly agree). The survey was reviewed by colleagues and then by the Committee on Human Research Subjects (CHRS) to ensure that the rights of the participants were protected.

Sound choice of population or sample. With respect to this third criterion, sampling methods are usually divided into two types: probability sampling and non-probability sampling. For the present study, eight classes were selected randomly from among all the courses offered in the school of education at an American Pacific island university in the fall semester of 2005. This university—the only 4-year institution of higher learning in Micronesia—was defined as a minority university by the U.S. Department of Education (90% of the students of this university were of non-European descent). The courses selected for the survey were both foundations courses and teacher education courses in undergraduate and graduate programs. The population of the study was the entire group of students enrolled in education courses during that semester. The demographic information of the study participants (N = 174) is summarized in Table 1.

Reliable and valid instruments. With respect to this fourth criterion, a survey questionnaire should contain items pertinent to the objectives. In brief, "valid data come from surveys that measure what they purport to measure" (Fink, 1995b, p. 5). The survey was reviewed to ascertain that the extent to which inferences and uses made on the basis of scores from the survey instrument were reasonable and appropriate (validity) and that the questionnaire items would be clearly understood by the participants (reliability). The following guidelines for developing useful survey instruments by Wiersma (2000) were considered in developing the questionnaire of the present study:

- Except for possibly a few items that request background or demographic information, items should relate directly to the research questions;
- Items should be clear and unambiguous;
- Only one concept should be included in a single item;
- The use of leading questions should be avoided;
- Only information that the respondent is able to provide should be requested;
- Shorter items are to be preferred to longer items; and
- Simpler items are to be preferred to complex items.

The present survey was pilot tested using 31 students independent of the sample of respondents used in the study. The reliability coefficient (Cronbach's alpha) from the results was .920. This suggested that the survey instrument was stable enough to determine students' perceptions of technology experiences. According to Chen and Krauss (2004), however:

... reliability coefficients only inform about the relative amount of random inconsistency of individuals' responses on a measure. A test with a Cronbach's alpha of .90 suggests that the test is more internally consistent than another test with a Cronbach's alpha of .70. However, both reliability estimates do not provide absolute indications regarding the precision of the test scores. (p. 955)

Appropriate analysis. With respect to this fifth criterion, although surveys can use a variety of conventional statistical procedures to analyze the data, the appropriate analysis depends on the survey aims (such as description, comparison and correlation) and the size of the sample.

The overall means (M) and standard deviations (SD) for all the respondents by all the questions were calculated. Then ANOVA procedure was conducted to answer four questions that informed the research objectives; the F statistics generated from the analysis. A predetermined level of significance (alpha = .01) was chosen for the analysis. Qualitative data (student essays on technology use and self-directed learning) were also analyzed to support quantitative data. Graduate students ($N = 25$) in two classes participated in this essay project in fall 2005.

Accurate reporting of the results. With respect to this sixth criterion, Fink (1995b) has noted that accurate survey reports require knowledge of how to use tables and figures to present information. In this survey, both nominal data and ordinal data (i.e., categorical data such as gender and age) were summarized in tables. Tables are useful and effective in most cases, although it should be noted in passing that Patten (2001) is of the opinion: "Generally, figures are more eye-catching, and many people find them easier to interpret than tables" (p. 90).

Table 1. Demographic information of the survey participants

	N	Percent
Gender		
Female	120	69.0
Male	54	31.0
Total	174	100.0
Ethnicity		
Chamorro	86	49.4
Asian Filipino	55	31.6
Micronesian	14	8.0
Asian other	3	1.7
Caucasian	9	5.2
Black	2	1.1
Other	5	2.9
Total	174	100.0
Age		
20 or younger	39	22.4
21-25	48	27.6
26-30	32	18.4
31-39	31	17.8
40-49	18	10.3
50 or older	6	3.4
Total	174	100.0
Academic status		
Freshman	21	12.1
Sophomore	30	17.2
Junior	36	20.7
Senior	21	12.1
Graduate	66	37.9
Total	174	100.0

Table 2. Descriptive statistics for perceptions of computer technology experiences

Questions		Strongly Agree	Agree	Not Sure	Disagree	Strongly Disagree
Q1.	I am very comfortable using a personal computer.	126 72.4%	39 22.4%	4 2.3%	3 1.7%	2 1.1%
Q2.	I rely on computers in doing school assignments.	115 66.1%	52 29.9%	2 1.1%	3 1.7%	2 1.1%
Q6.	I use computers to help keep me organized.	67 38.5%	72 41.4%	14 8.0%	20 11.5%	1 0.6%
Q7.	I use computers to produce artistic, innovative projects.	95 54.6%	54 31.0%	9 5.2%	13 7.5%	3 1.7%
Q11.	I like to play computer games.	65 37.4%	59 33.9%	17 9.8%	24 13.8%	9 5.2%
Q12.	I read and send e-mail messages almost every day.	72 41.4%	60 34.5%	13 7.5%	25 14.4%	4 2.3%
Q18.	I use word processing more than any other program.	72 41.4%	65 37.4%	18 10.3%	17 9.8%	2 1.1%
Q22.	Internet access is essential if I am to do a good job in my class.	82 47.1%	56 32.2%	15 8.6%	17 9.8%	4 2.3%
Q24.	I read most of my news on the Internet.	67 38.5%	67 38.5%	9 5.2%	27 15.5%	4 2.3%
Q25.	I use the Internet for research more than the library.	92 52.9%	46 26.4%	11 6.3%	21 12.1%	4 2.3%
Q36.	I enjoy online chat rooms or discussion groups.	29 16.7%	43 24.7%	19 10.9%	53 30.5%	30 17.2%
Q42.	I can create a PowerPoint presentation.	97 55.7%	41 23.6%	11 6.3%	19 10.9%	6 3.4%
Q49.	I believe technology helps teachers teach better.	96 55.2%	44 25.3%	12 6.9%	14 8.0%	8 4.6%
Q50.	I believe technology helps students learn better.	93 53.4%	51 29.3%	19 10.9%	8 4.6%	3 1.7%

Note: N = 174

Results and Discussion

A total of 174 responses were usable for the questionnaire research. As seen in Table 1, 69% of the participants were female and 31% male. This contrast was expected because 62% (registrar's office) of the entire student body of this university were female; and, the majority of students in the school of education, particularly in the teacher education program, were female in this university. About 38% of the participants were graduate students, and 62% undergraduate students (12.1% freshman; 17.2% sophomore; 20.7% junior; and 12.1%

senior). The largest ethnic group was Chamorro (49.4%), which was expected because 44% of all the students of this university were Chamorro (Registrar's Office). The next largest group was Filipino (31.6%). Other Pacific Islander (mainly Micronesian) made up 8.0%, other Asian 1.7%, Caucasian 5.2%, and Black 1.1%. Finally, 22.4% of the participants were at age 20 or younger, 27.6% between 21 and 25, 18.4% between 26 and 30, 17.8% between 31 and 39, 10.3% between 40 and 49, and 3.4% over 50, respectively.

Computer Technology Experiences

Among the 62 questions in the survey, 14 were selected to determine the students' perceptions of computer technology experiences. The reliability coefficient alpha across the 14 questions was .808, suggesting that these questions were measuring the same thing. The overall results of descriptive statistics indicated that students of this sample perceived that

Table 3. Means and standard deviations for student perceptions of computer technology and distance education

	N	Min.	Max.	Mean	SD
Q1	174	1.00	5.00	4.6322	.72311
Q2	174	1.00	5.00	4.5805	.71472
Q6	174	1.00	5.00	4.0575	.98961
Q7	174	1.00	5.00	4.2931	.98559
Q11	174	1.00	5.00	3.8448	1.21363
Q12	174	1.00	5.00	3.9828	1.13011
Q18	174	1.00	5.00	4.0805	1.00540
Q22	174	1.00	5.00	4.1207	1.07107
Q24	174	1.00	5.00	3.9540	1.12674
Q25	174	1.00	5.00	4.1552	1.12463
Q36	174	1.00	5.00	2.9310	1.38358
Q42	174	1.00	5.00	4.1724	1.16010
Q49	174	1.00	5.00	4.1839	1.15332
Q50	174	1.00	5.00	4.2816	.95325
Q54	174	1.00	5.00	3.8218	1.11603
Q55	174	1.00	5.00	3.7931	1.07131
Q56	174	1.00	5.00	3.8563	1.04081
Q60	174	1.00	5.00	3.8333	1.03736
Q61	174	1.00	5.00	3.8046	1.09480

Table 4. Analysis of variance summaries for student perceptions of computer technology

Scale	SS	df	MS	F
Gender				
Between Ss	6.125	1	6.125	.275
Within Ss	3824.800	172	22.237	
Ethnicity				
Between Ss	128.456	6	21.409	.966
Within Ss	3702.469	167	22.170	
Academic status				
Between Ss	214.526	4	53.632	2.506
Within Ss	3616.399	169	21.399	
Age				
Between Ss	66.580	5	13.316	.594
Within Ss	3764.345	168	22.407	

the use of computer technology was a positive learning experience (see Table 2). The three most "strongly agree"-occurring questions were: "comfortable using a personal computer" (72.4%); "rely on computers in doing school assignments" (66.1%); and "can create a PowerPoint presentation" (55.7%).

As seen in Table 3, overall, students of this sample are "very comfortable using a personal computer" (M = 4.63; SD = .72) and "rely on computers in doing school assignments" (M = 4.58; SD = .71). For them, "Internet access is essential to do a good job in the class" (M = 4.12; SD = 1.07). They use computers "as word processors" (M = 4.08; SD = 1.01), "to read and send e-mail messages" (M = 3.98; SD = 1.13), "to organize the course work" (M = 4.06; SD = .99), "to produce more artistic, innovative projects" (M = 4.29; SD = .99), "to create a PowerPoint presentation" (M = 4.18; SD = 1.15), "to search for research references" (M = 4.16; SD = 1.12), "to read daily news on the Internet" (M = 3.95; SD = 1.23) and "to play computer games" (M = 3.84; SD = 1.21), but they do not "join online discussion groups" (M = 2.93; SD = 1.38). The students of the sample fairly strongly believe: "technology helps teachers teach better" (M = 4.18; SD = 1.15); and "technology helps students learn better" (M = 4.28; SD = .95).

The fact that the students "read and send e-mail messages almost every day" (41.4% marked "strongly agree"; and 34.5% "agree") suggests that through e-mail students are able to contact each other with questions about assignments and collaborative work, strengthening communication and ties among classmates. The integration of the e-mail system into learning is very much a "student-led process"; the adoption of e-mail by students has transformed university cultures, as departments have used it as a channel for faculty-student contact (Breen, Lindsay, Jenkins, & Smith, 2001). As previously mentioned, in addition to the laptop computer, the e-mail system is making a significant difference in college students' study habits (Demb et al., 2004).

The results of the ANOVA analysis indicated that gender ($F(1, 172) = .275, p > .01$), ethnicity ($F(6,167) = .966, p > .01$), academic status ($F(4,169) = 2.506, p > .01$) and age ($F(5,168) = .594, p > .01$) were *not* statistically significant factors for the students of this sample (see Table 4). There were no differences in student perceptions of computer technology experiences (1) between females and males, (2) among different ethnic groups, (3) among various academic status groups, nor (4) among various age groups. The fact that none of these demographic variables are statistically significant strongly suggests that perceptions of computer technology experiences are different individually and are *not* influenced by demographic factors.

As Lim (2004) has noted, another implication for instructional practice is that technology-enhanced learning can empower students' self-directed, inquiry-based learning by increasing student involvement and responsibility for their own learning. As previously pointed out, the following five stages of the inquiry-based learning system should be clearly understood: Articulate own problems; design problem-solving strategies; explore resources for solving problems; provide solutions; and discuss the implications for further refinement. This learning system *will* definitely become ever more important in higher education in the digital age.

In the history of American higher education, people have commonly perceived professors differently: In the colonial period, the professor has failed as an instructor if a student has not learned; in the 19th century, the professor should help students develop the capacity to become independent learners; and in the 20th century, the professor should be less directive and act more as a facilitator for students' learning. In the 21st century, as Janicki, Schell, and Weinroth (2002) have noted, the role of the professor is shifting fundamentally from an *expert* dispensing knowledge (i.e., refers to professor as expert model, textbook as primary source and emphasis on product or outcome) to a *resource* or a *guide* (i.e., refers to professor as facilitator, variety of sources or media, and emphasis on process and experience). This shift accelerates "resource-based" teaching, which in turn "emphasizes the use of computers and software, encourages student and faculty contact, encourages cooperation among students, encourages active learning, gives prompt feedback, emphasizes time on task, communicates high expectations and respects diverse talents and ways of learning" (Matthews, 2000, p. 58).

Most participants of this survey were in the teacher education program. Upon completion of the general preparation component of their program, prospective teachers should meet the following National Educational Technology Standards for Teachers (ISTE, 2000):

- Technology operations and concepts (e.g., demonstrate continual growth in technology knowledge and skills to stay abreast of current and emerging technologies);
- Planning and designing learning environments and experiences (e.g., design developmentally appropriate learning opportunities that apply technology-enhanced instructional strategies to support the diverse needs of learners);
- Teaching, learning and the curriculum (e.g., use technology to support learner-centered strategies that address the diverse needs of students);
- Assessment and evaluation (e.g., use technology to collect and analyze data, and communicate findings to improve instructional practice and maximize student learning);
- Productivity and professional practice (e.g., use technology resources to engage in ongoing professional development and lifelong learning); and
- Social, ethical, legal and human issues (e.g., promote safe use of technology resources).

What is more, keeping up with current and emerging technologies, prospective teachers have to provide *technology-enhanced* instructional strategies as well as *learner-centered* strategies to improve teaching and maximize student learning, promoting *life-long learning*.

As this study has revealed, college students are very familiar with computer technology and its applications, confirming Sheard and Lynch's (2003) study that college students' affective responses to the Internet-based learning environments are often related to their familiarity with the learning environment, and their skills and confidence with technology.

Distance Education

The overall results of the descriptive analysis indicated that students' attitudes toward distance education were fairly positive (see Table 5). The results confirm Larson and Strehle's (2001) observation: "Technology holds the promise of bringing learning to students in individualized ways with the ability to frequently assess responses to their learning needs" (p. 30).

The participants, as seen in Table 3, are relatively "familiar with the concept of distance education" (M = 3.82; SD = 1.12) and recognize "a growing need for distance education" (M = 3.79; SD = 1.07). They would like to take a distance course "if it would help them graduate sooner" (M = 3.86; SD = 1.04), or "just for the new experience" (M = 3.83; SD = 1.04). They also believe: "distance education could help them go further in school" (M = 3.80; SD = 1.09).

The above five questions were combined as one variable, representing student attitudes toward distance education (the reliability coefficient alpha across the five questions was .925). The results of ANOVA indicated that gender ($F(1, 172) = 2.372$ $p > .01$), ethnicity ($F(6, 167) = .905, p > .01$), academic status ($F(4, 169) = 1.438, p > .01$) and age ($F(5, 168) = .663, p > .01$) were *not* statistically significant factors for this sample, supporting Peters' (n.d.) observa-

Table 5. Summary statistics for attitudes toward distance education

Questions	Strongly Agree	Agree	Not Sure	Disagree	Strongly Disagree
Q54. I am familiar with the concept and function of distance education	61 35.1%	49 28.2%	42 24.1%	16 9.2%	6 3.4%
Q55. I think there is a growing need for distance education in higher learning	58 33.3%	44 25.3%	55 31.6%	12 6.9%	5 2.9%
Q56. I would take a distance course if it would help me graduate sooner	58 33.3%	53 30.5%	48 27.6%	10 5.7%	5 2.9%
Q60. I believe that distance education could help me go further in school	56 32.2%	53 30.5%	50 28.7%	10 5.7%	5 2.9%
Q61. I would take a course via distance education just for the new experience	57 32.8%	52 29.9%	46 26.4%	12 6.9%	7 4.0%

tion that despite many variables, gender does not significantly affect student perceptions of distance learning. These five questions from the present study were too general, however. Future studies should replicate, for instance, Richardson's (2005) study, which focused on students' perceptions of academic quality and approaches to studying in distance education with the Open University in the United Kingdom (UK). In Richardson's investigation, both age and gender were associated with scores on "approach" items (specifically "deep approach," such as seeking meaning; "strategic approach," such as time management; and "surface approach," such as syllabus-boundness) but not to scores on course experience items, such as good teaching, clear goals and standards, appropriate workload, appropriate assessment and emphasis on independence. This finding by Richardson (2005) suggests that demographic characteristics and perceptions of the academic environment are individually salient but mutually independent influences on approaches to studying.

Students' Voices on Technology

The students of two graduate classes of educational research courses participated in developing a one-page essay about their perceptions of computers and IT based on four specific questions. Many of the participants were K-12 schoolteachers and administrators. The typical answers of the participants for each question are summarized next:

1. How will the new information tools change the process of education and learning?
    -   "Information technology has already changed the entire landscape of higher education."
    -   "One can utilize the computer and the Internet to conduct research online by accessing libraries and universities without stepping out the door."
    -   "Information today is at your fingertips. It is out there at your convenience."
    -   "Modern technologies allow students with disabilities to integrate in the educational system."
    -   "In addition to e-mail, chat rooms provide opportunities to learn more about each other."
    -   "The flow of information and interactions from the teacher to students, and among the students as well, can take place with ease."
    -   "Online courses do not require students to interact with the professor and classmates face to face. This may affect the quality of education, since it is not always easy to fully explain complex concepts via e-mail and other online resources."

2. How are you prepared for the challenges of the information age?
    -   "I will continue to develop the skills necessary to utilize new and emerging technologies."
    -   "I constantly seek new information by surfing the Internet and reading current journals."
    -   "I use technology to create worksheets, lesson plans, report cards, newsletters and teaching materials for my middle school students."

- "I am taking computer applications and computer programming courses."
- "Proper assimilation of both organizational and research information tools into the teaching and learning process will be the best way for teachers."
- "Adequate preparation for information age involves familiarization with information tools."

3. Do you possess the skills and motivation required for self-directed, life-long learning?

- "I embrace challenges, dynamic, information-rich society by keeping my senses active."
- "I am very motivated to learn things through formal and informal education."
- "I am always searching for new ideas and alternative perspectives."
- "I am an independent and autonomous learner who takes responsibilities for my learning."

4. How can professors help students to better prepare and improve information literacy skills?

- "By setting a good example. It is always exciting to take a course where the professor energizes enthusiasm for learning by introducing new electronic media into the curriculum."
- "By forcing students to use the various technologies as part of the course assignments."
- "By creating venues in which information literacy skills can be utilized in the curriculum."

In summary, many of the students that participated in this essay project pointed out that today both professors and students have unlimited resources to teach and learn, providing accommodation to a range of people with a variety of needs for learning. The participants are ready to assimilate *new* experiences that become available in education to support the learning process. They also realize that they must adopt the attitude of a risk-taker, remaining open-minded to innovative possibilities and *new* alternatives. Finally, students have emphasized that in the past decade, the number of distance-learning and computer-based degree programs have been tremendously explored. This has made it possible for individuals who previously would not have had an opportunity to participate in degree programs, especially in graduate studies.

Future Trends

The use of the Internet in higher education is still in the early stages, but has the huge potential to enhance at least three learning dimensions: (1) distance learning; (2) communication skills in collaborative learning; and (3) constructive learning (Cheung & Huang, 2005). Also emphasized by Cheung and Huang is that distance learning and constructive learning correlate positively with general learning and collaborative learning: "Internet use may support and enhance comprehensive learning activities for university students. ... Internet use may help students heighten their constructive learning by enhancing their constructive learning motive and strategy" (p. 247).

Advancements in online technologies facilitate a convergence of distance and campus-based learning, offering *new* opportunities for all students through better access to resources, increased interaction between faculty and students, and greater flexibility in place and time of instruction (Bennett & Lockyer, 2004). As repeatedly stated in this study, the transition to online teaching and learning presents *new* challenges as the roles and expectations of both faculty and students evolve. One such challenge is that of adapting student-centered approaches to the online environment, which requires the development of *new* skills and changes to the process of education and learning and teaching practice. In consideration of various instructional approaches discussed in this chapter, the following future trends can be highlighted:

Constructive learning. Constructivism is a "psychological-philosophical orientation that views the central problem in explaining cognitive development as one of understanding how the mind succeeds in constructing relationships among objects and events" (Lefrançois, 1999, p. 48). In other words, constructivism views that human beings are active learners who construct their knowledge on experience and on their efforts to give meaning to that experience (Frank, Lavy, & Elata, 2003). In the 1980s and 1990s, constructivism and multiculturalism as educational movements have combined roots in the philosophies of humanism, progressivism, existentialism and reconstructionism (McNergney & Herbert, 1998). In a study by Frank et al. (2003) on the perceptions of college students in a project-based learning course in engineering, students were required to construct their knowledge by means of active experience and learning by "trial and error." In this learning environment, students *do* construct their own knowledge through active learning and interaction with teammates and faculty based on a constructivist approach. Perhaps constructive learning (i.e., the teacher's role is seen as aiding students' construction of knowledge) will become an appropriate theory for practice in the information age.

Paperless learning. Unquestionably, future higher education courses will be increasingly paperless, and all course materials (such as syllabus, assignments and supplemental information) will be included on a course Web page so students can visit the Web site, which will become an "open door" to the classroom (Koepke, 2000). The Web site for each course will grow throughout the semester, including pages on a course's background and development, the syllabus and all assignments, student projects and guest speakers. Right now, professors try to create a sense of community in the classroom. As Koepke maintains, however, the Web site will creates a "sense of community" among class members; eventually, the Web site will become a great way to inform and engage students across the curriculum in what this class is doing.

Partnerships among librarians and faculty. Information overload and rapid technology changes are among the most significant challenges to all educational professions and librarians (Roldan & Wu, 2004). Nevertheless, little is known about the effectiveness of partnerships among librarians and faculty members that result in "context-based" library instruction. According to Roldan and Wu's report, a management information systems professor and a librarian collaborated to improve information literacy and library research skills. Through this collaboration effort, students developed greater confidence with course activities and increased students' use of high-quality resources available to them in the library, increasing estimates of the amounts of time they expect to spend on preparation of research papers.

Online partnership. The University of Guam launched an online partnership in 2005 with Gatlin Education Services to provide a variety of online courses to the community ("Online Courses," 2005). Unlike the traditional university setting, where there is a certain time a student can enroll and register for classes, students are able to enroll in this program and register whenever they would like. The courses are also self-paced. The courses are non-credit and designed to enhance skills for professional development and life-long learning purposes. Through this partnership, open and life-long learning will be facilitated as adult continuing education. Certainly, it will be a future trend in the outreach program.

Conclusion

Academic institutions of today are in transition, and much of the change is due to economic pressures from mounting costs and demands by the business world for graduates with the ability to function well in the information age (Palloff & Pratt, 1999). Schools and universities of today are also becoming more ethnically, culturally and racially diverse. It is generally viewed that technology should increasingly fit *all* learners and that teachers are challenged to provide meaningful, relevant and motivating educational interventions to *all* learners. The institutional, managerial, staff and student levels all need to be considered when encouraging the adoption of new technologies for learning. Universities must combine their traditional roles of extending the boundaries of knowledge and passing on that knowledge to the leaders of tomorrow with a commitment to make higher education available to *all* individuals through massively extended university outreach and the provision of opportunities for mass higher education through the use of media, educational technology, libraries and distance education (Dodds, 2003).

The survey reported in this chapter was conducted in a university, where the student population was no more than 3,000, in the western Pacific. As the study has indicated, overall, students' attitudes toward IT are highly positive. There are no differences in students' perceptions of computer technology experiences between females and males, among various ethnic groups, among various academic status groups and among various age groups. One practical explanation for the results may be that this university is situated in a small island and people go to the same high schools and, consequently, their patterns of thoughts, expectations and behaviors are merged through their academic and social interactions.

While professors are becoming more self-proficient using technology, they are not yet at the point of enhancing their pedagogy (Nisbet, 2005). However, Nisbet's emphasis is the following:

... research has become part of every professional role today and, in education, one task of professional or faculty development is to weave a research element into the expertise of their teaching, leading them to adopt at a personal level the self-questioning approach, which leads to reflection and understanding and from there into action. (p. 43)

As cited in the beginning of this chapter, the teacher-researcher movement has brought momentous changes in professional development for teaching professions. It is useful for faculty members to conceptualize a reciprocal relationship between teaching and research. Teaching gives direction and purpose to research endeavors while, simultaneously, research ensures that teaching is continuously updated and improved. It is true, indeed, that technology has enormous potential to enhance instructional practice, including pedagogical knowledge, beyond what traditional methods allow. By expanding the use of technology both in research and in teaching, faculty members can help university students use technology to enhance their learning.

This study was conducted based on three inquiries: (1) Are today's college students well prepared for the challenges of the information age? (2) Do students possess the skills and motivation required for self-directed, life-long learning? and (3) How can educators help students to better prepare and improve information literacy skills? It is fair to say that students of the current study sample are prepared for the challenges of the information age, and are motivated for self-directed, life-long learning. By maintaining and updating their Web site for the course, professors are able to demonstrate how to access Internet information from different sources, such as online databases and instantaneous communication with experts worldwide. This will help students find timely information for the course work and improve information literacy skills as well. Professors using the Web in the classroom demonstrate to students that their mastery of technology, knowledge and skills in teaching are up to date. In due course, professors have to learn how to create a Web page, download a graphic or even create an audio file, just as once they had to learn how to use the overhead projector or tape recorder (Ko & Rossen, 2004).

The questionnaire research reported in this chapter was a small, exploratory study conducted in the school of education at a university in the western Pacific. Future research is definitely required that is sampled in such a way as to ensure that the findings can be generalized to the entire student body of this university. Future research can be conducted with a different population sample and improvement of the research instrument. In this university, research on technology integration into teaching and learning is in its infancy. Research endeavors are very much needed so that reinforcement of faculty and student training, technical support for faculty and students, and classroom maintenance are recommended to administrators and policy makers to use technology for reshaping the diverse learning environment in higher education.

Postscript

Improving Reliability and Validity in Questionnaire Research

Survey questionnaires are a practical method for obtaining many types of information from people and, in many circumstances, are the most economical method. A common misconception is that it is easy to design and conduct a survey questionnaire. However, as Litwin (1995) has noted: "There are good surveys and bad ones ... good surveys yield critical information and provide important windows into the heart of the topic of interest" (p. 1).

To improve future studies, it is necessary to discuss the limitations of the questionnaire reported here. First, although the instrument was reviewed by other researchers, it might still not have been as valid (Note: Validity is the extent to which differences found with a measuring tool reflect true differences among those being tested) and as reliable (Note: reliability is a measure that is reliable to the degree that it supplies consistent results) as standardized or published instruments. To achieve reliability, test-retest reliability should be applied (having the same respondents complete a survey at two different points in time). Or alternate-form reliability should be performed using differently worded items or changing the order of items to measure the same attribute. These tests are useful, even though in practice their usefulness can be limited by the fact that people might "become familiar with the items and simply answer based on their memory of what they answered the last time" (Litwin, 1995, p. 13). Second, a 7-point scale might have yielded more accurate results than the 5-point scale used, because the mean scores suggested that there was no clear distinction regarding the importance of each item (Table 3).

Finally, a cover letter, an essential part of any questionnaire, introduces individuals to the purpose and nature of the questionnaire and motivates a response (Wiersma, 2000). In regard to recipients completing the questionnaire in an accurate and timely manner, Wiersma's following observations are useful: "... the purpose of the questionnaire is clearly stated, confidentiality is assured, a deadline is given for the return of the questionnaire and appreciation for completing the questionnaire is expressed" (p. 173). Absolutely, without respondents, questionnaire analysis is impossible and the cover letter is the passage to the successful questionnaire research.

Note

The author is grateful to Mark C. Goniwiecha at the University of Guam for his thoughtful suggestions on earlier drafts of this chapter.

References

Agre, P. E. (1999). Information technology in higher education: The global academic village and intellectual standardization. *On the Horizon, 7*(5), 8-11.

Beller, M. (1998). The crossroads between lifelong learning and information technology. *JCMC, 4*(2). Retrieved April 24, 2005, from www.ascusc.org/jcmc/vol4/issue2/beller. html

Bennett, S., & Lockyer, L. (2004). Becoming an online teacher: Adapting to changed environment for teaching and learning in higher education. *Educational Media International, 41*(3), 231-244.

Breen, R., Lindsay, R., Jenkins, A., & Smith, P. (2001). The role of information and communication technologies in a university-learning environment. *Studies in Higher Education, 26*(1), 95-114.

Burge, E. (1998). Gender in distance education. In C.C. Gibson (Ed.), *Distance learners in higher education* (pp. 25-45). Madison: Atwood.

Chen, P. Y., & Krauss, A. D. (2004). Reliability. In M. S. Lewis-Beck, A. Bryman, & T. F. Liao (Eds.), *The SAGE encyclopedia of social science research methods* (pp. 952-956). Thousand Oaks, CA: Sage.

Cheung, W., & Huang, W. (2005). Proposing a framework to assess Internet usage in university education: An empirical investigation from a student's perspective. *British Journal of Educational Technology, 36*(2), 237-253.

Delamarter, S. (2005). Theological educators, technology, and path ahead. *Teaching Theology and Religion, 8*(1), 51-55.

Demb, A., Erickson, D., & Hawkins-Wilding, S. (2004). The laptop computer alternative: Student reactions and strategic implications. *Computers & Education, 43*, 383-401.

Dodds, T. (2003). *Universities, adult basic education, open and lifelong learning and new technology*. Retrieved April 24, 2005, from www.eldis.org/static/DOC13384.htm

Eynon, R. (2005). The use of the lute met in higher education: Academics' experiences of using ICTs for teaching and learning. *Association of Special Libraries and Information Bureau Proceedings, 57*(2), 168-180.

Fink, A. (1995a). *The survey handbook*. Thousand Oaks, CA: Sage.

Fink, A. (1995b). *How to design surveys*. Thousand Oaks, CA: Sage.

Frank, M., Lavy, I., & Elata, D. (2003). Implementing the project-based learning approach in an academic engineering course. *International Journal of Technology and Design Education, 13*, 273-288.

Friesen, N., & Anderson, T. (2004). Interaction for lifelong learning. *British Educational Communications and Technology, 36*(6), 679-687.

Gefen, D., & Straub, D.W. (1997). Gender differences in the perception and use of e-mail: An extension to the technology acceptance model. *MIS Quarterly, 21*(4), 389-400.

Ila Parasnis, V. J. (2005). Deaf college students' attitudes toward racial/ethnic diversity, campus climate, and role models. *American Annals of the Deaf, 150*(1), 47-58.

Inoue, Y. (1999-2000). The university student's preference for learning by computer-assisted instruction. *Journal of Educational Technology Systems, 28*(3), 277-285.

International Society for Technology in Education (ISTE). (2000). National educational technology standards for teachers (brochure). Author.

Janicki, T. N., Schell, G. P., & Weinroth, J. (2002). Developing of a model for computer supported learning systems. *International Journal of Educational Technology, 3*(1). Retrieved July 5, 2005, from www.outreach.uiuc.edu/ijet/v3n1/janicki/index.html

Ko, S., & Rossen, S. (2004). *Teaching online: A practical guide.* New York: Houghton Mifflin.

Koepke, M. L. (2000). Portfolio development: Multimedia presentations for designers. In D. G. Brown (Ed.), *Teaching with technology* (pp. 178-182). Boston: Anker.

Kompf, M. (2005). Information and communications technology and the seduction of knowledge, teaching, and learning: What lies ahead for education? *Curriculum Inquiry, 35*(2), 213-233.

Koohang, A. (2004). Students' perceptions toward the use of the digital library in weekly Web-based distance learning assignments portion of a hybrid programme. *British Journal of Educational Technology, 35*(5), 617-626.

Larson, R. C., & Strehle, G. P. (2001). Edu-tech: What's a president to do? In P.S. Goodman (Ed.), *Technology enhanced learning* (pp. 21-59). Mahwah, NJ: Lawrence Erlbaum.

Lefrançois, G. R. (1999). *The lifespan.* Belmont: Wadsworth.

Lim, B-R. (2004). Challenges and issues in designing inquiry on the Web. *British Educational Communications and Technology, 35*(5), 627-643.

Litwin, M. S. (1995). *How to measure survey reliability and validity.* Thousand Oaks, CA: Sage.

Madsen, N. (2004, Winter). Diversity in music education. *Illinois Music Educators,* 50-51.

Matthews, G. E. (2000). Circuit simulation software in electronics courses. In D. G. Brown (Ed.), *Teaching with technology* (pp. 55-62). Boston: Anker.

McNergney, R. F., & Herbert, J. M. (1998). *Foundations of education.* Needham Heights, MA: Allyn & Bacon.

Metzger, M. J., Flanagin, A. J., & Zwarun, L. (2003). College student Web use, perceptions of information credibility, and verification behavior. *Computers & Education, 41*(3), 271-290.

Moore, D. (1999). School + technology = changes. *School Planning & Management, 38*(3), 11.

Nisbet, J. (2005). What is educational research? Changing perspectives through the 20th century. *Research Papers in Education, 20*(1), 25-44.

Online courses at UOG offer enhanced education. (2005, May 16). *Triton's Call (University of Guam Campus Newspaper), 23*(4), 2.

Palloff, R. M., & Pratt, K. (1999). *Building learning communities in cyberspace.* San Francisco: Jossey-Bass.

Patten, M. L. (2001). *Questionnaire research.* Los Angeles, CA: Pyrczak.

Peters, L. (n.d.). *Student perceptions of online learning.* Retrieved June 18, 2005, from www.collegedegreeguide.com/articles-fr/perceptions.htm

Richardson, J. T. E. (2005). Students' perceptions of academic quality and approaches to studying in distance education. *British Educational Research Journal, 31*(1), 7-27.

Roldan, M., & Wu, Y. D. (2004, July/August). Building context-based library instruction. *Journal of Education for Business*, 323-327.

Sheard, J., & Lynch, J. (2003). Accommodating learner diversity in Web-based learning environments: Imperatives for future developments. *International Journal of Computer Processing of Oriental Languages, 16*(4), 243-260.

Sofia, Z. (1998). The mythic machine: Gendered irrationalities and computer culture. In H. Bromley & W. Apple (Eds.), *Education/technology/power* (pp. 29-51). State University of New York Press.

Stafford, T. F. (2005). Understanding motivations for Internet use in distance education. *IEEE Transactions on Education, 48*(2), 301-306.

Thompson, M. M. (1998). Distance learners in higher education. In C. C. Gibson (Ed.), *Distance learners in higher education* (pp. 9-24). Madison: Atwood.

Van Soest, D., Canon, R., & Grant, D. (2000). Using an interactive website to educate about cultural diversity and societal oppression. *Journal of Social Work Education, 36*(3), 463-479.

Wiersma, W. (2000). *Research methods in education*. Needham Heights, MA: Allyn & Bacon.

Williams, M. L., Paprock, K., & Covington, B. (1999). *Distance learning*. Thousand Oaks, CA: Sage.

Chapter VIII

Internet Overuse on College Campuses:
A Survey and Analysis of Current Trends

Mary Jane Miller, University of Guam, USA

Abstract

The changes wrought in the last 10 years alone are sufficiently awesome to astound and confuse any Rip Van Winkle who may have managed to sleep through the decade. As with all man-made marvels, however, along with the much touted fabulous benefits and glittering accomplishments, it seems there always exist undesirable side effects. One side effect of the technological revolution with the potential to cause harm is an inclination by some people, most notably students in higher education, for excessive and compulsive Internet use. Often called Internet addiction, this disorder is particularly prevalent on the campuses of colleges and universities, and for some students, it has the potential to be as destructive as excessive use of alcohol, tobacco or drugs. This chapter talks about Internet overuse on college campuses in general and discusses a survey of 305 University of Guam students regarding their Internet use.

Introduction

Modern technology has quite conspicuously ushered us into the 21st century with a roar of rocket engines, the lilt of synthesized music, the spark of pacemakers and the unmistakable click, click, click of a million keyboards. Computers have piloted our space craft through the distant cosmos and sent back incredible photographs of planetary features heretofore unknown to man. They have guided our robotic explorations of alien planets and gathered particles of dust from a passing comet. Computers have helped us explore the tiniest realms of the known universe, providing solutions to outlandishly long, complicated and difficult mathematical models of atomic structure. It was the power of computers that allowed us to unravel the sequence of the human genome and that gives us functional models of exceedingly complex processes, such as global climate trends and world economies.

From the rarified atmosphere of exotic sciences to the most basic chores of daily life, computers are increasingly an indispensable tool, not a mere luxury. Computerized systems are used to schedule a dentist's appointment, to regulate the traffic lights in busy intersections, to organize the shipping and delivery of international packages, to access medical history, to obtain a copy of high school transcripts or to remind you to pick up bread on the way home from work. Perhaps the most vital and indispensable use of computers, however, is the universal access it gives to enormous stores of information and the easy communication that e-mail allows with formerly impossible-to-reach researchers, authors, movie stars, business leaders, politicians, scientists, personal physician and even far-away family and friends. There is little doubt that technology is increasingly changing the face and pace of American life.

Background

The pattern is well established that computer usage, most significantly uses of the Internet and the World Wide Web, grow in variety, importance and numbers in the Western world every day. But the impact of technology is felt around the world, including here on our small Pacific island of Guam. A recent study by Miniwatts International (2005) shows that there are more than 872 million Internet users in the world. This is a 146.9% growth in Internet use during 2000-2005. Of this 872 million, nearly 16-1/2 million Internet users live in Oceania. This is a 113.5% increase during the same time span. With a population of 165, 575, Internet use in Guam has increased enormously in the last few years. It has grown by a nearly unbelievable 900% since 2000 (Miniwatts International, 2005).

A recent issue of *Popular Science* magazine talks about some of the technological marvels currently under development for kitchens in tomorrow's homes. Can you imagine calling your refrigerator on your cell phone to see if you have milk? How about asking your trash compactor to generate a shopping list for you based on the items discarded in the past week (Wardell, 2004). There are few who debate the benefits that computers and computerization have had on every facet of modern life. Rather, the debate centers on the real quality of life that all this technology has brought to the average person: you, me, members of the family next door and our children. Like every other frontier or man-made marvel, all these technological capabilities have the potential for miraculous benefits, but also possess the potential for a darker side. The lure of virtual worlds; the thrill of becoming invincible in a video killing game; winning scads of money from nameless, faceless opponents; exploring a shopping center full of brand-name products and well-known stores with only a few keystrokes; or chatting for hours on end with virtual strangers who think you are successful, brilliant, charming and witty, perhaps even an ideal mate, can seem quite compelling and very much worth the investment of an enormous amount of time and care. A decade ago, few people spent the majority of their leisure time on the computer other than those who were professionals in the technology industry. Today, however, surfing the Web has become an activity as acceptable, sometimes as sociable, and often as marketable as bar hopping, beach parties and going to movies. As the World Wide Web and similar Internet hosts have become an integral part of everyday life, some mental health professionals have noted that a percentage of people using the Web do so in a compulsive and out-of-control manner (Internet Addiction, 2004).

Using the Internet on Today's College Campuses

Given the fact that Internet use is a vital part of university life that is not going to diminish in the near future, it is worthwhile looking at how university students say they are spending most of their Internet hours. One study reported in 2004 that in addition to academic and research pursuits, the online activities that university students most commonly engage in are:

- *Exchanging e-mails with friends and family;*
- *Scanning newsgroups to stay current with the latest information about favorite movies, TV shows and bands;*
- *Engaging in online chat groups to vent frustrations, develop friendships, romances or to experiment with different personal;*
- *Engaging in ongoing online games that seem to never end where the player is rewarded for accumulated online time;*
- *Downloading pornographic photos and other forms of cyberporn; and*
- *Endlessly surfing Web pages on any topic that catches their eye.* (Webb, 2004)

It may seem excessive to suggest that the use of a positive, dynamic force such as the Internet can become a negative, debilitating factor in some people's lives, but the fact is that just as the use of alcohol, food, prescription medications or the purchase of material things can become excessive and compulsive, so too can an interest in and preoccupation with using the Internet (Webb, 2004). Although the overuse of the Internet can occur in any setting, among any population and within all ages, races, genders and socio-economic groups, college campuses appear to be a breeding ground for Internet abuse. Many students find themselves spending longer and longer amounts of time online. The Internet is a near indispensable resource tool for students seeking to find information; communicate with friends, family and professionals; and as a means of entertainment. Some students, however, find that they begin to use the Internet to fill all their time, avoid other life responsibilities or neglect normal social interactions. Internet use then may become detrimental to their studies, work and social lives as they grow increasingly dependent on their Internet time and Internet friends (Webb, 2004).

One of the great benefits of Internet use is its ability to connect people nationally and internationality, and Internet abuse is clearly not just a Western phenomenon. A study by Chen (2004) of National Taiwan University reports on what he calls pathological Internet use among college students in Taiwan. His results show that of 1,336 students surveyed, 9.7% self reported that they are likely addicted to the Internet. A large study of Internet use among various races in the Unites States (U.S.) by Korgen, Odell and Schumacher (2001) showed that there was some disparity between the races and the amount of Internet use, with African Americans tending to use it the least and Caucasians and Asians the most. This difference in Internet use would have a corresponding effect on instances of Internet abuse. The study indicated that the primary reason for the difference in Internet use was the presence or absence of a computer in the home (2001).

A quote by a college freshman at Duke University in a research study by John Lubans (1999) captures the essence of how important the Internet has become to campus life in the last decade:

As a college student, I can hardly remember life before I was born into the world of e-mail. I use electronic mail and the World Wide Web to communicate with family and friends ...to ask questions of professors, to gather information about current events and to learn about topics ranging from Shakespeare to strawberry Pop Tarts. (p. 1)

This quote becomes particularly telling when it is noted that it was written back in 1997, a half a dozen lifetimes ago in technology years. Since then, online information seeking and Internet use have proliferated at an extraordinary rate.

Recent research has begun to explore more thoroughly the phenomenon of excessive and obsessive Internet use, often referred to as Internet addiction, Internet dependence or pathological Internet computer use. Briggs (2001) writes of a disorder he terms Internet behavior dependence (IBD), defining it as a form of Internet addiction. He says IBD is a correctable condition used to compensate for lack of satisfaction in other areas of life (2001). An increasing number of research studies explore the complex interactions between the Internet, society and behavior, and many of them focus primarily on university student Internet use.

Anderson (2000) studied 1,300 college students from eight institutions of higher education. The students were surveyed about their Internet use and how it affects their social and academic lives. This study supports the view that college students may be particularly susceptible to problems related to Internet use, specifically excessive Internet use. The results report that the average length of daily Internet use is 100 minutes per day. However, there was a small group of students who reported more than 400 minutes per day of Internet use, and approximately 10% of the Internet-using students said they have used the Internet to the degree that they felt their usage meets criteria similar to those identifying other forms of addiction (2000). "While in all areas, the respondents did not indicate they felt much negative impact due to their Internet use, the high-use group did report more negative consequences than the low-use group" (Anderson, 2000, p. 6). Indeed, excessive Internet use has become a concern at colleges and universities across the country. "College officials are increasingly concerned about the growing number of students who are unable to control the amount of time they spend with their computers. These students are being called 'Internet Vampires,' because they emerge from computer labs at dawn" (DeLoughtry, 1996, p. 3).

Internet Addiction

Whether or not one agrees with the terminology, the phenomenon of compulsive Internet use has been termed Internet addiction. This is based on its similarity, at least superficially, to commonly acknowledged addictions, such as smoking, drinking and gambling. Some mental health professionals and research psychologists have called Internet addiction an actual psychological disorder, but at this time there seems to be no overall consensus of opinion about the character of Internet addiction or the appropriateness of the name (Internet Addiction, 2004).

Although no one disputes the fact that some people do use the Internet compulsively, some researchers disagree with the use of the term "Internet addiction," because they contend that people are not addicted to the Internet itself; rather, they are addicted to a particular content contained within the Internet, such as shopping, chatting, gambling or even pornography (Holmes, 1997). Possibly they liken the Internet to a vehicle of delivery, such as the syringe of a heroin addict, but maintain that the content of the Web, like the content of the syringe, is where the addiction lies. Psychologist Kimberly S. Young (1998) compares Internet addiction to other pathological conditions, addictions such as pathological gambling. She makes the comparison because they both involve lack of impulse control but neither involves use of an intoxicant (Stonecypher, 2001). Conversely, in his paper, *Internet Addiction Guide*, Grohol (1999) states:

Do some people have problems with spending too much time online? Sure they do. Some people also spend too much time reading, watching television and working, and ignore family, friendships and social activities. But do we have TV addiction disorder, book addiction and work addiction being suggested as legitimate mental disorders in the same category as schizophrenia and depression? I think not. ... What most people online who think they are addicted are probably suffering from is the desire to not want to deal with other problems in their lives. (p. 2)

In a true addiction, a person becomes so compulsively dependent upon a particular kind of stimulation that obtaining a steady supply of that stimulation becomes the central focus, even the entire focus, of his or her life. An addicted person will increasingly neglect work duties, relationships and ultimately even his or her own health in the overwhelming need to remain stimulated. In some cases with alcohol or drug addiction, a phenomenon known as "tolerance" occurs. Tolerance means that more and more stimulation is required to produce the same pleasurable effect. Also in a true addiction, a related phenomenon called "withdrawal" can occur. During withdrawal, an addict who has come to depend upon a particular source of stimulation will experience enormously unpleasant and even potentially fatal reactions when he goes without it.

"Sources of addictive stimulation can be chemical, as with alcohol, cocaine, nicotine and heroine; sensual, as in sex; or even informational, as in gambling or workaholism" (Internet Addiction, 2004, p. 2). What all these potential sources of addiction have in common is that they produce a strong reaction in the person using them. The more the user indulges in his stimulation of choice, the greater the compulsion to seek out the source of that stimulation on a regular, usually increasingly frequent basis. While many people like to smoke or gamble or engage in sexual relations or drink alcoholic beverages because of the enjoyment they draw from those activities, it is certainly true that not everyone who does so is an addict. This is also true of Internet abuse. Many people indulge in excessive use from time to time and are neither Internet addicts nor pathological users. The term "addiction" only applies when someone's need for a particular stimulation, in this case a need to use the Internet, gets to the point where it begins to interfere with his or her ability to function normally at school or at work or to maintain personal relationships. Dr. John Grohol, who does not appear to be a proponent of the term "Internet addiction," has spent a considerable amount of time studying compulsive Internet use. He says the type of useful information that would make it easier to specifically define disorders related to Internet use and abuse is missing. According to Grohol, this is primarily because of flaws in the first investigative surveys that do not substantiate causal relationships between specific behaviors and their perceived causes (1999).

It seems appropriate that many researchers are using the same criteria that are applied to well-accepted addictions to define Internet addiction and to determine its presence or absence in an individual. The American Psychiatric Association (APA) has established seven criteria to assist with the determination of whether a person may be suffering from some form of an addiction. In her paper, *Internet Addiction Disorder: Causes, Symptoms and Consequences*, Ferris (1998) describes these seven criteria in detail. She applies the seven criteria suggested by APA for determining an addiction to the problem of excessive Internet use. The application of the seven criteria includes the following:

1. Tolerance: This refers to the need for ever-increasing amounts of time on the Internet to achieve satisfaction or to significantly diminish effect with continued use of the same amount of time on the Internet.

2. Two or more withdrawal symptoms developing within days to 1 month after reduction of Internet use or cessation of Internet use, and these must cause distress or impair social, personal or occupational functioning. These include: psychomotor agitation, such as trembling or tremors; anxiety; obsessive thinking about what is happening on the Internet; fantasies or dreams about the Internet; voluntary or involuntary typing movements of the fingers.

3. Use of the Internet is engaged in to relieve or to avoid withdrawal symptoms.

4. The Internet is often accessed more often, or for longer periods of time than was intended.

5. A significant amount of time is spent in activities related to Internet use; for instance, reading books about the Internet, trying out new World Wide Web browsers, researching Internet vendors.

6. Important social, occupational or recreational activities are given up or reduced because of Internet use.

7.   The individual risks the loss of significant relationship, job, educational or career opportunity because of excessive use of the Internet.

If three or more of the above criteria are present at any time during a 12-month period, then a diagnosis of Internet addiction may be considered.

Recent research has identified other characteristics of addiction, as well. One characteristic is a feeling of restlessness or irritability when attempting to cut down on the amount of Internet use or stop its use altogether. An additional characteristic is that the Internet is used in an effort to escape problems or relieve feelings of helplessness, guilt, anxiety or depression. A third characteristic, in addition to those listed by APA, is exhibited when an Internet user lies to family members or friends in an effort to hide the amount of time spent online or about the extent of involvement with the Web. And a final characteristic is noted when an Internet user continues to return to a particular site in spite of excessive fees (Egger & Rauterberg, 1996).

Internet Use and Overuse on College Campuses

Why do university students seem to be vulnerable to excessive Internet use? More than one researcher has suggested it is partially because of the unlimited availability of the Internet in many computer labs and dorm rooms. They also suggest that a sense of security arising from the anonymity of the Internet also makes it attractive to users on college campuses (Anderson, 2000). Quoting from Young in her 2001 paper, one sophomore physics student stated, "Staying up late at night on the Internet is the best time I have at school. After a while, it was all I wanted to do, all I thought about. It was all so fascinating" (p. 2). This young student was formerly an outstanding math and science scholar who allowed her grades to plummet before she recognized that her obsessive Internet use had seriously jeopardized her career ambitions.

Young has compiled a list of several factors that seem to contribute to excessive Internet use among college and university students. These factors include:

1.   **Free and unlimited Internet access:** It is common when freshmen register that one of the things they receive is a free, personal e-mail account at the university. They often have no further online fees to pay and sometimes have no limits on their online time. In some cases, computer labs are open 24 hours a day.

2.   **Huge blocks of unstructured time:** Most college students attend classes for 12 to 16 hours per week. The rest of the time is for studying, working, socializing or exploring their new environment. Some students forget all about these activities and concentrate on just one thing: using the Internet.

3.   **Newly experienced freedom from parental control:** Many college students are away from home and parental supervision for the first time. Traditionally, students have exercised their new-found freedom by doing, thinking, eating and drinking things their parents would not approve of. Today, students often utilize their free time by hanging out in cyberspace with no parent to complain about the amount of time they

spend online, excessive service fees, lack of social time with the family or refusal to do chores.

4. **No monitoring or censoring of what they say or do online:** At home, most parents were on the watch for appropriate Internet use. At work, bosses will be watchful of employees, but in a university computer lab, monitors are usually student volunteers who are there to help with problems, not to tell students what they can and cannot do.

5. **Full encouragement from faculty and administrators:** Most school administrators and faculty want the students to make full use of the Internet's vast resources. Many instructors give assignments that require Internet research, and individual courses often have their own Web sites. E-mail is frequently considered the best way to communicate with a professor.

6. **Adolescent training in similar activities:** Most college freshmen will enter the university having spent years staring at video game terminals, surfing the channels on cable TV, programming movies or re-runs on the home theater screen or closing out the world around them with MP3 players. PowerPoint presentations by students are an expected part of many high school courses. College students are well prepared to slip into aimless Web surfing, even if they had never done so in high school.

7. **The desire to escape college stressors:** Many university students are under heavy pressure to make high grades, fulfill personal or parental expectations and, after graduation, to succeed in spite of fierce competition for good jobs. The Internet makes it easier for students to do their necessary course work as quickly and efficiently as possible. However, some students, rather than use the Internet productively, turn to their Internet friends to hide from their feelings of inadequacy, fear, anxiety and depression.

8. **Social intimidation and alienation:** The population on some university campuses is well more than 30,000 students. On any campus, especially on such large ones, students can easily feel lost in the crowd. Sometimes university cliques and in-crowds are even harder to penetrate than those in high school. But when students reach out to join the faceless community of the Internet, they find that with little effort they can be popular with new friends from all over the U.S., Europe, Asia and sometimes even South America. This leaves little incentive to risk personal confrontation for acceptance when acceptance is readily available on the Internet.

9. **A higher legal drinking age:** With the drinking age at 21, fewer undergraduate college students can socialize in bars or openly drink alcohol. What can you do on a dateless Saturday night? The Internet is always open; no ID required and no closing hour. Internet use can stealthily segue its way into the position of substitute drug of choice.

Warning Signs for Students

Many higher education students are rightfully quick to point out their belief that Internet use has greatly enhanced their academic performance, ability to communicate and overall educational experience. They use search engines to research topics for assignments and projects, and to access materials from online libraries. They use e-mail to keep in touch with study groups, friends, classmates, family and professors. For most college students, the Internet is a useful and powerful tool, one that has greatly enhanced their ability to gather information, to communicate and work with group members and friends. The Internet also provides an almost unlimited variety of stimulating and affordable entertainment resources, as well.

How is a student to know when he or she has crossed the boundary of what may be considered normal Internet use and slipped into the realm of Internet addiction? Nicola Webb, a clinical psychologist at Edith Cowan University, suggests that if a student is concerned about the possibility of suffering from Internet addiction, an honest appraisal of several factors could help in the determination. Webb suggests that a student may be addicted to use of the Internet if he or she can relate to most of the following signs:

- *Uses the Internet as a way of escaping from problems or feelings of helplessness;*
- *Uses the Internet to relieve feelings of depression, anxiety, guilt;*
- *Has jeopardized or lost a significant relationship, job, educational or career opportunity because of Internet overuse;*
- *Often thinks about previous online activities and is anticipating the next online session;*
- *Feels restless, moody, depressed or irritable when attempting to cut down or stop Internet use—may get "cybershakes"; and*
- *Frequently stays online longer than intended or lies about Internet usage.* (p. 4)

Normal Internet Use

There are approximately 14,500,000 students in institutions of higher learning across the U.S., and the demographic profile of traditional college students has changed little over the past decade, with slightly more women than men enrolled in college (Jones, 2002). However, one characteristic that sets apart today's university students from past generations is their degree of familiarity with the Internet. Most college students today were likely to have been introduced to the computer at an early age. Many have little or no recollection of a world without computers, e-mail and the World Wide Web. The great majority of college students today own their own computer and more students than not use at least two e-mail addresses (Jones, 2002).

A 2002 joint study by 360 Youth and Harris Interactive Market Research found that 92% of college students own a personal computer. The study also said that 93% of college students in 2002 had access to the Internet, making them the most connected segment of the nation's population (Torabi, 2003). The percentage of students who possess personal computers and who daily access the Internet could only have increased since 2002.

In a study of Internet usage among college students, Steve Jones and his team of researchers analyzed surveys from 2,054 respondents attending 27 diverse public and private 2- and 4-year colleges and universities. The Jones study, *The Internet Goes to College*, found that college students seem to find the Internet a very useful tool, and most believe that it has a positive impact on their overall educational experience and academic performance. The majority of the students surveyed (89%) expressed a positive attitude about the Internet as well as its communication tools. Most of the students reported that their Internet time was generally split between academic and social uses, and indicated that they found it enjoyable and useful for both purposes. In addition, the study gives the following partial summary of its findings:

- 20% of college students began using the computer between the ages of 5 and 8. By the time they were 16 to 18 years old, the Internet was a commonplace item.

- 86% of college students have gone online, compared with 59% of the general population.

- 72% of college students frequently look for e-mail, at least once per day.

- 49% began using the Internet in college, while 47% began using it at home before college.

- 78% of college Internet users say that at one time or another they have gone online just to browse for fun.

- 60% of college Internet users say they have ever downloaded music files.

- On a typical day, 26% of college Internet users utilize instant messenger.

Table 1. Responses to survey of UOG student Internet use

Less than 1 hour	1.0 -1.9 hours	2.0-2.9 hours	3.0-3.9 hours	4 or more hours	Total responses
1. About how many hours per day do you spend online?					
41	92	77	35	60	305
13.4%	30.2%	25.2%	11.5%	19.7%	100%
2. About how many hours per day do you spend playing computer games?					
197	47	31	13	17	305
64.5%	15.4%	10.2%	4.3%	5.6%	100%
3. On average, how many of your on-ine hours are for school or work?					
57	107	69	37	35	305
18.7%	35.1%	22.6%	12.1%	11.5%	100%

Internet Use at the University of Guam

Increasing awareness of the apparently widespread existence of Internet abuse and even pathological Internet use among university students has led to an examination of the way students at the University of Guam (UOG) use their Internet time. A survey was administered to 343 students in the College of Professional Studies, the College of Natural and Applied Sciences and the College of Language and Social Sciences at UOG during the spring and summer terms of 2005 to determine how much time an average student spends using the Internet and to ascertain whether Internet use for research, communication or entertainment purposes has affected the students' academic and social lives. After discarding 38 surveys for various reasons, 305 surveys were tabulated and the results are shown in Table 1, with analysis and discussion following each section of the survey.

Questions one, two and three of the survey address the amount of time that the university students spend online for academic or entertainment purposes. It should be noted that the surveys were administered to students who were enrolled in university classes, so Internet use for research and scholarly purposes was likely to be at a high point.

Student responses to questions one, two and three show that:

- Most of the UOG students (55.4%) average 1 or 2 hours per day using the Internet;
- 31.2% reported spending 3 or more hours per day on the Internet and, of these, 19.7% indicate that they use the Internet for 4 or more hours;
- Only 13.4% average using the Internet less than 1 hour every day;
- Although most UOG students (55.4%) replied that they spend 1 to 2 hours each day using the Internet, 18.7% said that less than an hour of this time is spent on academics;
- A total of 46.2% report they spend 2 or more hours per day working on academic or work related activities; and
- The majority of UOG students (64.5%) state that they spend less than 1 hour per day playing computer games or never play them at all.

Of all the UOG students surveyed, 9.9% report that they spend at least 3 hours per day playing computer games, whereas 64.5% say they spend less than 1 hour per day playing games or never play at all.

While 19.7% of the UOG students surveyed report that they spend 4 or more hours per day on the Internet, the portion of these students who say they are doing so for work or academics is 11.5%, leaving 8.2% of the respondents using the Internet 4 or more hours per day for other purposes, such as shopping, chatting and gaming. Comparing the 8.2% reported by UOG students to the Jones (2002) study of universities across the U.S., where about 10% of the college students said they use the Internet primarily for entertainment, UOG seems slightly less than average in student reported use of computer time for entertainment purposes.

Questions 7 through 11 of the survey address how Internet use has impacted the students socially and academically.

Table 2. Responses to survey of UOG student Internet use

Yes	No				Total Responses
8. Do you feel guilty when you have spent more time online than you intended to?					
87	218				305
28.5%	71.5%				100%
9. Does your online use ever prevent you from getting seven hours of sleep a night?					
138	167				305
45.2%	54.8%				100%
10. Do you sometimes miss out on social or recreational activities because of the time you spend online?					
49	256				305
16.0%	84.0%				100%
11. Is your academic work affected because of the time you spend online?					
73	232				305
23.9%	76.1%				100%

- The majority of UOG students, 49.5%, report that they rarely or occasionally consume meals or snacks at their computer terminals.
- 16.4% said they never consume meals or snacks at their computer terminals, while 16.7% do so very often. Some even commented, "all the time."
- The response with the highest percentage of students, 31.1%, indicates that students occasionally (about twice in 2 weeks) have meals or snacks at their computers.
- 28.5% of the students surveyed said they feel guilty when they spend more time than they intended to on the Internet, with 71.5% reporting no guilt for the extra time investment. Frequently, a response indicating no guilt felt was accompanied by an explanation that the extra Internet use was related to school work.
- 45.2% of students reported that their Internet use sometimes interferes with their ability to get 7 hours of sleep per night, while 54.8% said that this never happens.
- 16% of student respondents stated that they sometimes miss out on social events because of their Internet use. This was often explained as necessary to complete homework assignments or school projects, but occasionally because the user became so engrossed in the Internet activities he or she did not want to leave.

- 84% of the students state that they never miss out on social engagements because of their Internet use, commenting that family and friends come first.

- 23.9% of the responses indicated that the students' academic work was affected by their Internet usage. A number of student comments indicated their belief that the impact of the Internet on their overall academic performance was positive and that their grades had improved as a result. A few students reported that Internet use had adversely affected their academic performance, because time spent online interfered with their ability to complete assignments and study for tests.

Overall, the results of this survey indicate that Internet use at UOG for the most part is healthy and beneficial, similar to Internet use on other college campuses. However, as is also the case elsewhere, there is that small element of the surveyed population whose responses indicate their Internet use is great enough and compulsive enough to suggest they are at risk of becoming victims of Internet addiction.

What is a Student to Do?

With more than half of all college students reporting that their instructors require the use of Internet sources in their assignments and 73% of students saying that they prefer to use the Internet over going to the library to do research (Jones, 2002), it becomes quite impossible for university students to avoid the Internet completely. In truth, refraining from Internet use altogether would certainly be counterproductive for a college or university student in this day and age. Moreover, evaluating Internet abuse based primarily on the number of hours spent using it and whether or not it interferes with academics and social activities may not be in-depth enough to give an entirely accurate picture. It is, however, a first step in identifying a pool of candidates within which those who do exhibit symptoms of the compulsive, obsessive and life-disrupting nature of an addiction disorder may be found.

Normal users of Internet services, no matter how many hours they spend on the Internet, do not *need* to get online and they do not neglect their friends, families, studies or jobs in order to do so. The characteristics of pathological Internet use from Webb (2004) stated earlier could help researchers, medical personnel, parents or students themselves identify when Internet use has gone beyond the realm of normal and appropriate work, academics or entertainment applications and may become problematic.

Colleges and Universities Respond

The issue of Internet abuse can be a very touchy one with college administrators, who are concerned that they have spent millions of dollars for an educational tool that some students are using for self-destructive purposes by spending inordinate amounts of time chatting, playing interactive games, gambling online, day trading, downloading pornography or just surfing the Web (Young, 2001). Most tertiary institutions have implemented Internet use policies that all students are supposed to abide by—at least on university-controlled networks and machines. These Internet policies frequently require all students to read and sign acknowledgement of time constraints and content parameters that are allowed by the institution. There is little an institution can do to regulate individual or private use of Internet services on personal computers, even in dorm rooms on campus. Through their medical or counseling departments, universities and colleges are increasingly providing services to students who may be suffering from symptoms of pathological Internet use. They may make referrals to psychologists or counselors who are not university employees. They also provide students with management strategies, which can help students take control of their Internet overuse. Webb (2004) recommends the following strategies:

1. **Assess online time:** Keeping a log for a week can help a student recognize actual Internet use time. If accurately kept, the log also makes it difficult for a student to deny the amount of online involvement.

2. **Recognize what is missing:** Since Internet use may be a substitute for something missing in one's life, it is important to assess how much time and the quality of the time spent with partners, family or friends. Also look at time spent on routine activities, such as sleep, TV, exercise, hobbies and social events.

3. **Use time-management techniques:** The student should identify his or her usage pattern, then find external stoppers, possibly something important he or she needs to do or a place he or she wants to go, to remind him or herself when to log off. The student will need to make special efforts to cultivate alternative activities. There is no mandate to go "cold turkey" and quit Internet usage altogether. Incorporating planned Internet time into each day or week can assist with time management. Consider cutting time online by half and planning just one Internet session per day.

4. **Find support in the real world:** Even if a student finds that he or she has been cut off from friends, family or partners, that student needs to make diligent efforts to become reconnected with people. It can be important to replace the camaraderie often experienced with online friends with face-to-face social or support groups.

5. **Recognize addictive triggers:**
   - The student needs to consider his or her feelings when heading towards the computer. Does he or she feel bored, lonely, depressed, anxious, angry or stressed?
   - How does he or she feel when engaged in his or her favorite Internet activity?
   - It is important for the student to recognize what his or her flings are before and during Internet use. Recognizing the differences in feelings before and during online use allows the student to see what he or she may be attempting to escape and could clarify what he or she hopes to gain online. Each time the student logs on in response to a trigger, he or she faces a choice point, and changing behavioral patterns at choice points is crucial.

6. **Carry positive reminder cards:** Reminder cards are just that: reminders. They list the main problems caused by obsessive Internet use and the main benefits of cutting down. The cards are a useful way for a student to remember what he or she wishes to avoid and what he or she wishes to accomplish for himself.

7. **Take concrete steps to address the problem and listen to the voices of denial:** The student should take steps to actively change aspects of his or her former routine that led into addiction-like behaviors into a more functional one.

In his paper, Orman (1996) says that no matter how much initial success you have in eliminating an addiction, unintended relapses are just around the corner. Something unexpected might happen in life or someone might succumb in a moment of weakness. He suggests that plans should be made that anticipate the possibility of a relapse and prepares the individuals to deal with them successfully. He emphasizes the importance of understanding that the word "relapse" is not to be equated with the word "failure," and that the primary objective is to insure that a 2-day relapse does not become 5 days. Students should have an outrageous game plan in mind that they hope they will never need to use, but that they are committed to execute if the need arises (Orman, 1996).

Future Trends

Current research shows that computers, computer technology and Internet services are already a mainstay of Western life and increasingly a part of everyday life around the globe. It is not anticipated that this technological involvement—not only in education but in all aspects of society—will lessen; instead, it will only increase as new innovations, lower prices and more reliable service in even the most remote areas become the norm.

The future of technology in education very likely holds a trunk full of surprises, and it will undoubtedly play a dominant role in meeting the needs of diverse learners and in performing routine chores and organizational functions. This will surely spill over into the home as well as into other professions. The list of potential improvements, inventions and scientific advances stemming from technological improvements and innovations is well beyond the scope of a segment in this chapter; it is an entire paper in its own right. Applications of new technologies in the world of academia, in the home, at work, in our modes of transportation and means of communication, health care options and much more are on the drawing boards, just waiting to merge into our daily lives. Immediate access to information, however, seems to be the most powerful application of all. In a 2002 paper on Internet use, the Pew report predicts that current university students are so accustomed to having easy, unlimited, high-speed Internet access that they are likely to expect the same level of access after graduation in their businesses and homes. The Pew report says that college graduates will want to keep the same level of communication, file sharing and streaming video watching with which they have become accustomed.

Young agrees with this assessment and states that the high level of reliance among college students upon the Internet as an information and reference source indicates they will very likely want and expect to use the same level of service in the future (2004). It would appear that the future of computerization in general and Internet in particular has already been written in the trends of the last 2 decades. The educational applications are numerous, and the trend toward utilization of technology to individualize education is established. There are those who predict that a computerized future will leave people isolated, alone and without the will to socialize. There are others who see social problems arising from computerization and an excessive use of the Internet as basically growing pains. In his 2005 paper on *Internet Addiction*, Grohol says he believes that most people will eventually attain a balanced, normal use of the Internet, although some people do get caught into an obsession or enchantment for a time. "Just like a teenager learns to not spend hours on the telephone every night on their own (eventually!), most adults online will also learn how to responsibly integrate the Internet into their lives" (p. 3).

Conclusion

Computers are an indispensable and inescapable part of our lives in the modern world, and they are likely to have an even greater presence in the years to come. Computerization and technological innovations are not just fads that our century will see come and go; this is a revolution in how most of the world lives, interacts and does business. Much of what has been developed and what is to come will be hailed as marvels of progress and a boon to humankind, and for the most part that is true. But, as with all revolutions, the potential for abuses and misuse is inherent. One problem area of potential significance is that of what is sometimes termed Internet addiction. This compulsive and obsessive use of the Internet that leaves the user with all the symptoms typical of other addictions is already a problem on some college campuses. Universities and colleges, recognizing the destructive potential of pathological Internet use, have taken steps to assess the problems and implement some interventions. Several research studies have been commissioned to study the problem, and this chapter looks at Internet use at UOG.

Internet use at UOG generally follows studies done on other college campuses. The current study shows that most students at the university view the Internet as a vital and indispensable educational tool, one that can occasionally be used for entertainment purposes, as well. Like most university students, those at UOG tend not to allow Internet usage to interfere with academic or professional goals nor family and social life. There are, however, a handful of survey respondents whose answers suggest that they could be potential victims of pathological Internet use. As a whole, the Internet is a marvelously efficient and effective information, communication and entertainment tool. The vast majority of college students recognize it as such a tool and use it improve themselves and their understanding of the world, find entertainment and pleasure in the numerous Web sites offered, communicate regularly with friends and family, and then continue about their daily lives in a healthy manner. Will those students whose Internet use becomes pathologically compulsive eventually mature into adults who lead normal and productive lives? Counseling and intervention help. Awareness of the problem is the first big step, but the final answer lies somewhere in the future, and only within the individual.

References

American Psychiatric Association (APA). (1994). *Diagnostic and statistical manual of mental disorders* (4th ed.). Washington, DC: Author.

Anderson, K. (2000). *Internet use among college students: An exploratory study.* Troy: Rensselaer Polytechnic Institute.

Briggs, R. (2001). Psychosocial parameters of Internet addiction. *Journal of Mental Health Counseling, 23*(4), 312-327.

Chen, S. (2004). *Prevalence of Internet addiction among college students in Taiwan*. Retrieved February 3, 2005, from www.laapsy.org/25icap/common/P962.htm

DeLoughry, T. (1996, March 1). Snared by the Internet: College officials debate whether students spend too much time on line. *Chronicle of Higher Education, 42*(12), A14-15.

Egger, O., & Rautenberg, M. (1996). *Internet behavior and addiction*. Swiss Federal Institute of Technology: Zurich. Retrieved February 7, 2005, from www.ifap.bepr.ethz.ch/~egger/ibq/res.html

Ferris, J. (1998). *Internet addiction disorder: Causes, symptoms, and consequences*. Virginia Institute of Technology. Retrieved April 2, 2005, from www.chem.vt.edu/chem-dept/dessy/honors/papers/ferris.html

Grohol, J. (1999). *Internet addiction guide*. Retrieved February 7, 2005, from http://psychcentral.com/netaddiction

Holmes, L. (1997). *What is normal Internet use?* Retrieved February 7, 2005, from http://mentalhealth.com/Jlibrary/weekly/aal_O_QM

Internet addiction. (2004). *CenterSite, LLC*. Retrieved April 2, 2005, from www.mentalhelp.net/poc/center_index.php?id=66&cn=66

Jones, S. (2002). *The Internet goes to college: How students are living in the future with today's technology*. Retrieved February 7, 2005, from www.pewinternet.org/report

Korgen, K., Odell, P., & Schumacher, O. (2001). Internet use among college students: Are there differences by race/ethnicity? *Electronic Journal of Sociology, 5*(3). Retrieved February 9, 2005, from www.sociology.org/content/vol005.003/korgen.html

Lubans, J. (1999). *How first year university students use and regard Internet resources*. Duke University. Retrieved February 7, 2005, from www.lib.duke.edu/lubans/docs/1styear/firstyear.html

Miniwatts International. (2005). *Internet usage and populations in Oceania*. Retrieved February 7, 2005, from www.internetworldstats.com/stats6.htm

Orman, M. (1996). *Common causes of computer stress*. Retrieved March 14, 2005, from www.stresscure.com/hrn/common.html

Stonecypher, L. (2001). *Are you addicted to the Internet*. Retrieved March 2, 2005, from http://kudzumonthly.com/kudzu/jul01/addiction.html

Torabi, F. (2003). *Hi-tech devices move from luxury to necessity for college students*. Columbia Universty. Retrieved March 14, 2005, from www.youngmoney.com?technology/tech_trends/030417_02

Wardell, C. (2004). House of the future: The souped-up kitchen. *Popular Science, 264*(3), 30-40.

Webb, N. (2004). *Dynamics that make universities ripe for Internet overuse*. Edith Cowan University Counseling Service. Retrieved February 9, 2005, from www.ecu.edu.au

Young, K. (1998). Internet addiction: The emergence of a new clinical disorder. *CyberPsychology and Behavior, 1*(3), 237-244.

Young, K. (2001). Surfing not studying: Dealing with internet addiction on campus. *Student Affairs On-line.* Retrieved February 7, 2005, from www.studentaffairs.com/eiournal/ Winter_2001/addiction.html

Chapter IX

Adoption of Online Courses in Higher Education:

Evaluating the Readiness of Business Students and Faculty

Anita Borja Enriquez, University of Guam, USA

Abstract

This chapter examines the state of readiness towards adopting online distance education (DE) courses between undergraduate business students and business faculty at the University of Guam (UOG). The study was timely, given the infancy planning stage of online education delivery at UOG. Preferences among business student respondents, based on generation groups, ethnicity and occupation status, were reviewed. The following research questions were posed to guide this study: (1) At what stage of the undergraduate program do undergraduate business students recognize the importance of using the Internet for online education use?; (2) What factors explain the rate of adoption towards Internet use by undergraduate business education students and business faculty at UOG?; and (3) Are there significant differences between undergraduate business education students and UOG business faculty in the perceived state of readiness of adoption of online distance education? Overall, business students expressed willingness to pursue this delivery format.

Introduction

This study purports to evaluate the perceptions and attitudes towards adoption and diffusion of Internet use by undergraduate business students and business faculty at UOG as a basis for determining their state of readiness towards adopting online DE courses. It comes at an opportune time, as UOG is at its infancy stage of offering online DE courses. Rogers' (1995) model on diffusion of innovations explains in part the early reluctance of a majority of people on the adoption of any innovation, given the timing of educational reform on instructional technology due to information technology (IT) advances (Tsang-Kosma, 2005). In the study reported in this chapter, all undergraduate business administration majors and business instructors at UOG were surveyed using an attitudinal survey instrument. The state of readiness towards online DE courses was examined between business students and faculty respondents. In addition, differences between business student respondents' "state of readiness" by ethnicity and occupation status were examined.

To guide the present study, the following research questions were posed: (1) At what stage of the undergraduate program do undergraduate business students recognize the importance of using the Internet for online educational use?; (2) What factors explain the rate of adoption towards Internet use by undergraduate business education students?; and (3) are there significant differences between undergraduate business education students and faculty in the perceived state of readiness of adoption of online DE courses?

Background

Tremendous research exists concerning the adoption of instructional technologies by faculty in higher education (Macchiusi & Trinidad, 2001; Yohon, Zimmerman, & Keller, 2004). According to Nachmias and Segev (2003), there is a rapid increase in the use of the Internet as an instructional tool in higher education. However, research is scant (Limayen & Hirt, 2000; Singh & Pan, 2004) on the reasons associated with student adoption of online courses. The introduction to the early majority of (instructor) users should be related to their perceived program and process needs (Carr, 1999; Rogers, 1995). Beggs (2005) asserts that as faculty members are asked to utilize new technologies in their pedagogy, some accept while others resist. This reluctance to adopt a new technology is common among people in general (Wilson, 2004). The challenge of infusing technology into instruction can be attributed to the need for more technological training (Duhaney, 2001; Means, 2001). Yohon et al. (2004) suggest that training on Web-based teaching tools should include pedagogy and student engagement solutions so that faculty members understand how to effectively use technology tools. Luke, Moore and Sawyer (1998) contend that for students to be better prepared to learn with technology, teachers should be better prepared to teach with technology. New technology adoption, according to Yan and Fang (2004), starts from faculty consensus to adopt this technology.

Finley and Hartman (2004) posit that people need to feel comfortable that they either have or will be able to attain the required skills and knowledge prior to adopting any innovation. This kind of confidence is associated with building faculty confidence towards integrating technology into a course, as suggested by Nisan-Nelson (2001). What is critical for early majority success is the ease of use and low risk of failure, which are likely through support and training (Carr, 1999; Gallant, 2000; Guhlin, 2002). Faculty development is seen as the key to address the new generation of student learners (Moore, Moore, & Fowler, 2005). Web-based contents have become a major component in many academic courses (Nachmias, 2002). Young, Klemz, and Murphy (2003) suggest that students view technology simply as a tool involved in implementing the instructional method. There is a belief that presentation of educational contents on the Internet is highly valuable for students who enjoy visual presentation of information and supplements to materials taught in lectures (Cummings, Bank, & Jacobs, 2002). The perceived value of these online resources, according to Soong, Chan, and Chua (2001), needs to be examined. Nachmias and Segev (2003) assert that there is little empirical evidence available on the actual use of learning materials available through academic Web sites.

How can higher education address differences in course delivery preference by different generations? A review of generational differences has become a focal point only recently, where it is assumed that each generation requires a different teaching format (Hay, 2000). The generation groups examined in this study are: (1) Baby Boomers, born between 1946 and 1964; (2) Generation X (Gen-Xers), born between 1964 and 1977; and (3) Net Generation (Net-Geners), born between 1977 and 1999. How do most higher education institutions address their lag in technology literacy and proficiency in contrast to the level of proficiency of students referred to as Gen-Xers (Smith, 2005) and Net-Geners (Hartman, Moskal, & Dziuban, 2005)? The Net-Geners is a much larger population than the Baby Boomers. Members are inclined to be more Internet savvy, as they are a generation immersed with digital technology culture (Tapscott, 1998). They are the first to come of age in the digital age (Nelson Buchanan & Oostergard Ptc Ltd., 2005). The Net-Geners are purported to have a huge edge in IT over the Baby Boomers. They have a greater understanding of the need for interconnectivity to the growing worldwide economy (Alch, 2000). They tend to display a curious blend of collaboration, interdependence and networking to achieve their ends (Moore et al., 2005). Alch (2000) states the following:

Distance learning will be something this generation will be interested in once established in a job and deciding to further skills or begin crossing over to another occupation. Whether in a formal degree or certificate program or individual courses, the Internet will be used more and more as a business tool, at a time the adult worker prefers and with an ability to join the class online with the instructor, thus making it more of a personal education experience. (p. 18)

What will be important is the extent to which technological and pedagogical approaches by faculty will yield more interaction and positive outcomes for student learning. One will need to take into account the different preferences among the various generations of learners. Perhaps, hybrid or blended learning approaches that combine face-to-face and online education formats may be the best approach to bridging the generations, particularly in satisfying the need for face-to-face contact by Baby Boomers, the need for independence by Gen-Xers and the need for interaction and sense of community by Net-Geners (Hartman et al., 2005).

Issues, Controversies and Problems

Online course delivery is a new phenomenon at the School of Business and Public Administration at UOG. No courses are currently offered through this education delivery format, which is unusual given the regional charge in the school's mission to serve its neighbors in the Western Pacific region. The school has made some effort in moving towards online DE courses by providing DE training workshops to a handful of business faculty. However, this effort is at its infancy, and given the momentum and direction the school is taking towards exploring DE offerings, the findings presented in this chapter come at an opportune time. This is particularly useful for planning purposes, given the preference indicated by students and faculty assessed under this study. Furthermore, the advantage of closing spatial distance through this medium, coupled with requests from residents of neighboring islands in the Commonwealth of the Northern Mariana Islands (CNMI), the Federated States of Micronesia (FSM), the Republic of Palau (Palau) and the Republic of the Marshall Islands (RMI) to offer DE courses in their locations, serve as an opportunity for the school, particularly as a means to increase enrollment. However, prior to taking advantage of such an opportunity, the school should be prepared to take on this challenge.

Aside from the issue of infrastructure capability, "state of readiness" of business faculty and students needs to be examined. Much research on the diffusion of adoption is made available for instructors, but much more needs to be explored among students (Poindexter, 2003). What factors will ease the transition from face-to-face course delivery to online education? Are the School of Business and Public Administration students indeed prepared for this challenge? Like the business faculty, however, distance learning may be a new phenomenon for the majority of students, as online courses are not currently available at the school. One threat that needs to be considered is whether or not the school will be at risk of losing students in the future if online courses are not available. The extent of this threat may be assessed through the expressed preference for online DE courses by students within this study. If there is a greater preference for the face-to-face format, then the urgency for the school to implement DE may not be required.

If there appears to be a strong preference among business students for online courses, then where does this preference fall among the generations of students in terms of adoption? IT literacy has become the norm. Net-Geners (referred to as Echo Boomers) have been differentiated as the first generation to grow up surrounded by digital media. For a generation that is perceived more computer literate due to computer use and exposure in high school, it has become a "sort of life online." Computers and digital technologies are commonplace to Net-Geners. The Baby Boomers are purported to have about the same Internet usage as Gen-Xers who follow them; and Baby Boomers tend to be wealthier and better educated than generations before them; therefore, they tend to have higher Internet usage at work and at home (Hodge, 2005). Because the School of Business faculty are primarily Baby Boomers, with two exceptions who predate the Baby Boom generation, generational differences among faculty members were not addressed in this study. It can be purported that the predominant college-bound generation groups (Net-Geners and Gen-Xers) are more computer literate and Internet savvy. Would there be a risk of the business school being at a competitive disadvantage if these generation groups prefer, or are inclined to enroll in, courses that challenge this digital age competency?

The Case of Business Faculty and Undergraduate Students

The basis for Internet use needs to be understood, especially as the initial orientation towards offering online DE courses. Business faculty at UOG at present provide students with an opportunity to use the Internet for course requirements by either performing research online or accessing course-specific notes or files posted on the UOG's Web site. Where the adoption of online course delivery is still in its infancy at UOG, it is important to determine the reasons behind the lag in the diffusion of this instructional technology, particularly in business education courses, and to determine the preferences by business students towards fully adopting online course delivery in place of the traditional face-to-face format. The availability of a computer and Internet access, whether it is at home or at the university campus, would be a prerequisite to online course adoption by students and faculty. Of specific interest is the number of business administration students at UOG who currently have access to such technology.

Because of the unique demographic composition of students at UOG, particularly the Business School, relative to its counterparts in the United States (U.S.), descriptive responses by ethnic groups and generation groups were also examined. Compared to the predominantly white, black and Hispanic demographic composition of US-based institutions of higher learning, the undergraduate student population (approximately 2,500) at UOG consists primarily of Asian-Pacific Islanders (91%), followed by whites, blacks and Hispanics (6%, 1% and less than 1%, respectively) (UOG student enrollment by ethnicity and gender, 2005). At UOG, a more detailed breakdown of the Asian-Pacific Islander classification is maintained due to the ethnically diverse makeup of Asians and Pacific Islanders who attend this institution. The composition of Asian students represents those of Chinese, Filipino (the largest at 30%), Indian, Japanese, Korean, Thai, Vietnamese and others. The composition of Pacific Islander students represent those of Chamorros (indigenous people of Guam, who encompass the largest at 45%) and those located in the neighboring islands, who represent 6% of the overall UOG student population. Within the Business School, 94% represent Asian or Pacific Islanders, while less than 5% represents white, non-Hispanic, and black, and less than 1% of the business student population represents Hispanics. The majority of these students originate from Guam and the surrounding regional islands, such as CNMI, FSM, Palau and RMI, wherein online DE is either non-existent or, at best, at an infancy stage, due to isolation and IT infrastructure challenges.

Survey Questionnaire

Two survey questionnaires on the use of the Internet and state of readiness for online DE were used to assess perceptions of business students and faculty at UOG. Descriptive statistics and correlations were used as the bases of this assessment. Of the 385 business administration majors enrolled in courses at UOG in spring 2005, 140 (36%) responded to the survey. Of the 17 full-time and part-time faculty, 7 (41%) responded to the survey.

The first research problem addressed in this study centered on the following: At what stage of the undergraduate program do undergraduate business students recognize the importance of adopting the Internet as a medium for education-related use? Descriptive statistics revealed how early in their program undergraduate business students began using the Internet, and if differences in student generation groups exist on the start of the use of the Internet due to course requirements. The second problem focused on the factors that explained the rate of adoption of Internet use by undergraduate business students and faculty. Descriptive statistics revealed whether undergraduate business students and faculty differ in their responses on factors that relate to adoption and use of the Internet. Additionally, the findings revealed which factors explain the adoption of Internet use among the generational groups. The third research problem addressed whether there are significant differences between undergraduate business students and faculty in the perceived state of readiness towards adopting online DE. Descriptive statistics revealed whether business students appear to have a stronger preference towards online education than business faculty. In addition, is there a perceived difference between generational groups of students in the preference towards adopting DE? Are there differences between the ethnic groups regarding their preference for online DE vs. traditional face-to-face learning formats? Finally, do undergraduate business students have a higher confidence level than business faculty toward adopting online DE?

Findings

Of the 140 business students surveyed, 37% of the respondents were male and 63% were female; 62% of those surveyed were employed (26% full-time; 36% part-time).

Demographics

Student distribution by generation. Most of the student respondents represented the Net-Geners (86%). The Gen-Xers group followed at 10% and 4% represented the Baby Boomers. The large concentration of Net-Gener respondents, followed by Gen-Xers, is indicative of the relatively high percentage of the business student population who are technology literate and proficient, as posited by Smith (2005) and Hartman et al. (2005).

Student distribution by class level. Determining the concentration of Net-Geners by class level is a factor that would be useful for anticipating how soon online courses could be made available to this technology-savvy generation. Additional observations include the breakdown of generation groups by class level at UOG. Overall, the Net-Geners dominated the representation across all class levels. Seniors represented the largest class level (50%), of which 84% were Net-Geners, 13% were Gen-Xers and 3% were Baby Boomers. The juniors represented the second largest (32%), of which 84% were Net-Geners, 11% were Gen-Xers and 4.5% were Baby Boomers. Sophomores comprised the third largest (17%), with 96% representing Net-Geners and 4% representing the Baby Boomers. The freshmen were represented solely by Net-Geners.

Student distribution by ethnicity. The distribution of student respondents by ethnicity is provided in Figure 1. This resembles the ethnic distribution of the student population. Chamorro-Pacific Islanders make up the largest representation, followed by Filipino-Asians. Other Asians represented the third largest group of student respondents, followed by Other Pacific Islanders. White-non-Hispanics, Hispanics and blacks represented the smallest groups, at 1.4% each.

Figure 1. Distribution of business student respondents by ethnic group

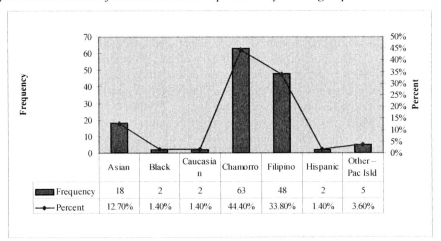

Faculty distribution by generation. Of the seven faculty respondents, five were Baby Boomers and two pre-dated the Baby Boom generation. It was determined that differences in responses by faculty generation groups would not be a part of this study.

Faculty distribution by ethnicity. Of the 17 full-time and seven part-time faculty, there were seven Chamorros (Pacific Islanders), four Asians (two Chinese; one Filipino; one Korean) and six white-non-Hispanics. This is indicative of the diverse ethnic makeup of faculty at UOG. When accounting for the full-time business faculty respondents, the ethnic composition is somewhat similar to UOG's overall faculty composition. Based on U.S. federal classification of ethnic groups, as of this study, 50% of the full-time faculty at UOG were white-non-Hispanics, 42% were classified as Asian-Pacific Islanders, 1% were Hispanics, 4% represented others, and only one was black.

Comparison between Faculty and Students on Average Internet Hours Spent

The average number of hours one spends per day on the Internet may help to explain the extent to which respondents use the Internet. The findings revealed that faculty spent an average of 3 hours on the Internet per day, as compared to students, who spent slightly less than 3 hours on the Internet per day.

Student average Internet hours spent, by ethnicity. In examining the breakdown of students by ethnic groups, Hispanic/Latino respondents averaged the greatest daily use, at 9 hours; Other-Pacific Islander respondents averaged the second highest, at 5 hours per day; black respondents followed with 3 hours; Filipino-Asian respondents at slightly less than 3 hours; Chamorro-Pacific Islander respondents averaged slightly more than 2 hours per day; and white-non-Hispanic respondents represented the least use, at 2 hours per day.

Student unlimited computer and Internet access at home. The number of students who had unlimited access to a computer and the Internet at home was examined, as presented in

Table 1. Frequency distribution of business students with unlimited access to computer and Internet at home (By ethnic group and employment)

Ethnicity	Employed Full-Time	Employed Part-Time	Not Employed
Asian-Other	2	4	9
Black	1	0	1
White-Non-Hispanic	0	0	0
Chamorro-Pacific Islander	19	18	17
Filipino-Asian	7	21	17
Hispanic/Latino	0	1	1
Pacific Islander-Other	3	0	2
Total	32	44	47

Table 1. Here, the number of Asians with unlimited access to a computer and the Internet at home was 88%, or 15 of 17 respondents. All black respondents had unlimited access, while none of the white-non-Hispanic respondents had access at home. The largest representation of unlimited computer and Internet access at home was the Chamorro-Pacific Islander respondents, at 87%, or 54 of 62. However, 94% of Filipino-Asian respondents had unlimited access, or 45 of 48 respondents. Finally, all of the Hispanic/Latino respondents had access, and 71%, or 5 of 7, of other Pacific Islanders had unlimited access to a computer and the Internet at home.

Also noteworthy is the comparison of students employed and not employed, given their unlimited access to a computer and the Internet at home. Employed Chamorro-Pacific Islander and Filipino-Asian respondents represented a majority of those who had unlimited access to a computer and the Internet at home, as compared to those in their respective ethnic groups who were not employed. In contrast, Asian students who reported they were unemployed had more unlimited access than those who were employed. Some factors may explain this difference, but will be recommended for further research. Observations of the different generational groups were also made. About 88% of students claimed they had unlimited access to a computer and Internet at home. Net-Geners had the highest number, at 88%. And 86% of Gen-Xers claimed they had unlimited access, and 80% of Baby Boomers claimed they had unlimited access.

Findings on Stage of Internet Adoption for Course Requirements by Student Class and Generation Group

To determine if undergraduate business students originally started to use the Internet as early as their first year at UOG for course requirements, respondents were asked how early they began Internet use due to course requirements. The possible responses ranged from as early as high school to as late as their senior year in college. From an analysis of the data, 66% of student respondents started using the Internet for classroom assignments as early as high school, while 24% during their freshman year in college, 7% in their sophomore year, 1% in their junior year and 1% in their senior year. The generational differences were evident in that 73% of Net-Geners started using the Internet in high school, while 72% of Gen-Xers and 75% of Baby Boomers started as freshmen in college. There were notable differences between the groups, particularly with those who took a computer class as early as high school. Most of the Net-Geners respondents (79%) took a computer class in high school, compared to only 43% of Gen-Xers. Of the Baby Boomers surveyed, none of the respondents took a computer class in high school. For the Baby Boomers, the unavailability of the Internet during their high school years (as recent as 1982 for those born in 1964) could explain this phenomenon.

Findings on Factors that Explained Internet Adoption by Students and Faculty

The second problem focused on the factors that explained the rate of adoption of the Internet by undergraduate business education students and business faculty at UOG. Descriptive statistics revealed factors that explain why both sets of respondents adopted the use of the Internet, as presented in Tables 2 and 3. The social factor (refers to social communication with friends and family as a preference, in comparison to work-related or academic-related reason) came out as the leading reason for students, while online research or academic reason was ranked first by faculty. Both sets of respondents ranked the availability of a computer at home as the second top factor that influenced the beginning of their use of the Internet. It is important to note that students rated online research as the third top reason that influenced their start of Internet use. For faculty, online research and the availability of the

Table 2. Factors that influenced students' start of Internet use

Rank	Factor	Frequency
1	Communicate with friends and/or family	120
2	Availability at home	111
3	Course requirement for online research	90
4	Availability at school	79
5	Communicate with classmates	76
6	Download music, games or movies	54
7	Order products or services online	53
8	Communicate with instructors	43
9	Computer/Internet training course	39
10	Other	9

Note: N = 140

Internet at home were tied as the top reason, while communication with faculty colleagues, communicating with friends and/or family, and availability of the Internet at school all tied for second. Another noteworthy finding was that faculty did not perceive accessing music, games or movies as a motivating factor for this purpose, while students ranked this sixth as an influencing factor to initial Internet use.

Table 3. Factors that influenced faculty's start of Internet use

Rank	Factor	Frequency
1*	Online research	6
1*	Availability at home	6
2**	Communicate with faculty colleagues	5
2**	Communicate with friends and/or family	5
2**	Availability at school	5
3***	Communicate with students	2
3***	Order products or services online	2
4***	Computer/Internet training course	1
4	Other-specify	1
None	Download music, games or movies	N/A

*Note: N = 7, *tied for first, **three-way tie for second, ***two-way tie for third*

Table 4. Factors that influenced students' start of Internet use by generational group

Rank	Factor	Net- Geners	Gen-Xers	Baby Boomers	Total
1	Communicate with friends and/or family	106	11	3	120
2	Availability at home	97	2	2	111
3	Course requirement for online research	81	7	2	90
4	Availability at school	72	6	1	79
5	Communicate with classmates	67	8	1	76
6	Communicate with instructors	52	2	0	54
7	Order products or services online	48	5	0	53
8	Communicate with instructors	38	4	1	43
9	Computer/Internet training course	31	7	1	39
10	Other	6	2	1	9

What factors explain the adoption of Internet use among the generation groups? Table 4 provides a distribution of responses by each generational group on the factors that helped to explain their start of the use of the Internet.

As shown in Table 4, the ranking by the Net-Geners mirrors those overall for students, reflected in Table 2. From the distribution, 88% of student respondents who ranked communicating with friends and/or family as the primary reason were Net-Geners, with 9% representing Gen-Xers and 3% representing the Baby Boomers. Note that for all three generational groups, this came out as the top-ranked reason to commence use of the Internet. For the Net-Geners, availability at home, course requirement for online research, availability of the Internet at school and communicating with classmates ranked as the second, third, fourth and fifth reasons for initial use of the Internet. The distribution for Gen-Xers, on the other hand, reveals that the two top reasons for start of Internet use was to communicate with friends, family and classmates. This reflects the social reasons. Course requirement for online research for the Gen-Xers ranked as the third top reason, followed by the availability of the Internet at school ranking fourth and ordering online ranking fifth. For Baby Boomers, communicating with friends or family also ranked as the top reason, with availability of the Internet at home and online research for course requirement ranking tied for second, and availability at school communicating with classmates and instructors, access to computer and Internet training, and research for work tied for third.

Motivating Factors for Continued Use of Internet

The motivation factors for continued use of the Internet were also examined for both groups of respondents. Tables 5 and 6 display the frequency of responses for each group, which help to explain which factors serve as the primary reasons they use the Internet. Overall, the social reason still ranked as the top reason, with academic (online research) ranking second for both groups to continue use of respondents. A review for differences across generation groups and ethnicity was also made. In observing the generational differences, the ranked responses were very similar to those reflected in Table 5.

Finally, in reviewing for potential differences in responses of students by ethnic groups, none were found, as the distribution was relatively the same across all groups. Faculty respondents revealed very similar results in their distribution of responses, as presented in Table 6. Here, faculty ranked social contact with friends and/or family as the top reason for using the Internet, and online research as the second top reason. Overall, the reasons for using the Internet appear job related. When compared to the responses by students, downloading music, games or movies was not as a priority for them. When comparing for gender differences, the rankings by female and male faculty were consistent overall. However, male faculty respondents were more inclined to use the Internet to order products online than their female counterparts.

Table 5. Ranked reasons business students use the Internet by generation group

Rank	Factor	Frequency	Percent Net-Geners	Percent Gen-Xers	Percent Baby Boomers
1	Communicate with friends and/or family	131	87.6	8.5	3.9
2	Course requirement for online research	127	87.2	9.6	3.2
3	Communicate with classmates	124	88.5	8.2	3.3
4	Order products or services online	118	88.8	8.6	2.6
5	Communicate with instructors	118	87.5	8.6	3.4
6	Download music, games or movies	106	91.3	5.8	2.9
7	Other	31	77.4	16.1	6.5

Table 6. Ranked reasons business faculty use the Internet

Rank	Factor	Frequency of responses
1	Communicate with friends and/or family	7
2	Course requirement for online research	6
3	Communicate with faculty colleagues	6
4	Communicate with students	5
5	Order products or services online	5
6	Other	1
7	Download music, games or movies	1

Findings on State of Perceived Readiness between Students and Faculty

The third area of review focused on determining if there was a difference in the perceived state of readiness of adopting online DE between undergraduate business students and faculty. These were considered to help explain the state of readiness, and business students and business faculty were asked to state whether or not they agreed to online related activities, along a five-point Likert-scale. To make this determination, a correlation of related factors first needed to be examined among the following variables:

1.   Unlimited access to computer at home for Internet use
2.   Unlimited access to computer at UOG for Internet use
3.   Comfortable using computer to do online research

4.   Recognize importance of accessing Internet for course assignments

5.   Prefer to use Internet vs. UOG library to get information for research projects

6.   Prefer to use Internet to communicate with instructors via e-mail and/or online chartroom

7.   Prefer to use Internet to communicate with classmates via e-mail and/or online chartroom

8.   Internet is helpful to locate reference materials for course assignments and/or research

9.   Prefer accessing course syllabus via Internet vs. accessing face-to-face

10.   Internet is the best place to post class exercises

11.   All my instructors should require Internet-based research

12.   Prefer to access my grades via the Internet through UOG Web site

13.   Prefer submitting my course assignments to instructor via Internet

Separate correlations for both groups were run, using Pearson's correlation coefficient determinants, to identify the variables that help explain the readiness for online learning for business students and faculty. Strong relationships were found among 10 of the 13 variables between the faculty and students. Because no significant correlations were found among the following variables, they were excluded from the state of readiness construct: "I prefer to have unlimited access to computer at UOG for Internet use"; "I recognize the importance of accessing the Internet for course assignments"; and "I prefer to use the Internet vs. UOG's library to get information for research projects." The preceding factors, with the exception of preference to have unlimited access to the computer at UOG for Internet use, were included in the state of readiness correlated variables identified for business students. Hence, only 10 variables were used, as a means to compare the state of readiness between business faculty and students.

Most notable was a strong direct relationship, based on a correlation coefficient of 1.0, between faculty's comfort in using the computer to do online research and their preference to have unlimited access to a computer at home for Internet use, at the 99% confidence level. From a 95% confidence level, strong relationships ($r = .825$) were also found between faculty's preference to post student grades online via UOG's Web site, and their preference to use the Internet to communicate with colleagues online. A strong relationship was also found between faculty's preference to receive course assignments from students via the Internet, and their preference to communicate with students online. There was also a strong relationship between faculty's preference to require Internet-based research for course assignments and/or research projects, and their assertion that the Internet is helpful in locating reference materials for course assignments and/or research projects. A significant level of confidence at 99% was found in strong relationships between faculty's assertion that the Internet is the best place to post class exercises, and their preference to provide course syllabi online via UOG's Web site.

Comparison of Preferences between Business Faculty and Students

The mean responses for both groups, using a five-point Likert scale of agreement, are displayed in Table 7. No difference was found between faculty's and students' perception of state of readiness for online learning. The computed *t*-statistic (1.345) was less than the critical value for the one-tailed test (2.82) and the two-tailed test (3.249) at the .01 level of significance. For the sake of discussion, based on the responses, it can be purported that both groups agree on most of the factors presented, with a few exceptions. Business students appeared to be less comfortable using the computer to do online Internet research than the faculty. The faculty respondents' comfort level can be attributed to the greater exposure in conducting research in general. This could explain the difference in mean responses on preference for the Internet vs. UOG library for research projects. The faculty mean responses

Table 7. Comparison of online state of readiness means between business students and faculty

	Factors	Student Mean	Faculty Mean
1.	Unlimited access to a computer at home for Internet access is important to me.	4.02	4.71
2.	I am comfortable using the computer to do online Internet research.	3.68	4.86
3.	I prefer to use the Internet to communicate with instructor/students via e-mail and/or online chat room.	4.40	3.71
4.	I prefer to use the Internet to communicate with my classmates/faculty colleagues via e-mail and/or online chat room.	3.82	4.14
5.	The Internet is a helpful way to locate reference materials for course assignments and/or research projects.	4.77	4.57
6.	I prefer accessing/providing a course syllabus for all my courses via the Internet (UOG Web site), vs. distributing it via face-to-face interaction in the classroom.	4.86	3.43
7.	The Internet is the best place to post class exercises.	4.34	3.29
8.	All my instructors (or I) should require Internet-based research for course assignments and/or projects.	4.80	4.29
9.	I prefer to access student grades via the Internet (UOG Web site)/student survey. I prefer to post student grades via the Internet (UOG Web site)/faculty survey.	4.23	3.29
10.	I prefer submitting course assignments to my instructor via the Internet (e.g., electronic mail)/student survey. I prefer receiving course assignments from my students via the Internet (e.g., electronic mail)/faculty survey.	3.96	3.00

again showed strong agreement, compared to the weak agreement by student respondents. However, the weak agreement was also reflected through the mean responses of the different generation groups, as explained later in this section. With a mean score of 4.40, it appears that students have a stronger preference for using the Internet to communicate with instructors than do the business school's faculty, as indicated by a faculty mean response of 3.71. Business faculty expressed they were not sure of their preference in a number of factors, while business students expressed solid agreement in these same factors. These included access to course syllabi, class exercises and grades on the Internet (via UOG Web site). Students also preferred to submit course assignments via e-mail. Business student female respondents expressed slightly stronger agreement in all cases than their male counterparts who participated in the study.

Student State of Readiness by Ethnicity

Differences on state of readiness variables among business students were examined based on ethnicity. There was general agreement across all ethnic groups, with a few exceptions towards some variables. The white-non-Hispanic and other-Pacific Islander respondents were not sure if they preferred to submit their course assignments to instructors via online. The Chamorro-Pacific Islander and Filipino-Asian respondents on average tended to not be sure, or rather, expressed very weak agreement towards instructors requiring online research. The black respondent tended to disagree with this preference. The Asian and black respondents were not sure that they would rather use the Internet vs. the UOG library to conduct research. All ethnic groups showed relatively strong agreement towards the following variables: "I prefer unlimited access to computer at home for Internet use"; "I am comfortable using computer to do online research"; "I recognize the importance of accessing Internet for course assignments"; "The Internet is helpful to locate reference materials for course assignments and/or research projects"; and "I prefer to access grades through online through UOG's Web site."

Finally, an examination for differences on business students' state of readiness for online courses, according to employment status, was also performed. There was general agreement across all variables. However, part-time and not-employed students expressed less preference towards accessing course syllabi online, as compared to their full-time student counterparts. All three groups expressed slight agreement for using an online Web site to access class exercises. All three groups showed weaker agreement towards wanting to conduct online research. Those who were not employed were not as inclined to prefer accessing their grades online.

Preference Toward Online Education

Preference for the extent of online education delivery was assessed. As indicated in Table 8, the results of student preference for online DE courses vs. traditional courses were somewhat similar. Along a 3-point scale, "1" measured a preference for online, "2" measured a preference for traditional and "3" measured a preference for both, or a hybrid (or blended) approach. The mean score of 2.34 for students supports the preference by students for a

Table 8. Comparison between business students and faculty on preferred learning format

	N	Mean	Standard Deviation
Student preference towards DE vs. traditional learning format	140	2.34	.716
Faculty preference on teaching DE vs. traditional format	7	2.43	.535

more traditional approach to learning in a face-to-face classroom setting, with a possibility of adopting both. From the mean score results of 2.43 for faculty, faculty appear to prefer the traditional approach, and are likely to adopt a hybrid approach of both learning formats.

Assessing State of Readiness through Level of Confidence and Preference Toward Online Education

The breakdown of preferences by percentages revealed the following: 14% of student respondents preferred online; 38% traditional approach; and 48% both or blended approach. Of those who expressed they were "not at all confident," one preferred online, while seven preferred traditional. There was no preference for the blended approach. Of those who expressed that they were "unsure," 3 preferred online, 27 traditional approach and 19 blended format. Of those who expressed "somewhat confident," 6 preferred online, 13 traditional and 29 both. Of those who expressed "confident," 10 preferred online, 5 traditional and 18 both.

Observations for differences in responses by generation groups, ethnic groups and gender were also examined. In examining differences between the generational groups of business students, as reflected in Figure 2, the Baby Boomers' mean response of 2.5 implied that there is a preference for a hybrid approach to classroom learning, similar to their Baby Boomer and older counterparts within the faculty group surveyed. When the question was inverted, and students were asked if they preferred to meet in a traditional face-to-face, vs. online, classroom setting, the Net-Geners agreed, while the Baby Boomers and Gen-Xers followed with slightly lesser agreement towards the traditional approach.

In assessing their preference to meet in a traditional face-to-face, vs. online, learning environment, there were notable differences by ethnic groups. Black respondents expressed a strong preference for both, based on a mean response of 3.00, with Hispanics/Latinos, Asians and Filipino-Asians expressing mid-point preference between traditional and both, with mean responses of 2.50, 2.44 and 2.40, respectively. Chamorro-Pacific Islander respondents and other-Pacific Islanders leaned more towards the traditional face-to-face preference, with mean responses of 2.29 and 2.00, respectively. White-non-Hispanics expressed a preference for the traditional approach based on a mean response of 2.00.

Overall, male and female student respondents' preferences leaned towards a traditional approach, with mean responses of 2.31 and 2.34, respectively. In reviewing business students' responses on their preference, by employment status, there were identifiable differences within the groups. For full-time employed business respondents, 46% had a preference for

Figure 2. Comparison between generation groups on preference for online DE vs. traditional face-to-face learning format

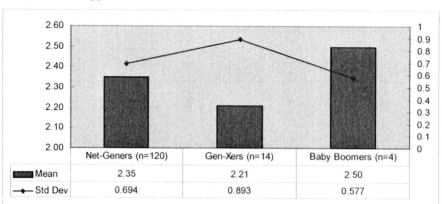

	Net-Geners (n=120)	Gen-Xers (n=14)	Baby Boomers (n=4)
▉▉ Mean	2.35	2.21	2.50
◆ Std Dev	0.694	0.893	0.577

the blended approach, 34% traditional and 20% online. For part-time employed respondents, 47% preferred the blended approach, 39% traditional and 14% online. For students who were not employed, 49% preferred the blended approach, 40% traditional and 11% online. Affirmation of the findings was further assessed when the question of preference was inverted. Here, both student and faculty respondents were asked if they preferred to meet in a traditional face-to-face classroom setting with each other, vs. online. From the analysis of the means, as displayed in Table 9, both students and faculty agree that they prefer to meet each other in a traditional face-to-face classroom setting, vs. online. A review for gender differences revealed that business male and female students expressed similar agreement for this format of learning, although the mean ranking for male students was slightly higher than that of their female counterparts (by .15 points). The comparison results for faculty respondents were similar to students, in that the mean ranking for male faculty was slightly higher (by .25 points) than that of their female counterparts.

Did the study reveal if there was a difference between generational groups of students in the preference towards adopting DE? Significant differences appeared in how the generational groups of students responded to the following questions: "I prefer to access course syllabus via the Internet, vs. accessing face-to-face from instructors"; and "The Internet is the best place to post class exercises." Along a five-point Likert scale, with 1 measuring "strongly

Table 9. Comparison between students and faculty on preference for classroom setting

	N	Mean	Standard Deviation
Prefer meeting my instructor and classmates in traditional face-to-face classroom setting, vs. online.	140	4.06	.984
Prefer meeting my students in a traditional face-to-face setting, vs. online	7	4.14	.900

disagree" and 5 measuring "strongly agree," the Baby Boom generation tended to be unsure about whether or not they (1) preferred to access course syllabi via the Internet, vs. accessing face-to-face from instructors, and (2) that the Internet was the best place to post class exercises. The Net-Geners students, on the other hand, showed slight agreement in their responses, while the Gen-Xers were solid in their agreement. Additionally, in determining the preference to use Internet to communicate with Instructors via e-mail or online chat rooms, there was no significant difference found between the three generational groups. The findings revealed that all generation groups agree on the preference to use the Internet to communicate with instructors. Further analysis of business students' perceived preference towards online-related learning formats was reviewed by comparing their responses on traditional face-to-face vs. online learning format, along a four-point Likert-scale of agreement. There is perceived agreement among all three generational groups towards a traditional classroom meeting format, as opposed to an online format. This differs from the preference to communicate with instructors.

Student Net-Geners in general expressed stronger agreement, with a mean of 4.10, as compared to their Gen-Xers and Baby Boomer counterparts, with means of 3.79 and 3.80, respectively. Of business students, those who were unemployed and worked part-time expressed stronger agreement than those who worked full-time. In examining for gender differences, agreement among male and female students was about the same. Differences between the ethnic groups on the preference for online DE vs. traditional face-to-face learning formats were also reviewed. To measure this, students were asked if they would prefer an online, traditional (face-to-face) or both (blended) approach to courses. The black respondent expressed a preference for both, while the Hispanic/Latino, Asian and Filipino-Asian respondents were mid-way in their preference between traditional and blended approaches. Chamorro-Pacific Islander, other-Pacific Islander and white-non-Hispanic (Caucasian) respondents, on the other hand, leaned towards the traditional approach. Another way to measure the preference was through an inverted question, wherein students were asked if they preferred meeting with their instructors and classmates in a traditional face-to-face learning format, vs. online. Among the different ethnic groups, the Hispanics/Latinos expressed the strongest preference for the traditional learning format (mean of 5.0). Those who expressed lesser agreement were the other-Pacific Islander and black respondents.

Another indicator for preference for online education is a survey of how many online DE courses, if any, business students and faculty would be willing to pursue each semester. For students, this would include the online courses they would be willing to enroll in; for faculty, the online courses they would be willing to teach. As shown in Table 10, Net-Geners who responded to this question expressed a willingness to enroll in an average of two online courses per semester. The ranges of responses were from 0 to 10 courses. The responses of the Gen-Xers and Baby Boomers were similar, in that they expressed an interest to enroll in an average of one online course. Because the Net-Geners represented a relatively large percentage of respondents (at 88%), the mean of student respondents leaned towards an average of two online courses overall. Male and female students who responded to this question expressed similar results, to enroll in an average of two online courses. Upon a review of student responses by employment status, all groups responded similarly in their willingness to enroll in an average of two online courses.

Differences among student respondents by ethnic group were also examined. All of the Asian, black, white-non-Hispanic, Chamorro-Pacific Islander and Filipino-Asian respon-

Table 10. Breakdown of student groups by generation on number of courses enrolled and number of courses willing to take online by semester

Generational Group	N	Average Number of Courses Enrolled	Standard Deviation	N	Average Number of Courses Willing to Enroll Online	Standard Deviation
Net-Geners	120	4.82	1.139	119	2.11	1.627
Gen-Xers	13	3.81	1.319	14	1.32	1.067
Baby Boomers	4	3.00	1.155	3	1.33	.577
Total	137	4.67	1.214	136	2.03	1.577

dents expressed a willingness to enroll in an average of two online courses per semester. All other-Pacific Islander respondents indicated a willingness to enroll in two to three online courses. Only one of the two Hispanic/Latino respondents expressed a willingness to enroll in online courses.

Business faculty who responded to this question were willing to teach an average of one course per semester. Notice the range of responses, indicating that at least one faculty member expressed no interest in teaching an online course. As indicated in Table 11, part of the analyses included measuring students' and faculty's confidence levels in students adopting vs. faculty teaching DE, or online, courses. Responses were measured along a four-point Likert question scale, with 1 measuring "Not at all Confident," 2 measuring "Unsure," 3 measuring "Somewhat Confident" and 4 measuring "Confident." The student confidence levels in online DE courses were relatively low, with a mean response of 2.8. Results of faculty confidence level in teaching online DE courses were similar, with a mean response of 2.9.

Differences across gender were also examined. For students, male respondents expressed they were somewhat confident in enrolling in online DE courses, based on a mean of 2.9, while their female counterparts expressed a lower confidence level, based on a mean response of 2.7. Faculty female respondents expressed they were slightly confident in teaching online DE courses, based on a mean of response of 3.00, while their male counterparts expressed less confidence, based on a mean response of 2.75. Observations for potential differences in business students' responses by ethnicity group and employment status were also made.

From Figure 3, less than 10% of student respondents (white-non-Hispanics, Hispanics/Latinos and other-Pacific Islanders) showed greater confidence levels, with Chamorro-Pacific

Table 11. Comparison between business students and faculty on confidence level toward online DE courses

	N	Mean	Standard Deviation
Student confidence in taking DE courses	140	2.77	.881
Faculty confidence in teaching a DE course	7	2.86	1.069

Figure 3. Distribution of business student responses on confidence level toward online DE courses by ethnic group

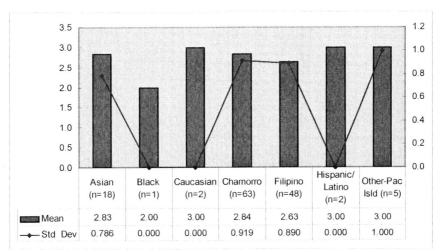

	Asian (n=18)	Black (n=1)	Caucasian (n=2)	Chamorro (n=63)	Filipino (n=48)	Hispanic/ Latino (n=2)	Other-Pac Isld (n=5)
Mean	2.83	2.00	3.00	2.84	2.63	3.00	3.00
Std Dev	0.786	0.000	0.000	0.919	0.890	0.000	1.000

Islander, Asian and Filipino-Asian respondents expressing relatively weak confidence level. The black respondent expressed that he was unsure.

In observing the mean responses among the generational groups, Gen-Xers expressed they were "somewhat confident," based on a mean response of 3.07, while Baby Boomers and Net-Geners expressed slightly lesser confidence levels by .25 points, based on mean responses of 2.75 and 2.72, respectively. Finally, in reviewing confidence levels of students towards online DE courses by employment status, most of the students expressed stronger confidence levels than those who expressed they were unsure or not at all confident. Of the 24 full-time employed respondents, 50% expressed confidence and 46% unsure, and 4% not at all confident. Of the 63 part-time employed respondents, 68% expressed confidence, while 27% unsure and 5% not at all confident. Of the 53 unemployed respondents, 53% expressed confidence, while 40% unsure and 7% not at all confident.

Willingness to Pay Higher Tuition for Online Courses

When business students were asked if they would be willing to pay a slightly higher tuition, the mean responses at all employment levels were about the same. This meant they were not sure, so there was no disagreement by students. When compared across the generation groups, the responses were very similar, in that all three groups expressed they were "un-sure." The white-non-Hispanic and the Hispanic/Latino respondents, representing relatively few numbers, expressed they would be willing to pay a slightly higher tuition for online courses. Hence, should online courses be offered, UOG should be aware that the majority of business students from this study expressed they were not willing to pay a premium for online DE courses. This may be a challenge given the additional resources required to support online DE infrastructure and the additional faculty time required to deliver courses through this format.

Solutions and Recommendations

Technology enables ease of communication between colleagues. The Internet, in particular, enables smooth and expedient communication via e-mail. In this study, students expressed a preference to communicate either by e-mail or online chat rooms with classmates and friends. Faculty, as well, prefer this mode of communication between colleagues. There appeared to be no differences among the three student generational groups in their preference towards a traditional face-to-face learning format. This is a surprise, given that this group would yield a preference towards the online learning format. Although the traditional face-to-face meetings were clearly preferred by the majority of student and faculty respondents, indications of willingness to engage in online course learning, or course delivery for faculty, prompt that both sets are ready for online education. Faculty, however, indicated that much needed resource support is required to improve their confidence level towards engaging in online education. The literature presented earlier in this chapter supports this need.

Future Trends

Despite the expressed willingness to engage in online learning, students in teaching institutions will continue to have a desire for some degree of traditional face-to-face learning environment. A hybrid, or blended approach, using a combination of face-to-face instruction and online delivery, to course delivery and learning may become the norm, as opposed to full online access to education, or face-to-face access. The varying generations, from the Net-Geners to the Baby Boomers, will find the compromise of this approach addresses various needs. Although not homogenous in their reasons for adopting online education, each generation will find that ease of communication, ready access to information, the need to expand and maintain social networks, and need for entertainment can all be met through this communication medium. The blended approach satisfies the need for visible social contact implied through both student and faculty's primary use for the Internet, or rather a sense of community that traditional face-to-face learning provides. Institutions of higher education can capitalize on this approach, and further studies are needed to assess the extent to which this approach to course delivery and learning can truly yield positive student learning outcomes, indicators popularly advocated by professional business accreditation agencies for the purpose of outcomes assessment.

Conclusion

This study was instrumental in assessing the state of readiness of business students and faculty at UOG, and the extent to which traditional face-to-face course delivery was preferred over online delivery. Despite the availability of computers and the Internet at home, students and faculty expressed the importance of access at the university campus, as well. Further, although several business faculty have expressed (outside of this study) that students are not ready for online education, students in the study appeared to have a higher level of confidence, and some have expressed exposure to online education already. The findings from both groups, on preference to have face-to-face meetings outside of class time, call, however, for a combination of both, or a hybrid (blended) approach. This concludes that business students at UOG are indeed prepared to engage in online education. Online education accessibility has become more of the norm than the exception, leaving strategic implications for institutions of higher learning that do not make this mode of education available in general, at least through a hybrid or "blended" approach. These educational institutions may be prone to a competitive disadvantage, and could very well compromise enrollment numbers. For UOG, the business students' expressed willingness to enroll in at least two online DE courses reflects a demand that should not be ignored. In view of the findings revealed in this study, the disadvantage of not making these courses available would be a lost opportunity of prospective student markets that prefer this mode of delivery.

References

Alch, M. L. (2000, July). Get ready for the net generation. *USA Today*. Retrieved July 26, 2005, from www.findarticles.com/p/articles/mi_m1272/is_2662_129/ai_63668116

Carr, V. H. (1999). *Technology adoption and diffusion*. The Learning Center for Interactive Teaching. Retrieved from July 18, 2005, from www.au.af.mil/au/awec/awcgate/innovation/adoptiondiffusion.htm

Cummings, J. A., Bank, C. J., & Jacobs, F. R. (2002). Twenty-first century college syllabi options for online communication and interactivity. *Internet and Higher Education, 4*, 1-19.

Duhaney, D. C. (2001). Teacher education: Preparing teachers to integrate technology. *International Journal of Instructional Media, 28*(1), 23-30.

Finley, L., & Hartman, D. (2004). Institutional change and resistance: Teacher preparatory faculty and technology integration. *Journal of Technology and Teacher Education, 37*, 161-175.

Gallant, G. (2000). Professional development for Web-based teaching: Overcoming innocence and resistance. *New directions for Adult and Continuing Education, 88*, 69-78.

Guhlin, M. (2002). Teachers must push technology's tidal wave. *Journal of Staff Development, 23*(1), 40-41.

Hartman, J., Moskal, P., & Dziuban, C. (2005). *Preparing the academy of today for the learner of tomorrow.* Educating the Net Generation. University of Central Florida. Retrieved July 26, 2005, from www.educause.edu/contents.asp_?page_id=6062&bhcp=1

Hay, L. (2000). Three generations of learners. *The School Administrator Web Edition.* Retrieved July 26, 2005, from www.aasa.org/publications/sa/2000_04/hay_side_learners.htm

Hodge, P. (2005). *Living younger longer: Baby boomer challenges.* White house conference on aging policy committee hearing. Retrieved July 26, 2005, from www.genpolicy.com/articles/2005_WHCoA_Policy_Committee.html

Limayen, M., & Hirt, S.G. (2000). Internet-based teaching: How to encourage university students to adopt advanced Internet-based technologies. *Proceedings of the 33rd Hawaii International Conference on System Sciences, 1*(1), 1055. Washington, DC: IEEE Computer Society.

Luke, N., Moore, J., & Sawyer, S. (1998). *Authentic approaches to encourage technology using teachers.* Charlottesville: Association for Advancement of Computing in Educating Press.

Macchiusi, L., & Trinidad, S. (2001). *Information and communication technologies: The adoption by an Australian university.* Retrieved July 26, 2005, from http:lsn.curtin.edu.au/tlf/tlf2001/machiussi.html

Means, B. (2001). Technology use in tomorrow's schools. *Educational Leadership, 58*(4), 57-61.

Moore, A. H., Moore, J. F., & Fowler, S. B. (2005). *Faculty development for the net generation.* Retrieved July 26, 2005, from www.educause.edu/FacultyDevelopmentforthe-eNetGeneration/6071

Nachmias, R. (2002). Research framework for the study of campus-wide Web-based academic instruction project. *Internet and Higher Education, 5*(3), 213-229.

Nachmias, R., & Segev, L. (2003). Usage of contents in Web-supported academic courses. *Academic Exchange Quarterly, 7*(1). Retrieved July 26, 2005, from www.rapidintellect.com/AEQweb/cho23003w.htm

Nelson Buchanan & Oostergard Pte Ltd. (2005). *Knowledge management.* Retrieved from www.nbogroup.com/articles/knowledge.htm

Nisan-Nelson, P. (2001). Technology integration: A case of professional development. *Journal of Technology and Teacher Education, 9*(1), 83-103.

Poindexter, S. (2003). *The case for holistic learning.* Retrieved July 26, 2005, from www.findarticles.com/p/articles/mi_1254/is_1_35/ai_95907512/print

Rogers, E. M. (1995). *The diffusion of innovations* (4th ed.). New York: Free Press.

Singh, P., & Pan, W. (2004). Factors affecting student adoption of online education. *Academic Exchange Quarterly, 8*(1). Retrieved July 26, 2005, from www.rapidintellect.com/AEQweb/cho25934w.htm

Smith, G. P. (2005). *Baby Boomer versus generation X managing the new workforce.* Retrieved July 26, 2005, from www.businessknowhow.com/manage/genx.htm

Soong, M. H. B., Chan, H. C., & Chua, B.,C. (2001). Critical success factors for online course resources. *Computers and Education, 36,* 101-120.

Tapscott, D. (1998). *Growing up digital-the rise of the net generation.* Retrieved July 26, 2005, from www.bizsum.com/growingupdigital.htm

Tsang-Kosma, W. (2005). *Rogers' diffusion and adoption research: What does it have to do with instructional technology?* Retrieved July 18, 2005, from www2.gsu.edu/~mstswh/ courses/it7000/papers/rogers/.htm

University of Guam. (2005, Spring). *Student enrollment by ethnicity and gender.* Guam: University of Guam, Admissions and Records Office.

Wilson, A. (2004). *If you lead them to e-learning, will they use it?* Retrieved July 26, 2005, from http://lsn.curtin.edu.au/tlf/tlf2001/macchiusi.html

Yan, Y., & Fang, X. (2004). *Technology adoption in e-commerce education: A case study.* Retrieved July 26, 2005, from http://isedj.org/isecon/2004/3164/ISECON.2004.Yan. pdf

Yohon, T., Zimmerman, D., & Keller, L. (2004). An exploratory study of adoption of course management software and accompanying instructional changes by faculty in the liberal arts and sciences. *Electronic Journal of e-Learning, 2*(2), 313-320.

Young, M. R., Klemz, B. R., & Murphy, J. W. (2003). Enhancing learning outcomes: The effects of instructional technology, learning styles, instructional methods, and student behavior. *Journal of Marketing Education, 25*(2), 130-142.

Section V

Development and Implementation of Technology and Diversity in Learning

Chapter X

A Collaborative Learning Environment to Support Distance Students in Developing Nations

Michelle Dottore, San Diego State University, USA

Steve Spencer, San Diego State University, USA

Abstract

In developing nations, information and communications technologies (ICT) offer dramatic opportunities for economic and social transformation. Such nations hope to jump-start economies and actualize human potential by providing ICT-based education and training to individuals in remote areas. Educational institutions seeking to outsource programs internationally face complex cultural, political and technological considerations not found within traditional student populations. Virtual learning environments (VLEs) are tools that provide electronic access to campus services. However, distance educators are challenged to develop VLEs that also support critical social elements of student life. The San Diego State University Interwork Institute is partnering with community colleges in the Western Pacific to offer degrees using a unique educational model. Through partnership and technology, this model blends virtual technologies with site-based facilitators and services, enabling Pacific Islanders to access advanced degrees without having to travel abroad.

Introduction

At the threshold of the 21st century, the transition from the Industrial to the Information Age is well underway. The explosion of new and sophisticated information and communications technologies (ICT) is causing a gradual, yet fundamental shift in social and economic systems worldwide (ILO, 2001; Knight, 2002). The possibility of marginalization and scarcity is real for those who lack the equipment or skills to participate in this new electronic frontier. Not wishing to be excluded, technologically underdeveloped nations are identifying resources to build infrastructure and equip residents with the skills needed to access ICT's vast potential. Many have drafted national plans to implement widespread education and training at the secondary and tertiary levels (Palau MOE, 1999; UNESCO, 2001). Conversely, governments and universities are responding by ramping up the delivery of educational programs internationally. Yet, many educational organizations lack systems and strategies to support international students, who present complex cultural, political and technological issues not typically found within traditional student populations.

Reputable distance education organizations must think beyond mere delivery of quality content. An exemplary online degree program not only offers comprehensive and targeted student support services, but also provides students with opportunities for social connectedness through access to a rich academic community. VLEs are tools that provide electronic access to some or all aspects of campus life, including libraries, program advisement and financial aid. However, distance educators are challenged to develop VLEs that also foster critical social elements of student life.

Educational organizations are applying emerging technologies to deliver high-quality instructional programs to developing nations. In this chapter, we will describe trends and critical factors affecting these efforts and present a model being implemented by the Interwork Institute at San Diego State University, in partnership with community colleges in the Western Pacific. Through partnership and technology, this model blends virtual technologies with site-based support and services, enabling Pacific Islanders to access advanced degrees without having to travel abroad. At the same time, it allows regional 2-year colleges to build capacity to meet critical educational challenges that will position their citizens with the skills and aptitudes needed in the 21st century.

New Educational Opportunities for Developing Nations

ICT has impacted societies worldwide, touching all but the furthest reaches of civilization. With the worlds of work and education converging, life-long learning will become a fundamental aspect of job security and employability in the digital age. Meanwhile, access to current and sophisticated education and training resources will provide a competitive advantage to employees, businesses and governments (ILO, 2001; Quibria, Ahmed, Tschang, & Reyes-Macasaquit, 2002). With the half-life of the latest technical innovations currently at 1 to 2 years, and quickly shrinking to just a few months (Kurzweil, 2005), technological fluency is a constantly moving target. Critical skill sets will be characterized by the ability to transform existing knowledge into new knowledge. In remote and developing nations, ICT offers dramatic opportunities for economic and social transformation. These nations hope to jump-start economies and actualize human potential by leveraging ICT to increase workforce skills and knowledge (Bloom, 2001; Quibria et al., 2002; Singh 2001; Tellei, 2004). Global policymakers concur that investment in education for third-world and developing nations is key to achieving economic growth and access to the global market. "Investment in basic and higher education is the most critical policy tool available to governments [who wish] to reap the benefits of ICT" (ILO, 2001, p. 323). Consequently, these nations are taking action to establish a solid education platform by seeking to import ICT-based degrees and programs. To access secondary and tertiary educational programs, they are exploring partnerships with foreign universities who offer distance education internationally (Knight, 2002; Rumble, 2000a; UNESCO, 2001).

Governments, private industry and universities are taking keen notice of the vast market potential in distance education, and are quickly ramping up delivery of programs to learners in remote geographic locations (Dolence & Norris, 1998; Rumble 2000a; Tait, 2003). The organization for General Agreement on Trade in Services (GATS) and the World Trade Organization (WTO) have developed initiatives for outsourcing education to developing nations, much to the concern of many who feel that these policies have been prematurely developed without proper research or enough stakeholder input. At risk are inappropriate or fiscally unsound agreements for implementing educational solutions to target populations within developing nations (Currie, 2001; Knight, 2002; UNESCO, 2005). In response to the GATS initiative and international trends in general, the United Nations Educational, Scientific and Cultural Organization (UNESCO), in collaboration with the Organization for Economic Cooperation and Development (OECD), recently held a Global Forum on International Quality Assurance, Accreditation and Recognition of Qualifications. Observing that trade in higher education is a billion-dollar business, and the demand for higher education internationally is growing into a very lucrative market, the forum's objective was to respond to emerging ethical challenges and dilemmas as a result of the globalization of higher education (UNESCO, 2001). Based on outcomes of the forum, UNESCO and OECD are now drafting a set of guidelines on "Quality provision in cross-border education" (UNESCO, 2005). The draft addresses issues surrounding transnational partnerships, local capacity building, relevance of curriculum, technical infrastructure and accessibility of education for all sectors of underdeveloped populations. From these efforts will evolve a set of recommendations to educational institutions and to nations for delivering or receiving programs via distance.

Reinventing Education to Maintain Viability

Some futurists are predicting a dramatic shift of educational responsibility to the private sector (Sokolowski, 1999). Students will be turning to the university as only one of many resources available to meet their needs, forcing universities to reinvent their role in society (Dolence & Norris, 1998). It is only through rapid and dramatic transformation that universities and educational institutions will be able to keep abreast of sophisticated learning technologies and maintain market share. Grasping the implications of this suddenly very competitive environment, many universities are searching for ways to retain life-long learners and to effectively position themselves with uniquely desirable degrees, courses and training (Gibbons,

2001; Howell, Williams,& Lindsay, 2003; Rumble, 2000b). Governments, too, are looking at educational outsourcing as an important means for continued economic development. Education is now Australia's third-largest service export (DEST, 2004). With a fiercely guarded reputation for providing quality higher education internationally, Australia is undergoing a national inquiry to refine its vision and framework for international educational programs, as evidenced in its Education for Students Overseas (ESOS) Act passed in 2000. A recent evaluation of the ESOS legislation recommends further clarification of legislative objectives, including implementing systems and policies to assure Australia's continued outstanding reputation as an international provider of educational programs (DEST, 2005).

In response to education's sudden popularity as an internationally traded commodity (Altbach, 2002), accrediting bodies, such as the Western Association of Schools and Colleges, (WASC), the Council for Higher Education Accreditation (CHEA) in Washington, DC and the Council of Europe (COE) have developed policies and best practices for distance and international education programs. These policies assert that in addition to rigorous curriculum and engaging learning experiences, quality distance education programs must be in alignment with an institution's mission and policies, and must demonstrate a commitment for support. To achieve accreditation from these agencies, a new distance education program undergoes intense scrutiny. Accreditation requirements cover the gamut of academic standards, educational best practices and student support services, ensuring that distance students receive the same quality education as that of campus-based programs. These agencies also explicitly stress the need for systems that encourage student interaction and the establishment of learning communities.

In this new market, students are becoming savvy shoppers for customized educational programs that best suit their needs and lifestyle (Howell et al., 2003). Choice points include institutional reputation; quality and relevance of instruction; flexibility in schedules; and robust, easy-to-access student support systems (Tait, 2003). Another important trend is the shift in consumer interest from availability of individualized courses toward full online degree programs. A recent study indicates that programs offering full degrees have a 4:1 success rate over programs that only provide courses without a degree outcome (Abel, 2005).

Distance Students Need Comprehensive Support

As previously mentioned, with the mobilization of distance education worldwide, concerns are being raised about academic quality and value. Problematic areas include danger of student isolation; curriculum becoming a packaged good; and "globalization of content, with reduction of cultural diversity and richness" (Rumble, 2000b, p. 2). It has been observed that retention rates for distance programs are typically 10% to 20% lower than campus-based programs (Howell et al., 2003; Miller & Elbert, 2003). Research indicates that many students are dropping through the cracks for a variety of reasons, including personal crises, non-resolution of technical issues and difficulty with admissions and bureaucratic processes (Abel, 2005).

The shift from student support on a course-by-course basis to comprehensive support throughout an entire online degree creates a new dilemma for distance education institutions—that of tracking and guiding a student throughout a program of study, from start to finish. Best practices outline many critical services that should be made available to students in an online educational program. The list is long, but includes information for prospective students, online registration, admissions assistance, financial aid, library resources, academic advisement, career services, support for students with disabilities, personal counseling, tutoring, and technical training and support (Krauth & Cargajal, 1999; Shea & Armitage, 2003). Finally, almost all best-practice guidelines stress the need for services that promote a sense of community, inside and outside the virtual classroom (Chambers, 2004; LaPadula, 2003; Levy, 2003; Ludwig-Hardman & Dunlap 2003; Tait; 2003; Wright, 2001).

Student services are an integral part of any college or university experience. They serve to decrease attrition, ease transition into college and contribute to academic success (LaPadula, 2003). Traditional campus-based student support models offer a wide array of services. However, most campuses do not offer support mechanisms that allow provision of services to distance students. Traditional campus-based student service centers are specialized and autonomous, with little interaction or sharing of information between other service centers. Organizational stove-piping obstructs a holistic approach to monitoring and supporting distance students across an academic life cycle, particularly for students with unique needs in remote regions. Interestingly, universities are finding that alongside distance education students, the new, technically savvy "Net Generation" college student is demanding a "One Stop" approach that allows students to access multiple services via single online portal (La-Padula, 2003; Oblinger & Oblinger 2005). With students in the more powerful consumer role, universities will need to find better ways to respond to the needs and desires of the non-traditional student.

Lack of adequate student services can be discouraging and isolating for the distance student (LaPadula, 2003; Tait, 2003). Even if universities were to allocate resources and staff specifically to distance programs, it is not easy to convert existing site-based services into an electronic format. Libraries, for example, have devoted extensive time and resources to making reference and academic material available online. So too, with special education services—the creation of virtual support systems for students with disabilities has involved several years of concentrated effort.

Unbundling Traditional Roles

Starting from the ground up, distance education organizations are "unbundling" traditional university functions and roles, including that of the instructor, and redefining what it means to teach and support learners at a distance (Levy, 2003; Tait, 2003). With the tremendous logistical and technical effort required to deploy an online course, instructors are no longer expected to run the show alone. Instead, technical and administrative support teams assist with coordination and delivery, while instructors are tasked to focus on providing meaningful content and instructional activities, and to take responsibility for the achievement of learning outcomes. Instructors may be assisted by facilitators, who are typically assigned small groups of students to support throughout a course. Facilitators' roles may also be expanded to that of academic advisor, tutor or learning coach, providing a consistent and familiar point of connection to students throughout an academic lifecycle (Riffee, 2003; Rumble, 2000; Tait, 2003). With flexible start dates, unique costing models and an atypical student base, distance education programs rarely fit into the existing university structure. Distance administrative support personnel take on much broader roles than their campus-based equivalents. Distance staff must often provide individualized guidance through the academic bureaucracy, closely monitoring the receipt of records, entrance exams and payment of fees. Often, administrative personnel in distance education centers have special arrangements with admissions, financial aid and records offices on campus that enable them to provide services to students that fall outside of the norm. These administrative personnel also work with libraries and campus bookstores to allow distance students access to services outside of the regular session timetable.

Connectedness through a Virtual Learning Environment

Distance education's Achilles' heel can be found within the isolation that students feel when interactivity and collaborative activities are absent from the curriculum, where courses become little more than independent study with low success rates and high learner dissatisfaction (Ludwig-Hardman & Dunlap, 2003; Tait, 2002). In fact, 90% of the student population attending Open University, United Kingdom (UK), report that they want interaction with other students (Tait, 2003). Over the years, distance education programs have become adept at incorporating interactivity *within* a course through group activities, class-wide dialog and managed interaction between participants. However, the model fails at the programmatic level, *outside* of the virtual classroom. The resulting sense of isolation is linked to attrition, lower achievement levels, reduced satisfaction with the learning experience and a disconnectedness with the university (Krauth & Carbajal, 1999; Ludwig-Hardman & Dunlap, 2003).

It is widely agreed that the cumulative effect of a college degree goes beyond that of becoming knowledgeable in a particular field of study. Rather, the "College Experience" treasured by most graduates conjures up a myriad of social, emotional and cognitive events that, over time, culminate into a transformational rite of passage. The next question, then, is how to deliver a rich and meaningful academic experience in an online environment? The answer provided by distance education research almost always points to the interaction with classmates, instructors, advisors and educational coordinators to create a sense of mutual support and growth, as an academic community:

Our communities today are formed around issues of identity and shared values; they are not place-based. There is a dynamic whole that emerges when a group of people share common practices, are interdependent, make decisions jointly, identify themselves with something larger than the sum of their individual relationships and make long-term commitment to well-being (their own, one another's and the group's). (Palloff & Pratt, 1999, p. 26)

The challenge to distance educators is that of providing a comprehensive student services network while simultaneously forging an academic learning community using ICT-based tools and strategies. Dillenbourg (2000) describes a VLE as an information space that is "populated" and where educational interactions occur. VLEs are inherently social, and use the word "place" to emphasize that notion. As in the real world, participants are able to modify virtual "rooms" to serve their unique needs and interests. Dillenbourg suggests that the VLE allows members to co-construct the virtual space, extending the level of participation from that of merely being *active* to the role of *actor*. In these early stages, it is important to note that most virtual environments overlap with physical environments. Electronic environments are still in the experimental stages, with several university VLEs currently providing a narrow range of support services and interactive experiences geared to specific student populations. Ideally, VLEs provide a single point of entry for students, faculty and staff to access courses, student services and a thriving academic community.

Online learning communities are products of the skillful blending of technology and pedagogy (Dillenbourg, 2000). To proliferate, they require nurturing and motivated effort on the part of learners and instructors. They evolve as a course progresses but, too often dissipate with the close of the course and assignment of the grade. Sometimes the learning community reconvenes, through collaborative activities in courses further down the road. However, in many online programs, there is no vehicle for sustained community interaction. A conscious effort must be made to put structures in place that further the dialog and social exchange.

Despite the sparseness of information conveyed through electronic communication tools, relationship and community can thrive in an online environment. If tools and spaces are made available within a VLE, camaraderie and dialog can continue to occur outside of the classroom, allowing students to form lasting bonds, similar to those found among college students on any campus. If we are seeking an engaged and thriving academic community that centers around a program and an institution, the electronic learning environment must not only simulate campus-based support services, but also integrate engaging activities that build and sustain social and collaborative interests. Lesser, Fontaine and Slusher (2000) add four key challenges in building virtual communities; the technical, social, management and personal challenge:

1. *The technical challenge: Design human interfaces that not only make information available, but help community members think together;*

2. *Social challenge: Develop communities that share knowledge and still maintain enough diversity of thought to encourage differences;*

3. *Management challenge: Create a support network that allows members to accomplish intended activities easily without technical or participant obstruction; and*

4. *Personal challenge: Maintain openness to the ideas of others and a thirst for new knowledge.* (p. 34)

Cognizant educational institutions recognize that even student support systems developed for "traditional students" must become fluid and dynamic service portals to meet the needs and expectations of online and "Net Generation" students. The VLE is designed to extend beyond the walls of the virtual classroom and into the university community. It is tasked with the goal of providing both managed and spontaneous opportunities for student support, learning and academic community building. Although VLEs can help colleges improve student support systems, implementation of a VLE within most universities will require organizational culture change and re-engineering of business processes within colleges (JISC, 2003).

Regional Implications to Education by Distance

Gibbons defines the term "globalization" as the adaptation and marketing of existing solutions to local environments (2001, p. 5). When exporting education to foreign countries, institutions must seek to harmonize programs against regional standards and policies so they may best meet the needs of foreign populations. Alignment efforts often involve activities such as cross articulation of courses, identification of cross-border financial aid, reevaluation of degrees by accrediting bodies such as WASC or CHEA, and clearance by Ministries of Education or local educational agencies (McBurnie & Ziguras, 2001; UNESCO, 2005). Finesse and expertise is required to "hybridize" academic standards and learning outcomes that integrate and support the cultural diversity and richness of the populations served. Without losing focus on learning outcomes and pedagogical rigor, curriculum and instruction should address a variety of cultural, environmental and technical aspects at the local level.

Increasing diversity requires increased learner support (McCracken, 2004). Prior to program design and implementation, cultural, physical and technical aspects of the local environment should be assessed to ensure the use of appropriate learning solutions. For example, in some non-Western cultures, ancient learning traditions were based in oral and real-world activities such as storytelling and apprenticeship (Rechebei & McPhetres, 1997; Tellei, 2004). For these cultures, curriculum that is text laden may be less effective than the use of graphics, visual and audio material alongside field-based activities. Similarly, activities involving egalitarian class-wide discussions may be a new experience for these populations and, therefore, extremely challenging. The situation may be exacerbated when English is a second language (ESL). Interestingly, distance tools seem well suited to shy, inhibited or ESL individuals, allowing them to "post" or "submit" ideas only after they have had time to formulate and edit them. In a final example, group work is another area that may push against traditional boundaries, with members of varying clans and ranks expected to forgo cultural norms to complete project activities as a team. Sensitivity to these and other cultural issues during the design and implementation phases helps to ensure successful learning outcomes.

When considering local educational facilities, assessment should include classroom size and availability as well as local access to textbooks, research materials, and libraries. It is also important to identify learning spaces and community resources that support authentic activities, including fieldwork and practicum. Evaluators should make determinations regarding computer labs, Internet availability and speed (throughout various times of day and seasons), configuration of local servers, and student access to computers at home or on the job. In developing nations, shortwave radio is also a viable means for delivering education. In ICT-based programs, even evaluation and identification of e-mail providers can become an important activity. Students with no personal computer do better with Web-based e-mail accounts that allow them to access their e-mail from any Internet-ready machine. In low Internet-bandwidth areas, e-mail accounts that offer minimal graphic interfaces, such as Gmail, are preferable to high-graphic interfaces, such as Yahoo or Hotmail.

Perhaps most critical to the success of online programs offered to international students is the implementation of site-based facilitators. Best practices indicate that providing students with facilitators or mentors helps ensure successful completion rates (Riffee, 2003; Tait, 2003). In a study of high-quality, international educational institutions, Roberts (2004) identifies local and individualized student support systems as resulting in improved completion rates.

The study recommends the presence of local facilities and resources, academic advisement and mentoring, and allowance for learner input in decisions regarding program design and implementation. The study also concluded that international educational programs should find ways to encourage participation by students, facilitators and instructors in a community of learning.

Case Study: VLEs to Support Pacific Partnerships

In the emerging knowledge-based economy, there is a causal link between education and economic growth (ILO, 2001). Developing nations have the opportunity to "leapfrog" traditional phases of economic development by leveraging ICT. However, without access to adequate educational resources, workforces will not be able to take advantage of ICT potential. As part of their economic growth plan for the new millennium, entities in the Western Pacific region are seeking ways to implement widespread access to 4-year and graduate degree programs (Palau MOE, 1999; UNESCO, 2000). In the Federated States of Micronesia (FSM) alone, there are approximately 1,600 teachers, about 30% of whom are educated at the high school level, 40% holding AA or AS degrees, 20% holding a third-year teacher certificate and only 10% with a bachelor of arts (BA) (ADB, 1998). Most teachers serving in FSM have had no formal teacher training courses, with an overall low literacy rate in FSM directly related to teachers lacking the skills needed to provide adequate instruction.

The population rate of children in FSM is increasing, while at the same time, formally educated teachers are leaving FSM for more profitable jobs on the U.S. mainland and other countries. These two factors put the projected need of new teachers at 160 annually. Yet the college system within FSM is able to graduate a significantly lower rate of new teachers per year with an AA degree. Currently, there is no comprehensive training program for incumbent teachers. As a case in point, FSM demonstrates the need throughout the Western Pacific to ramp up new teacher education programs in the region that can realistically respond to the urgent need for qualified teachers. FSM and other Pacific entities have elevated teacher education to a top priority, and have developed national policies to support this effort (Palau MOE, 1999; UNESCO, 2005). Unfortunately, on island, existing 2-year colleges are not able to respond to the magnitude of need for BA-level training.

The potential for exciting new opportunities to meet current and future educational needs of remote and developing nations can be found within close partnerships between local community colleges and external 4-year colleges. Over the past 25 years, the Interwork Institute at San Diego State University (SDSU) has provided education and training to the emerging nations of the Western Pacific. Programs and services have been delivered in American Samoa, FSM, Republic of the Marshall Islands, Guam, Commonwealth of the Northern Marianas Islands and the Republic of Palau. Inherent to its mission and vision, SDSU Interwork Institute has forged several partnerships with community colleges and other government agencies in the Pacific region that allow bachelor's- and master's-level programs to be delivered locally, on island. This regional collaborative model for education is strategically different than the student-driven model, in which individuals seeking an education must work with foreign universities to gain admittance and matriculate through a program—essentially conducting all college activities without the benefit of local support services. For international students, the admissions process alone can be formidable. The result is that many potentially good students drop out even before coming under the radar of university administrative staff. In direct contrast, this regional collaborative model offers a comprehensive program negotiated in partnership with a local community college or Ministry of Education. The model allows high-quality curriculum of a well-developed distance education program to be effectively implemented in rural Pacific island settings, and enables degree programs to be offered in partnership with local 2-year colleges.

The partnerships are designed to leverage the strengths of each institution, to offer comprehensive student support jointly. Marketing, recruitment, advisement, financial aid and other logistics are predominately handled through the local educational institution. SDSU focuses on delivering high-quality, upper-division and graduate-level courses via distance as well as providing sophisticated educational resource tools to support the academic community. Students participating in the program have local access to Internet-ready computer labs and technical support, a community college library and classrooms. Research-quality materials, professional journals and reading resources are provided through the SDSU university library portal, alongside other electronic and non-electronic university support systems. This joint partnership approach minimizes fragmentation and confusion for students by providing knowledgeable support staff on island, who are usually faculty members and employees of the local college. Students identify with being affiliated with the local college while attending a well-known university. External resources provided by SDSU are seen as complementing local resources and building local capacity, rather than as goods offered by an outsider who is trying to sell something that might not fit local needs.

This collaborative model has become a successful means for a 2-year community college within a developing nation to be able to "broker" bachelor's- and master's-degree programs without having to become a 4-year educational institution. The potential for this model is significant, as most of these developing entities do not have the resources to support an advanced degree offering. The win-win situation allows local community colleges in rural/remote Pacific island settings to present opportunities for students to fully participate in advanced degree programs without having to leave the island. Local colleges then gain further credibility and recognition by providing the means to meet their own critical national educational goals. For this type of model to work effectively, all members of the collaborative must have a sense of trust and mutual respect. There are many hurdles and "square pegs" to be fit into "round holes," requiring a strong commitment by all parties in order to reach a successful conclusion.

Interwork Student Information System-VLE: Tools and Techniques

To address student needs in the Pacific at both the course and programmatic level, SDSU Interwork Institute is implementing a VLE that combines ICT and face-to-face activities in a blended format. The blending of technology with live human interaction at a local level firmly positions the Pacific community colleges or Ministries of Education as a central figure in the degree offering and as advisor for regional and cultural aspects of the program. The Interwork Student Information System (ISIS) VLE integrates social spaces, online grade books, electronic portfolios and other campus support mechanisms to provide an academic network for students in multiple time zones and throughout a degree lifecycle. The ISIS-VLE is composed of a suite of ICT applications that enables students and instructional staff to access information and services using an Internet Web browser. Interwork Institute has been developing and testing the ISIS-VLE system over the past year. The applications and tools at this point are still somewhat disconnected. In the coming year, SDSU Interwork Institute will be integrating the individual tools into a single platform. It is important to note that ISIS-VLE is designed to be "bandwidth friendly" and fully accessible for students with disabilities. We have several students within and outside of the U.S. who are using dial-up access, or are limited in bandwidth at their campus or on island. We also have several students who use screen readers or require captioning or alternative forms of multimedia and materials. It is imperative to us that students are able to fully participate in a robust and engaging learning experience through unobstructed access to content, faculty, staff and each other.

The ISIS-VLE Administrative Support Tool

A technology tool that sustains an academic program requires seamless and integrated information management. The ability to track a student from initial contact through application, coursework, graduation, and alumni phases contributes to effective and individualized support. Prior to implementation of ISIS-VLE, the incredible detail required to enroll and manage our distance students caused duplication of effort, loss of historical details, and confusion for students and staff. The new ISIS-VLE consolidates information within a single system, enabling administrative personnel to determine the status of an individual immediately (see Figure 1).

Using an activity tracking tool (see Figure 2), support personnel are able to capture and retrieve narrative information and commentary. This type of information can be important, for example, when making personal contact, and allows for further personalization of student support and tracking. In ISIS-VLE, support personnel can also hand off tasks to other personnel through a task assignment form. Once assigned, the task is e-mailed to the designee for follow-up. Using a Web browser, personnel can view all open tasks assigned to them or others through various options in the system.

ISIS-VLE Student Portal

Throughout our years of delivering Web-based distance education, students have continually requested spaces outside of the virtual classroom for sharing of information with colleagues and faculty. Similar to the powerful community spaces designed within the popular Yahoo! Groups or other public Internet portals, the final ISIS-VLE will include personal Web pages (see Figure 3), directories, blogs and discussion places. The student portal provides students with a snapshot their of current academic status, direct access to classes, news and headlines specific to each program, ability to purchase books online and access to the library, grades and more. It also provides an electronic portfolio where they can share their progress and showcase their work to the academic community.

Students can update their profile and email address, or share favorite sites and resources using the tools provided by ISIS-VLE (see Figure 4).

Figure 1. Program activity matrix allows for customization of program requirements and procedures

Group	Activity Description	Repetition	Status	Display Order	Action
Admission	SDSU Application	No	Yes	1	✎ ✗
	SDSU Application Fee	No	Yes	2	✎ ✗
	Program Application	No	Yes	3	✎ ✗
	Department Recommendation Form	No	Yes	4	✎ ✗
	GRE Score	Yes	Yes	5	✎ ✗
	TOEFL	No	Yes	6	✎ ✗
	Transcripts	Yes	Yes	7	✎ ✗
	Letter of Recommendation	Yes	Yes	8	✎ ✗
	Interviews	Yes	Yes	9	✎ ✗
	RSA Scholarship Agreement forms	No	Yes	10	✎ ✗
	SDSU Foundation Forms (TAX)	No	Yes	11	✎ ✗
	Admitted to Dept	No	Yes	12	✎ ✗
	Admitted to University	No	Yes	13	✎ ✗
					Update Activity Order
Program	Program Start	No	Yes	1	✎ ✗
	Advisory Assignment	No	Yes	2	✎ ✗
	Listsrvs	No	Yes	3	✎ ✗
	Send Students Startup Materials	No	Yes	4	✎ ✗
	Foundation cert. For eligibility form	No	Yes	5	✎ ✗
	Taxation of scholarship	No	Yes	6	✎ ✗

Figure 2. Activity tracking enables support personnel to view contact details and status of support activities; personnel may also assign tasks to themselves or others

Interwork Student Information System Student Info Administration Reports Logout

E HISTORY | FOLLOW-UP REQUIRED | ACTIVITY HISTORY | Coordinator Logged in: Young H. Jang

• Add New Activity   • Add New Student

Student Name	Mr. John Dow	Profile Type	Pre-Admission
Street (1st)	5555 Main St.	Email: Home	john.dow@yahoo.com
Street (2nd)	N/A	Email: Work	johnd@work.com
City	San Diego	Program Interest	Assistive Technology
State	CA	Interest Level	Very Interested
Zip Code	92111	Advisor	Linda Libsack
Day Phone	(619) 555-4231	Referral	Friends
Night Phone	(619) 554-3256		

ACTIVITY HISTORY

Activity #	DATE/FOLLOW-UP RQD	ACTIVITY / BY WHO / COMMENTS	ACTION	STATUS
11	3/11/2005 1:17:15 am	**Phone Call - In / Young Jang** Mr. John Dow called for assistance on finnacial service for tuition.	Add Comment Cancel Activity	OPEN 0/1 Done 1 Open
11.1	3/11/2005 1:19:28 am assigned to Tom Turner Due By 3/16/2005	**Phone Call - Out / Young Jang** Tom, please give him a call by next Wednesday and assist him on financial aids. Thanks.	Add Comment Cancel Activity	OPEN
9	3/11/2005 12:55:39 am	**Email Received / Young Jang** Mr. John Dow sent an email request for more information about Assistive Technology Certification program.	Add Comment Cancel Activity	OPEN 0/1 Done 1 Open
9.1	3/11/2005 1:03:24 am assigned to Linda Libsack Due By 3/23/2005	**Send Email / Young Jang** Linda, please send the program information packet to Mr. John Dow before 3/23. Thanks.	Add Comment Cancel Activity	OPEN

The virtual campus gateway (see Figure 5) allows access to the student portal and other university-based academic support tools. Here, students will find additional services, such as resources for financial aid, technology and orientation tutorials, as well as places to interact with fellow students, faculty and distance learning staff. Although graphics and visual appeal tend to lose their importance after an initial period of use (Dillenbourg, 2000), we chose to correspond functional areas within the virtual campus to physical images on our campus. We hope this will serve to increase the affinity and connection to the university. This may change if usability tests indicate they should be replaced with a more linear, text-based gateway to the virtual campus.

Figure 3. Student portal allows students to access current records, classes and their electronic portfolio

Figure 4. Student profile area gives students a place to share personal and academic information about themselves

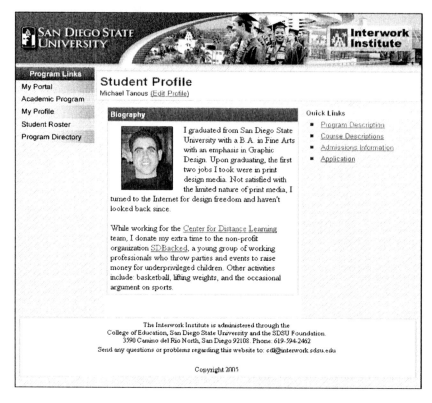

Course-Based Tools and Technologies

As mentioned earlier, most distance courses regularly provide multiple opportunities for intellectual and social interaction. In our case, we would like to share two techniques in particular that have resulted in strengthening the academic community. To meet diverse learning needs, SDSU faculty and instructional designers are continually searching for ways to collect information that will inform the design of culturally appropriate curriculum. We have successfully engaged students and instructors in a "getting to know you" introductory discussion board during the design phase of each course several weeks before it goes live. In these boards, faculty members inquire about students' knowledge and background in specific subject areas. Questions range from sharing of personal knowledge and experiences

Figure 5. Virtual campus provides a gateway to student support in the larger context, simulating services provided at the university

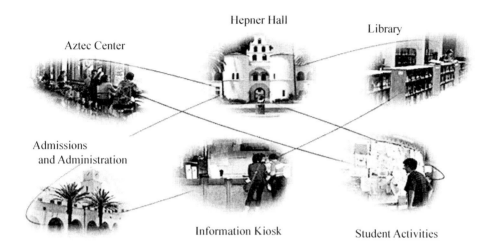

to requests by the instructor for regional curriculum standards and textbooks used on island. This information then serves to guide the course development process. The discussion board also gives students and faculty a chance to "meet" and get to know each other before the course starts. Students are enthusiastic about meeting their instructors and having a chance to disclose fears or lack of knowledge in a safe and casual environment, outside of the classroom. At the same time, faculty members enjoy discovering more about their students culturally, professionally and academically.

The site based "Circle Group" activity is another technique we have used successfully with learners in the Pacific. The power of the Circle Group is in the negotiation of meaning and the sharing of local experiences and perspectives with classmates on other islands. During the week, individuals explore a central theme or topic through readings and online activities. Students then meet face to face with local facilitators to continue exploration of the topic through guided questions. At the close of the Circle Group session, a student volunteers to summarize the group dialog using an online webform. Once submitted, the group's summary is automatically sent out to other student groups via email. When individuals in the same class are spread across geographically diverse locations, they delight in comparing the similarities and differences between groups. Circle Groups are particularly invaluable for pods of learners situated across multiple locations or islands.

Electronic Grade Book

Although many course management systems provide grading tools, few offer space for rich commentary and feedback. We implemented an electronic grade book several years ago and it remains one of the most important tools in our VLE suite. Moving the grading process from spreadsheets and e-mail to a central Web-based environment has helped to metamorphose what was once a logistical nightmare into a valuable feedback and tracking tool (see Figure 6). Students and instructional staff can review the grade book from any Web-ready computer, reducing interruption in feedback activities due to travel or computer difficulties.

A Regional Facilitation Model

An important factor in the success of this distance education model is the involvement of facilitators at the local level. We implemented facilitators into the online program to serve two important functions: introduce a formal structure for capacity building at the local level, and promote and support the specific learning needs of students in the online degree program.

Figure 6. A Web-based grade book provides a central location for feedback accessible from any Internet-ready computer

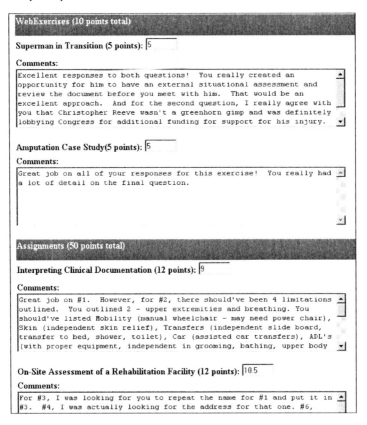

As the program is implemented, community college faculty or professionals within the field of study are selected to serve as facilitators. In this role, they gain new teaching skills and are able to broaden their use of technology to teach and learn.

Using a strategy that blends an online format with facilitated local support allows individuals to participate in advanced degree programs while remaining in current jobs, without impact to families and the local community. Until now, educational programs that require participants to leave island have often resulted in these individuals never returning, a phenomenon frequently referred to as "brain drain." This becomes a cost-effective and practical solution to teacher and workforce development. As evidence of the success of this model, three of the four current presidents of the 2-year colleges in the Western Pacific have participated in programs offered through SDSU.

The SDSU facilitated online regional model has evolved over the past several years from a program implemented in the FSM to deliver teacher-training courses in special education. This widely successful program enabled students, who were distributed across four states, multiple islands and 3,000 miles, to have access to courses not available locally. During its 3 years of implementation, all four courses in the program were completed by more than 150 teachers, many of whom were using computers and the Internet for the first time. The program demonstrated high retention rates (85%-90%) and enthusiastic learners who were able to apply newly gained skills and knowledge directly to the classroom. Even more exciting were reports of networking and professional affiliation among teachers across vast distances. These teachers delighted in meeting their virtual classmates at national and international conferences and in sharing regional differences and similarities in policy and educational activities. Based on course evaluations, the comments below are typical of the impact that this model served (personal communication, December 2, 2001):

- "I think I would not learn from traditional course as much as I have learned from this distance education. So thank you very much for such a wonderful opportunity, I just wish more teachers would take it."

- "Communication was out of this world! Support was very helpful. I almost dropped out, but thanks to my facilitators, it didn't happen."

- "We had an excellent group. I enjoyed working with and sharing with my fellow students in this course. [The facilitator] was with us all the way, making sure we stayed on task and resolved any problems we had and helped us when we got 'stuck.' He valued our input and worked with us."

Interwork Institute SDSU is continuing to refine and expand the facilitated model. Recently, it partnered with Palau Community College (PCC) to develop a distance learning program that will allow individuals who have achieved an AS degree through PCC to complete an inter-disciplinary bachelors degree program specifically designed for educators. Using the ISIS-VLE alongside the facilitated online regional model, the bachelor's degree is conferred through SDSU. The program is designed to prepare teachers with skills and expertise necessary to provide high-quality instruction for the students of Palau. Integral to the success of the program is a teacher training curriculum that incorporates practical applications within the context of Palau. There is an immediate theory-to-practice approach for students. The island-based course facilitators work with SDSU professors to integrate local needs into the curriculum and determine ways to practically apply skills within the public schools of Palau. Courses have been adapted to incorporate local context and cultural issues, particularly in the critical content areas of mathematics, literacy and technology.

Within this model, the facilitator helps to assure student success by offering logistical support and guidance throughout the learning process. As an essential member of the educational delivery team, the facilitator establishes meeting dates, motivates and monitors students, and serves as a liaison between the students, instructors, and university. He or she will also assist with access to technology and meeting spaces, notify students or instructors of situations or events impacting the class, etc. Thus facilitators are tasked with a variety of jobs that are vital to maintaining a consistency and flow within a program, from beginning to end. A vital contribution made by the facilitator is that of "learning guide," helping students find value in course and program goals. Figure 7 compares roles played by the instructor and facilitator in the facilitated online regional model.

Pedagogical strategies used by the facilitator include techniques to help students conceptualize, clarify, synthesize and localize the content (Figure 8). Facilitators must provide sustained learning support throughout the entire degree, maintaining the momentum between courses. The support role thus extends over long periods of time, and is instrumental in establishing and maintaining the learning community as well as the community college/university affiliation.

Figure 7. A comparison of roles played by the instructor and facilitator

Facilitated Online Regional Model: Instructor and Learning Facilitator Roles	
Instructor	**Learning Facilitator**
Presents the Theories	Facilitates Practice and Application
Provides the "What"	Facilitates the "So What"
Provides the "Big Picture" *-Global-*	Facilitates "My Picture" *-Local-*
Provides Cutting-Edge Content	Facilitates Synthesis of Content

Figure 8. Pedagogical strategies available to the learning facilitator

Pedagogical Strategies Provided by the Site-Based Learning Facilitator	
Conceptualize	Using the material and activities provided online, the facilitator assists students in formulating new concepts relevant to personal experiences, current work experiences and future job goals. The facilitator may accomplish this through large-class face-to-face discussions and e-mail follow-up to questions. The facilitator may also provide input to online discussions.
Clarify	The facilitator plays an important role in helping clarify key concepts and theories. Given the diverse background and experiences of the learners, it is important to work with each student to ensure that major concepts are being internalized with practical considerations for implementation. The facilitator may provide this guidance during periodic large- or small-group meetings and by serving as mentor to individuals.
Synthesize	The facilitator assists students to use the information and concepts being presented online in conjunction with their unique circumstances to formulate new understanding. Facilitators work with learners to negotiate meaning and generalize ideas.
Localize	The facilitator works with students to transfer "theory" into "practice." The facilitator provides a local context to assist students in formulating practical individual and group projects that directly relate to the working environment. Through application of theory, students interact within the local setting for case study and experiences relevant to their needs.

The partnership between the university and local educational institutions has proven invaluable in getting these programs underway, with each institution making critical contributions to program success. Island community colleges and Ministries of Education dedicate resources, such as classrooms, computer labs, technical and administrative staff, and local faculty, who serve as facilitators. Local institutions have also been instrumental in identifying students for the programs and assisting with the admissions process. Due to its success in the first year at Palau Community College, the facilitated online regional model has allowed SDSU to partner with institutions throughout the Western Pacific to offer a bachelor's degree for teachers as well as a second bachelor's degree with an emphasis in special education.

Distance Support Staff

It is imperative that we mention the critical role played by distance support staff. When offering a program internationally, support staff are geographically disparate, yet must be in continuous communication. For example, the admissions process requires extensive time and attention to detail on both sides. Staff must work closely with Academic Affairs and Admissions offices on each campus to track submission of applications and fees, transcripts, completion of entrance exams, and other activities necessary for admission to the university.

Support staff also manage logistical tasks such as travel arrangements for visiting professors, shipment and duplication of course materials, provision of technical support in computer labs, tracking down missing students, maintaining current email addresses and listservs, turning in grades, and a myriad of other duties that keep the program running smoothly. As a side note, we have found instant messaging (IM) to be a fundamental tool for communication with our remote teams in the Pacific. Through IM we can work out specifics that were not clearly communicated over email, or quickly resolve small issues that arise. IM is helpful in supporting and sustaining partnership. This "ounce" of an application has provided a "pound's" worth of value, particularly when work schedules across time zones overlap by only a few hours.

Conclusion

Going to college is much more than attending class. It is an opportunity to develop a sophisticated set of skills and knowledge that will support an individual throughout a lifetime of learning. A quality distance education program must find ways to incorporate into the curriculum the rich and memorable academic, social and transformational experiences held so dear to college graduates around the world. Beyond the narrow walls of the virtual classroom lies a lively and robust academic community. Best practices suggest that in addition to the availability of meaningful and sustained social interaction, students should have access to comprehensive academic support services made available through an online, easily accessible format. Several additional layers of complexity are introduced when distance education programs are delivered internationally. The presence of site-based facilitators and local support systems have proven to be critical to the success of international distance education programs. Facilitators can function in a multitude of roles, including learning guide, liaison between university and student, technology champion, and advisor on cultural and local learning needs.

In the technical arena, VLEs strive to embody all elements of a college experience, including access to library resources, financial aid, disabled student services as well as providing means to support the social aspects of student life—sharing of interests, learning experiences, and mutual support—outside of the classroom. VLEs are, by nature, technologically based. They integrate Web tools, databases, software applications, graphics and more. However, at the heart of a VLE are engaging learning spaces and human interaction, found both electronically and in the natural environment.

The "college experience" should be an opportunity available to all students, including distance learners. Integrating the notion of a VLE into the big picture serves to guide the vision of student support networks for universities wishing to export programs internationally. It is our prediction that VLEs developed out of necessity by distance education centers today will come full circle, to inform future solutions for universities facing the onslaught of the consumer-oriented "Net Generation."

Michael Fullan, renowned educational reformist suggested, "The society that will most successfully face the challenges ahead is one that is truly a learning society" (1993, p.131). San Diego State University, Interwork Institute has integrated technology and human touch to develop a facilitated online regional model for distance education that is VLE supported. While providing tools for monitoring and tracking individual students across an entire academic lifecycle, this model blends virtual environments with face to face contact to achieve social interaction and nurturing of the academic community. Collaboratively, local community colleges and Ministries of Education form partnerships with a prominent university to offer bachelor's and master's degrees, expanding access to educational programs that would not be available otherwise. The blending of technology and pedagogy fosters a free flow of knowledge across borders, allowing for a global, yet customized learning opportunity. The collaborative partnership shared by SDSU and its Pacific neighbors have so far provided all participants—students, instructors, facilitators, and support staff—with a unique capacity building opportunity to teach, learn, and grow academic communities. It is through this endeavor and others like it that Pacific island residents, and eventually populations within other developing nations will create and demonstrate new paradigms for education that help lead the way to an equitable and dynamic learning society.

References

Abel, R. (2005). *Achieving success in Internet-supported learning in higher education.* Alliance for Higher Education Competitiveness. Retrieved February 2, 2005, from www.a-hec.org/research/study_reports/IsL0205/TOC.html

Altbach, P. (2002). Knowledge and education as international commodities: The collapse of the common good. *Current Issues in Catholic Higher Education, 2*(22), 55-60.

Asian Development Bank (ADB). (1998). *Annual report.* Retrieved February 2, 2005, from *www.adb.org/Documents/Reports/Annual_Report/1998/default.asp*

Bloom, D. (2001). Higher education in developing countries: Peril and promise. *Society for Research in Higher Education (SRHE) International News, 46.* Retrieved November 2, 2005, from www.srhe.ac.uk/documents/inewsglobalisation.pdf#print

Chambers, D. P. (2004). From recruitment to graduation: A whole-of-institution approach to supporting online students. *Journal of Distance Learning Administration, 7*(4). Retrieved July 18, 2005, from www.westga.edu/%/7Edistance/winter74/winter74.htm

Council for Higher Education Accreditation (CHEA). (2002). *Accreditation and assuring quality in distance learning.* CHEA Institute for Research and Study of Accreditation and Quality Assurance. Retrieved March 1, 2005, from www.chea.org

Currie, J. (2001). Gumnut University as an enterprise university: An Australian case. *SRHE International News, 46.* Retrieved November 2, 2005, from www.srhe.ac.uk/documents/inewsglobalisation.pdf#print

Department of Education, Science, and Technology (DEST). (2004). *Auditing the offshore activity of Australian higher education providers.* Retrieved June 2, 2005, from www.dest.gov.au/sectors/international_education/policy_issues_reviews_issues_reviews/reviews/quality_auditing_of_offshore_delivery

Department of Education, Science, and Technology (DEST). (2005). *Evaluation of the education services for overseas students act 2000.* Retrieved June 2, 2005, from www.dest.gov.au/sectors/international_education/publications_resources/profiles/evaluation_report.htm#abstract

Dillenbourg, P. (2000). *Workshop on virtual learning environments: Learning in the new millennium. EUN Conference.* Retrieved June 2, 2005, from http://tecfa.unige.ch/tecfa.unige.ch/tecfa/publicat/dil-papers-2/Dil.7.5.18.pdf

Dolence, M. G., & Norris, D. M. (1998). *Transforming higher education: A vision for learning in the 21st century.* Ann Arbor: Society for College and University Planning.

Gibbons, M. (2001). Globalisation in higher education: A view for the south. *SRHE International News, 46.* Retrieved June 2, 2005, from www.srhe.ac.uk/documents/inews-globalisation.pdf#print

Howell, S. L., Williams, P. B., & Lindsay, N. K. (2003). Thirty-two trends affecting distance education: An informed foundation for strategic planning. *Online Journal of Distance Learning Administration, 7*(3). Retrieved November 10, 2005, from www.westa.edu/~distance/ojdla/fall63/howell63.html

International Labor Organization (ILO). (2001). *World employment report 2001: Life at work in the information economy.* Geneva: Author.

Joint Information Systems Committee (JISC). (2003). MLEs and VLEs explained: MLE briefing paper 1. *JISC MLE Information Pack.* Retrieved August 10, 2005, from www.jisc.ac.uk/mle/reps/briefings/bp1.html

Knight, J. (2002). Trade in higher education services: The implications of GATS. *The Observatory on Borderless Higher Education.* Retrieved March 10, 2005, from www.obhe.ac.uk/products/reports/publicaccesspdf/March2002.pdf

Krauth, B., & Carbajal, J. (1999). Guide to developing online student services. *Western Cooperative for Educational Telecommunications.* Retrieved May 10, 2005, from www.wcet.info/resources/publications/guide/guide.htm

LaPadula, M. (2003). A comprehensive look at online student support services for distance learners. *The American Journal of Distance Education, 17*(2), 119-128.

Levy, S. (2003). Six factors to consider when planning online distance learning programs in higher education. *Online Journal of Distance Learning Administration, 6*(1). Retrieved July 1, 2005, from www.westga.edu%7Edistance/ojdla/spring61/spring61.htm

Ludwig-Harwman, S., & Dunlap, J. C. (2003). Learner support services for online students: Scaffolding for success. *International Review of Research in Open and Distance Learn-*

ing, 4(1). Retrieved May 5, 2005, from www.irrodl.org/content/v4.1/dunlap.html

McBurnie, G., & Ziguras, C. (2001). The regulation of transnational higher education in Southeast Asia: Case studies of Hong Kong, Malaysia, and Australia. *Higher Education, 42*, 85-105.

McCracken, H. (2004). Extending virtual access: Promoting engagement and retention through integrated support systems. *Online Journal of Distance Learning Administration, 3*(1). Retrieved July 1, 2005, from www.westga.edu/%7Edistance/jmain11.html

Miller, P. E. (2003). *Lessons from afar: Concerns of distance students.* Paper presented at the 10th Annual International Distance Education Conference. Retrieved July 1, 2005, from www.cdlr.tamu.edu/dec_2003/decProceedings/20-Miller-Lessons%20from%20afar.pdf

Oblinger, D., & Oblinger, J. (2005). *EDUCAUSE e-book: Educating the net generation.* Retrieved July 1, 2005, from www.educause.edu/educatingthenetgen

Palau Ministry of Education (Palau MOE). (1999). *Palau 2000 master plan for educational improvement.* Palau: Palau Ministry of Education, Bureau of Curriculum and Instruction.

Palloff, R. M., & Pratt, K. (1999). *Building learning communities in cyberspace: Effective strategies for the online classroom.* San Francisco: Jossey-Bass.

Quibria, M. G., Ahmed, S. N., Tschang, T., & Reyes-Macasquit, M. L. (2002). *Digital divide: Determinants and policies with special reference to Asia.* Asian Development Bank. (Economics and Research Department Working Paper Series No. 27). Manila Philippines.

Rechebei, E. D., & McPhetres, S. F. (1997). *History of Palau: Heritage of an emerging nation.* Koror: Palau Ministry of Education.

Riffee, W. H. (2003). Putting a faculty face on distance education programs. *Syllabus Magazine.* Retrieved July 1, 2005, from www.campus-technology.com/article.asp?id=7233

Roberts, D. (2004). *Learner support in South African distance education: A case study.* Third Pan-Commonwealth Forum on Open Learning, July 4-8. Dunedin, New Zealand.

Rumble, G. (2000a). Student support in distance education in the 21st century: Learning from service management. *Distance Education Melbourne: 2000, 21*(2), 216-235.

Rumble, G. (2000b). *The globalization of open and flexible learning: considerations for planners and managers.* Retrieved July 1, 2005, from www.westga.edu%7Edistance/ojdla/fall33/fall33.html

Shea, P., & Armitage, S. (2003). *Beyond the administrative core: Creating Web-based student services for online learners.* Retrieved March 1, 2005, from www.wiche.edu/telcom/resources/publications/guide/guide.htm

Tait, A. (2003). Editorial: Reflections on student support in open and distance learning. *International Review of Research in Open and Distance Learning, 4*(1). Retrieved May 10, 2005, from www.irrodle.org/content/v4.1/tait_editorial.html

Tellei, P. U. (2005). *Omesubel a ureor: Workforce development in Palau from pre-contact to 1999* (unpublished doctoral dissertation). San Diego: University of San Diego.

UNESCO. (2001). *Global forum on quality assurance, accreditation and the recognition of qualifications in higher education: Information note.* Retrieved June 10, 2005, from www.unesco.org/education/studyingabroad/highlights/global_forum/gf_info_note. shtml

UNESCO/OECD. (2005). *Global forum in international quality assurance, accreditation and recognition of qualifications.* Retrieved June 1, 2005, from http://registration. wascsenior.org/wasc//Doc_Lib/GoodPracticesDeD.pdf

Wright, T. (2001). Toward a holistic view of staff development of regional tutorial staff at the Open University. *Systematic Practice and Action Research, 6*(14), 735-762.

Chapter XI

Research in the Pacific:
Utilizing Technology to Inform and Improve Teacher Practice

Denise L. Uehara, University of Hawaii, USA

Abstract

Pacific Resources for Education and Learning (PREL) Regional Educational Laboratory (REL) initiated the Pacific Communities with High-performance In Literacy Development (Pacific CHILD) research project in response to an overwhelming need in PREL's service region to improve teachers' knowledge and instructional practices in early reading. A conscious effort was made to use indigenous knowledge while at the same time satisfy the federal requirement of adhering to a set of rigorous methodological standards. The research design is a balance of scientific research methodology and the incorporation of cultural, language, political, social and environmental realities of the Pacific. This chapter highlights some of the technological methods used to collect data from staff members who provided on-site professional development. Data was also collected via video cameras that offered immediate feedback to teachers regarding strategies acquired during professional development activities. Also described are the rewards and potential pitfalls of utilizing technology for both formative and summative use.

Introduction

PREL is an independent, non-profit organization that serves the educational community in the United States- (U.S.) affiliated Pacific islands, the continental U.S., and countries throughout the world. One of PREL's largest programs is the REL, funded by the Institute of Education Sciences (IES) through the U.S. Department of Education. PREL seeks to bridges the gap between research, theory and practice in education and works collaboratively with schools and school systems to provide services that range from curriculum development to assessment and evaluation. The REL contract is primarily a research endeavor that consists of six tasks that focus on supporting the efforts of Pacific region entities, districts, schools, communities, institutions of higher education and others to develop high-performing learning communities in the region.

The region served includes 10 U.S. affiliates in the Pacific region (i.e., American Samoa; Commonwealth of the Mariana Islands (CNMI); Federated States of Micronesia (FSM), which are Chuuk, Kosrae, Pohnpei, Yap; Guam; the state of Hawaii; the Republic of the Marshall Islands; and the Repulic of Palau), whose political status ranges from statehood to free association. In addition to economic and political diversity, these Pacific entities are characterized by a multiplicity of cultures and languages. At least nine different Pacific cultures are prominent in the region. The languages of instruction in the region's schools include English, as well as a dozen or more Pacific languages. In the region outside of Hawaii, there are approximately 410,183 students attending 446 schools, including private institutions.

The academic achievement of children whose first language is not English has long been a major educational concern. Those who come from cultural and linguistic minority backgrounds have been shown to fall short in school achievement. Measured through grading, retention in grade level, teachers' judgments of student ability and standardized tests, the academic performance of limited English proficient students generally lags behind other elementary school students (Moss & Puma, 1995). Other mitigating factors further contribute to the region's literacy dilemma, including lack of sufficient pre- and in-service training for teachers, lack of materials in local and English languages, unclear reading content standards and shifting orthographies in Pacific languages. With the institutionalization of accountability measures mandated by the No Child Left Behind (NCLB) Act of 2001, the pressure to provide high-quality education for our students has been made explicit.

Many students in the region are not learning to read in part because their teachers lack adequate preparation in content, and pedagogical knowledge and skills to teach effectively. Poor teacher preparation is a general education problem, but it is particularly relevant to those who teach reading. Significant numbers of teachers in the Pacific language-dominant entities hold only a high school diploma or associate's degree. These numbers are not surprising, since the minimum requirement to teach in most of these entities is a high school diploma (see Table 1).

In a study of teacher education and reading instruction released by the National Reading Panel (NRP) (n.d.), the panel drew the following conclusions:

Based on the analysis, the NRP concludes that appropriate teacher education does produce higher achievement in students. Much more must be known about the conditions under which this conclusion holds. Some issues that need to be resolved include determining the optimal combination of preservice and inservice experience, effects of preservice experience on inservice performance, appropriate length of interventions for both preservice and

Table 1. Number and percent of teachers' highest level of education by entity*

	A. Samoa		Chuuk		CNMI		Guam		Hawaii**		Kosrae		RMI		Palau		Pohnpei		Yap	
	n	%	n	%	n	%	n	%	n	%	n	%	n	%	n	%	n	%	n	%
n	203		124		332		301		12,400		144		74		159		179		189	
HS	24	12	22	18	4	1	6	2		0	22	15	34	46	26	16	18	10	80	42
AA	74	36.5	60	48	8	2.5	9	3		0	85	59	29	39	44	28	66	37	64	34
BA+	87	43	29	23.5	282	85	268	89	12,400	100	26	18	1	2	76	48	79	44	25	13

Note:

* *Total number of teachers based on representative sample from The Retention and Attrition of Pacific School Teachers and Administrators (RAPSTA) Study: (1999), with the exception of Hawaii. Hawaii teacher data from Hawaii DOE personnel services. Percentages may not equal 100 because of no response to survey or other categories.*

** *While it was reported that all teachers in Hawaii hold at least a Bachelor of Arts (BA) degree, there are numbers who do not hold a BA in education.*

inservice education, and best ways to assess the effectiveness of teacher education and professional development. (p. 5)

The results of the NRP study, among others, have convinced PREL that an important initiative to improve reading performance among students in the region is to improve the knowledge and skills of teachers who teach reading. PREL's REL initiated the Pacific CHILD research project in response to an overwhelming need in PREL's Pacific service region to improve teachers' knowledge and instructional practices in early reading. The components of the professional development (PD) model have been evolving for 3½ years through the REL. The key components that inform the model were studied in nine schools throughout the Pacific region, five of which were designated research sites where intense data collection took place.

Purpose: One question provided the focus and direction for the research agenda: *What are the components of an effective PD model for early reading improvement?* This question guided the inquiry. To answer the research question, quantitative and qualitative research methodologies were determined to be the most logical and appropriate. This chapter highlights technological methods used to collect data from staff members who provided on-site PD. Data was also collected via video cameras that offered immediate feedback to teachers regarding strategies acquired during PD activities. The purpose of this chapter is to describe the rewards and potential pitfalls of utilizing technology for both formative and summative uses within diverse contexts.

Background

Indigenous knowledge (IK), or the conscious effort to honor, respect and celebrate the various cultures in the Pacific and, at the same time, learn from and engage local participants in the research process, guided the research of the REL research team. "IK refers to the unique, traditional, local knowledge existing within and developed around the specific conditions of women and men indigenous to a particular geographic area" (Grenier, 1998, p. 1). In addition, IK systems are dynamic, where new knowledge is continuously added. Such systems generate change from within and will also internalize, use and adapt external knowledge to suit the local situation. Paying attention to and incorporating local indigenous knowledge can yield the following attributes:

1.   Creating mutual respect, encouraging local participation and building partnerships for joint problem resolution

2.   Facilitating the design and implementation of culturally appropriate development programs, thereby avoiding costly mistakes

3.   Identifying techniques that can be transferred to other regions

4.   Helping identify practices suitable for investigation and adaptation

5.   Helping build a more sustainable future

A conscious effort was made to utilize indigenous knowledge while at the same time satisfy the federal requirement of adhering to a set of rigorous methodological standards. The research design is an attempt to balance scientific research methodology and the incorporation of cultural, language, political, social and environmental realities of the region. This author was strongly committed to the process of "indigenizing" the REL work by drawing upon the traditional bodies of knowledge and corresponding codes of values present within the communities of the Pacific.

Teacher Diversity and Professional Development

While there are an abundance of research studies that identify exemplary PD practices (Guskey, 1985; Joyce & Showers, 1995; Loucks-Horsley, Hewson, Love, & Stiles, 1998; Sparks, 1983), they have largely been conducted with little or no regard for teachers from diverse backgrounds. In fact, very little research has focused on providing PD utilizing practices that incorporate the rich and diverse backgrounds of, for example, Pacific island teachers.

The current U.S. teaching force in public K-12 schools and institutions of higher education is overwhelmingly white and middle class. Although the sheer number of teachers with diverse backgrounds is increasing slowly (according to NCES [1996], there are approximately 350,000 teachers of color in U.S. schools), students of color are the clear majority in many of our country's largest school districts. The clashes that occur between the predominantly white teaching force and students and teachers of color has created a dichotomous situation that does not promote academic success for students nor professional satisfaction for the teachers of color.

Why do pre- and in-service teachers of color feel invisible, isolated and marginalized in both school and university settings (Delpit, 1995)? How can the culture clash between white teachers and diverse teachers and students be resolved? How can a dominant culture-based institution be transformed into a learning environment that recognizes respects, affirms and embraces the diversity of its community?

While teaching and learning principles have been afforded increased attention in the education of students from diverse cultural and linguistic backgrounds, many researchers in teacher education, school reform and related areas also have begun to realize the importance of well-prepared, competent teachers and their impact on student achievement (Darling-Hammond, 2000b). That is, a parallel development in work focused on improving educational outcomes for students has been the realization that effective instructional environments depend upon well-trained, reflective teachers who are adequately supported in terms of PD (Darling-Hammond, 2000a). Rather than trying to develop "teacher-proof" curriculum and teaching practices, recent work has focused on fostering professional communities of learners and life-long support programs (Sprinthall, Reiman, & Thies-Sprinthall, 1996). The growing number of teachers who teach in diverse contexts and are themselves from diverse backgrounds must be included in this conversation.

One critical aspect of this work is the realization that PD for teachers, in the most basic sense, is a learning activity that parallels the learning of students in the classroom. That is, the conditions that facilitate learning for children should not in principle differ from those that facilitate learning for adults. This is not to argue that there are no differences between children and their adult teachers. Clearly, adults may have different and more organized background knowledge, be more strategic in how they learn, have different motivations for learning and may be more aware of their learning such that they monitor and self-regulate it more effectively. However, the claim made here is that the principles describing effective teaching and learning for children in classrooms should not differ from those for adults in general and teachers in particular. The principles should be broad enough to encompass diverse backgrounds.

Best Principles and Practices of Professional Development

Keeping in mind the limitations of research findings in the area of PD for teachers from different backgrounds, it is important to present the models, practices and strategies that have been identified as effective by experts in the field. Many are appropriate for all teachers when implemented with cultural sensitivity. Elmore (1995) elaborates on what we know about the characteristics of successful PD:

It focuses on concrete classroom applications of general ideas; it exposes teachers to actual practice rather than to descriptions of practice; it involves opportunities for observation, critique and reflection; it involves opportunities for group support and collaboration; and it involves deliberate evaluation and feedback by skilled practitioners with expertise about good teaching (p. 2)

However, the knowledge we have about how to organize successful PD so that it influences practice in greater numbers of schools and classrooms continues to elude educators. More specifically, how do we organize successful PD practices for diverse teachers within diverse environments? This is one question the Pacific CHILD research sought to answer.

What we do know thus far is based on solid investigations into PD that provided a starting point for our work. Showers, Joyce, and Bennett (1987) suggest that strong implementation is not achieved until a new strategy has been used in approximately 25 teaching episodes. This seems to imply that long-term PD is a necessary component for changing teaching behaviors. In 1976, Berman and McLaughlin introduced the idea of "mutual adaptation" —the modification and adaptation of new practices into a teacher's environment. In some cases, both environment and practice are modified until implementation occurs. Constructivism has been a useful approach for working with adults and has emerged as an important educational paradigm for PD (Joyce & Showers, 1995; Lambert et al., 1995; Lyons, Pinnell, & DeFord, 1993; Lyons & Pinnell, 2001). Lyons and Pinnell (2001) suggest the following set of eight principles for organizing and implementing PD:

1.   *Encourage active participation;*

2.   *Organize small-group discussions around common concerns;*

3. *Introduce new concepts in context;*

4. *Create a safe environment;*

5. *Develop teachers' conceptual knowledge through conversation around shared experiences;*

6. *Provide opportunities for teachers to use what they know to construct new knowledge;*

7. *Look for shifts in teachers' understanding over time; and*

8. *Provide additional experiences for teachers who have not yet developed needed conceptual understanding development.* (p. 4)

The work of Guskey (2000) addresses the desired results of PD-improved student outcomes—and encourages educators to evaluate the effects and effectiveness of activities. In the past, however, researchers have tried unsuccessfully to determine the true impact of PD in education. Although various forms of in-service education and staff development endeavors continue to be enormously popular and highly valued, relatively little is known about what difference they make.

Recent studies have attempted to isolate particular elements of PD that can be correlated to improved teacher knowledge and/or student performance. The results from a national sample of teachers of mathematics and science provide the first large-scale empirical comparison of effects of varying characteristics of PD on teachers' learning (Garet, Porter, Desimone, Birman, & Yoon, 2001). These researchers found that sustained and intensive PD is more likely to have an impact than shorter PD. In addition, integrating PD focusing on specific content gives teachers opportunities for "hands-on" activities and is more likely to result in enhanced knowledge and skills. Using the core features that emerged from that study, the following 3-year longitudinal study conducted by Desimone, Porter, Garet, Yoon, and Birman (2002) examined the effects of PD on teacher instruction. They found that PD focused on specific teaching practices increased teachers' use of those practices in the classroom. Further, the data indicated that the likelihood of changing teachers' classroom practices is higher when PD activities have shared participation of teachers from the same school, department or grade; contextualized learning opportunities, such as reviewing actual student work or obtaining feedback on teaching practices; and increased coherence by linking to other activities or building on teachers' existing knowledge.

Likewise, the study conducted by Frey and Kelly (2001) found that providing PD through a learning community format coupled with modeling and coaching resulted in several changes at the teacher level. For example, of the teachers who were active long-term participants in the study, concerns regarding teacher-centered classroom management issues shifted to concerns regarding student-centered learning/pedagogy issues. In addition, the researchers noticed the teachers learned what was taught but did not use what they learned beyond the lessons. This finding offers PD providers insights about increasing implementation of new teaching behaviors through ongoing classroom support for specific strategies.

The results of a quasi-experimental study designed to measure the impact of two components (interactive course and year-long collaboration) of a PD model on K-12 teachers' attitudes, beliefs and teaching practices showed an improvement in all three areas. This study also measured the impact on student learning of early reading skills. Greater gains were made by the students of teachers who participated in the PD program than control group teachers who did not participate in any PD activities. The course was every day for 2½ weeks; was 3½ hours in length; and focused on early reading and spelling difficulties, assessments for diagnostic purposes and teaching strategies to address reading and spelling difficulties. Collaboration took the form of project staff teaching and modeling instructional strategies for teachers and assessing individual students, assisting the teacher as the teacher taught, observing the teacher in teaching situations, debriefing after in-class activities, sharing information and identifying resources (Bos, Mather, Narr, & Babur, 1999). This study reflects an on-going effort to isolate specific factors within PD that lead to empirically based evidence of change.

Web-Based Data Collection to Identify a PD Model for Teachers from Diverse Backgrounds

Adhering to the notion of indigenous knowledge, local professional educators were hired to provide the PD to teachers at research sites. Most of the local-based REL PD providers were either from the community of the school or from the same island and spoke the language of instruction. In an effort to collect comprehensive data on PD, REL researchers designed a Web-based, weekly PD activity log. The log is designed to document (and monitor) the early literacy PD activities conducted by REL staff. The log provides key data on the PD experience at each site. This data informed the model by factoring out such components as content, duration and format. The Web-based instrument provides such information as the number of PD activities that take place during a week, the location of the PD, the grouping format and strategies used and grade levels served. There are also places for narrative information, such as reflection and turning points noted by REL staff. The log provides opportunity to code the PD content (early reading) and process (instructional strategies). This coding provided better alignment with the other data collection instruments. This instrument was submitted weekly via Web site or, in places where Internet connection was not stable, an Excel version was available. On a monthly basis, a Web-based version of the PD log was also submitted. It was designed to target subjective accounts of change over time. The use of a Web-based data collection instrument presented several challenges, such as the inconsistency of Internet access across research sites, the variability of staff skills utilizing the Web-based instrument and varying computer configurations across staff throughout the region. Negotiating these challenges to ensure research integrity while simultaneously responding to the needs of our constituents made for interesting and fulfilling work.

Based on preliminary analysis of the activity log data (school year 2003-2004), the emerging salient components confirm what we already know about effective PD. For example, the majority (80%) of PD took place at the school. The remaining 20% was reported to occur at the PREL Service Center. And 62% of the PD was conducted individually with one teacher, while 15% involved the whole group format, 13% with small groups and 10% in dyads. In addition, several different types of PD strategies were recorded. The following list describes the kinds of PD strategies that were provided and reported on:

1. **Coaching:** 16% of PD strategies involved one-on-one learning focused on improving teaching practices. In some instances, the PD provider worked with two teachers in an intimate setting where teaching strategies were shared within a safe setting. Coaching and collegial/professional conversation seemed to be very similar strategies as the data was further analyzed.

2. **Modeling:** 16% of PD strategies provided teachers the opportunity to observe REL staff or a colleague demonstrating a particular lesson, strategy and so forth. Prior to and after a demonstration, conversation typically took place between the teacher(s) and the PD provider.

3. **Guided observation:** 4% of PD strategies presented a forum where teachers observed REL staff or another teacher demonstrating a particular lesson and strategy. Under the guidance of another REL staff member, questions can be answered immediately, important moments can be brought to attention and significant behavior can be described *as it occurs*. The observation sessions were typically conducted live with a lead teacher as model and a PD provider facilitating the conversation and observation in the back of the classroom. The live sessions were met with considerable resistance by the observers (teachers) as they watched a demonstration. None of the observers asked questions on features during the demonstration. After several inquiries, we discovered that the teachers felt very uncomfortable speaking when a lead teacher was teaching. Although the merits of this strategy were carefully explained, the teachers felt it was extremely rude to be speaking when they should be watching. As the data illustrates, this particular strategy was not utilized very often and offers further inquiry into cultural norms and standards.

4. **Study group:** 11% of PD strategies offered teachers the opportunity to come together to address issues of teaching and learning, with implications that new learning will take place. Study groups allow teachers to inquire and ask questions concerning a specific or particular topic over a period of time and in a collaborative, supportive environment. This particular strategy was often described in the logs as more of a focused conversation facilitated by the PD provider. However, study group as defined by Lyons and Pinnell (2001) refers to a focused study of a single concept or idea over a period of time and can be facilitated by any member of the group. In many cases, isolated topics of conversation were reported, suggesting that exploration of a particular topic or idea over a course of weeks or months did not occur. However, we recognized that the study group as defined by the PD staff was an important component of the project. Accepting this adaptation of the Lyons and Pinnell definition is an example of incorporating contextual experiences into research.

5. **Training:** 10% of PD strategies typically involved a presenter or a team of presenters, including the following formats:

    a. large group presentation and discussions

    b. workshops

    c. seminars

    d. colloquia

    e. demonstrations

    f. role-playing

g. simulations

h. micro-teaching

This PD strategy was primarily seen at the beginning of the research project, since its formats were the most familiar to staff members. However, as REL PD providers gained knowledge and skills in PD, they diversified their repertoire of strategies and were able to offer varying modes of delivery.

6. **Collegial or professional conversation:** 25% of PD strategies involved conversation around the development of new knowledge and skills (extended learning). This is not limited to the classroom or school setting. Preponderance of focused conversation, dialog and discussion is a characteristic of extended learning. In many instances, coaching activities were described more in terms of rich conversations around an instructional strategy or literacy content. This particular PD strategy requires an established relationship between PD provider and teacher and, in most cases, takes a while to develop.

7. **Information, resources and materials sharing:** 18% of PD strategies provided teachers with resources, such as books, journal articles, video and audiotapes, and handouts to inform teaching practices (Guskey, 2000; Loucks-Horsley, Hewson, Love, & Stiles, 1998; Lyons & Pinnell, 2001). After reviewing the data, we inquired about whether or not some type of instructional conversation took place during the dissemination of information, resources and materials. In most cases, there were rich conversations and, often times, these conversations led to a coaching, demonstration or other PD activity pertaining to the information or resource that was shared.

The pie chart in Figure 1 depicts the breakdown of various strategies in use by REL staff.

These percentages are further substantiated by open-ended questions included in the activity log. The questions were designed to provide more information on PD activities recorded for the week. The questions served two research purposes: (1) Elicit detailed information

Figure 1. The breakdown of various strategies in use by REL staff

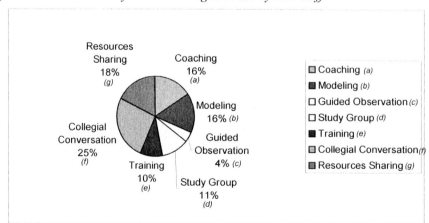

about the kinds of PD activities that occurred at research sites, and (2) provide a reflective practitioner forum for PD provider(s) to focus on thoughts and strategizing.

To analyze this narrative data, the methodology of grounded theory was employed. Grounded theory is a specific methodology in which the researcher attempts to develop a theory by using several stages of data collection and refinement, making the inter-relationship of information categories explicit (Strauss & Corbin, 1990). Two primary features of this design are the continual comparison of emerging categories and the theoretical sampling of different groups to enhance the similarities and differences of information (Creswell, 1994). For the purpose of answering the research question, we used the first feature of conducting simultaneous data collection and analysis to generate categories and build thematic strands, as recommended by Merriam (1998) and Creswell (1994). Similar to other forms of qualitative research, the investigator is the major instrument of data collection and analysis, assuming an inductive posture and aiming to gather meaning from the data. The end result of this type of research is a theory that emerges from, or is *grounded*, in the data.

Data were coded and the information was compared within and between categories. Also termed as *constant comparative analysis* (Glaser & Strauss, 1967), this technique occurs as data are compared and categories and their properties emerge or are integrated (Anfara, Brown, & Mangione, 2002). A better term for the narrative data analysis is *evolutionary comparative analysis*, where the content of the narratives reveals changes over time. After several iterations of mining the data from the activity logs, a consistent theme group emerged: *PD Indirect Indicators of Good Practice*. This referred to the notion that quality PD provided active learning opportunities for teachers, including practice, feedback and reflection. However, if teachers are to be reflective, PD providers must also model such practices. The data also showed that teachers were beginning to initiate PD activities in both content and process. Utilizing a Web-based data collection instrument, these results provided some evidence for factoring out the components of an effective PD model for early reading improvement.

As a result of the PD provided by REL staff, teachers at the research sites were expected to demonstrate a significant improvement in their early language and literacy instructional practices. The Early Language and Literacy Classroom Observation (ELLCO) Toolkit was an instrument used to gauge improvement of general classroom practices. The ELLCO instrument provides "a means to identify the practices and environmental supports that can nourish children's early literacy and language development in early childhood and early elementary classrooms" (Smith & Dickinson, 2002, p. 2). The instrument includes a detailed technical appendix that provides in-depth information on the research that undergirds the ELLCO and its psychometric properties, including general statistics on its use, validity and reliability analyses, measures of stability and change, and its relationship to other commonly used classroom observation tools. The instrument consists of three parts: a literacy environment checklist, classroom observation and teacher interview, and literacy activities rating scale. Observations using this instrument were conducted three times per year (fall, winter and spring) during the 2003-2004 school year and twice per year (fall and spring) during the 2002-2003 school year. They were conducted by trained staff with the required inter-rater reliability scores to utilize the instrument. It must be noted that the psychometric properties of the ELLCO was based on East Coast U.S. classrooms and may, therefore, be inappropriate for use in rural Pacific classrooms. However, the general content of the Toolkit provided a stable measure of growth as well as a set of standards to strive for when teaching early

Table 2. Mean scores for the ELLCO Toolkit, school years 2002-2003 and 2003-2004

Date	N	Mean Sum Literacy Environment Checklist	Mean Sum General Classroom Environment	Mean Sum Language, Literacy and Curriculum	Mean Sum Observation Total	Mean Sum Literacy Activities Rating Scale
2002	23	10.5*	8.52	10.83	20.35	4.26
2003	44	17.27**	11.00	13.77	25.80	5.43
2004	28	19.89	12.39	16.18	30.43	5.75

Note:

* Refers to 19 missing values.

** Refers to 14 missing values. The Literacy Environment Checklist was not used in some classrooms during the first year of administering the ELLCO Toolkit.

These scores are based on the results of observations at the five research sites.

literacy. A more culturally contextual classroom observation instrument was developed and used for the purposes of the REL research project. Its reliability and measurement properties are elaborated in another research paper submitted for publication in another venue. Table 2 illustrates the results of the ELLCO Toolkit.

In every category, a marked improvement in mean scores is noted. Teachers appeared to be improving in how they set up their classrooms; in general classroom practices; in reading instruction; and the types of activities they provide for reading and writing.

Challenges of Completing the Web-Based Activity Log

While the Web-based, weekly activity log provided a convenient way to manage and organize the PD data, it was not necessarily the most convenient for region staff to complete. In some areas, the Internet connection was very slow and unpredictable, often times taking more than 1½ hours to complete the activity log. The length of time that it took to complete the logs frequently resulted in frustration and discouragement among PD staff members. In other places, mere access to the Web site proved difficult with server, computer or software application problems. This instability in accessing and completing the Web-based weekly log resulted in inconsistent input of data. To address this issue, REL researchers developed an Excel version of the activity log, where staff can input the information and send it via e-mail or fax.

The Excel version added an extra step in the data collection and analysis process; however, it addressed the environmental conditions that often hindered the research agenda. Yet at some sites, staff felt uncomfortable accessing the Web-based version and the Excel version. Because a majority of region-based staff members were primarily service providers, spending a majority of their time at the school, the requirement to complete the logs was often seen as an additional task that took time away from the site. Also, many staff were not proficient in using Excel. Therefore, a printable version of the Excel formatted log was developed so that staff members could print it out, hand write the information and fax it to the Honolulu office for input.

While REL administrators stressed the importance of completing the logs for research purposes, making the activity one of several responsibilities of their job, log completion and log timeliness were often problematic. To receive the data, REL research staff often called region-based staff and asked for verbal accounts of their PD activities for the week.

Lights, Camera, Action! Using Video to Inform Teacher Practices in the Pacific

This section describes the use of videotaping teachers to inform their practice. While not a key component of the REL research agenda, videotaping was a result of site-based PD providers wanting to enhance their own PD practices. Teachers at these particular sites were open to using videotape as another vehicle for their PD. The use of videos in teacher education and PD is well documented (Capraro, Capraro, & Lamb, 2001; Hong & Broderick, 2003; Kain, 1994; Parkin & Dogra, 2000; Strickland & Doty, 1997). In particular, videotaping a teacher's instructional episode for self-evaluation/reflection and feedback provides authentic assessment of their teaching performance (Eckart & Gibson, 1993; Martin-Reynolds, 2001; McCurry, 2000; Smith & Diaz, 2002; Stough, 2001).

At some of the REL research sites, teachers were videotaped during a language arts lesson. The videotape allowed teachers to sit with the PD provider (coach) and review the lesson for both content and process. In terms of content, the teacher can see whether or not he or she was able to cover the intended early literacy domains or targets for that particular lesson. At the same time, the teacher and PD provider critically review instructional strategies that focus on content. By viewing the videotape together, within a safe environment, both teacher and PD provider are afforded a rich opportunity to reflect on and discuss comfortable and appropriate ways in working with students. The videotape format also allowed the PD provider to attend to differing learning needs of teachers as well as respond to the various cultural contexts that arise within small Pacific communities. Because the site-based PD providers were local and understood the nuances of the culture, videotaping was left to the discretion of the teachers and the PD provider. In other words, REL researchers depended on the site-based staff to render judgment regarding indigenous knowledge and what were appropriate or inappropriate PD practices within the realm of the research agenda. Grounded in theories of self-assessment and self-reflection, the use of videotape parallels the aforementioned constructivist approach within PD. Video captures the complexities and realities of the classroom that include facial expressions, body language, and accurate visual and verbal evidence of an actual teaching episode, while simultaneously providing time for analysis and reflection. As opposed to live guided observation, the issue of speaking and commenting during an actual lesson is addressed.

Prior to the REL study, videotaping of teachers for self-analysis was not commonly practiced throughout most of the research sites. When videotaping was introduced, understandably, at one site teachers were apprehensive and uncomfortable. They were limited in their experiences with videotaping. In one instance during an actual filming, teachers asked if they could stop and start the lesson from the beginning. Eckert and Gibson (1993) suggest setting up the video recorder in the classroom for periods of time so that both students and teacher can become comfortable and familiar with the equipment. If students and the teacher are taped informally, the presence of the equipment and technician will be less distracting. Additionally, these informal tapings can serve as baseline data that will provide information about the teacher's practices in the classroom over time. Once the initial apprehension of being videotaped is overcome, the discrete actions of teacher's behaviors are then able to be analyzed.

Termed "pedagogical readiness," viewers must first gain a level of comfort with seeing how they look and sound on videotape before they can analyze their performance. The idea of guiding the viewer's attention during playback is a critical component to overcome a seemingly natural tendency to focus on personal characteristics. In so doing, perhaps, teachers miss the actual purpose of the taping process (Martin-Reynolds, 2001). Such focus on self did hinder initial attempts to gain insights into the teaching experience, where teachers commented on appearance, sound of voice and other non-related personal factors.

In a typical individual PD session utilizing videotape, the teacher initially met with the PD provider and described the lesson to be observed. The teacher may ask the PD provider to observe particular instructional strategies, such as execution of a shared reading lesson or an interactive writing activity. Depending on time and available coverage, immediate feedback based on the video playback can be given as an initial response to the observed lesson, with a longer follow-up session scheduled within the next couple of days. This provides an opportunity for the teacher to respond to his or her own lesson as well as respond to the PD provider's initial feedback. In many cases, the teacher immediately shared his or her perception of the lesson. The video playback details the extent to which the lesson did or did not go as planned. The ability to pause, stop and rewind allows both the teacher and PD provider the opportunity to pinpoint potential areas where improvements can be made. The videotape serves as the basis for subsequent PD sessions that target specific content or processes.

Challenges of Using Videotape in Diverse Contexts

Technology is only useful if the environment can support and facilitate its function. In some classrooms, electricity is simply not available. The tropical setting of the Pacific plays host to a number of environmental hazards that can cause power outages. While most REL research classrooms were equipped with electrical outlets, occasional power outages occur. When utilizing technology that requires electricity, backups are necessary. A fully charged video camera battery is an important item to have when videotaping a lesson.

Another key feature to have when videotaping teachers is a talented videographer. The videographer must be well trained in using the videotape recorder, understanding the functions of the equipment as well as capturing the nuances of the lesson being videotaped. During a previous research endeavor, many REL research site staff members were provided training on videotaping classrooms. Therefore, they were quite familiar with basic rules and standards of classroom filming. At one particular research site, the Ministry of Education requested a video compilation of "best practices" of the REL teachers for use in large group trainings. The process of filming, editing and producing an effective video for group training purposes was critical and also required specific computer skills. While the videographer had the necessary filming skills, he did not have the editing skills or appropriate equipment to produce the training video. However, support and resources were sought, resulting in the production of an effective, high-quality training tape. Thus, a challenge to consider when videotaping teachers is having accessibility to equipment and the competency to operate the equipment. In some Pacific island locales, such equipment may not be available or are outdated or damaged due to the environment. In other Pacific island areas, high-quality, well-maintained equipment are available but limited to who can use it and when. Personnel who have the competencies to operate the equipment may be limited in time. Scheduling becomes very essential to this process.

The involvement of the videotaped teachers during the editing stages of the video proved to be another important aspect in the production of the training tape for PD purposes. Teachers appreciated the opportunity to comment on their performance and highlight strategies as a voiceover during the video. One of the biggest challenges of videotaping as reported by a REL PD provider was supporting teachers to overcome their initial anxiety about being filmed. Teachers were not automatically comfortable with being filmed regardless of the purpose and proposed benefits. The possibility of making mistakes while being filmed was a common objection. The fear of other teachers possibly viewing the tape was another lament. Alleviating their worries and anxieties by establishing a close and trusting relationship was crucial to the videotaping process.

Equally important was facilitating teachers' understanding of critical reflection informing practice, proposed by Dewey (1916) and elaborated by Scöhn (1983) as "reflective practitioner." The video offers the reflective practitioner a tool to gather information about the self in authentic settings (McCurry, 2000). Prior to and after the videotaping, much discussion takes place. These conversations allow the teacher to mentally and emotionally prepare for videotaping. Typically, an informal videotape was made of the classroom, minimally focusing on the teacher and more the surroundings, such as displays, environmental print, students and centers. A relaxed discussion occurred while viewing the tape with some feedback on teaching. In many instances, once getting past the novelty of seeing and hearing oneself on tape, teachers were able to constructively critique themselves related to the content and context of the video. This initial practice serves to put the teacher at ease with seeing him or herself on tape and also convey the utility of videotaped feedback.

Future Trends

The use of technology to support research endeavors has always been common practice, particularly during the analysis stage. No longer considered novel, technology such as Web-based surveys for data collection purposes is becoming routine. In many places, its mere use provides a simpler, standardized, efficient and effective way to collect, analyze and report data. However, in remote places, such as the western Pacific region, where basic Internet access is often times inadequate, technology becomes more of a hindrance than a benefit. As local and state governments experience the benefits of technology, more and more schools and educational settings in the Pacific ought to have easy access and support. Continued assistance must also be provided through training and in-services so that a technologically literate society can flourish.

The desire to develop teachers who are reflective practitioners able to critically think about their own practice is continually talked about in the teacher education literature. As part of teacher training curriculums and teacher PD programs, the use of videotapes as a means to facilitate this skill will hopefully continue. With the level of teacher comfort in sharing the videotapes with other teachers and schools, the benefits of providing feedback and reflection offers an opportunity to scale up this PD effort. The use of digital video is a foreseeable way to further improve this PD strategy. The impact of NCLB is made explicit, leaving teachers accountable for improving student achievement. The videotape is an effective accountability tool for demonstrating teacher quality and commitment in a field where evidence for improvement is mandatory.

Conclusion

REL's Pacific CHILD research project addressed the concern for well-qualified, competent teachers and aimed to improve the knowledge and skills of reading teachers by identifying essential components of an effective PD model. To answer the question, *What are the components of an effective PD model for early reading improvement?*, both qualitative and quantitative research methods were determined to be the most appropriate and logical. The focus of this chapter was to describe the rewards and potential pitfalls of utilizing technology for both formative and summative uses within diverse contexts.

Technology should be a tool that supports educators and researchers to meet the educational needs of all students. With the increase of technological tools throughout the world, the remote location of some Pacific entities must be addressed. Accessibility should be a right, not a privilege, so that all educational systems begin on equal footing. This technology should be used to enhance teacher practice, facilitating self-reflection and evaluation. It is important that within diverse contexts and general contexts, teachers are empowered to make informed decisions about their own classroom practices. The importance of planning, infrastructure, preparation and evaluation of the potential impact of technology on teacher education and learning in general be accounted for and addressed. Teachers, PD providers, principals and researchers need to be willing and ready to utilize these tools appropriately so that maximum benefits are realized. PD using technology is a process involving consistent support and follow-up. Like any unfamiliar or new educational endeavor, the realization of improved student outcomes can only be realized if educators themselves believe in the tools.

Note

The research described in this chapter was conducted during the author's tenure at Pacific Resources for Education and Learning, 2000-2005 Regional Laboratory contract. Dr. Uehara is currently an assistant professor at the Center on Disability Studies at the University of Hawaii at Manoa.

References

Anfara, V. A., Brown, K. M., & Mangione, T. L. (2002). Qualitative analysis on stage: Making the research more public. *Educational Researcher, 31*(7), 28-38.

Berman, P., & McLaughlin, M. W. (1976). *Federal programs supporting educational change, Volume VIII: Implementing and sustaining innovations.* Santa Monica: Rand Corporation.

Bos, C. S., Mather, N., Narr, R. F., & Babar, N. (1999). Interactive, collaborative professional development in early literacy instruction. *Learning Disabilities Research and Practice, 14*(4), 227-238.

Capraro, R., Capraro, M. M., & Lamb, C. (2001, October). *Digital video: Watch me do what I say.* Paper presented at the Consortium of State Organizations for Texas Teacher Education, Corpus Christi, TX (ERIC Database # ED459697).

Creswell, J. (1994). *Research design: Qualitative & quantitative approaches.* Thousand Oaks: Sage.

Darling-Hammond, L. (2000a). Reforming teacher preparation and licensing: Debating the evidence. *Teachers College Record, 102*(1), 28-56.

Darling-Hammond, L. (2000b). Teacher quality and student achievement. *Education Policy Analysis Archives, 8*(1). Retrieved March 12, 2003, from http://epaa.asu.edu/epaa/v8nl

Delpit, L. (1995). *Other people's children.* New York: The New Press.

Desimone, L., Porter, A. C., Garet, M. S., Yoon, K. S., & Birman, B. F. (2002). Effects of professional development on teachers' instruction: Results from a three-year longitudinal study. *Educational Evaluation and Policy Analysis, 24*(2), 81-112.

Dewey, J. (1916). *Democracy and education.* New York: Macmillan.

Eckert, J. A., & Gibson, S. L. (1993). Using camcorders to improve teaching. *Clearing House, 66*(5), 288-292.

Elmore, R. (1995). *Investing in teacher learning: Staff development and instructional improvement in community school district #2, New York City.* New York: National Commission on Teaching and America's Future.

Frey, N., & Kelly, P. R. (2001). The effects of staff development, modeling, and coaching of interactive writing on instructional repertoires of K-1 teachers in a professional development school. *National Reading Conference Yearbook, 51*, 176-185.

Garet, M. S., Porter, A. C., Desimone, L., Birman, B. F., & Yoon, K. S. (2001). What makes professional development effective? Results from a national sample of teachers. *American Educational Research Journal, 38*(4), 915-945.

Glaser, B. G., & Strauss, A. (1967). *The discovery of grounded theory: Strategies for qualitative research.* Chicago: Aldine.

Grenier, L. (1998). *Working with indigenous knowledge: A guide for researchers.* Ottawa: International Development Research Centre.

Guskey, T. R. (1985). Staff development and teacher change. *Educational Leadership, 42,* 57-60.

Guskey, T. R. (2000). *Evaluating professional development.* Thousand Oaks: Corwin Press.

Hong, S. B., & Broderick, J. T. (2003, spring). Instant video revisiting for reflection. *Early childhood research and practice: An Internet journal on the development, care, and education of young children* (ERIC Database # ED475620).

Joyce, B., & Showers, B. (1995). *Student achievement through staff development.* White Plains: Longman.

Kain, K. T. (1994). Staff development videos provide catalyst for learning. *T.H.E. Journal, 22*(3), 84-85.

Lambert, L., Walker, D., Zimmerman, D. P., Cooper, J. E., Lambert, M. D., Gardner, M. E., et al. (1995). *The constructivist leader.* New York: Teachers College Press.

Loucks-Horsley, S., Hewson, P. W., Love, N., & Stiles, K. E. (1998). *Designing professional development for teachers of science and mathematics.* Thousand Oaks: Corwin Press.

Lyons, C. A., & Pinnell, G. S. (2001). *Systems for change in literacy education: A guide to professional development.* Portsmouth: Heinemann.

Lyons, C. A., Pinnell, G. S., & DeFord, D. E. (1993). *Partners in learning: Teachers and children in reading recovery.* New York: Teachers College Press.

Martin-Reynolds, J. (2001). The effects of a self-evaluation model on the focus reaction of student teachers during split-screen videotape feedback. *Journal of Educational Research, 73*(6), 360-364.

McCurry, D. S. (2000). Technology for critical pedagogy: Beyond self-reflection with video. *Society for Information Technology & Teacher Education International Conference: Proceedings of SITE 2000, 1-3* (ERIC Database # ED444459).

Merriam, S. B. (1998*). Qualitative research and case study applications in education.* San Francisco: Jossey-Bass.

Moss, M., & Puma, M. (1995). *Prospects: The congressionally mandated study of educational growth and opportunity. First year report on language minority and limited English proficient students.* Washington, DC: U.S. Department of Education.

National Reading Panel (NRP). (2000). *Teaching children to read: An evidence-based assessment of the scientific research literature on reading and its implications for reading instruction.* Bethesda: National Institute of Child Health and Human Development.

National Reading Panel. (n.d.). Teacher education and reading instruction. Retrieved August 10, 2005, from www.nichd.nih.gov/publications/nrp/ch5.pdf

Pacific Resources for Education and Learning (PREL). (1999). Retention and Attrition of Pacific School Teachers and Administrators Study (RAPSTA). Honolulu, HI: Author.

Parkin, A., & Dogra, N. (2000). Making videos for medical undergraduate teaching in child psychiatry: The development, use and perceived effectiveness of structured videotapes of clinical material for use by medical students in psychiatry. *Medical Teacher, 22*(6), 568-571.

Schön, D. (1983). *The self-reflective practitioner: How professionals think in action.* New York: Basic Books.

Showers, B., Joyce, B., & Bennett, B. (1987). Synthesis of research on staff development: A framework for future study and a state-of-the-art analysis. *Educational Leadership, 45,* 120-129.

Smith, J., & Diaz, R. (2002). *Evolving uses of technology in case-based teacher education.* Philadelphia: National Center on Adult Literacy.

Smith, M., & Dickinson, D. (2002). *User's guide to the early language & literacy classroom observation toolkit.* Baltimore: Brookes Publishing.

Sparks, D. (1983). Synthesis of research in staff development for effective teaching. *Educational Leadership, 41,* 100-107.

Sprinthall, N. A., Reiman, A. J., & Thies-Sprinthall, L. (1996). Teacher professional development. In J. Sikula (Ed.), *Handbook of research on teacher education* (pp. 666-703). New York: Macmillan.

Stough, L. M. (2001, April). *Using stimulated recall in classroom observation and professional development.* Paper presented at the annual meeting of the American Educational Research Association, Seattle, WA.

Strauss, A., & Corbin, J. (1990). *Basics of qualitative research: Grounded theory procedures and techniques.* Newbury Park: Sage.

Strickland, J. F., & Doty, K. (1997). Use of videotapes of exemplary mathematics teaching for teacher preparation. *Education, 118*(2), 259-261.

Section VI

Opportunities and New Challenges in Technology and Diversity

Chapter XII

Using Video to Productively Engage Learners

Nancy Schmitz, University of Guam, USA

Abstract

This chapter focuses on the different uses of video technology for instruction and assessment. The use of video technology allows performance-based skills, knowledge and disposition for learning to be demonstrated and recorded for a number of uses. The uses of video technology provide ways for students with different backgrounds and experiences as well as language differences to effectively engage with their performance and develop their skills, knowledge and dispositions. Through engagement in performance recorded via video technology, students become more motivated to prepare effectively. Action-oriented videotaping allows those students with less language skills to make use of alternative ways to demonstrate their skill, knowledge and disposition to learn in an effective and supportive environment. Each of the uses for video technology utilizes different strategies and techniques. Successful examples of each use of video technology are provided within this chapter for using video effectively in undergraduate as well as K-12 settings.

Introduction

Video technology has made a profound impact on modern life. We respond daily to the visual images created via video technology regarding events close to our home or across the globe. We learn about science, history, geography, cultures and the arts through the medium of video technology. Because of its visual and auditory content, the video medium provides a means to collect images and sound that impact education because it is demonstrative and interactive. Video technology, for the purpose of this chapter, is defined as the use of recorded images and sound via different media formats—including videotape, videodisks, digital desktop video, multimedia, CD-ROM, interactive TV and Web-based media—to achieve a practical purpose. It is an ever-evolving technology, leading to evolving practical uses. The use of video technology in education has evolved into complex combinations with other forms of media, including audio, data, graphics, text, tape, CD, DVD and computer (Thornhill, Asensio, & Young, 2002). According to the United States Department of Education (U.S. DOE) (1993), the increasing affordability and popularity of video recorders and hand-held cameras has affected the use of this technology within schools; accordingly, teachers find video technology to be highly motivating and educationally valuable.

This chapter focuses on different applications of video technology to improve learner outcomes and develop more engaged learners. In particular, focusing upon the nature of the instruction delivered and opportunities for increasing student engagement, knowledge and disposition for learning, this chapter provides specific strategies that should be used in the classroom. The chapter also provides strategies that teachers and teacher candidates can use for their own self-reflection. Finally, the chapter looks forward to the challenges created by continued development of the integration of digital video technology with computers.

Background

Aided by the development of video home system (VHS) videotape by Japan Victor Company (JVC) of Japan in 1976 and the increasing miniaturization of camera technology, video use became affordable and accessible to the public (Center for Enhancing Learning and Teaching, n.d.; Pogue, 2000). Thornhill et al. (2002) noted that research on the use of moving images in education goes back as far as 1918. According to Von Schoff, Sherman, Davies, and Messman (2004), by the mid-1970s, the use of film and video in the classroom became an area of intense research; and by the early 1980s, many universities had access to video technology for recording and playback purposes. These cameras and recording decks were cumbersome and too expensive for most K-12 school settings. However, the smaller cameras and decks developed for home use in the late 1970s opened the door to public use of video (Pogue, 2000). As the medium became more public, teachers found video equipment highly motivating and valuable as an educational tool (U.S. DOE, 1993). The advent of videotape provided teachers with the power to pause, quickly rewind and replay sections of the videotape for further study by their students. The ease of operation quickly established video as a media of choice in schools.

Educational reform of the 1990s centered on making radical changes in the way children were educated. Many education professionals saw technology as a means to reform schools (U.S. DOE, 1993). The U.S. DOE viewed technology as a means of involving students with complex, authentic tasks. Reformers saw that with the new, complex, authentic tasks mediated by technology in the classroom, changes to the primary organization would need to occur to accommodate more interdisciplinary and cooperative learning.

According to Miller (1998), a 1997 teacher survey indicates that teachers believe that video is a valuable educational tool that assists them to be more effective and creative. This same poll found that 75% of teachers believe that video enables students to understand content more effectively, especially those students who are visual learners. In this same survey, teachers point out the effectiveness of the use of video for motivating learners, especially those who are reluctant learners, students with disabilities or students from at-risk populations.

Following a constructivist viewpoint of learning based on teaching basic content knowledge and skills through authentic and complex problems, video technology became a key element in reform suggested during the 1990s (U.S. DOE, 1993; Von Schoff et al., 2004). According to the U.S. DOE (1993), sufficient evidence supports the theory that comprehension, reasoning, composition and experimentation are acquired by the learner through interaction with the content rather than through the rote learning of facts. This study (US DOE, 1993) cites research by Resnick in 1987 and a separate 1989 study by Collins, Brown, and Newman that support interactive learning as superior to traditional learning. Because of the interactive nature of video technology as well as other educational technologies, they are believed to support learning more effectively as they also model expert thought processes and provide for collaboration and new teacher roles to assist students in achieving higher levels of cognitive thinking than students would accomplish on their own (U.S. DOE, 1993). Von Schoff et al. (2004) cite a 1998 study prepared by Reeves for the Bertelsmann Foundation that summarizes 40 years of research showing that television programs produced for the explicit purpose of education have positive effects on learning. Research by Bates (2003) concludes that "active, effortful processing of television results in better learning outcomes than passive processing" (p. 72).

Using authentic tasks in the classroom mediated by video technology brings a new role for the teacher. According to the CEO Forum on Education and Technology (2001), technology transforms the learning environment so it is student-centered, problem- and project-centered, collaborative, communicative, customized and productive. The teacher is freed from use of a textbook curriculum and lecturing on what the student should know. Instead, the teacher develops meaningful tasks for the students based on state and national standards and serves as a guide or coach who models inquiry skills, supports students as they apply similar skills and diagnoses where students are having difficulty (CEO Forum, 2001). These teacher behaviors require a higher degree of teaching skill and require specific pre-service and in-service training to support implementation of educational technology and the assessment of learning derived from its use (U.S. DOE, 1993).

Every classroom, course or research project potentially can use video technology. The CEO Forum (2001) report suggests that when well-trained teachers adequately integrate video technology across the curriculum, dramatic, positive results are produced. Specific benefits include improved standardized test scores, increased application of knowledge for real-world problems and tasks, increased student learning strategies and promotion of achievement for students with a variety of special needs, as well as increased overall knowledge of content, inquiry and investigation skills. Additionally, the CEO Forum (2001) report notes that use of video technology at all grade levels improves basic skills, digital age literacy skills, inventive thinking, communication and social skills, as well as productivity. According to the report, students need 21st-century skills, including digital literacy, inventive thinking, effective communication, teamwork and the ability to create high-quality products. The CEO Forum (2001) report suggests that "the impact of technology proves most powerful when focused on specific, measurable educational objectives" (p. 6) and "combined with other key factors that increase achievement, such as parental and community involvement, increased time spent on task, frequent feedback and teacher subject matter expertise" (p. 7). A study conducted by Apple Computer of student responsiveness to technology-rich classrooms shows improved attendance, lower dropout rates, increased independence and self-responsibility for learning (Von Schoff et al., 2004).

Video technology assists educators in a variety of ways that foster product documentation, analysis, self-reflection on products of learning and independent learning. The use of video provides an informative (and entertaining) means for students to present complex subjects to others (CEO, 2001; Thornhill et al., 2002; Von Schoff et al., 2004). Video technology can be used to capture aspects of interactions between individuals or groups, preserving sound, gestures, gaze, body posture, movement, spatial use, costume, setting and manipulations of objects. It allows for repeated observations of the same event and microanalysis of the event from a variety of perspectives. Video technology can be applied to almost all content areas.

Applications of the Use of Video Technology

The use of video technology allows performance-based skills, knowledge and disposition for learning to be demonstrated and recorded for a number of uses. One major use of video technology is to document performance. This allows both the teacher and student to observe, analyze and evaluate a performance or a series of performances. Another major application of video technology is to foster reflection on learning. Still another application is to supplement instruction. Further, video technology can provide the medium through which students communicate their learning to teachers and peers. It can serve as a medium for collaborative reflection and problem solving. Video technology can be used to create assessments to evaluate knowledge and skills. Additionally, it can serve as a resource for substitute teachers as needed. It can also be used to monitor student behavior (Mohnsen, 1995).

The use of video technology provides ways for students with different backgrounds and experiences as well as language differences to effectively engage with their performance and develop their skills, knowledge and dispositions. Through engagement in performance recorded via video technology, students become more motivated to prepare effectively. Their skill level rises both from the motivated preparation and through interaction with the product. Video technology allows those students with less language skills to make use of alternative ways to demonstrate their skill, knowledge and disposition to learn in an effective and supportive environment (Thornhill et al., 2002; Von Schoff et al., 2004). According to Bruce and Levin (1997), interactive, multimedia technology provides a means to "draw upon children's natural impulses" (p. 5). Multimedia technology brings all the media to-gether as a means to expand the range of learning and engage the learner actively. Within the experience, students can control what they see and do within the media experience. Through placing control with the student, his or her learning is adjusted to his or her needs and interests (Bruce & Levin, 1997). Prior to the development of the personal analog video camera, athletic coaches used cumbersome and expensive 8- or 16-millimeter filming of games as a means to analyze the game play of their own players as well as the game play of opponents (Mohnsen, 1995). This assessment provided the coach opportunity to make ap-propriate adjustments to the game plan as different teams were encountered. The game film normally resulted from an assistant coach filming a game or practice session of an opponent several weeks in advance of a scheduled game. Processing of the movie film, analysis of the game by the coach and scheduling of a session for the team to view the film with a play-by-play discussion all contributed to lag time between the performance and viewing of the film by the team as well as discussion and practice of strategies needed to be successful against the opponent. A coach could use film of his own team during scrimmages and game play to analyze deficits in techniques or strategies and to prepare appropriate drills for practice. Dance choreographers and dancers also used film to record performances and to analyze them for choreographic and performance improvements (Mohnsen, 1995). However, lag time due to processing and analyzing also affected the process.

The advent of personal video technology provided athletic teams and choreographers initially with a less expensive and more time-sensitive alternative to filming performances (Mohn-sen, 1995). As equipment advanced and more options on cameras for home use became available, individuals found increased use for the new technology, including the recording of major life events, performances and sporting events. The immediacy of the recording of the event to the playback of the event provided opportunity for use of replay for the purpose of augmenting the performer's knowledge of results in a more immediate way than pos-sible with film. Knowledge of results is a means by which the performer makes use of the information provided by the sensory system (internal feedback) or some external source (augmented feedback) to change the next performance (Schmidt & Wrisberg, 2004; Schmidt & Lee, 2005). The ability of the video recording to provide knowledge of results within a short time frame of the performance substantiates a primary use of video technology for student use within educational settings. Secondarily, the opportunity for repetitive viewings allows students to analyze the performance and use the information gained to change future performances (Mohnsen, 1995).

As video camera technology improved, better quality recordings became possible. These cameras took advantage of longer recording time, remote monitoring, zoom lenses, lower light levels, less grainy results, as well as recording increasingly faster action. The cost of video cameras for the non-commercial market also decreased, so even the new digital tech-nology became well within the price range of many individuals and educational institutions. Additional technology allows the video camera to be configured for a variety of activities, including specialized mini-cameras, remote recording lenses, wireless microphones and underwater housings. These specialized video camera configurations allow recordings of events less conspicuously, with better sound quality and in environments too harsh for normal recording. Like the earlier use of film, video recordings provide a similar opportunity for analysis of performance. Videotape has advantages over film, as replay takes little more than a camera with a built in mini-tilt screen to begin the process or at most a video camera and a television monitor. A video camera equipped with a tilt screen becomes a mini studio for both recording and playback as well as analysis purposes. Instant replays of performance using only the video camera have several drawbacks that limit use to gross motor movement. The video camera screen is approximately four square inches, which makes subtle, fine motor movements almost impossible to see. Sound replay is not normally possible through the camera, making tracking of communication impossible. However, the use of a small-screen TV using the camera as a VCR allows rapid replay that for field purposes is usually effective. With the digital video camera and a computer with a video card, recordings can be easily downloaded to the computer for use with enhancement programs, uploading to LiveText (a Web-based portfolio tool) or cutting of a DVD for later use. The addition of time coding during initial recording or on subsequent downloading onto the computer makes precise reference to sections of the video possible.

For video applications in the classroom or in a space where there is ambient noise and the speaker needs to be heard clearly on the recorded medium, the addition of a wireless microphone system that plugs into the microphone plug on the camera is recommended. For teacher candidate or other clinical assessments, this additional equipment is more effective than straining to hear the speaker over the ambient noise in the tape or having the recorder interfere with the performance. This wireless microphone system also enables the supervisor to listen in to personal feedback given to students by the teacher candidate or for hearing communications between clinical nurse or social work students and their clients. This system is capable of receiving clear communication at distances of up to 100 feet. Many of these systems can be used for listening purposes even when the camera is not being used. The system is comprised of two main components: The one for the teacher candidate has a lapel microphone and transmitter. The component for the cooperating teacher or supervisor has an earphone, receiver and microphone jack. This system retails for less than $200. More expensive models are available. Some are specialized for a specific camera or brand of cameras.

Assessment works best when done as close to the event or behavior as possible. However, a videotape of the event extends the time frame in which participants and viewers can effectively assess data (Schmidt & Wrisberg, 2004). A videotaped event can be replayed immediately following the event. It also can be replayed later and repeatedly over time, lending itself to microanalysis (Mohnsen, 1995). While beginning learners may not respond to internal feedback, they are able to use the valuable augmented feedback provided by the videotape to assist in improving their performance. More experienced learners make better use of internal feedback and, thus, their reliance on augmented feedback such as video is lessened (Schmidt & Wrisberg, 2004). The use of video technology allows performance-based skills, knowledge and disposition for learning to be demonstrated and recorded for a number of uses. One major use of video technology allows both the teacher and student to observe and evaluate the performance or series of performances. In this application, a videotape is created to record the performance or behavior. The videotape is then played back on a monitor for teacher and student to observe. For performance-based skills, the viewing of one's own performance (augmented feedback) is an important opportunity for a student to self assess. The videotape provides the augmented knowledge of results needed for the student to analyze the performance and synthesize a personal plan of action. The tape also allows the teacher to assess the performance in order to develop strategies to assist the student in mastering the skill. The viewing of the video provides an opportunity for teacher and student to interact effectively about a shared viewing experience, reducing tension between teacher and student. This opportunity to share an event and, if needed, to replay it, allows both teacher and student to comment upon what is seen and heard rather than what is remembered. Thus, the documentation diffuses controversy about the event.

To increase the benefits of the experience, the teacher prepares a series of questions and/or a rubric to use as a basis of discussion with the student. This assessment process provides opportunity for the teacher and student to engage in thoughtful discussion regarding the performance and assessment of it using the rubric. When instructing the skill, critical elements are used to focus the learner's attention on significant aspects. When these same critical elements are used for informal and formal assessment purposes, they provide a meaningful means for assessment of the skill during the video playback. When the rubric is presented during the practice phase and available to the students prior to the recording, students have a better idea of what is needed, as they perform the skill and are prepared to analyze their work more effectively. This increases motivation and communication in addition to promoting better performance.

Another major application of video technology is use of the product to foster reflection on learning. This application is closely allied to the previous one. For this, students use prerecorded performances to reflect on and assess their own performance. For some subject matter, skills need to be described as part of this reflection. For this description, the student writes down every movement, interaction or words that they observe in the video. This increases the attention of the student on the details of the skill performance. Second, the student compares and contrasts the performance of the skill with some other performance of the skill. This can be a previously recorded performance, a second performance completed after the first one on the tape, a peer's performance or an expert's performance. The comparison provides opportunity for further written reflection on the skill, critical elements of the skill and different levels of performance. The student can also compare the performance to criteria contained in a rubric. This process of reflection, including adequately observing the nuances of the skill performance, comparison of the performance with some other model, as well as assessing the performance to a set of criteria or rubric, develops the student's understanding of the skill and builds an accurate understanding of the student's own ability to perform the skill.

An example of this might be students from a sixth-grade class who develop skits on different events during the era of history they are studying. In this case, they are studying the middle ages. The assignment is to as accurately as possible depict life or event in the middle ages, including costumes, customs and the differences in social classes that existed as well as to cooperate with others to write the script, rehearse and perform the skit. Students are in groups of four to five students for this assignment. The rubric criteria included both content and performance areas. For content, the students are assessed on accuracy of their skit to the period, showing customs, differences in class behaviors and inclusion of an aspect of life or a significant event that took place during the middle ages. For performance, the group is assessed on aspects of play writing and performance, a clear beginning, middle and resolution, character development, use of props and set to help tell the story, as well as the quality of the performance, demonstrating adequate rehearsal. The students research and write their script, then videotape their skits during a rehearsal and use the video to self-assess their work, using the rubric the teacher provides. Using their self-assessment, the group decides on changes needed in the script or any aspect of the performance. After additional rehearsal, the group performs the skit for the class and the teacher. This performance is also videotaped. After the performance, students individually complete the self-reflection using the same criteria and rubric that the teacher supplied earlier. Each student completes a comparison of his or her performances as shown on the first and second videotapes. The teacher uses each student's self-reflective paper to note the student's cognitive processes, application of the criteria to his or her own performance and strategies for self-correction. Students with limited writing or language skills can also tape record their responses and transcribe the tape to prepare their reflection. In this assignment, students grow through the use of the video documentation and their reflection. Reflection is done as both an individual and a group process. Using the video documentation as a point for reflection allows more specific group response, as they can replay the video as needed. Group interaction allows the slower learner or one struggling with language skills to hear other participants' thoughts and to take the time needed to personally reflect as well as contribute to the group process.

At the teacher preparation level, teacher candidates complete many fieldwork assignments as well as one or more culminating student teaching practicum. While fieldwork students and student teachers may be videotaped weekly or biweekly for their informal reflective use, specific assignments requiring self-reflection of the videotaped teaching provide a meaningful way for the student teacher to build new delivery skills and assess skill, knowledge and disposition development. Besides comparing teaching behavior with best practices used by successful teachers, observation instruments can be used that focus on one or more specific instructional and managerial best practices identified by research or clinical practice. Time coding and analysis of the time spent during the teaching episode on instruction (instructing, lecturing, demonstrating and describing assignment or task), student engagement with the learning (reading, writing, singing, dancing, practicing the task), time spent waiting (for equipment or papers or books to be distributed, setting up equipment) and management time (time spent in disciplining students, grouping students, repeating protocols or instructions regarding how to proceed with task) provides a way for teacher candidates to see how much time within a lesson actually is devoted to meaningful engagement vs. what is wasted while waiting or on management. Conscious focus by teacher candidates on instructional time encourages improvement in lesson timing.

Another instrument that can be applied to the videotaped lesson is one that looks at feedback given to students as a group and as individuals. The teacher candidate uses this instrument to calculate what type of feedback is given during the lesson. The use of a wireless microphone during videotaping is helpful to record feedback given to individual students that would normally be given in a soft voice. Other instruments encourage teacher candidates to observe their pathway in the classroom and observe which students receive feedback or prompting. This knowledge of results then can be applied to improve room coverage as well as to foster more positive interactions with each student in the classroom.

The beginning teacher expectations as set out by the Interstate New Teacher Assessment and Support Consortium (INTASC) or those of the particular professional association related to the teaching area or school level, such as Association for Childhood Education International (ACEI), National Council for Accreditation of Teachers of English (NCATE), National Association of Sport and Physical Education (NASPE), National Council of Teachers of Mathematics (NCTM) and National Council for Social Studies (NCSS), can be applied to completely assess the development of teaching practices. Depending on length of the student teaching practicum, two to five lessons are recorded. Teacher candidates view their video and complete the instruments required. This requires looking at the videotape numerous times to complete each assessment instrument. Each time the videotape is reviewed while completing the appropriate instrument, the teacher candidate develops greater understanding of his or her strengths and weakness. The teacher candidate writes a complete self-reflection of the teaching using data from the various instruments to support a discussion of strengths and weaknesses. At the conclusion of the reflective paper, the teacher candidate creates a bulleted list of between five and eight areas that require further development. If the videotape is a subsequent one during the semester, the student compares the strengths and weaknesses seen in the previous tape with that of the subsequent one. If the videotape is the final tape before completion of the fieldwork or student teaching experience, the student retrospectively looks at self-development in teaching over all of the tapes recorded throughout the teaching experience and evaluates where specific growth is still needed.

Still another application of video technology supplements instruction. Supplemental instructional videos are made that provide instruction from class episodes that can be used to tailor activities to specific learners. The teacher can produce these instructional activities ahead of time or compile commercially produced video materials to effectively meet the remedial, ongoing or accelerated learning needs of the student. Students desiring more assistance can access and review the video needed prior to completion of their assignment. This works effectively for students who have missed a class or those needing repetitive demonstrations. A review station with TV and VCR or DVD or a computer that students can access readily in the classroom is needed. A similar application is the production of video sequences to be used by a substitute who may not be as familiar with the content. The substitute uses the video sequences either for entire lessons or for specific learning stations. The substitute monitors the class and provides guidance to the students as needed (Mohnsen, 1995). An example of this is providing a tape of a procedure, such as finding a ratio between two numbers. The teacher prerecords this demonstration on video or records the demonstration as it is presented to the class. This is either made into a videotape or CD or DVD, or directly inputted into a computer. Students needing to review this process are directed to review the tape, CD or DVD, and complete a practice sheet using the process. The student reviews the tape as many times as needed to become successful with the process. This repetition provides optimum learning through repeated contact with the process. Using the computer, the CD or DVD can also contain interactive aspects as the student completes problems using the process, getting immediate feedback on answers through the computer.

Some teachers use video technology to assist their students in learning class rules and procedures. At the beginning of the year, after a discussion of class rules, the teacher asks the students to self-select into small groups of three to five students. Each group is requested to develop a video presentation illustrating one rule. The students can make posters and explain the rule, create a skit to illustrate the rule, create an animated cartoon to illustrate and explain the rule or any other product that can be recorded via video technology. The students provide credits at the end of each presentation that serves as an introduction of each member of the group to the class. One benefit to the students is that they become engaged with the class rules and their specific meanings or situational uses. Another benefit is that students must engage in formative discussions regarding the rule they are illustrating and presenting. Still another benefit is that students are able to use their own best skills and interests in creating their own depictions illustrating the rule. Creating the credits to the video presentation provides students with still another way to use their creativity and show individuality. Videos allow the presentations to be saved for new students entering the class. When a new student arrives in the class, these video presentations provide an opportunity for the new student to learn the rules by viewing the work of other students and to get to know each of the students in the class through their presentations and credits. Then the new student can select a rule and create his or her own presentation, introducing themselves to the class and giving the class an opportunity to revisit that particular rule.

Assessment strategies to evaluate knowledge can use video technology. These strategies may include direct evaluation from the videotape or assessment instruments and rubrics. Students can look directly at the results of the videotape to apprehend key points of their performance of a presentation, an artistic performance, classroom behavior, teaching or athletic performance. They can use this direct apprehension to make changes in their performance or behavior. While this use of video is used for feedback purposes extensively, more focused use of videotape provides attention to the details of performance most appropriate to the student in their stage of development. Providing a rubric or checklist for the student to use as they view the videotape brings attention to the specific areas being addressed within the class.

Here's an example: A group of fifth-grade students are learning a unit in physical education on basketball skills. They learned to dribble and pass the ball in lower grades. This year they are adding the skills of shooting for a basket in various situations (lay-up, set shot and free throw). The teacher already provided direct instruction in the performance of each of these shots. She has also provided simple cues or key elements to use when performing each shot. They practiced their shots and completed self-checks of their performance using a rubric highlighting the same cues. They also completed a task where they worked with a partner. Each partner used a check sheet with a rubric using the cues or key elements to note those elements they saw each time their partner performed the task. The students also videotaped each other while practicing or performing one of these tasks. The teacher uploaded the data to a number of computers available within the gym setting for this task. Each child selected the appropriate file of his or her skill performance and used the video sequence on the computer to assess his or her own performance using the criteria set out in a rubric shown on the screen under the video segment. This reinforced the critical cues needed to perform as well as helped develop student self-reflective practices. The teacher set up the class to work in stations during each of the next class sessions, so that some students can be using the computers to access the videotaped segments while others attend to different tasks. The students working on the computers using their videotaped performances engaged effectively with their task and completed it within the allotted time segment with some assistance from the teacher, who monitored the task.

Another example comes from a class of pre-service teacher candidates who are studying methodology specific to teaching reading through direct instruction. They have already had traditional lectures and reading assignments about direct instruction. They have had numerous opportunities to observe students in a school setting being taught using direct instruction. Their professor provides the teacher candidates with key elements to look for and to use while teaching using this methodology. The teacher candidates schedule several sessions in the school setting to teach using this methodology. The classroom teacher videotapes each lesson taught by the teacher candidate. The teacher candidate uploads the digital videos to the LiveText site, observes his or her performance, analyzes the performance using the key elements that the instructor noted previously and posts a reflection of his or her teaching performance to LiveText for the professor to use for assessment purposes. The professor previously posted the reflection format and assessment criteria on the LiveText site for the teacher candidate to use. The professor views the uploaded performance and self-reflection applying the rubrics appropriate to this assignment to assess each teacher candidate. The professor also notes what additional instruction and experiences the candidate needs to further develop his or her teaching of reading.

Preparation of video examinations provides another use of technology to individualize assessment or show how students can apply knowledge. In this application, the teacher provides individual students, groups or the entire class with a recorded video or multimedia test showing applications of the learning. A series of questions are provided that each student must address for each application. This type of test demonstrates higher learning levels of analysis and synthesis. While this can be done using a videotape or DVD and a paper test, the test can also be presented as a PowerPoint presentation accompanied by a paper test, or a computerized test using the PowerPoint presentation with direct student response on the computer. It can also be created as an online assessment with student response and immediate feedback on results.

The last video application discussed is providing online distance instruction. The current use of video on most distance education formats provides limited opportunities for videotaped segments through streaming-video use. Streaming media include audio or video files sent in a constant stream from a source computer or Web site to the receiving computer. The media can be accessed and perceived in real time (as if it were happening in front of the viewer) (Ko & Rossen, 2004). Other than use of short Joint Photographic Experts Group (JPEG) video segments of video footage, distance education formats limit the use of video (Mohnsen, 1995). These JPEG segments can be selected to illustrate a skill that cannot be adequately illustrated solely through written format or a digital picture. Currently, if distance educators wish to use longer examples of methodology in the classroom or see the results of instruction in the school, they must do so using prepared materials distributed as videotape or conversions into CD or DVD. In the future, educators will be able to include longer digital footage directly or have students upload digital video to a distance education server so the instructor can access it. While not a distance education medium, LiveText provides opportunities for students and faculty to upload extended digitally videotaped segments for classroom use. With LiveText, the instructor and student can both upload digital pictures and digital video to their course or portfolio to allow access to the material for assessment and storage.

The use of video technology for student assessment and projects provides ways for students with different backgrounds, experiences and language differences to effectively engage with their performance and develop their skills, knowledge and dispositions. Through engagement in performance recorded via video technology, students become more motivated to prepare effectively. Student skill level improves because of the higher degree of motivation as well as through interaction with the product. Videotaping of assignments, tasks and projects allows those students with less language skills to make use of alternative ways to demonstrate their skill, knowledge and disposition. The use of self-reflection increases student understanding of the performance and the critical elements of that performance. By writing about his or her performance in light of the critical elements, the student practices language and writing skills, along with analysis skills. Students with limited writing skills can audiotape and transcribe their reflections onto paper. The students' self-reflections provide opportunity for the teacher to see the internal processes and dispositions of the students.

Future Trends

Video technology is merging with the use of computing devices as multimedia. New uses for video technology will emerge as the technology improves or new needs are recognized. One innovation will be the availability of connecting classroom video cameras to the Internet, either for a special occasion or for on-going use. This will allow parents to connect to the Internet to view in real-time their child's performance and behaviors in class. Parents will become more aware of the content of the class as well as their children's dispositions for learning within the class setting. Parents will be aware of what is expected of their child within the classroom and the level of competence needed for their work. They, too, can assess their child using rubrics provided by the teacher accessible on their Web page. Parent-teacher meetings, then, could be more focused on strategies to affect child academic or behavioral change as well as discussing artifacts reflecting the child's work, rather than be focused on explanations of what has been going on within the classroom setting (Mohnsen, 1995).

Interactive multimedia integrates text, graphics, animation, audio and full-motion digital video under the control of a computer program. The interactive technology captures students' attention by bringing instruction to life. It allows students to replay segments and delve deeper into areas of interest. Mohnsen (1995) notes that more than 30 research studies have indicated a reduction in average learning time for 50% of students using multimedia instructional programs. She also notes that students show 33% to 70% greater mastery "using interactive technology as compared to students using more traditional methods" (Mohnsen, 1995, p. 122). Students also have greater motivation, focus and learning with multimedia because they are actively involved. Interactive programs can be commercially available or developed by the teacher or students.

Thornhill et al. (2004) describe some of the benefits for the use of video streaming. They note that video is appealing to students. Students have most of the control over the image on the screen. This allows for dynamic presentations. Work can be completed independent of the classroom. The video contributes to the value of the text of the media presentation. Thornhill et al. (2004) noted that the subjects took in more information with the video streaming as compared to use of the textbook and the teacher's presentation because of the ability to stop and restart the tape. The subjects identified greater ability to see experts, examples and demonstrations that they can learn from anywhere or anytime. The look of the video streaming appealed to the subjects grabbing and retaining their attention. They were able to select what was of use and interest to them. The video streaming addressed students' different learning styles. Video streaming also complimented the specific chapter or module of study. Video streaming was seen as entertainment integrating Web resources. The visual aspects provide students with quicker information than text alone. This brings students with disabilities and less-developed language skills with greater access to the material. The use of the video streaming provides an interactive teaching environment with student support and feedback (Thornhill et al., 2004).

As real-time video viewing technology increases, higher education supervisors will be able to use this as a means to monitor teacher candidate development from the comforts of their offices. This will reduce the time needed for supervisors to travel from school to school observing their student teachers or teacher candidates doing fieldwork, as many observations can be made of a teacher candidate and immediate feedback can provided via the Internet in the time that is normally used for travel from school to school. These observations can be made at almost any time of day and can continue to be scheduled or non-scheduled. This will also facilitate viewing and assessing teacher candidate dispositions over more class hours and situations than possible under the current number of required observations of candidates. Sharing real-time video viewing of teacher candidates with candidates at earlier stages in development can be effective. Teacher candidates viewing the real-time video could complete observation instruments on best practices in teaching and discuss their findings with the instructor. Teacher candidates will benefit from observing others struggle with the various aspects of teaching and learning to apply rubrics that will be used later when they are completing their practicum. While this viewing of video documentation of others teaching is often used currently, it is prerecorded. Real-time viewing allows an immediacy that permits teacher candidates and instructor to enter into a discussion regarding what is freshly seen to each individual. Here, both instructor and teacher candidate can share their immediate reactions to what is seen and heard. As the cost and technology become more accessible, this real-time video use will increase. The advent of multi-configured cellular phones that can take digital photos and instantly e-mail one or more of them to others indicates a new market for cellular phones that take JPEG video files and upload them into the computer for later use. The availability of technology to everyone clearly highlights new possibilities for video use in classrooms and for teacher candidate reflection.

As multimedia technology develops, distance education will increase in its effectiveness to provide a means to tailor learning experiences for students with different needs (Ko & Rossen, 2004). Interactive digital television transmissions will provide a variety of viewing choices that will allow for customizing the broadcast for individual learning styles through viewer interaction (Miller, 2000). The classroom of the future will be equipped with technology "centers" that control access to programming accessible to teachers and students at all times. Professional development will be embedded into the resources to provide assistance as needed, with only the teacher having access to that part of the site. Individual educational plans will result from students interacting with the digital system for self-assessment of skills. Digitalization of television will allow for interactive learning to appear in homes, community centers, universities, K-12 schools and senior centers (Miller, 2000; Thornhill et al., 2002).

New Challenges

One challenge with video technology will continue to be the rapid change of technology in general. These changes to technology are occurring at a more rapid rate than in the past. Practitioners not only must use the video technology itself but also be able to use video technology imbedded in the newest computer applications that allow for video to be recorded, manipulated and made useful in a variety of contexts. They must also be capable of instructing students in the use of video technology to promote students to use higher-order thinking and become more engaged and motivated learners (Thornhill et al., 2002; Bruce & Levin, 1997; U.S. DOE, 1993). Another challenge will come with the cost of adding technology equipment to the classroom in technology "centers." According to Miller (2000), these centers will allow teachers to "control all access and use of electronically delivered learning resources" (p. 2) and students to interact with the digital system for individualization of learning content.

According to Thornhill et al. (2002), "the educational value that we give to video will be embodied in the use that we make of it with our students" (p. 17). The use of video in education as a teaching tool remains unrealized (Thornhill et al., 2002). Integration of video in instruction presents challenges for the future. Educational benefits of video technology use largely depend on the instructor's deliberate planning and capacity to use video technology within the overall learning design of a course or program (Thornhill et al., 2002). Thus, institutions of higher learning are challenged to integrate technology into their classrooms as models for teacher candidates as well as to provide training in the applications of video technology for teacher candidates and for professional development to in-service teachers.

Conclusion

In this chapter, evolving video technology is shown to provide increased motivation and engagement with learning. This engagement increases through the media itself as well as through the planning and guidance of the teacher. The teacher's role involves planning effective use of video technology to address state or national standards within the curriculum. The video technology is shown to assist teachers in observing, reflecting upon and assessing student performance as well as facilitating student assessment of their performance. The addition of a rubric for assessment allows student and teacher to share analysis of performances recorded using video and communicating this analysis to each other effectively. Video technology provides opportunity for students to show creativity and make meaningful compilations of their learning to effectively communicate this to peers and teacher. Interactive problems involving small groups increase verbalizations, exchanges of ideas and development of a product that extends individual learning.

The chapter demonstrated how video technology allows for the prerecording of demonstrations and procedures for reuse by students who need additional viewings to sequence properly the procedure or demonstrate the skill effectively. Teamed with the computer, student responses can be immediately assessed and strategies put into place to remediate or progress the student further. Video technology places a tool in the hands of students to investigate, create, record events, analyze events and synthesize them into meaningful learning experiences.

References

Bates, P. J. (2003). *A study into TV-based interactive learning to the home.* Retrieved October 30, 2005, from *www.pjb.co.uk/t-learning/contents.htm*

Bruce, B. C., & Levin, J. A. (1997). Educational technology: Media for inquiry, communication, construction, and expression. *Journal of Educational Computing Research, 17*(1), 79-102.

Center for Enhancing Learning and Teaching. (n.d.). *Educational technology.* Retrieved October 27, 2005, from www.csu.edu.au/division/celt/edtech/video/OVIEW/why.htm

CEO Forum on Education and Technology. (2001). *The CEO Forum school technology and readiness report: Key building blocks for student achievement in the 21st century.* Retrieved October 27, 2005, from www.ceoforum.org/downloads/report4.pdf

Ko, S., & Rossen, S. (2004). *Teaching online: A practical guide.* New York: Houghton Mifflin.

Miller, P. (1998). *TV in the classroom: Still good as gold.* Retrieved October 30, 2005, from www.knpb.org/commentsabouteducation/199802

Miller, P. (2000). *Convergence: Tomorrow's technologies experience a meeting of the minds.* Retrieved October 30, 2005, from www.knpb.org/commentsabouteducation/200004.asp

Mohnsen, B. S. (1995). *Using technology in physical education.* Champaign: Human Kinetics.

Pogue, D. (2000). *Movie: The missing manual.* Sebastopol: Pogue Press.

Schmidt, R. A., & Lee, T. (2005). *Motor control and learning.* Champaign: Human Kinetics.

Schmidt, R. A., & Weisberg, C. A. (2004). *Motor learning and performance.* Champaign: Human Kinetics.

Thornhill, S., Ascension, M., & Young, C. (Eds.). (2002). *Video streaming: A guide for educational development.* Retrieved October 29, 2005, from www2umist.ac.uk/isd/lwt/clickgo/the_guide/Guide-S2-learningandteaching.pdf

U.S. Department of Education (U.S. DOE). (1993). *Using technology to support education reform.* Retrieved October 29, 2005, from www.ed.gov/pubs/EdReformStudies/TechReforms/title.html

Von Schoff, E. L., Sherman, D. S., Davies, P., & Mossman, K. (2004). *Educational technology: From research to the classroom.* Retrieved October 29, 2005, from www.anon.aims. speeder.net/anon.aims/data/documentation/1011educationaltechnology.pdf

Chapter XIII

Higher Learning in the Pacific:
Reflections on Diversity and Technology in a Capstone Course

Kirk Johnson, University of Guam, USA

Jonathan K. Lee, University of Guam, USA

Rebecca A. Stephenson, University of Guam, USA

Julius C.S. Cena, University of Guam

Abstract

This chapter provides an overview of particular issues of diversity and technology within an island university. The chapter's central focus rests on the complexity of both concepts within the context of higher education in the Pacific. In particular, the chapter highlights both the challenges and opportunities that the university faces as it attempts to address the unique multicultural landscape of the Western Pacific region and its technological realities. It focuses on a capstone senior-level course as a case study, and explores the possibilities inherent in directly addressing issues of diversity and technology while at the same time accomplishing the course's prescribed academic goals. The chapter concludes by outlining 10 important lessons learned from the experience that others can benefit from, and establishes the importance of such a capstone experience for both students and faculty alike.

Introduction

In this chapter, we explore the topics of diversity and technology within higher education from an interdisciplinary perspective. We explore the complexity of each and, in the process, show the linkage of one to another. Much has been written on diversity and technology independently, within this volume and elsewhere. Thus, we feel it is important to illustrate in this chapter how both are not only intimately linked within the context of higher education but are especially salient features of today's increasingly globalized world. To illustrate this, a case study approach serves to explore the strengths and challenges of each within the context of a Pacific Island University. In doing so, we share lessons learned from an interdisciplinary capstone course designed for senior-level students at the University of Guam (UOG). The central thesis of this chapter is both descriptive and analytical. It is descriptive in the sense that it outlines and highlights the use of technology both by students and professors within the classroom setting and some challenges for each. Further, it seeks to describe the diverse landscape at UOG as well as within the particular capstone course under study. The chapter is analytical in that it seeks to explore ways in which diversity impacts the learning environment and learning outcomes within higher education. The chapter explores how technology has shaped these outcomes and, in turn, has engaged an extensive process of social change.

Scope of the Present Study

At the outset, let us define the boundaries of the concepts being used in this chapter. The concept of diversity is a commonly used term in academia and carries with it a great amount of baggage. Other terms often used synonymously (and sometimes incorrectly) with diversity include multiculturalism, pluralism, biculturalism and/or universalism. These concepts are complex, owing to their interpretation and policy implications both in terms of curricula development and classroom dynamics. For example, on the surface, one might think that proponents of diversity, multiculturalism and feminism may position themselves on the same side of the political and academic fence. However, it is multiculturalism that is taken to task by one of the leading feminist scholars of our time. In her essay titled "Is Multiculturalism Bad for Women?," Susan Okin (1999) takes the position that oppression of women is not adequately countered by formal provisions of equal opportunity and that there is often a serious tension that exists between feminism and multiculturalism in higher education that scholars have failed to adequately address. Some scholars argue that our focus on diversity and multiculturalism within the academy in recent decades has resulted in a decrease in standards of excellence (Griffin, 2000). Yet, its proponents feel that students must be prepared to enter a diverse world and the educator's role is to assist them in affirming their own unique cultural backgrounds while at the same time respecting others (Reissman, 1994). These are just a few illustrations that point to the complex nature of this field of inquiry. Technology is another area of inquiry within education that has garnered a great deal of attention in recent years. With the popularization of distance as well as other types of educational technologies, scholars have attempted to explore questions that relate technology to learning outcomes, content delivery and program assessment, to name a few. Scholars argue both for and against the benefits of technology, and the complexity of the issues grow deeper every day. Online education has in recent years become the subject of great debate as a growing number of universities vie with each other in trying to capture an increasingly mobile student population.

In this chapter, we first explore the literature that addresses diversity and technology within the higher education arena. We outline challenges and opportunities with both and then provide an overview of the context within which our study is situated. Finally, within our case study, we attempt to address the challenges and build on the opportunities of diversity and technology within the framework of the development and the teaching of a capstone course at UOG.

Diversity and Technology: An Overview

On Diversity

We are mindful that diversity is perhaps an inherent part of the multicultural landscape present within post-secondary education. But, what is the multicultural landscape? Multiculturalism, as such, appears in many different forms. Pieterse (2004) suggests a comparison of the concepts of *cultural differentialism, cultural convergence, cultural mixing* and *cohabitation* as dominant forms of multiculturalism. According to Pieterse, *cultural differentialism* is concerned with apartheid. Cultural separateness is preferred and, perhaps, even the obvious goal. People make considerable efforts to keep each other at an arm's length. *Cultural convergence,* on the other hand, appears to speak to the process of assimilation. But the concept of the melting pot is incorrect in this instance. Instead, the dominant group commands and maintains the cultural center. Other groups are kept in their place, which is clearly at the periphery. *Cultural mixing* as a form of multiculturalism highlights integration. No one gives up his or her cultural identity. A colloquial term for this situation, referred to here and there in the extant literature, is mixed salad. *Cohabitation*, when it happens in the context of multiculturalism, if successful, can be expected to yield new and unique cross-cultural patterns of differences. Such differences may add incredible variety to the experiences of being human.

Relevant to a discussion of multiculturalism is the matter of social capital. According to Pieterse (2004), not merely in-group but also intergroup social capital is of major significance. That is, within multicultural societies, to what extent do people within groups perceive that they need each other? And, to what extent is reciprocity a significant cornerstone of the phenomenon of social capital? Should multiculturalism, in fact, be seen as "an archipelago of separate communities?" (Pieterse, p. 36). Perhaps, it is more creative to view multiculturalism as "… intercultural interplay and mingling, a terrain of crisscrossing cultural flows, in the process generating new combinations and options" (Pieterse, p. 36). In short, the optimistic view suggests considerable positive energy and unique developments as significant outcomes of multiculturalism. To what extent is diversity truly found within multiculturalism? If the two concepts engage each other, how can the concept of diversity be understood? One practical definition of diversity is as follows:

Diversity is "otherness" or those human qualities that are different from our own and out-side the groups to which we belong, yet are present in other individuals and groups. It is important to distinguish between the primary and secondary dimensions of diversity. Primary dimensions are the following: age, ethnicity, gender, physical abilities/qualities, race and sexual orientation. Secondary dimensions of diversity are those that can be changed, and include, but are not limited to: educational background, geographical location, income, marital status, military experience, parental status, religious beliefs and work experience. "Otherness" provides strengths for us, as well as weaknesses. "Otherness" empowers us, as well as undermining who we are and what we do. (The University of Maryland, 2001)

On Technology

Technology, in recent years, has entered the academy by leaps and bounds. Over the past decade in particular, there has been great debate regarding the future of higher education in the new era of academic technology (Privateer, 1999). This debate, however, is not new. The Carnegie Commission on Higher Education (1972) issued a report titled *The Fourth Revolution: Instructional Technology in Higher Education* some 30 years ago. The report focused on the relatively limited experience with educational technology that has obviously expanded since then. The report established educational goals for the development of instructional technology by 1980, 1990 and 2000. Important questions posed that we are still grappling with in higher education included: If students learn at different rates and respond differently to a given instructional approach, how can we continue to address students primarily utilizing one technique? How can we enrich our courses and instructional approaches to meet the needs of students? How can we assess learning outcomes effectively unless we use adequate instructional objectives? (Carnegie Commission on Higher Education, 1972). These are the questions that remain at the forefront of discussions in terms of course development and objectives, learning outcomes and assessment within the context of higher education today.

Diversity in Higher Education

Diversity, multiculturalism, pluralism, biculturalism and universalism are difficult terms to define, and there is much debate among scholars to agree on a single working definition. For example, Powell (2003) illustrates that "attempting to define multiculturalism is like trying to pick up a jellyfish—you can do it, but the translucent, free-floating entity turns almost instantly into an unwieldy blob of amorphous abstraction" (p. 156). Where once diversity and its aggregates referred to an individual's national origin, religion, race and/or ethnicity, it is now inclusive of gender, sexual orientation, caste, class and/or language (Gordon, 1992). To add to the hodgepodge, diversity can also refer to employment status, family status, family responsibilities, place of residence and/or technological savvy of an individual (Pascarella & Terenzini, 1998). Every imaginable social division can be categorized as a culture—this is cultural diversity as it exists today. Rather than attempting to define diversity, as an attempt to do so is beyond the scope of this chapter, we will present an overview of the history of diversity within the academy.

The study of diversity in higher education is generally considered to have emerged out of the civil rights movement of the 1960s, with the primary focus on African American students gaining access to predominately white institutions (Osei-Kofi, 2003). The discourse on diversity grew in popularity, blossoming into major political, social, economic and academic agendas in the 1980s and 1990s. To address legislation and litigation, academic institutions have been accepting higher percentages of ethnic minority students by providing enhanced opportunities for enrollment in the form of financial assistance, and demographic projections indicate that the number of ethnic minorities will increase in coming years (Justiz, 1994). The rhetoric has changed, however, from a policy geared toward affirmative action to one that emphasizes that having a diverse student population will help students to be better prepared to enter today's multicultural society (Rubenstein, 1996).

Enrolling larger numbers of students from diverse ethnic and racial backgrounds may be only one simple answer to a complex issue. As researchers discovered at the University of California at Berkley, minority students tended to gather in racial and ethnic "enclaves" and would ostracize themselves from students of different backgrounds, a phenomenon termed *balkanization* (Duster, 1991, cited in Antonio, 2001). Rather than ameliorating racial tensions between ethnic groups, this type of self-segregation ostensibly exacerbated the problem of ethnocentrism. In a 3-year longitudinal study of an ethnically diverse university, Antonio (2001) reported that although ethnic minority students perceived the social environment to be ethnically and racially segregated, most of the participants in the study had heterogeneous friendship groups. In other words, the participants who maintained friendships with others from diverse backgrounds believed they were the exception to the balkanized norm. This finding supports the framework for a multidimensional model in exploring multicultural-ism on campus set forth by Hertado et al. (1998). According to this perspective, the racial climate is made up of four disparate, but interrelated, elements: (1) the institution's historical background on the inclusion/exclusion of ethnic/racial minorities; (2) the structural diversity, or the representation, of ethnic/racial minority groups; (3) the psychological climate of how individuals perceive relationships between and within ethnic/racial groups; and (4) the behavioral climate, distinguished by observable inter-group relations. Because of potential deleterious effects on the psychological climate, or "surface-segregation," as described by Antonio (2001), of the university milieu, scholars have redirected efforts to exploring strategies that could be interpreted into practice to inform institutional transformations that would best enhance intercultural and interracial harmony (Chang, 2002a; Hurtado, Milem, Clayton-Pedersen, & Allen, 1998).

The current body of research has informed policy and practice and has aided institutional leaders, administrators and faculty in nurturing the diverse student population in efforts to engage diversity on university campuses. One outcome has been the creation of numerous diversity courses in the academic curriculum, as well as the promotion of ethnic/cultural clubs and workshops. Chang (2002b) reported that students who had continued exposure to diversity courses made significantly more favorable judgments of blacks than those that had less exposure. To interpret the findings, Chang suggests that students who learn to think "broadly" about racial and cultural differences are instilled with a heightened sensitivity regarding human differences that often extend far beyond the topic of a particular course. This finding is consistent with other studies reported in the literature (Hurtado, 1996; Milem & Hakuta, 2000).

Another strategy employed by institutions to engage diversity is the establishment of learning communities. Learning communities combine opportunities to help students maximize their learning experiences. Shapiro and Levine (1999) define four types of learning communities: (1) paired or clustered courses; (2) cohorts in large courses or first-year interest groups (FIGS); (3) team-taught courses; and (4) residence-based programs, also known as living-learning programs. In a study on living-learning programs, Inkelas and Weisman (2003) suggest that providing students additional opportunities outside the curricula greatly increases students' awareness of issues related to diversity as well as results in a higher standard of academic achievement.

Cultural diversity in the academy is a widely researched topic and includes an extensive body of literature both empirical and theoretical. Much of the current research has been successful in inspiring institutional transformations that have revolutionized the academic canon. The population of universities is becoming incredibly diverse, and it is imperative that institutions not lose sight of their mission to prepare students to enter a rapidly changing society.

Technology in Higher Education

Technology is transforming the face of society and is one of the major forces driving the engine of globalization. Advances in technology are bringing together people in different parts of the world in new ways. Pundits have coined terms such as the *information age, the digital age, the wired age* and *the broadband age* to describe the changing times in the new *global village.* And at the vanguard of the information frontier is the academy. Entering today's technological world, a student's probability of success is increasingly being measured by the ability to effectively utilize technology, termed "information literacy (IL)" (Mackey & Jacobson, 2004; Ragains, 2001; Wright, 2000). This presents new challenges to educators. Foster (2001) highlights that institutions of higher learning must now: (1) Accommodate the educational needs of non-traditional learners; (2) integrate the philosophy of students as life-long learners; (3) compete with distance education programs for student enrollment; and (4) provide cost-effective learning despite legislation that calls for costly technological restructuring.

There is a growing body of literature to inform institutional leaders on how best to integrate technology into educational settings, because many educators believe that technology can act as a catalyst to enhance the quality of education (Doty, 2002; Jacobson & Mark, 2000; M. A. Miller, 1995). Some institutions are embracing the technological revolution and have made information literacy a priority for students, while others are struggling to keep up. Faculty are making a transition to multimedia instructional materials, such as educational DVDs and videos that are being shown to students to enhance traditional lectures. Faculty are also utilizing powerful presentation software, adding greatly to class presentations as well as discussion groups on the Web, where students can ask questions day or night. The virtual classroom, video conferencing and distance-learning programs are providing access to learners who were previously denied access to higher education because of geographical location or time. Technology is making possible educational instruction "anytime, anywhere" (Pascarella & Terenzini, 1998). Although technology has become pervasive in everyday life in higher education, perhaps the two areas that have been most affected are the traditional library and social and academic interactions.

There is a plethora of knowledge available on the World Wide Web (it is no wonder they call it the information age!). Libraries are being restructured to integrate electronic databases, including electronic references and full-text journal articles, into their collections. Research can now be conducted by remote access from the convenience of one's home rather than at the library. Despite the added convenience, there are drawbacks. Before the rise in Internet use, libraries maintained stringent filtering processes to weed out unreliable or questionable sources. However, now that the Internet has become, in the words of Wright (2000, p. 28), the "one-stop-shop for information," there is an inherent danger associated with the over-use and over-reliance of information resources. IL has become erroneously associated with "information management" rather than "information processing." It is on this ground that Purdue (2003) criticizes the IL rhetoric. Purdue offers the view that IL discourse is jargonizing and befuddles the non-privileged members. Rather than offering the umpteenth definition of IL, Purdue examines the functional view of IL to help students become actively literate to be able to critically engage any source of information, whether through personal interactions or through text. Thus, IL is not simply a skill that one either possesses or does not possess; it becomes something that prepares the student to learn over his or her lifetime.

Social and academic interactions are another area of life in the academy transformed by technology. The ubiquitous use of e-mail has revolutionized interactions between and among faculty and students. Faculty are utilizing e-mail to communicate and collaborate with other faculty within and between institutions. Students are using e-mail for communications with friends, family members and professors. E-mail has become perhaps an inseparable part of daily life in the university, but there is little research investigating outcomes associated with its use. Gatz and Hirt (2000) suggest that although e-mail is enhancing certain areas of university life for students, that it might also reduce time spent on other activities. That is, the time spent e-mailing takes away from time spent participating in activities more favorable to social integration, such as campus clubs and organizations. Thus, the impact of technology on higher education seems to be a paradox. On the one hand, technology has an added element of convenience and enhancement on the dissemination of knowledge for both educators and students. On the other hand, technology is not without potential detrimental effects on the social integration of the student population. In either case, there is a need for more empirical and theoretical research to inform policy and practice of technology integration in the academy.

The Technology of Diversity and the Diversification of Technology

Since its inception, the mission of higher education has not changed. Its goal has always been to prepare students to enter and excel in society as model citizens. However, there are new added responsibilities presented to the university, because society is rapidly changing. Society is becoming increasingly diverse and technology is an inseparable part of today's world. Gordon (1992) states that:

U.S. society has been rapidly overcome by modernity (i.e., efficiency of communication, transportation, commerce and technology) that has served to destroy the cultural enclaves in which ethnic identities were formerly celebrated and maintained. This destruction has forced interaction and assimilation. (p. 408)

And the destruction appears to be resulting in a process of Western and Eurocentric hegemony. The diversity of knowledge is becoming undiversified. Particularly in the Pacific region, indigenous ways of knowing and thinking are being subsumed and suppressed by Western world views (Johnson, 2000). Within any discussion of globalization, Antonio Gramsci's concepts of hegemony, ideology and consensus are important in understanding the conflict of oppositional forces (Femia, 1981). It is argued that dominance is maintained not just by force, but by encouraging consensus among diverse social groups. "Hegemony is attained through the myriad ways in which the institutions of civil society operate to shape, directly or indirectly, the cognitive and affective structures whereby men perceive and evaluate problematic social reality" (Femia, 1981, p. 24). Gramsci (Femia, 1981) believed that the production of meanings is closely connected to the social structure and, hence, to understand those meanings one must appreciate the structure and history that have produced them. C. Miller (1995) has argued that in the domain of culture, this contestation takes the form of the struggle for meaning, in which the dominant classes attempt to "naturalize" the meanings that serve their interests into the "common sense" of society as a whole. Subordinate classes, for their part, resist this process in various ways, and try to make meanings that serve their own interests (C. Miller, 1995). In the discourse of globalization, the mass media and its output have increasingly become areas of ideological struggle, which have ramifications for culture and its evolution. Thaman (2003) asserts as follows: "Globalization concerns the global spread of mainly Anglo-American knowledge, values and practices, rather than indigenous knowledge and wisdom" (p. 7). She argues that integrating indigenous views into the curriculum is essential in achieving a holistic understanding of the world, not just from a single perspective, but from a diverse perspective.

Technology is pervasive, and is invading every corner of the world, albeit some areas more slowly than others. In the Pacific region, there is an apparent disparity in the utilization of technology, primarily owing to reasons of cost or lack of services in the area. Thus, most of the "cyberdiscourse" on the Pacific and Pacific Islanders takes place among those living outside the region (Wesley-Smith, 2003). Ironically, this technology is about Pacific Islanders, rather than for Pacific Islanders. The underutilization of technology is leading to challenges for both educators and students alike.

In one instance, the primary author of this chapter was teaching an introductory sociology class that enrolled a number of "non-traditional" students from the rural outlaying islands of Chuuk in the Federated States of Micronesia. They had the highest quiz and test scores in the class and participated actively in discussions, demonstrating knowledge of the material. However, when the assignment was a research project, it became clear that none of these students knew how to use a computer. While showing the students how to use the electronic database, one student pointed to the flashing cursor and asked how it was being moved. It became clear that the great technological divide was, in fact, more enormous than great!

The literature on "diversity in higher education" and "technology in higher education" abounds. However, missing from the discourse is empirical and theoretical research that shows the linkage between the two. Meanwhile, academic policy is either ill informed or, in the worst case, uninformed. This presents challenges to educators and universities as they prepare students to enter today's increasingly multicultural and technologically advancing society. The university has always served as a paragon of society. To maintain its integrity in producing model citizens, there is a need to bridge the hiatus between diversity and technology in higher education for informed policy and practice.

Context for the Case Study; Micronesia, Guam and the University of Guam – Portraits of (Historical?) Diversity

In this chapter, we use our "paintbrush" to sketch the multicultural landscape, and through each brushstroke, the issues of diversity and technology are situated within this milieu. In this section, we position the islands of Micronesia and offer a brief history within the framework of diversity. We also introduce the island of Guam, its history and its place within the multicultural landscape of the Western Pacific. We then turn to UOG that is the home of the senior-level capstone course, the case study that we analyze in the second half of this chapter.

Micronesia is a sub-region of Oceania, together with Melanesia and Polynesia. The region of Micronesia, or "tiny islands," is further subdivided into three island groups; namely the Marshalls, the Carolines and the Marianas in the Western Pacific. Hundreds of years of colonial influence have left many Micronesians with feelings of perplexity owing to the varied interests, policies and attitudes of the foreign occupiers (Pelzer, 1950). Even Russian and French voyagers arriving before the other European colonizers had disagreements about what constituted the Micronesian people. Some considered the people of Micronesia a singular "type" of people, a "race"; and others simply a geographical region (Rainbird, 2003). These differences in views may in fact overshadow Micronesia's celebration of its rich ethnic, cultural and linguistic diversity. Micronesia as an entity includes the islands of Palau, the Commonwealth of the Northern Mariana Islands, the Marshall Islands, Kiribati, Nauru, the Federated States of Micronesia (further subdivided into Yap, Chuuk, Pohnpei and Kosrae) and the island of Guam. Each island or island group is inhabited by its indigenous people, with more than two dozen official languages in the Micronesian region alone. Guam

Table 1. Ethnic groups in Guam: 1920-1990 (Adapted from Schwab, 1998)

Ethnicity	1920	1940	1960	1980	1990	2000
Chamorro	12,216 (92%)	20,177 (90.5%)	34,762 (51.9%)	44,299 (41.8%)	49,935 (37.5%)	57,297 (37.01%)
Filipino	396 (3.0%)	569 (2.6%)	8,580 (12.8%)	22,447 (21.2%)	30,043 (22.6%)	40,729 (26.31%)
Caucasian /State sider	280 (2.1%)	785 (3.5%)	20,724 (30.9%)	26,901 (25.4%)	19,160 (14.4%)	10,509 (6.79%)
Other, including Asians and Micronesians	383 (2.9%)	759 (3.4%)	2,978 (4.4%)	12,332 (11.6%)	34,014 (25.5%)	46,270 (29.89%)
Total	13,275 (100%)	22,290 (100%)	67,044 (100%)	105,979 (100%)	133,152 (100%)	154,805 (100%)

is the only unincorporated United States (U.S.) territory in the region. Most of the other island communities in Micronesia maintain some type of independent association with the U.S. Although sharing some common history and identity and present political framework, each Micronesian island possesses a unique cultural identity that sometimes overlaps with others. It is possible that the island of Guam has the most diverse population in Micronesia, owing to its open in-migration of many people, most of them from Southeast Asia, since the US signed the Organic Act of 1950, granting U.S. citizenship to all of its inhabitants at that time. Guam is where U.S.'s day begins; with its territorial status, it is seen by many as the gateway to the U.S. and to the land of opportunity.

The tropical island of Guam is the southernmost island in the Marianas chain, about 3,700 miles west southwest of Hawaii. The natives of Guam are proto-Malays, seafarers who settled the island about 4,000 years ago (Iyechad, 2001). The colonial history has been the most dominant aspect of Guam's experience for the past 350 years. The native Chamorros on Guam have struggled to maintain some sort of identity throughout all these years of imperial dominance and continue today to hold on to their language, culture and traditions.

According to the most recent census (2000), the population of Guam totaled 154,804. Table 1 shows the ethnic breakdown of the island's inhabitants over the past century.

The celebration of Guam's ethnic, cultural and linguistic diversity is a source of great strength to the community and a source of tension at times. To a newcomer on the island, this diversity is very apparent, and one is struck by the warm and friendly interaction of the various constituents with each other. "But under the surface, like so many other diverse regions of the world, there are tensions. The deeper the cleavages run the more evident are these tensions" (Johnson & Inoue, 2003, p. 9). With the other Micronesian islanders making up close to 10% of the population today on Guam, the tensions between the various island peoples comes to a head when economic times are difficult. This conflict has been studied in some depth by Schwab (1998) but remains an area of inquiry that requires more probing. According to Johnson and Inoue (2003), Guam has five ethnic main players: the Chamorros; Filipinos; other Asians who originate from China, Japan, Taiwan, Korea, Hong Kong, India, Vietnam, Malaysia and Thailand; the Statesiders (U.S. in origin); and the Micronesians who originate from Micronesian islands other than Guam. They also state that:

Table 2. Ethnic profile of faculty and students at UOG (Source: University of Guam—Office of Records, September 2005)

Ethnicity	Student (percent)	Faculty (percent)
Chamorro	44.17	20.00
Filipino	34.41	5.37
Asian	5.17	10.24
Micronesian	6.13	1.95
"Stateside" Caucasian	7.05	58.05
"Stateside" Other	1.94	2.93
Other	1.12	1.46
Total	100.00	100.00

The Chamorro people are the indigenous people of the island and still the dominant group in regards to their size as well as the control of a number of resources, including the government and land holdings ... Filipinos ... began migrating in the 1940s after WWII, first as laborers after the war and then as immigrants bringing their families and making Guam their home ... [Filipinos] work primarily in the service and professional sectors of the economy ... their hard work and close family structure have contributed to their success educationally and financially. Asians make up a rather diverse yet visible and influential group, which continues to grow on Guam and will in the future play a larger role in the management of the affairs on the island. Statesiders or Caucasians for the most part consist of mainly professionals in business, law, banking and education, and the last major group consist of other Micronesians. [There are, of course,] great differences between the various Micronesia groups in terms of language and culture and ... [they are] the most economically disadvantaged on Guam and are often the most discriminated against in terms of everyday cultural interactions but also in terms of employment, housing and education. (p. 9)

Many Micronesian islanders also migrate and attempt to settle on Guam to search for better opportunities. This may be true for all immigrants to Guam, especially those who originate from South East Asia, who are often fleeing their country's economic hardships. Truly, Guam has become one of the most diverse island communities in the Western Pacific. And as the region's only 4-year land grant institution of higher learning, UOG is reflective of the island's social fabric, and the great diversity of faces and cultures of the Pacific Asian region.

UOG was originally known as the Territorial College of Guam, an institute for future educators that offered a 2-year teacher-training program. By the late 1960s, enrollment increased to 1,800 students, with faculty of 130. It is now a 4-year land-grant institution of higher learning accredited by the Western Association of Schools and Colleges. Although Guam lies somewhere in the middle of the traditional-modern continuum, UOG nevertheless follows the Western educational structure. By 2005, the number of full-time faculty on campus was nearing 200 and UOG had become home to 3,034 students (Moore-Linn, 2005). Some 60% of faculty members are of Caucasian-American descent, most of whom completed their education in the mainland U.S. In contrast, 90% of the student body is comprised of either indigenous Pacific Islanders or those of Asian descent (Johnson & Inoue, 2003).

Ironically, these so-called "minority students" outnumber the "majority faculty." About 44% of the students are Chamorros, 34% are Filipinos, 5% are Asians, 6% are Micronesians and some 7% are Caucasian. With a student population of almost 90% Asian/Pacific Islander and a faculty population of almost 60% Caucasian, the UOG campus makes for a very interesting ethnic mix. There is a great positivity among UOG faculty in embracing and celebrating diversity as seen both in their attitudes and in their actual practice within the educational pedagogy (Johnson & Inoue, 2003). For example, Johnson and Inoue have explored the concepts of multiculturalism within the context of UOG and, in particular, faculty attitudes and pedagogic practices in the classroom. The research yielded positive results; that is, the majority of professors strongly agreed that "multiculturalism is an asset that enriches the learning process" (Johnson & Inoue, 2003, p. 1), while that same majority actually takes concrete steps to reflect diversity and multiculturalism within the classroom environment. This is the context within which our case study is situated. The diverse environment of the region as well as the university makes for an interesting and sociologically important context within which to take a closer look at a particular senior-level course. This capstone course attempts to directly address both diversity and technology within the direct curriculum of the course itself, as well as the way the team approaches the subject matter of the class and the objectives set out in the course outline.

Case Study: Community Development Course

We now turn to a case study to help further explore and analyze the issues of technology and diversity within the landscape of higher education. AN/SO405 is a cross-listed course within the anthropology and sociology programs at UOG. The course is titled "Community Development" and is co-taught by two faculty, one from each department. The course provides an appropriate case study within this chapter since it uniquely addresses the central questions of this volume. By closely exploring this senior-level course at UOG, we seek to further bring to light the important issues within the discourse of diversity and technology in higher education. We also seek to add to our understanding of each as they relate to real life in the classroom for both faculty and students. The course AN/SO405 Community Development was offered in spring semester 2005 and enrolled 12 students. Imbedded within the class was a 7-day travel experience to Bali, Indonesia, in an effort to highlight the central questions of development theory and allow the students a first-hand look at development in practice. In addition to the two faculty who co-taught the course, nine other faculty from five additional universities participated in creating a learning experience for the students that excelled all expectations. The course was of great interest locally and beyond. Local print and television media covered the highlights and learning objectives for their audience, and a radio station from Australia interviewed participants, wanting to learn about how this endeavor contributed to their understanding of diversity cross culturally.

Celebrating Diversity in AN/SO405

Diversity, as mentioned above, calls attention to that which offers variety; that of a different kind, form and character; that which is multiple; different ways, means and the like. The motto of UOG is "Unity in Diversity." Paradoxically, this is the same motto of the country of Indonesia, the field site for the Community Development course. This is the site where we traveled with students in the Community Development course to observe a people and a culture both somewhat similar to and very different from our own. A valued feature of the capstone course is the diversity present within our team. In spring 2005, the team was comprised of faculty and students from the following cultures of origin: Bali, Indonesia; Chuuk, Federated States of Micronesia; Cook Islands; Cuba; Guam; Java, Indonesia; Mexico; Philippines; and the U.S. Other aspects of diversity apparent on our team included religious affiliation, age, gender, and marriage and family dynamics.

Within the Community Development course, globalization theory was utilized to inform us of the new(er) thinking concerning the world in general, and neighbors near and far in particular (e.g., Featherstone, 1990; Lewellen 2002; Roberts & Hite, 2000; Schech & Haggis, 2000; Yamashita & Eades, 2003). Eriksen (2003) takes the position that the contemporary world is "… one of global embeddedness, ubiquitous rights movements and reflexive identity politics, universal capitalism and globally integrated financial markets, transnational families, biotechnology and urbanization" (p. 2). Chiang, Lidstone and Stephenson (2004, p. vi) define globalization as: "supra-national ideas and processes that cross national borders with impunity." Such "ideas and processes" may appear to possess a will of their own, fostering

Figure 1. Celebrating diversity: The capstone course participants in Bali

closer links between cultures, societies and economies. But, do they? How do individuals, communities and nation-states actually respond to the forces of globalization? Yamashita (2003) and other researchers explore the concept of "glocalization," especially with reference to Southeast Asia. "Glocalization" suggests that the global is drawn in to the local by choice and, simultaneously, the local reaches out to embrace the global. The most important outcome suggests that which is local is highlighted, refreshed and reinvigorated. The local is reinforced especially because of being showcased on a global stage—more particularly in the context of international tourism. Chiang, Stephenson, Kurashina and Iverson (2002) consider this phenomenon with reference to Bali.

Finding Commonality in AN/SO 405

How, then, could we as a team of social science investigators, faculty and students studying community development attempt to find commonality within our group? How could we meaningfully create and then draw on commonality to make our diversity work for us? Commonality was essential to the success of our teaching and learning venture. An essential commitment was required of team members in our course, that of the willingness to become a team. Perhaps the most important part of our team building was the ways and means by which commonality emerged over time. We were able to learn valuable lessons from past ventures such as this; thus, team building became a central aspect of the community development course from the outset.

Contents of the Course

Living with Diversity

Within the capstone course that highlighted Bali, Indonesia, as the location of the site visit, we were mindful of significant similarities and differences of our team. In the point of view of Geertz (2000), cultural diversity is not easy to transcend:

A common view of cultural diversity is that it provides us with ... alternatives to us as opposed to alternatives for us. Other beliefs, values, ways of going on, are seen as beliefs we would have believed, values we would have held, ways we would have gone on, had we been born in some other place or some other time than that in which we actually were. ... But such a view seems to make both rather more and rather less of the fact of cultural diversity than it should. (p. 75)

Marcus (1998) has noted that: "... scholar(s) [are asked] to keep similarity and difference, the global and the local, in mind simultaneously, requiring of him or her the ability to see everything everywhere as the key to perceiving diversity" (p. 57), and also that "... diversity arises here not from some local struggle for identity, but as a function of a complex process among all sites in which the identity of someone or a group anywhere is defined in simultaneity" (p, 63).

Learning about Diversity

We began the course by acknowledging our varied diversity in terms of ethnic, cultural and academic backgrounds. Then we took some time to learn about diversity, and how our diversity was imbedded within our inquiry. For the teaching and learning process about diversity to be successful, we understood that a sense of trust was going to be essential. In an early session of the class, when most of the group members were relative strangers to each other, we conducted an outdoor exercise, holding hands in a big circle, and then moving about with no particular pattern into smaller circles, to form a human knot. The second part of the exercise was to "untie" the human knot, without letting go of hands. The physical exercise required teamwork, trust and getting "up close and personal" with each other, as we tried to reposition our bodies to reconstitute our original circle. Much laughter ensued, but the focused teamwork was essential to begin the process of building lasting trust among us.

Olivarez and Moore-Lin (2005), in highlighting the experiences of our team in Bali that link to diversity, quote UOG senior Jonathan Lee as follows:

One of the benefits of being at UOG is that we are not limited to the points of view of the scholars from our institution. Our professors network with scholars in other countries and universities to give us a more holistic education. The Bali experience has really given us the opportunity to hear different perspectives. (pp. 6-7)

Returning to our seminar classroom, and to more classic teaching and learning endeavors, students then worked in pairs to present the various assigned textbook chapters. As part of the in-class learning in this course, students read and discussed theories of development, continually seeking answers to one important question: Why are some nations more materially underdeveloped than others? Class members explored what it is like to live in the Third World, first by reading about it and then by traveling to Bali, a very different environment from their own, where they met and lived with people whose struggles the students were just beginning to understand. A week before our team traveled to Bali, we arranged for an academic colleague, Dr. Ir. D. K. Hayra Putra, from Udyana University in Denpasar, to come to Guam to guest lecture to the class on Bali's social organization and culture. It seemed centrally important for the students in the class to meet a Balinese professor prior to traveling to Indonesia and to learn from him in their own familiar environment. On the first morning after the team had arrived in Bali, when Dr. Putra walked up the stairs and into the Homestay in Ubud where we were living, students' eyes lit up to see a familiar face they had just encountered for a week back home at UOG.

An important process of discovery for students as well as professors occurred during a site visit to a remote part of East Bali. The team spent a night in a fishing village that is relatively impoverished compared with other parts of Bali. Team members were divided into pairs, and each pair spent the night with a village family. This experience was the highlight for the team, as the reality of being out of one's comfort zone kicked in and discomfort created an eye-opening experience that would have been impossible otherwise. Students could not communicate with their hosts due to a lack of knowledge of Bahasa Indonesia, the lingua franca. The living conditions proved to be a source of great distress and anxiety (e.g., bathing with very little water, squat toilets, very different food served on banana leaves). Yet students pulled through with flying colors as they leaned on each other for support. The issue of "poverty," which was discussed at great length back in the classroom, had now become more tangible. Students began to understand in a very personal way that "poverty" really means a lack of choices in life. They understood that their own choices far surpass those of the villagers living in Seraya.

Thus, diversity came to life through this capstone course by both living and learning, and students and professors grew as individuals and as team members because of these experiences.

The Technological Landscape

As with diversity, technology within higher education in the Pacific is complex. In terms of its applicability within this educational environment, UOG faces both strengths and challenges.

Strengths

UOG is an institution of about 3,000 students with close to 200 faculty. Guam is an island community with the highest per-capita income among Pacific Island nations, second only to Hawaii. This translates to a university environment with a relatively advanced technological base. Students are often more informed about technology than their professors, and are quite comfortable incorporating PowerPoint technology, video and multimedia into their classroom presentations. Thus, the technological advantages that UOG finds itself faced with are numerous and well established. In fact, UOG has the capacity for video conferencing and other forms of distance education delivery systems.

Challenges

While the strengths are many, UOG is an institution whose diverse student body represents a broad spectrum of capabilities in terms of technological know-how and use. In a 300-level class, it is not uncommon to find some students well versed in basic technology like Internet use, e-mail and PowerPoint design, while many other students do not have access to a home computer or an Internet connection. The outcome is a classroom environment that is often challenging for professors and students alike. Communication with students through e-mail as well as Internet-based assignments can be difficult when some students have not yet logged on to the World Wide Web. Since UOG is an open-enrollment university, it is not uncommon to find an incoming student, for example, from one of the outer islands in Micronesia, to have no basic knowledge at all of library use or computer technology. In fact, many of these students are coming to Guam from communities without electricity and running water. Many of these students have no prior knowledge of basic computer technology and, thus, finding their way on a campus that often assumes a certain knowledge base of all incoming students can be extremely challenging. These students are often initially at a disadvantage, but with hard work, dedication and understanding professors, by their sophomore or junior year, they are up to par with their fellow classmates and often excel in the classroom.

Learning about Technology

The Community Development course was designed to highlight for students the role of technology in the ever-changing nature of society. From the Agricultural Revolution to the Industrial Revolution, into the modern age of the Electronic and Communications Revolution, the one constant variable throughout history has been the link between technology and social change. In fact, change is perhaps most actively felt when it colors the rhythms of everyday life, and when technology continues to shape, mold and redefine our place in the world and our role in its development.

For the first 2½ months of the course, our group explored and discussed the literature on development and, in particular, the role of technology in creating and maintaining social change. Over the past four decades, there has been a plethora of research on this subject in an attempt to understand ways in which culture and social structure are shaped by and are in turn responsible for the production and design of technology. As the labor-intensive, economically disadvantaged countries have been pulled into an ever-shrinking global village, mass communication technologies and mass consumption have become the common thread linking communities across the planet. Scholars have tried to understand what impact this new market culture is having on these diverse societies. The students in the Community Development course came to an appreciation of the complexity of this equation.

To highlight what we were learning in the classroom and to help the students more fully understand the real questions that link technology, culture and social change, our team traveled to the island of Bali, Indonesia, for 1 week of intensive observation and structured inquiry. While in Bali, the team lived in a Home-Stay, which is a small family-run compound located in Ubud in South-Central Bali. Along with being informed through lectures given by Balinese and other visiting faculty from the region on a daily basis, our team engaged in service learning, field observations and a variety of other activities, impressing upon each of us some of the important questions facing Balinese society in the 21st century. To more fully understand the idea that "progress in the field of development largely depends on natural stirrings at the grassroots," the team traveled to the eastern tip of Bali to visit a relatively impoverished village to witness up close a revival of the traditional art of weaving. Students spent the night in village homes and saw some of the challenges people experience in this part of the world. "I was amazed to see how happy and content these villagers were, and yet they had so much less than we do," said anthropology major Julius Cena. "I think most of the students in the class would agree that the most memorable experience was spending the night in a traditional Balinese village." And according to senior psychology major Jonathan Lee, "This is a village that does not have running water or plumbing. We read about a lot of these issues going on in Third World countries in our textbooks, but they are abstract concepts. To be able to experience them first hand is an eye-opener." It was in this village that students came to appreciate the real meaning of traditional technology and its struggle to survive in a modern market-driven economy. Seraya is a fishing village of about 125 households. Each morning, village fisherman rise before dawn to make their way into the waters between Bali and Lombok to catch fish for their families. What they cannot eat they sell in the nearby market. Some of our students joined these fishermen in their small dugout canoes with their 100-pound nets and sails. These canoes appear much like the traditional flying *proa* found in our own region of the Mariana Islands.

Though the fishing expedition was fun, the primary purpose of our visit to this village was to learn about local efforts at reviving the traditional art of weaving. In ages past, this village along with others throughout the islands of Indonesia had been known for weaving beautiful textiles. Alas, due to a variety of modernizing forces, this art form has been threatened. Local people are selling off their looms and other equipment and moving to larger towns and cities for work, education and a new way of life. A non-profit organization based in Bali called Threads of Life is trying to help villagers to see the economic viability of weaving and provide them with a profitable outlet for their woven textiles. In Seraya, our team saw first hand what sustainable economic activity means. Local villagers grew the cotton and

Figure 2. Learning technology: Spinning cotton in Bali

indigo and prepared the dye and other materials needed for weaving, and were beginning to see the viability of such an enterprise.

The combination of theory in our UOG classroom and real-life development in practice in Bali allowed our students to appreciate learning as never before. In Bali, learning took place during lectures in the morning, while trekking trough the rice paddies in the afternoon and over delicious home-cooked meals in the evenings while discussing and debating issues with professors from a broad spectrum of disciplines and cultural backgrounds. According to one of our graduating seniors:

This course and our trip to Bali expanded my world view in so many ways by exposing me first hand to a different country, language and tradition. I experienced the different sights, smells, tastes and feelings that I know couldn't have been possible through a textbook.

And, according to another student and team member, "The world became our classroom and the buildings, plants and people around us became our textbook." We redefined the concept of distance education by actually taking students out of the classroom and placing them in a different country far from home.

Using Technology

In our efforts to design a capstone course at our university that would not only be a significant learning opportunity for students in terms of the content of the curriculum both within and outside of the classroom, we required that students engage a variety of technologies to complete important assignments throughout the course. This was especially significant in their final presentation, which was delivered to the UOG community at the end of the semester. The students presented a multimedia, 1-hour long presentation that included a documentary video and PowerPoint along with music and narrative about their semester-long work and learning outcomes. Both faculty and administrators along with students from across UOG attended this presentation. The 12 students that made up this capstone team worked for many weeks to prepare this presentation. The co-faculty of the course visited them at times in the students' homes, where all 12 had gathered, working well into the early morning hours. This experience of arranging for a university-wide official presentation put a great deal of pressure on the students. They took it upon themselves to create a presentation that would do justice to the course and to the people they had worked with and had gotten to know in Bali during the time that they were there. Co-faculty intentionally stood back and allowed the students to take full responsibility for the presentation outcome. The ownership of the project, then, was theirs and the final outcome demonstrated how well they worked together as a team and the pride they took in their work. This, of course, would not have been possible if it were not for the efforts made at team building from the start of the course and the struggles students went through during the course's 16 weeks that helped forge lasting bonds among the diverse student group. The outcome was transformative in every way. This capstone course encouraged students to interact with and learn more about other cultures, and in the process they learned more about themselves. According to Charleen Calip, one of the senior students in the course, "I'm going to graduate [from UOG] with an experience that has changed my life."

Ten Lessons Learned

The Community Development course involved spending many class-time hours analyzing, discussing and debating theories, models and case studies. Students made in-class presentations on a variety of relevant readings from both classic and contemporary literature. Several weeks were dedicated to familiarizing students with Indonesia and Bali within the context of culture, development and social change. Finally, towards the latter half of the semester, the team traveled to Bali for 7 days of intensive academic activities, ranging from on-site lectures to field observations, as well as service learning and site visits to remote villages. The goal was for the students to learn first-hand what development means on the ground; that is, for real people who struggle to make ends meet in their everyday lives. In this section, we would like to present some important considerations for faculty who are considering activities in their course development that take students out of the classroom and put them into the field in a foreign country. These are lessons we have learned from our own experiences and which continue to help and guide us as we further develop our activities and planning. Each lesson is directly related to the overall theme of this paper and this volume; that is, diversity and technology in higher education—some challenges. These, then, are some of those challenges and lessons learned from experiences with this capstone course.

- **Lesson 1:** Preparations must be considerable prior to traveling to another country, especially if that country is very different from one's own. A fairly well-grounded appreciation of the history of the country and current issues are essential for students to be able to ask informed questions and make salient observations. Prior to traveling, sufficient time must be spent in class to allow students to digest the information and discuss questions. Along with academic preparations, students must begin to understand the cultural climate and context within which they are being placed. Some of this involves fairly straightforward instructions, such as it is not acceptable to touch people on the top of their heads (in Indonesia), since this is regarded as the most sacred part of the human body. Some of the preparation time involves more complex matters, such as nuances of social relations and family dynamics within the country.

- **Lesson 2:** Students should acquire a very basic linguistic competence of the local language of the country to be visited. We recognize that we are not teaching a language course. Yet, when our students can address a local resident in Bali using very basic sentences in Bahasa Indonesia or in Balinese, the initial connection between the two people is greatly enhanced, as well as the student's sense of belonging. It is of considerable value if a visiting student can greet a local resident and ask, "How are you?" Likewise, if students can identify their countries of origin, explain why they are visiting the country, indicate a minimum knowledge of the local language and apologize for the latter, a significant connection between the visiting student and the local resident may well be underway.

- **Lesson 3:** A third consideration relates to culture shock. Prior to leaving for the field, we have learned that it is very helpful to engage students in a discussion about culture shock. Many students have never experienced culture shock before, and therefore, to speak with them about the stages of culture shock and to prepare them for what they are about to encounter will help them adjust to life away from home. When students are feeling out of their comfort zone, they can reassure each other about this particular stage of culture shock and help each other accept that their discomfort is normal and natural. Students are then able to begin to embrace and enjoy the very different setting that the overseas destination has to offer. Team discussions at the end of each day allow students to voice their concerns and their struggles and support others who are experiencing the same.

- **Lesson 4:** We have learned that spending enough time prior to travel on team-building exercises can significantly contribute to a positive experience for everyone during the overseas component of the course. Students join the course from different backgrounds and life experiences. Team-building exercises afford them the opportunity to find common ground, to become friends and to build respect for each other. As has already been mentioned, we take time in class to engage in exercises that contribute to solidifying these bonds. These include highlighting positive virtues of team members, trust exercises, weekend hiking trips, untying "human knots" outside on the lawn and a number of other activities that all contribute to forging friendships. Team-building exercises such as these occur before we travel and also continue within the host country to help create a positive sense of teamwork.

- **Lesson 5:** A fifth consideration concerns research permits. Scholars must not assume that they can travel anywhere in the world to conduct field research without official permission. In Indonesia, for example, a Research Permit must be issued by the National or Regional Government. Indeed, in today's world, it can be a time-consuming, laborious and costly endeavor for a foreign [outside] researcher to be granted a Research Permit in most countries. Accordingly, students may be encouraged to undertake systematic observations, listen and learn a great deal from the host community, which is an enormously valuable educational experience, but not to engage in research without permission. We help our students to understand why our team is not conducting research, *per se*, during our short visit to Bali. This is a lesson for all academics, including graduate students studying abroad. Stories abound of academics falling into serious trouble in many parts of the world (e.g., fines, incarceration, being denied exit to leave the country) for not having official permits.

- **Lesson 6:** While overseas in the host country, we feel it is important to have in hand a schedule of daily activities, and abide by the schedule as closely as possible. Students tend to experience less anxiety if they (and their families and friends back home) can view an outline of expected events that will occur during the entire stay overseas. If appropriate, students might be asked to assist in creating the schedule, which enhances their sense of ownership of the activities. Surprises, delays, unexpected opportunities and the like inevitably emerge during the field stay. But having a schedule to come back to is immensely helpful in keeping the course on track.

- **Lesson 7:** We found daily journaling to be helpful. Students are required to bring a journal with them to Bali, and write in it every day at certain appointed times, usually at the end of the day. Their daily entries must describe not only what happened, but also their personal responses and reflections. The requirement of journaling demands a time commitment for students and faculty alike—students must write and faculty must read. The faculty provide written feedback in the journals to each student on a daily basis. This system serves to reassure and keep the lines of communication open and meaningful between faculty and students while in the field. Students can often experience a high level of anxiety for a variety of reasons. Thus, journaling allows them the opportunity to reflect and think through those emotions and also keep faculty members in tune with what the class is going through.

- **Lesson 8:** It is essential to ensure the safety of students throughout their stay abroad. Students are given detailed instructions prior to leaving for Bali with regard to their health and well-being. On-site, students are encouraged to venture out in groups. Having both male and female faculty on the project ensures that students always have someone to talk to about personal as well as academic matters. We maintain a curfew out of respect for the family we stay with and so that each member of the team is well rested for the following day.

- **Lesson 9:** It is very important to make a concerted effort to meet and work with in-country scholars during a short-term stay overseas. If there is a local university, team members should make every effort to go to meet scholars in residence. In Bali, we greatly value the Indonesian scholars in anthropology, economics, primatology and tourism who are now our esteemed academic colleagues and greatly cherished friends at Udayana University in Denpasar. Our Indonesian colleagues have graciously accepted our invitations to guest lecture to our team at our Home-Stay, and their visits extend often to dinners and discussions late into the evening. Engaging local scholars in the inquiry can be a transformative experience for students and faculty.

- **Lesson 10:** A final consideration that can greatly add to the success of short-term study abroad courses is preparing the students for reverse culture shock on their return home. The first time the co-faculty taught a course such as this, we reasoned: "The students will only be in Bali for 7 days; how intense can the experience be? The students will not experience any reverse culture shock." We were wrong. The week in Bali was so intense, so full of new experiences and so out of the ordinary that, upon returning home, students had pronounced difficulties re-adjusting to their "old" lives. We have learned to counsel students to be especially sensitive to spouses/partners, close friends and fellow classmates back on campus who may feel "left out," since the students have had such life-changing experiences while being away. A part of our students' reverse culture shock involves difficulty coping with relative economics and cost comparisons. Knowing first-hand what one American dollar can buy in Bali, and reflecting that a cup of coffee in Guam costs about the same as what one person earns doing hard physical labor in Bali for 8 hours can be mind-bending, to say the least. Students need to be encouraged to discuss these matters freely when back on campus in the classroom. An important strategy that helps students readjust to being back home is a required lengthy reflection paper, to be read aloud in class during the first class period after the return. Students are asked to share what happened to them in Bali and what it meant to them. Laughter and tears and much more are an inevitable part of these reflections. Shared understanding and empathy serves to reinforce the uniqueness of the shared endeavor for all team members.

Taking university students out of their safe classroom environment and placing them in a foreign country must be approached carefully but with the full knowledge that this will be an experience of incredible value. Such endeavors likely become powerful learning experiences and life-changing episodes. When the considerations that we have raised are taken into account, we believe that short-term study-abroad courses can become especially meaningful as transformative and integrative experiences for undergraduate university students everywhere.

Conclusion

As we walked through the rice paddies waiting for the sun to rise over Mount Agung, local women made morning offerings, local men began to work in the fields and the children in their crisp uniforms walked to school. This was our first morning in Bali, Indonesia, for students enrolled in the Community Development course at UOG. In her final paper at the conclusion of the course, one senior student wrote:

This course has expanded my worldview in so many profound ways. It exposed me first hand to a different country, culture and tradition. I experienced the different sights, smells, tastes and emotions that I know couldn't have been possible through a textbook.

Diversity and technology within higher education have profound implications for the learning environment, learning outcomes and experiences of students and faculty alike. In this chapter, we have attempted to highlight some of these implications and in the process explore the experience gained from one senior-level capstone course at an island university in the Pacific. We have highlighted the strengths and challenges of both diversity and technology and illustrated how each can positively impact higher educational learning outcomes.

There remains, however, a great deal of uncertainty in the discourse on the future of higher education in an increasingly diverse world being taken over by technology. Many fear that the relationship between the professor and the student is being forever changed in this new age of distance and online education. We have attempted to show in this chapter an alternative model for higher education that takes full advantage of the reality of a diverse classroom in terms of learning about and living with diversity. We have demonstrated how technology can be employed both as a tool to enhance the learning experiences of students but also in terms of curriculum planning and engagement of students in the field. This volume, edited by Yukiko Inoue, attempts to explore the challenges of both diversity and technology in higher education in the 21st century. We strongly believe that, as long as the goals and objectives of education remain, the reality of diversity and technology can only help to advance the cause of education and realize its vision of ensuring a better world for present and future generations.

References

Antonio, A. L. (2001). Diversity and the influence of friendship groups in college. *The Review of Higher Education, 25*(1), 63-89.

Carnegie Commission on Higher Education. (1972). *The fourth revolution: Instructional technology in higher education.* New York: McGraw Hill.

Chang, M. J. (2002a). Preservation or transformation: Where's the real educational discourse on diversity? *The Review of Higher Education, 25*(2), 125-140.

Chang, M. J. (2002b). The impact of an undergraduate diversity course requirement on students' racial views and attitudes. *The Journal of General Education, 51*(1), 21-42.

Chiang, L-H. N., Lidstone, J., & Stephenson, R. A. (Eds.). (2004). *The challenges of globalization: Cultures in transition in the Pacific Asia region.* Lanham: University Press of America.

Chiang, L-H. N., Stephenson, R. A., Kurashina, H., & Iverson, T. J. (2002). Visitors' perceptions of cultural improprieties in Bali, Indonesia. *Journal of National Park, 12*(2), 156-169.

Doty, P. (2002). Fish, fire, and fallacies: Approaches to information technology and higher education. *Libraries and the Academy, 2*(4), 647-652.

Eriksen, T. (2003). *Globalisation: Studies in anthropology.* London: Pluto Press.

Featherstone, M. (Ed.). (1990). *Global culture: Nationalism, globalization and modernity.* Newbury Park: Sage.

Femia, J. (1981). *Gramsci's political thought.* Oxford: Oxford University Press.

Foster, L. (2001). Technology: Transforming the landscape of higher education. *The Review of Higher Education, 25*(1), 115-124.

Gatz, L. B., & Hirt, J. B. (2000). Academic and social integration in cyberspace: Students and e-mail. *The Review of Higher Education, 23*(3), 299-318.

Geertz, C. (2000). *Available light: Anthropological reflections on philosophical topics.* Princeton, NJ: Princeton University Press.

Gordon, E. W. (1992). Human diversity, cultural hegemony, and the integrity of the academic canon. *Journal of Negro Education, 61*(3), 405-418.

Griffin, M. (2000, April). *What is diversity?* Paper presented at the College of Arts and Sciences Research Conference, University of Guam.

Hurtado, S. (1996). How diversity affects teaching and learning: A climate of inclusion has a positive effect on learning outcomes. *Educational Record, 77*(4), 27-29.

Hurtado, S., Milem, J. F., Clayton-Pedersen, A. R., & Allen, W. R. (1998). Enhancing campus climates for racial/ethnic diversity: Educational policy and practice. *The Review of Higher Education, 21*(3), 279-302.

Inkelas, K. K., & Weisman, J. L. (2003). Different by design: An examination of student outcomes among participants in three types of living-learning programs. *Journal of College Student Development, 44*(3), 335-368.

Inoue, Y., & Johnson, K. (2002). Faculty attitudes toward diversity and multiculturalism in an American Pacific island university. *Research in the Schools, 9*(1), 51-59.

Iyechad, L. (2001). *An historical perspective on helping practices associated with birth, marriage and death among chamorros in Guam.* Lewiston: The Edwin Mellen Press.

Jacobson, T. E., & Mark, B. L. (2000). Separating wheat from chaff: Helping first-year students become information savvy. *The Journal of General Education, 49*(4), 256-278.

Johnson, K. (2000, March). *Globalization and culture: A framework for social change in the Pacific*. Paper presented at the 20th Annual Conference of the Guam Association of Social Workers, Hilton.

Johnson, K., & Inoue, Y. (2003). Diversity and multicultural pedagogy: An analysis of attitudes and practices within an American Pacific island university. *Journal of Research in International Education 2*(3), 251-276.

Justiz, M. J. (1994). Demographic trends and the challenges to American higher education. In M.J. Justiz, R. Wilson & L.G. Björk (Eds.), *Minorities in higher education* (pp. 1-21). Phoenix, AZ: Oryx Press.

Lewellen, T. (2002). *The anthropology of globalization: Cultural anthropology enters the 21st century*. Westport: Bergin and Garvey.

Mackey, T. P., & Jacobson, T. E. (2004). Integrating information literacy in lower- and upper-level courses: Developing scalable models for higher education. *The Journal of General Education, 53*(3-4), 201-224.

Marcus, G. E. (1998). *Ethnography through thick and thin*. Princeton, NJ: Princeton University Press.

Milem, J. F., & Hakuta, K. (2000). The benefits of racial and ethnic diversity in higher education. In D. Wilds (Ed.), *Minorities in higher education: Seventeenth annual status report* (pp. 39-67). Washington, DC: American Council on Education.

Miller, C. (1995). *Media, audience, and ethnography: Situating mass communication in everyday life* (unpublished manuscript). Montreal, Canada: McGill University.

Miller, M. A. (1995). Technoliteracy and the new professor. *New Literary History, 26*(3), 601-611.

Moore-Linn, C. (2005). *University of Guam enrollment up 3.8%*. Retrieved September 2, 2005, from www.uog.edu/newsandevents/index.htm

Okin, S. (1997). Is multiculturalism bad for women? *Boston Review (October/November)*. Retrieved July 27, 2005, from *www.bostonreview.net/BR22.5/okin.html*

Olivarez, M., & Moore-Lin, C. (2005, Summer). The Bali experience: University course changes views, lives. *University of Guam Magazine*, 7-8.

Osei-Kofi, N. (2003). Whose "I/Eye" counts?: The reproduction of mythical master narratives. *The Review of Higher Education, 26*(4), 487-496.

Pascarella, E. T., & Terenzini, P. T. (1998). Studying college students in the 21st century: Meeting new challenges. *The Review of Higher Education, 21*(2), 151-165.

Pelzer, K. (1950). Micronesia: A changing frontier. *World Politics, 2*(2), 251-266.

Pieterse, J. (2004). *Globalization and culture: Global melange*. Lanham: Rowman and Littlefield.

Powell, T. (2003). All colors flow into rainbows and nooses: The struggle to define academic multiculturalism. *Cultural Critique, 55*, 152-181.

Privateer, P. (1999). Academic technology and the future of higher education: strategic paths taken and not taken. *Journal of Higher Education, 70*(1), 60-79.

Purdue, J. (2003). Stories, not information: Transforming information literacy. *Libraries and the Academy, 3*(4), 653-662.

Ragains, P. (2001). Infusing information literacy into the core curriculum: A pilot project at the University of Nevada, Reno. *Libraries and the Academy, 1*(4), 391-407.

Rainbird, P. (2003). Taking the *tapu*: Defining Micronesia by absence. *The Journal of Pacific History, 38*(2), 237-250.

Reissman, R. (1994). *The evaluating multicultural classroom* (ERIC Database # ED379225).

Roberts, J., & Hite, A. (Eds.). (2000). *From modernization to globalization: Perspectives on development and social change.* Malden: Blackwell.

Rubenstein, N. (1996). Why a diverse student body is so important. *Chronicle of Higher Education, 42*(32), B1-2.

Schech, S., & Haggis, J. (2000). *Culture and development: A critical introduction.* Malden: Blackwell.

Schwab, G. J. (1998). *Ethnicities and masculinities in the making: A challenge for social work on Guam* (unpublished doctoral dissertation). Ann Arbor: University of Michigan.

Shapiro, N. S., & Levine, J. H. (1999). *Creating learning communities: A practical guide to winning support, organizing for change, and implementing programs.* San Francisco: Jossey-Bass.

Thaman, K. H. (2003). Decolonizing Pacific studies: Perspectives, knowledge, and wisdom in higher education. *The Contemporary Pacific, 15*(1), 1-17.

University of Maryland, The. (2001). *Diversity database: Moving towards community.* Retrieved September 1, 2005, from http://www.inform.umd.edu/EdRes/Topic/Diversity/Reference/diversity.html

Wesley-Smith, T. (2003). Net gains? Pacific studies in cyberspace. *The Contemporary Pacific, 15*(1), 117-136.

Wright, C. A. (2000). Information literacy within the general education program: Implications for distance education. *The Journal of General Education, 49*(1), 23-33.

Yamashita, S. (2003). Introduction – glocalizing: Southeast Asia. In S. Yamashita & J. S. Eades. (Eds.), *Globalization in Southeast Asia: Local, national, and transnational perspectives* (pp. 1-17). New York: Berghahn.

Yamashita, S., & Eades, J. (2003). *Globalization in Southeast Asia: Local, national, and transnational perspectives.* New York: Berghahn.

About the Authors

Yukiko Inoue, PhD, is a professor of educational psychology and research in the College of Professional Studies, University of Guam. Her research interests include interdisciplinary studies on student learning and development, educational technology for diverse learners, improving university teaching and learning, and the social contexts and learning with a higher-education focus. Inoue is the author of *The Educational and Occupational Attainment Process: The Role of Adolescent Status Aspirations*, and co-author of *Teaching with Educational Technology: The Case of the Asia-Pacific Region*. Inoue is also a poet and author of *Roses, You Must Be,* and *The Window That Reveals Tomorrow.*

* * *

Julius C. S. Cena was born and raised in Manila, Philippines. He graduated *cum laude* with undergraduate degrees in psychology and sociology from the University of Guam, and is currently pursing a second degree in anthropology with a minor in fine arts. His areas of research interest include culture and personality, music and the arts, and cross-cultural psychology. After completing his second degree, he plans to explore the areas of art and music therapy, filmmaking and psychological anthropology in graduate school.

Jose A. Cortes, MD, was born and raised in Puerto Rico. In 1984, he completed a Bachelor of Science in microbiology at Kansas State University and then studied medicine at Universidad Central del Caribe. He completed his internal medicine residency and fellowship at Cabrini Medical Center in New York City. Currently, he has an active private practice and work as the residency program director at Cabrini Medical Center. His profession interests include resident education, Latin American culture in health education and diversity in health management.

Michelle Dottore directs the Interwork Institute Center for Distance Learning (II-CDL) at San Diego State University, providing education and training throughout the United States and globally since 1995. She entered the field of information and communications technologies (ICTs) in 1984, with Apple Computer, and has pursued the merging of education and technology since. She is in the process of completing her doctoral program at Claremont Graduate University, California.

Anita Borja Enriquez, DBA, is an associate professor of marketing and administrative chair of the School of Business and Public Administration, University of Guam. She received a doctoral degree in business administration from the U.S. International University, a master's degree in business administration from the University of Guam and a Bachelor of Science in management from The University of Maryland. Her research interests are in strategic planning and competitive advantage. She has numerous publications related to competitive advantage factors in marketing channels and successful trading partner relationships.

Glenn Finger, PhD, is deputy director of the Centre for Learning Research and senior lecturer in the School of Education and Professional Studies at Griffith University, Gold Coast campus, Queensland, Australia. Finger lectures and researches in the areas of ICTs and technology education. Prior to his appointment at Griffith University in 1999, Finger had 24 years' experience as a primary school teacher and deputy principal in primary schools. He is a member of the Australian Council for Computers in Education, Australian Council of Educational Leaders and the Queensland Society for Information Technology in Education.

Paul Finger is a teacher education student undertaking a Bachelor of Education at Griffith University, Queensland, Australia. Finger has developed a strong interest and expertise in ICTs through the completion of formal studies in information technology (IT) systems and multimedia studies. His interests now include the use of ICTs for improving and transforming teaching and learning. Through his teacher education program, Finger is building upon his ICT skills and knowledge base to publish his personal stories of learning and to explore how this might be utilized in his role as a teacher.

Kirk Johnson, PhD, spent his childhood growing up in the rural mountainside of western India. As an associate professor of sociology at the University of Guam, he has made his home in Guam for the past 8 years with his wife Sarah and their son Aidan. Johnson received his doctorate in sociology from McGill University in Montreal, Canada. His research often takes him back to the villages of rural India, where he studies modernizing forces impacting social and cultural change. He has been a co-faculty for the university-sponsored field workshop in Bali since 2004. His areas of research inquiry include multicultural education, social change and globalization, and media.

Ray Johnson, EdD, has been a faculty member of the Department of Educational Administration at Fort Hays State University (FHSU) since 1995. His research interests range from a position as research associate on a national curriculum study conducted by Stanford University to the director of the first migrant education program at FHSU. He was the first recipient of the FHSU award for Creativity and Scholarship in Teaching with Technology. Johnson has designed and teaches a series of online courses in character education and community development and is a founding member of a Learning Community, a cross discipline group that provides staff development and professional growth.

Lucyann Kerry is a project director at the University of Guam for the funded distance education project, *Promoting Agriculture Education in the Western Pacific*. Her prior experience in distance education was at The University of Maryland, where she developed a training program for the state system's interactive video network. In 2002, she received a television industry fellowship from the National Association of Television Program Executives. She received a master's degree in film education from the University of Southern California.

Michelle LaBrunda, MD, has studied at multiple universities in the U.S. and Mexico. She completed a Bachelor of Science and a Master of Science in biology at Portland State University in Oregon, and continued her education in Mexico. She completed her graduate medical training at la Universidad de Monterrey in Monterrey, Mexico, and a 5th pathway program at New York Medical College in Valhalla. She is currently an internal medicine resident at Cabrini Medical Center in New York.

Jonathan K. Lee was born in Seoul, South Korea, and raised in Los Angeles. He received a bachelor's degree in psychology from the University of Guam with highest honors, and is currently pursuing a doctorate in clinical psychology from Suffolk University, Boston. He serves as a member of the committee on diversity, striving to enhance cultural awareness, and has been named an Outreach Fellow. His research areas include generalized anxiety disorder, post-traumatic stress disorder, and psychotherapy process and outcome. Lee hopes to return to Guam to teach after receiving his PhD.

Joyce K. McCauley, PhD, is an associate professor in the Department of Language, Literacy and Special Populations in the College of Education, Sam Houston State University. She teaches graduate and undergraduate courses in literacy and multicultural education and is actively involved in community-based learning projects with senior adults. In 1994, she retired from the University of Guam and was awarded professor emeritus in 1998. McCauley serves on the editorial board of *Micronesia Educator Journal* and is co-editor of *Reading Language Arts Teacher Educator Online Journal*.

Maret McGlasson is a tutor for the school of education and professional studies in the Faculty of Education at Griffith University, Gold Coast campus, Queensland, Australia. She also teaches within a primary school environment. With 15 years' experience in teaching aboriginal students ICTs, her areas of interest are digital portfolios, digital story telling and the seamless integration of ICTs into the education curriculum. She is currently teaching future teachers to take advantage of the potential of ICTs.

Mary Jane Miller, EdD, is an assistant professor in the School of Education, University of Guam. She received a Bachelor of Science from Arizona State University, Tempe; a Master of Science from Portland State University, Oregon; and a doctorate in education from the University of Sarasota, Florida. In her words, the age of technology was not yet fully upon us and computers were only for universities and science fiction stories.

Marilyn Rice, PhD, is an assistant professor in the Department of Curriculum and Instruction in the College of Education at Sam Houston State University. She teaches applications of technology in the planning, delivery and assessment of instruction at the undergraduate and graduate levels. Her areas of study are service learning and technology integration into the curriculum.

John Sanchez, PhD, is an associate professor in education and has worked in the education field for 20 years. Sixteen of those years were as a science teacher, guidance counselor and administrator within the Guam public school system. He has worked for the University of Guam since 2001, and his research interests include educational psychology, cross-cultural psychology, and human development and assessment. He uses technology to enhance his classroom and was recognized for his progress with the Award for Innovative Excellence in Teaching, Learning and Technology in 2005.

Nancy B. Schmitz, EdD, is an associate professor in the School of Education, University of Guam. Over the last 30 years, she has held full-time appointments at the University of Montana, Teachers College of Columbia University, University of Guam and University of Wisconsin – La Crosse. Her research has been presented at regional, national and international conferences, including the 1999 conference of the International Council for Health, Physical Education, Recreation, Sport and Dance in Cairo and the 2003 and 2004 AAHPERD Conventions in Philadelphia and New Orleans.

Christopher S. Schreiner, PhD, is an associate professor and administrative chair of English, communications and fine arts at the University of Guam. He taught at Hiroshima University and Fukuoka Women's University in Japan before arriving at the University of Guam in 2004. Schreiner has published more than 50 essays, book chapters and articles in the areas of literacy criticism and philosophy, with a special interest in the uses of phenomenology in interpretation theory and education.

Steve Spencer, EdD, has 30 years' experience in education program development, administration and evaluation. He currently serves as the director for the Center for Pacific Studies at San Diego State University, Interwork Institute, which seeks to expand access to advanced-degree programs within remote Pacific-island nations through use of innovative ICTs.

Rebecca A. Stephenson, PhD, is a professor of anthropology at the university and most recently co-edited *The Challenges of Globalization* (University Press of America). She was co-director of the Balinese Macaque Project in Indonesia from 1999 to 2002, and co-faculty for the University-sponsored field workshop in Bali (2004-2005). She has conducted extensive field research in the Cook Islands, Polynesia and in Micronesia and Guam. She was named an Honorary Life Fellow of the Pacific Science Association in 2003. She has many works in print in Pacific-Asian anthropology, especially in the areas of community development, ethnicity, identity and tourism.

Catherine E. Stoicovy, PhD, is an associate professor of language and literacy at the University of Guam. She received her PhD in administration, curriculum and instruction with an emphasis in language and literacy from the University of Nebraska - Lincoln. She also holds an MEd in reading. In addition to university teaching, she has 15 years of classroom teaching experience in the Guam public school system. Her research interests are technology and literacy, generation 1.5 English language learners, and culturally responsive literacy instruction for Pacific islanders.

Denise L. Uehara, PhD, served as senior research specialist at Pacific Resources for Education and Learning (PREL), conducting research on identifying components of an effective professional development model for early reading improvement. Over the last 7 years, she has conducted research in the former trust territories of the Pacific. As one of the lead researchers on the retention and attrition of Pacific school teachers and administrators and Pacific language use in schools studies, she provided much of the analysis and interpretation of the data. She is currently an assistant professor at the Center on Disability Studies at the University of Hawaii-Manoa.

Index